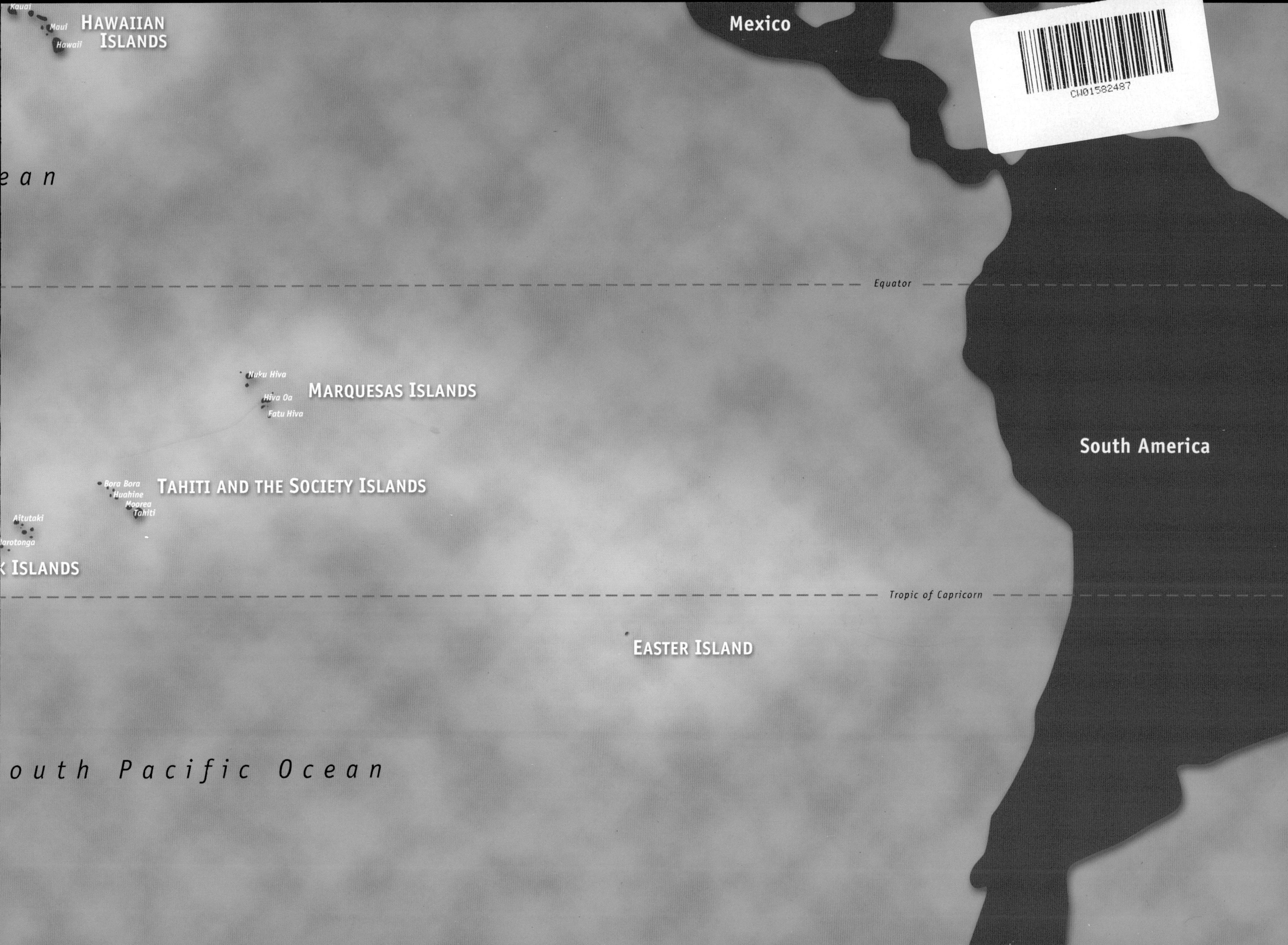
Kauai
Maui
Hawaii
HAWAIIAN ISLANDS
Mexico
ean
Equator
Nuku Hiva
Hiva Oa
Fatu Hiva
MARQUESAS ISLANDS
South America
Bora Bora
Huahine
Moorea
Tahiti
TAHITI AND THE SOCIETY ISLANDS
Aitutaki
arotonga
ISLANDS
Tropic of Capricorn
EASTER ISLAND
outh Pacific Ocean

Congratulations on the purchase of your property in Melbourne's premier lifestyle neighbourhood. To mark this special occasion, we present you with *Pacific Journeys,* a locally-produced book of photography.

With Compliments from Cayzer Real Estate
Real Estate with Real Service

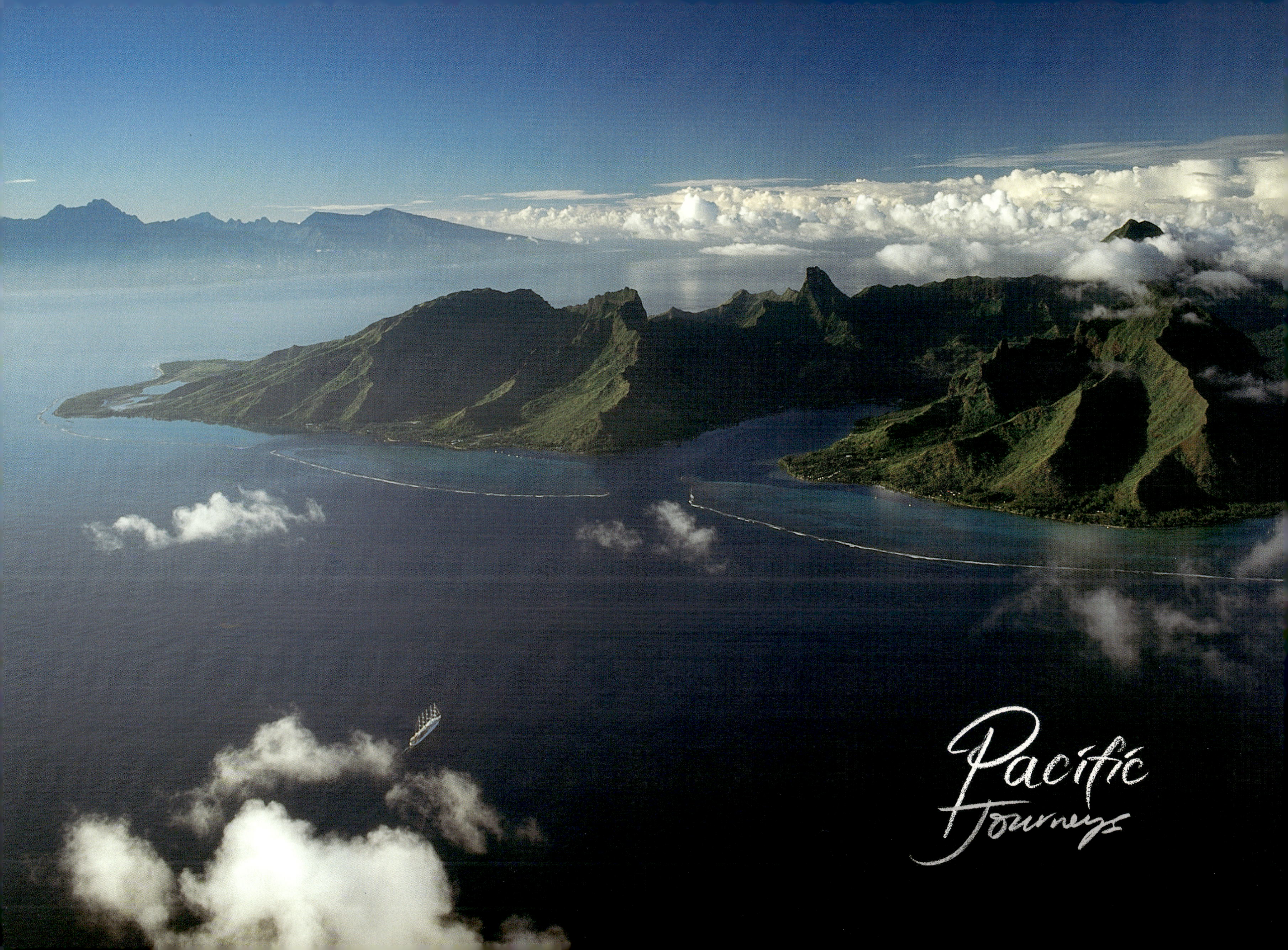
Pacific
Journeys

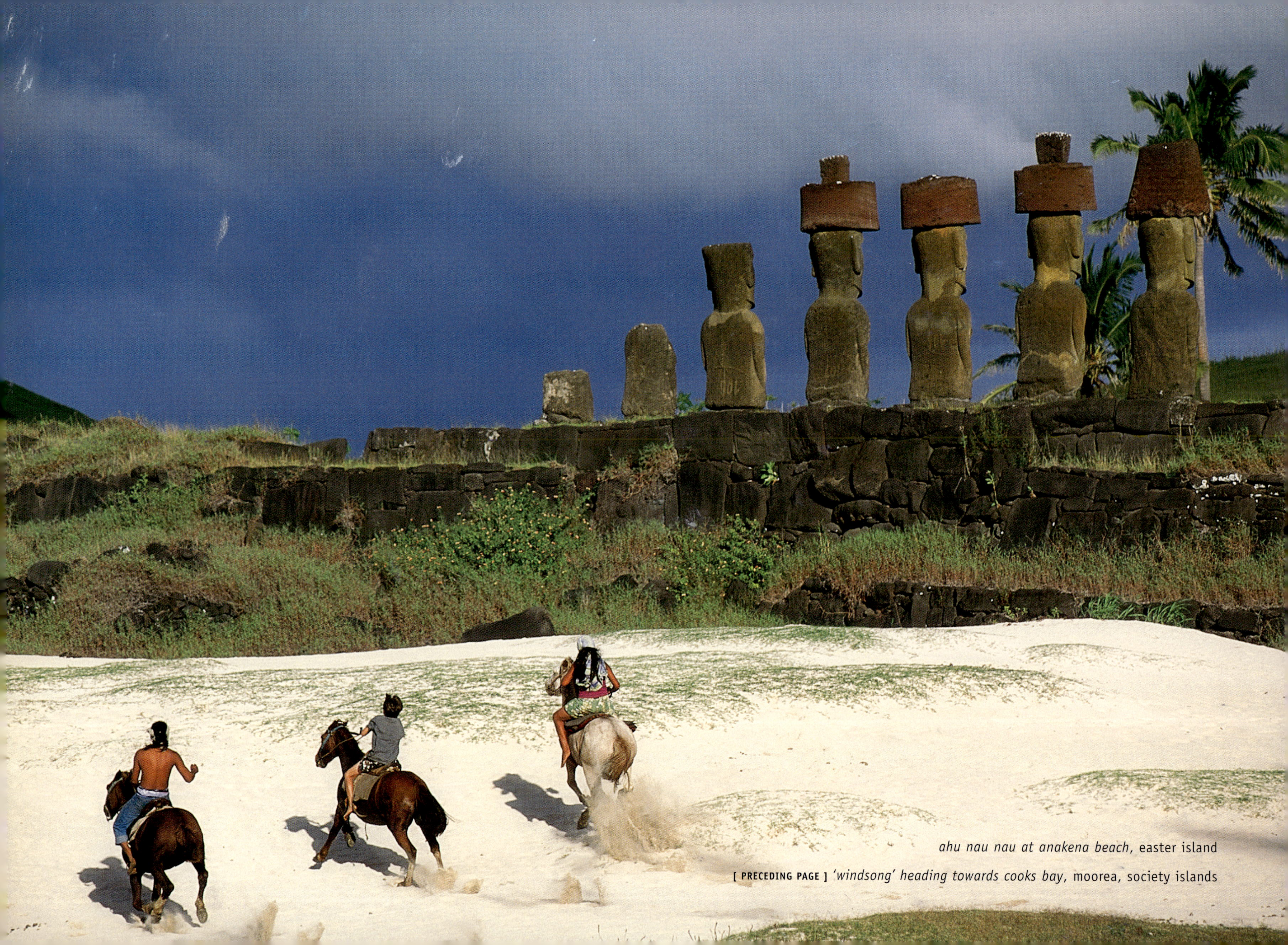

ahu nau nau at anakena beach, easter island

[PRECEDING PAGE] *'windsong' heading towards cooks bay*, moorea, society islands

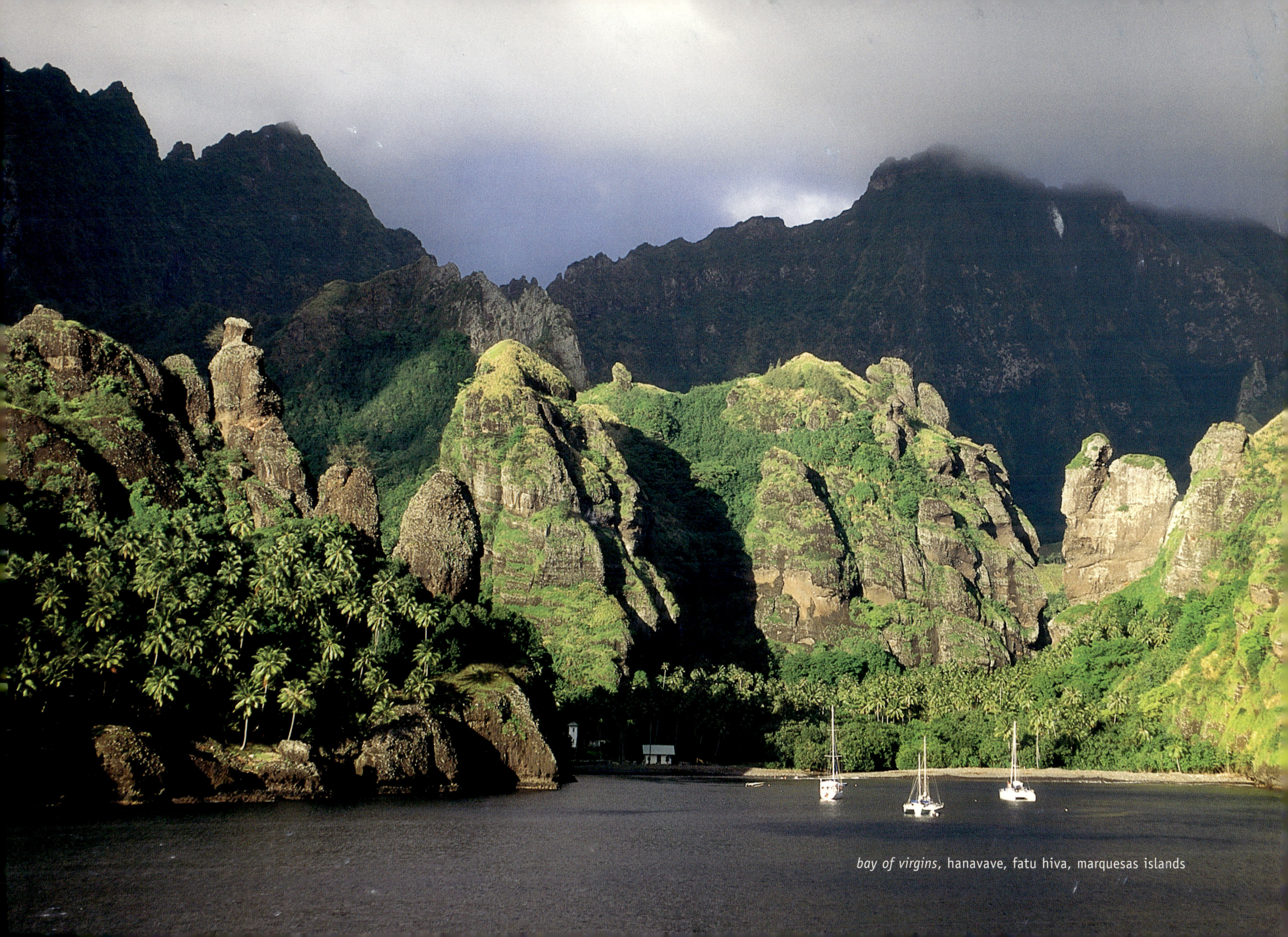

bay of virgins, hanavave, fatu hiva, marquesas islands

MY JOURNEY to the islands of the Pacific began by chance when an airline offered me the opportunity to discover a region close to me, but which had until then been little more than a blue expanse of water glimpsed from the window of an airplane.

From that first trip, I was to photograph another nine assignments before the magazine, *Pacific Panorama*, ceased publication. I realised then that I had the beginnings of a collection that I was to expand by another twenty two journeys of between one and three weeks duration.

I wish to express my sincere thanks to the people who I have photographed for this book. Nowhere else in my travels have I found such willing, open and enthusiastic subjects. I would also like to thank, Keira Lockyer – Editor *Pacific Panorama*, John Boyle, Lafi Onesemo and Ian Black from Samoa, George Cecil – Air Calin, Peter Schaap – Solomon Airlines, Michael Plumridge, Bill Burrows, Peter Wong, Anna Boetto, Brij Lal, Louelyn Wong and Alex Hendrie.

for **GEORGE** *and* **LYN**

Peter Hendrie

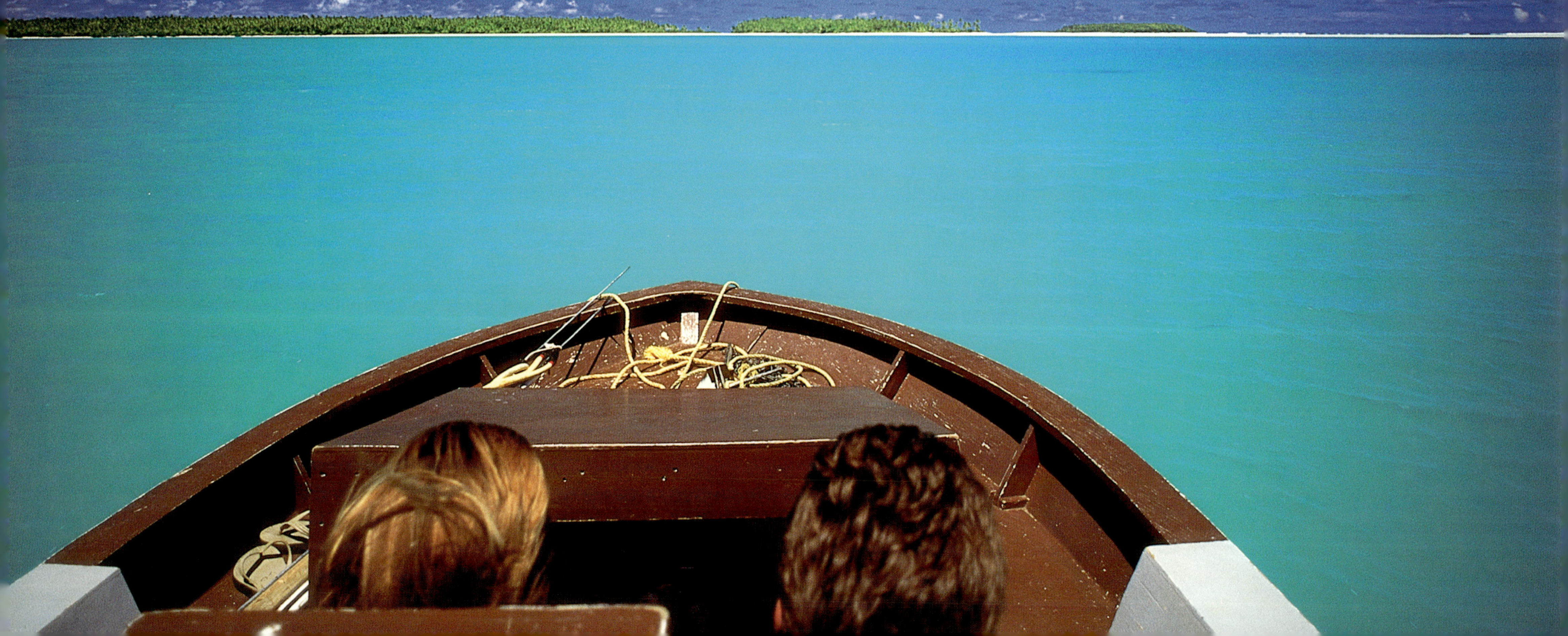

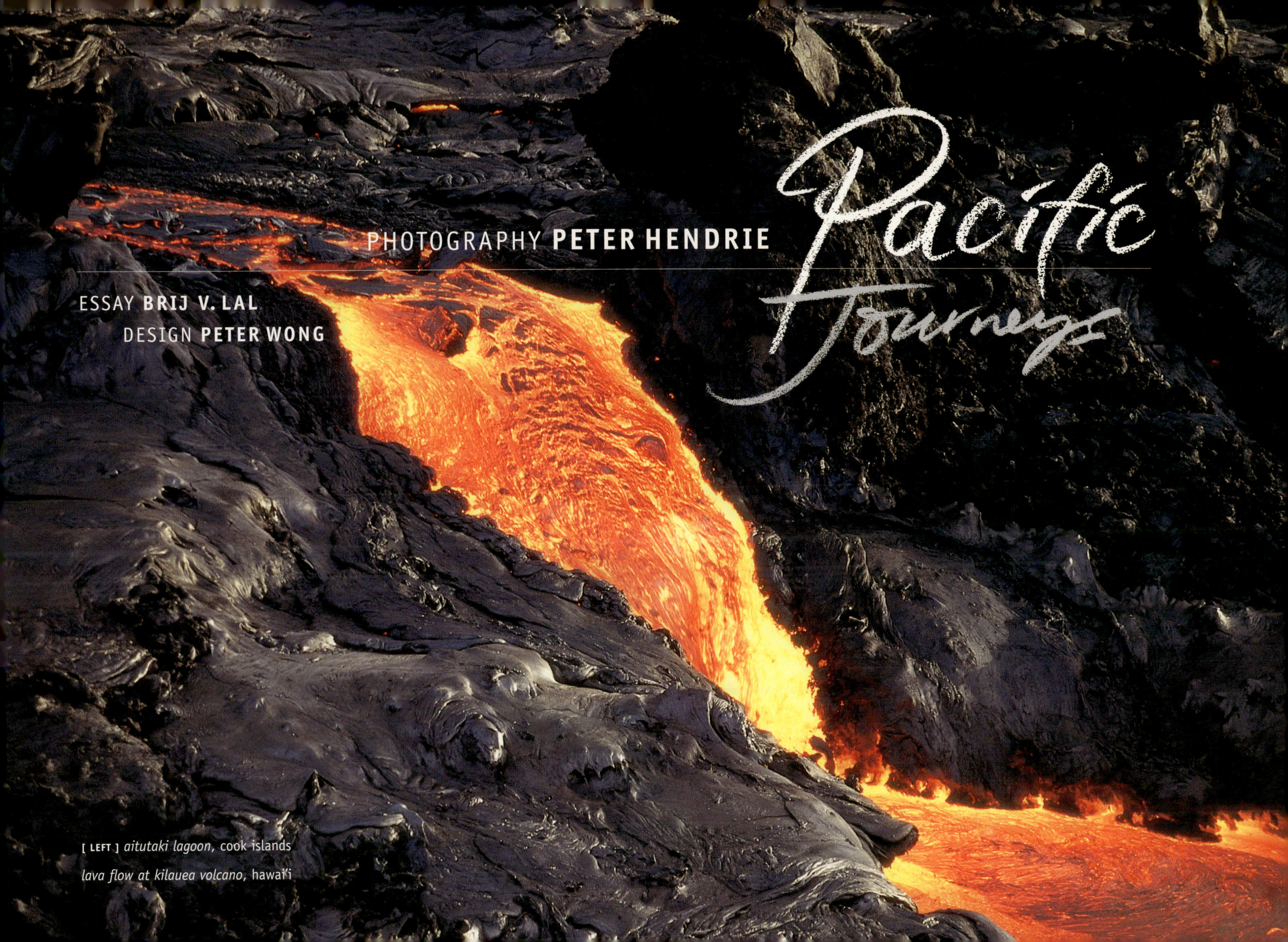

Pacific Journeys

PHOTOGRAPHY **PETER HENDRIE**

ESSAY **BRIJ V. LAL**

DESIGN **PETER WONG**

[LEFT] *aitutaki lagoon*, cook islands

lava flow at kilauea volcano, hawai'i

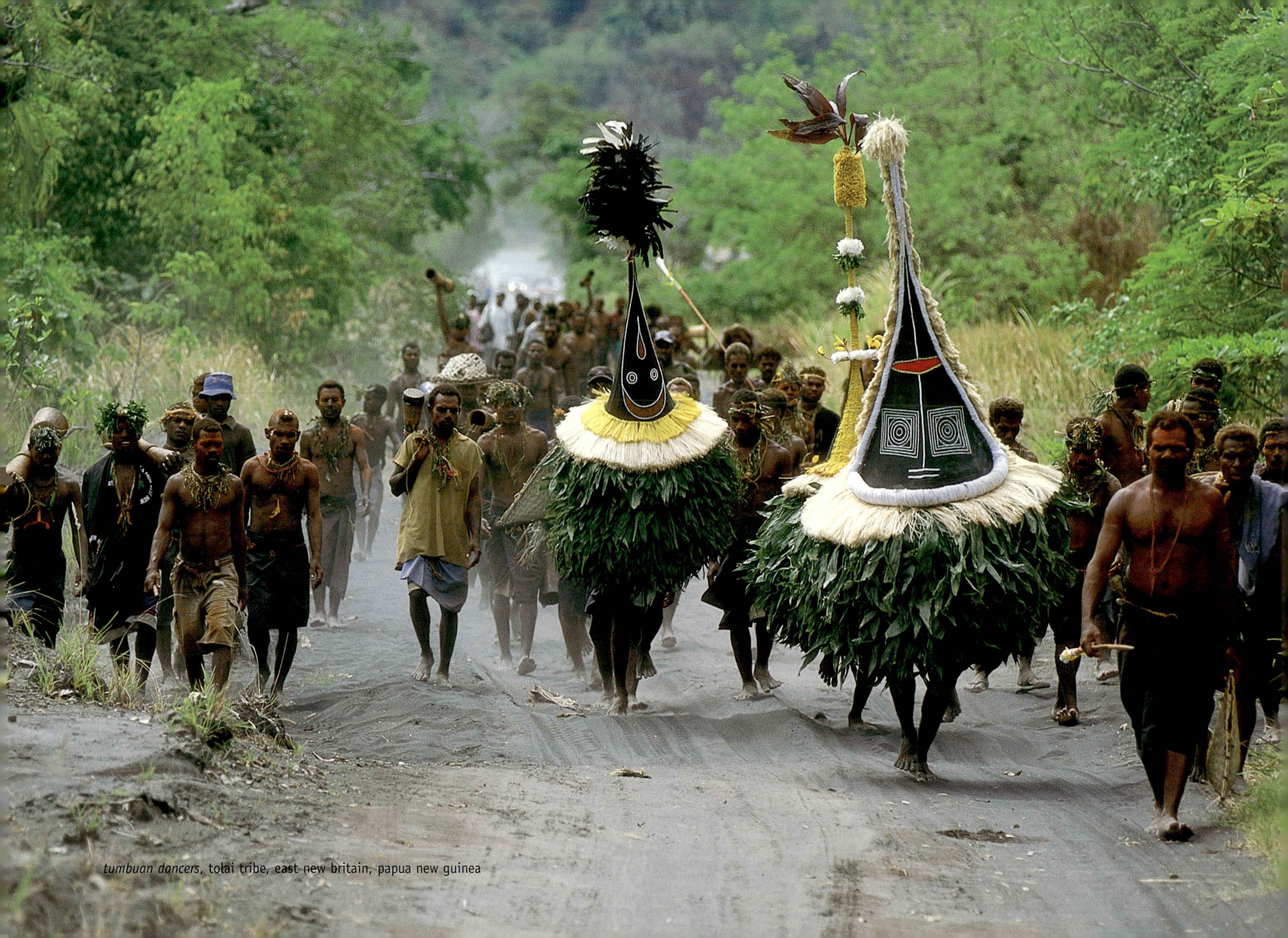

tumbuan dancers, tolai tribe, east new britain, papua new guinea

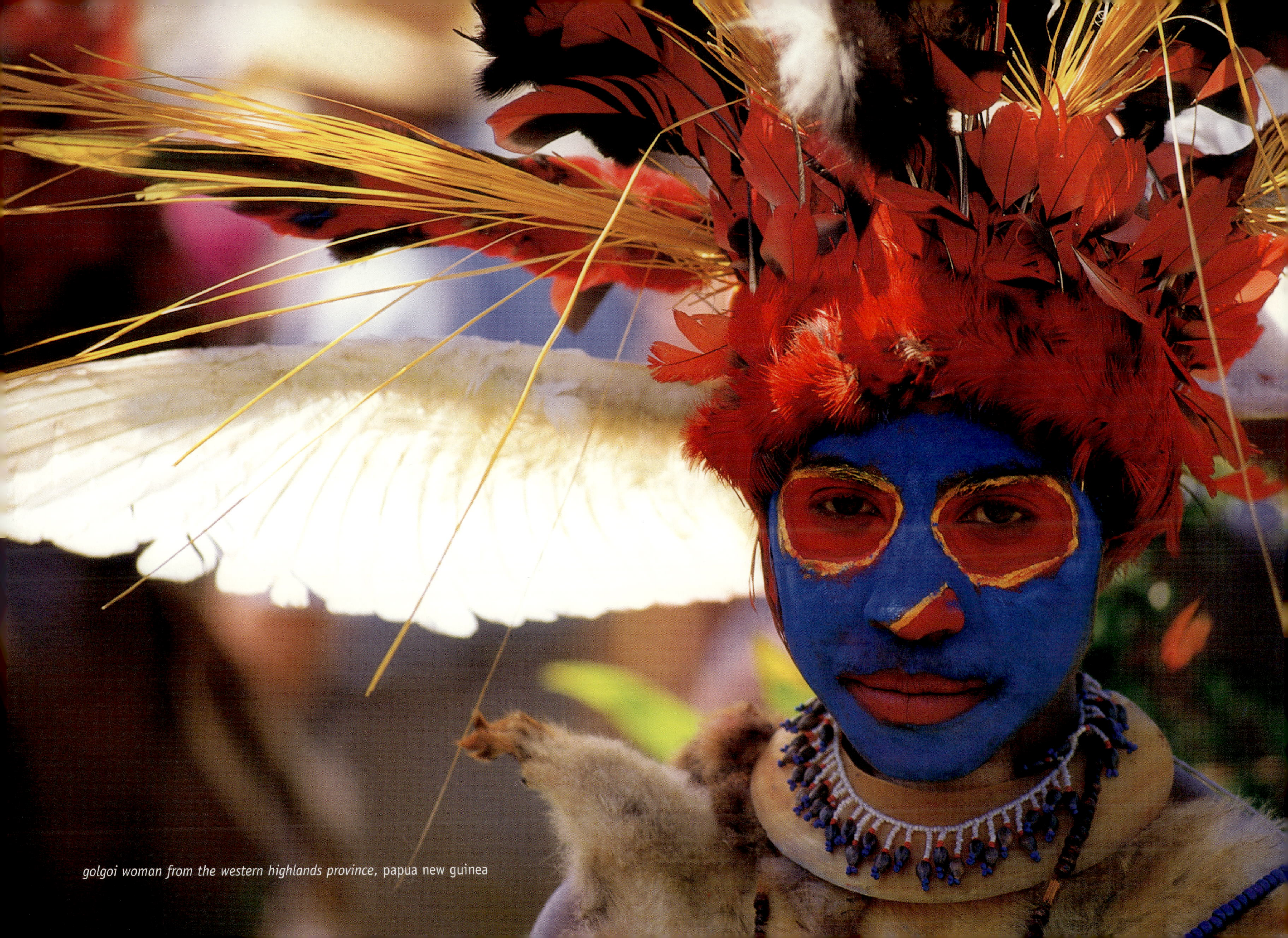

golgoi woman from the western highlands province, papua new guinea

CONTENTS

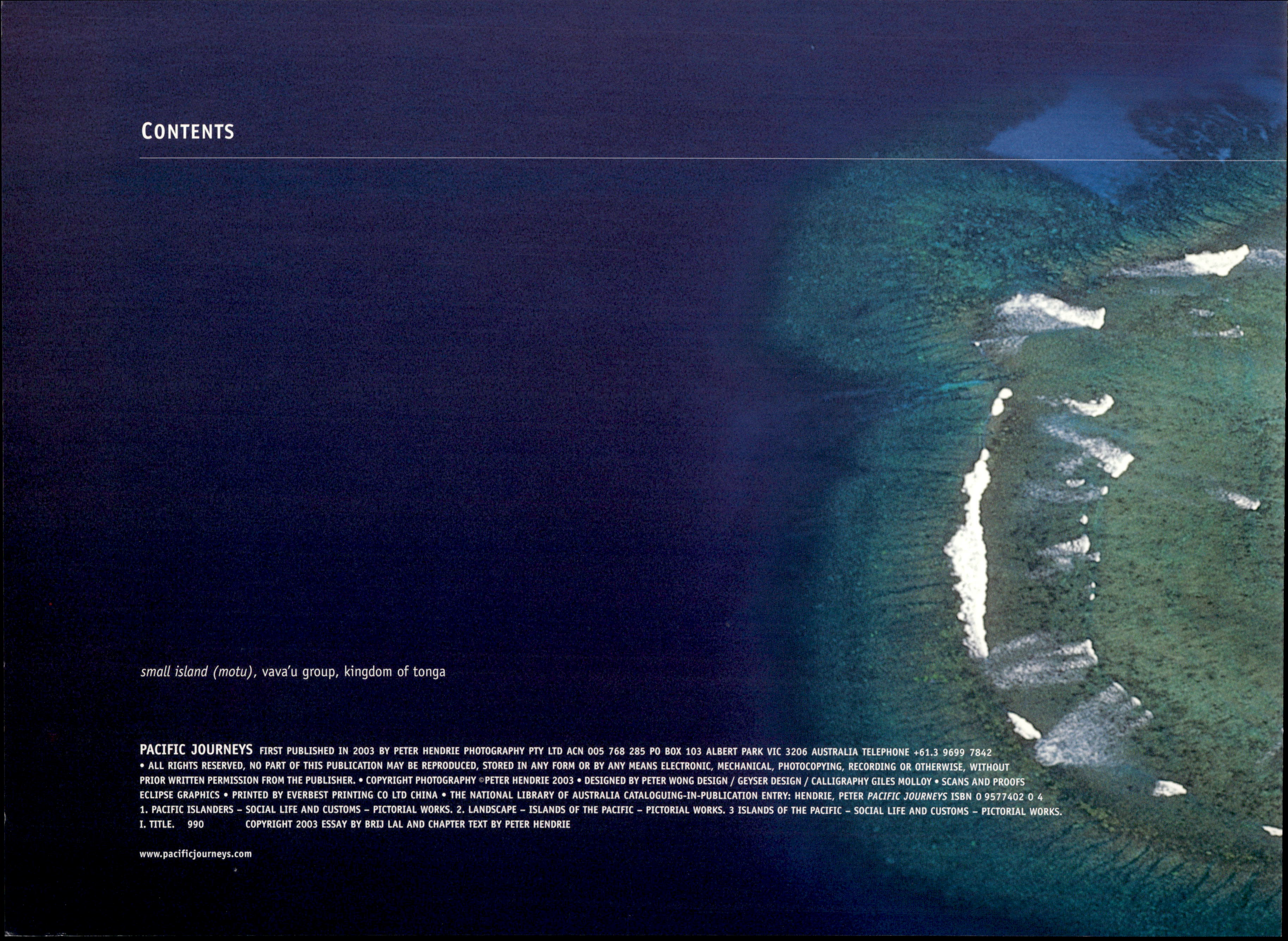

small island (motu), vava'u group, kingdom of tonga

PACIFIC JOURNEYS FIRST PUBLISHED IN 2003 BY PETER HENDRIE PHOTOGRAPHY PTY LTD ACN 005 768 285 PO BOX 103 ALBERT PARK VIC 3206 AUSTRALIA TELEPHONE +61.3 9699 7842

• DESIGNED BY PETER WONG DESIGN / GEYSER DESIGN / CALLIGRAPHY GILES MOLLOY • SCANS AND PROOFS ECLIPSE GRAPHICS • PRINTED BY EVERBEST PRINTING CO LTD CHINA • THE NATIONAL LIBRARY OF AUSTRALIA CATALOGUING-IN-PUBLICATION ENTRY: HENDRIE, PETER *PACIFIC JOURNEYS* ISBN 0 9577402 0 4
1. PACIFIC ISLANDERS – SOCIAL LIFE AND CUSTOMS – PICTORIAL WORKS. 2. LANDSCAPE – ISLANDS OF THE PACIFIC – PICTORIAL WORKS. 3 ISLANDS OF THE PACIFIC – SOCIAL LIFE AND CUSTOMS – PICTORIAL WORKS.
I. TITLE. 990

www.pacificjourneys.com

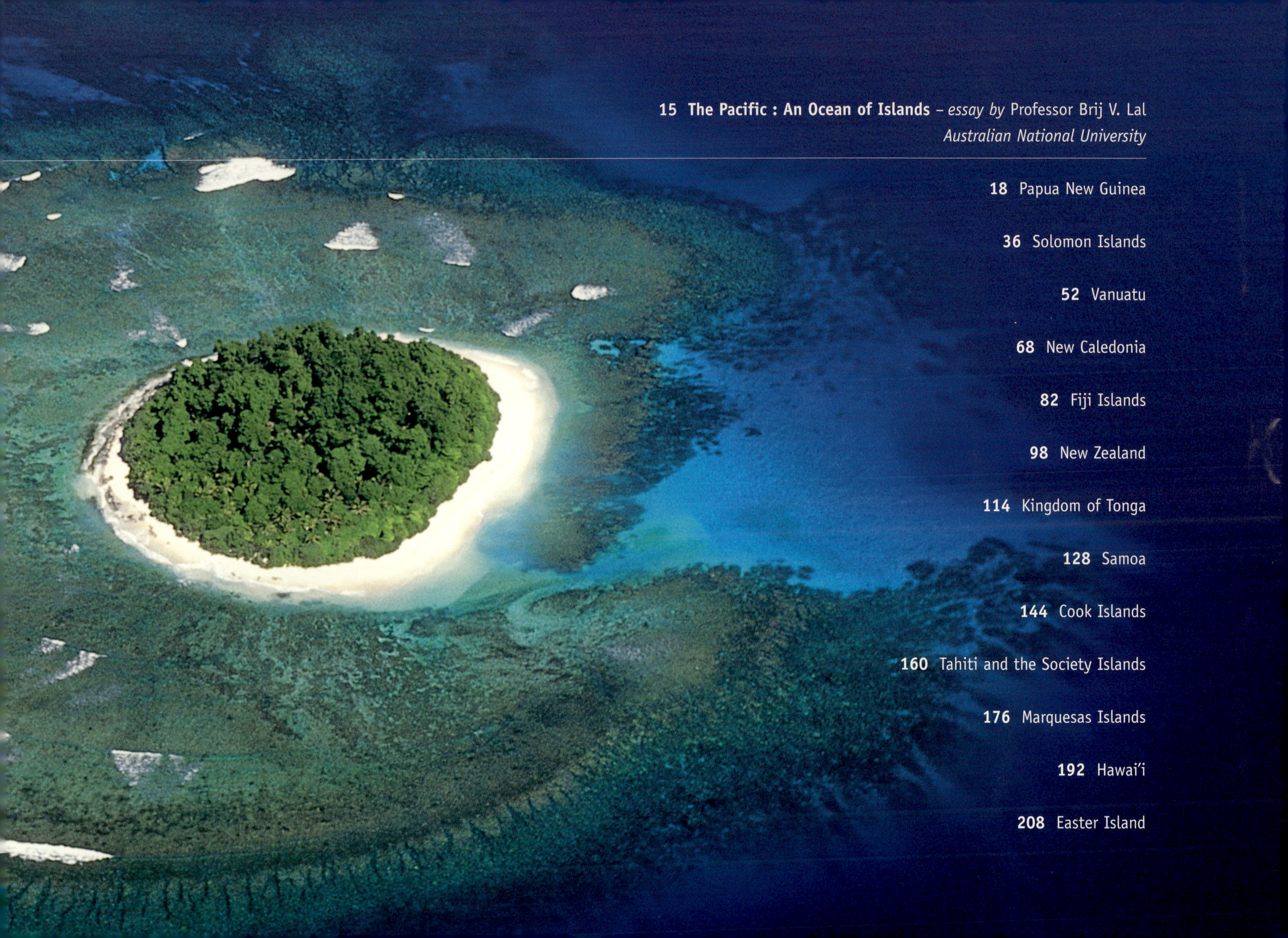

15 **The Pacific : An Ocean of Islands** – *essay by* Professor Brij V. Lal
Australian National University

18 Papua New Guinea

36 Solomon Islands

52 Vanuatu

68 New Caledonia

82 Fiji Islands

98 New Zealand

114 Kingdom of Tonga

128 Samoa

144 Cook Islands

160 Tahiti and the Society Islands

176 Marquesas Islands

192 Hawai'i

208 Easter Island

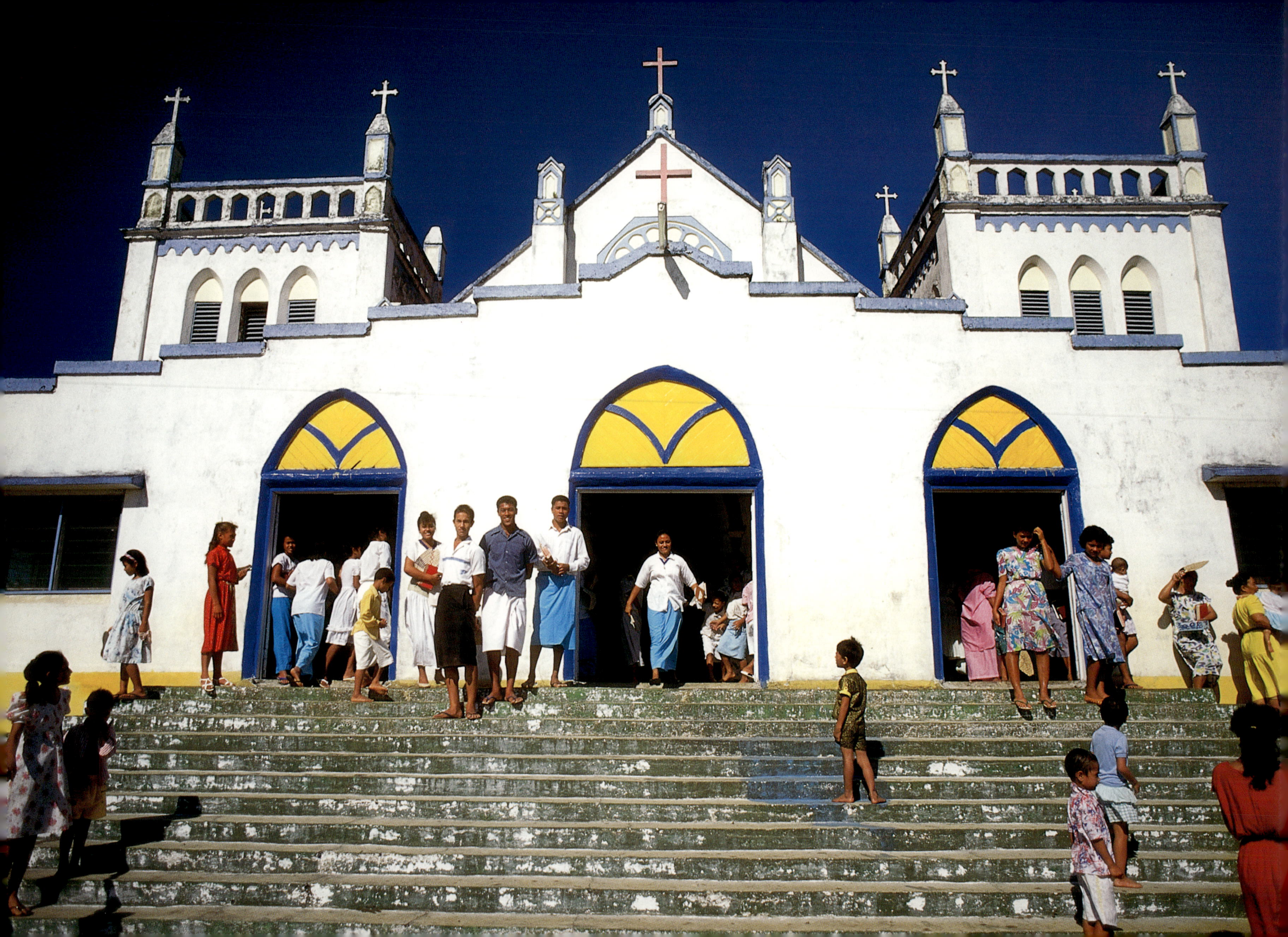

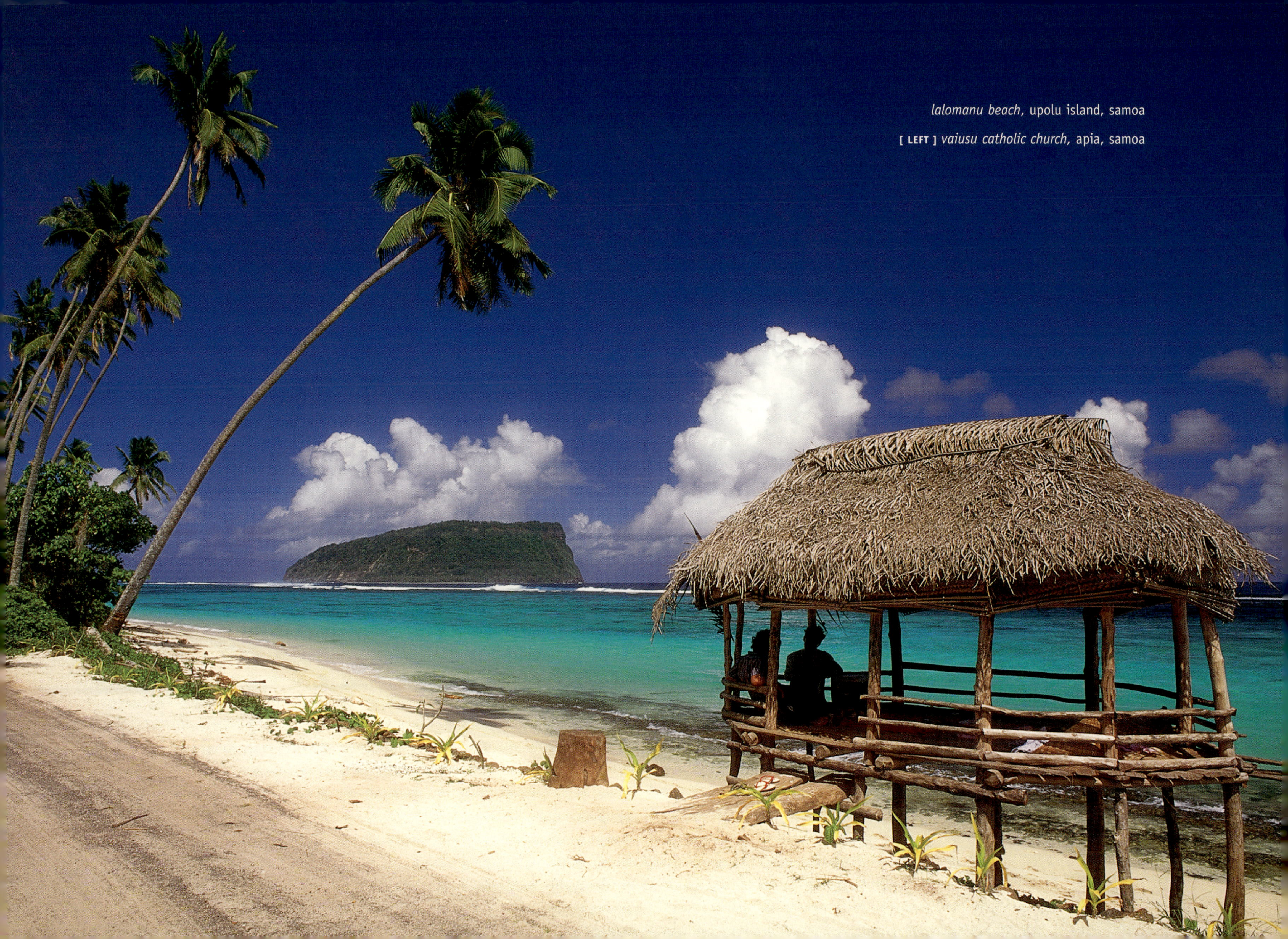

lalomanu beach, upolu island, samoa

[LEFT] *vaiusu catholic church*, apia, samoa

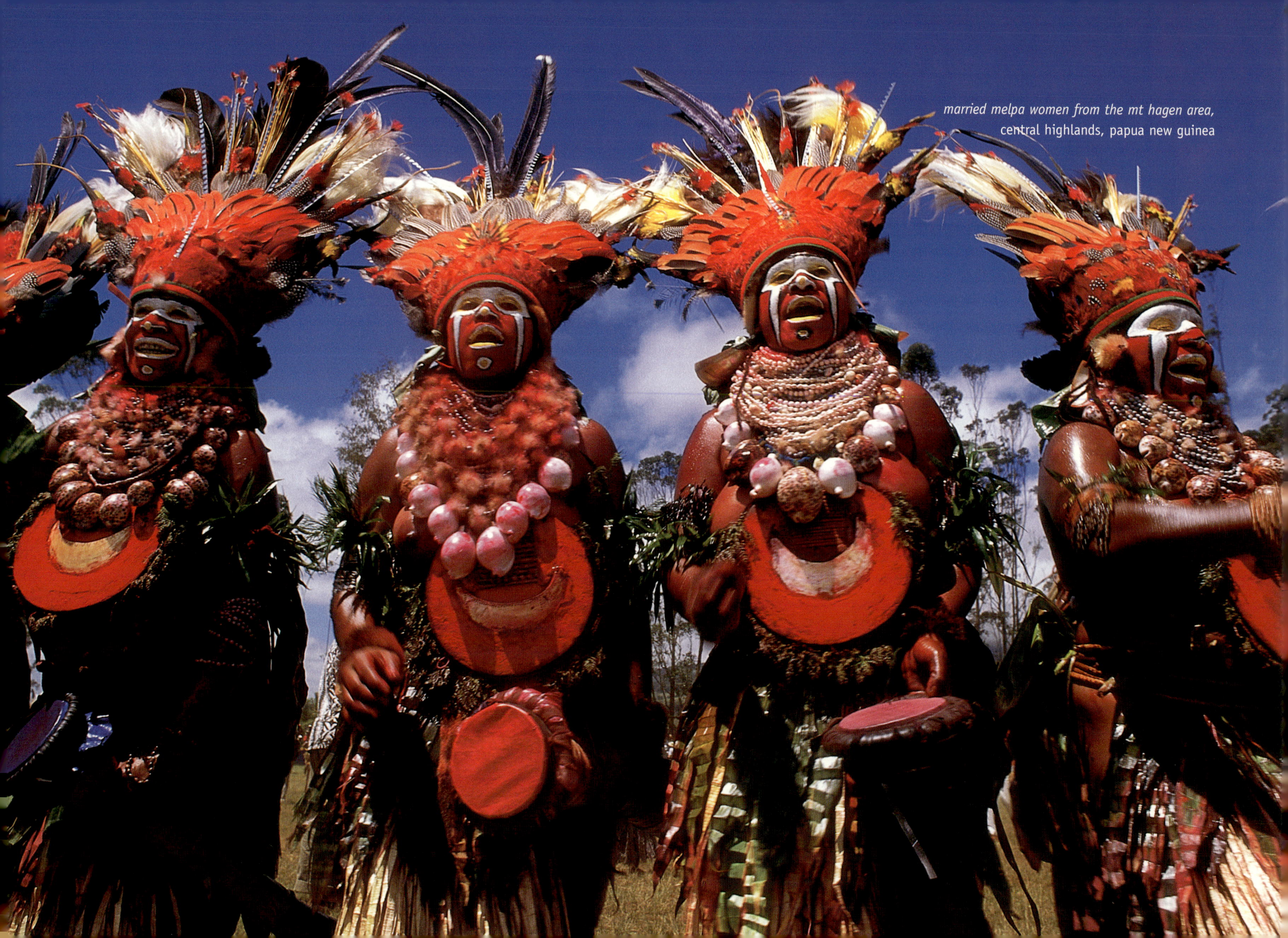

married melpa women from the mt hagen area,
central highlands, papua new guinea

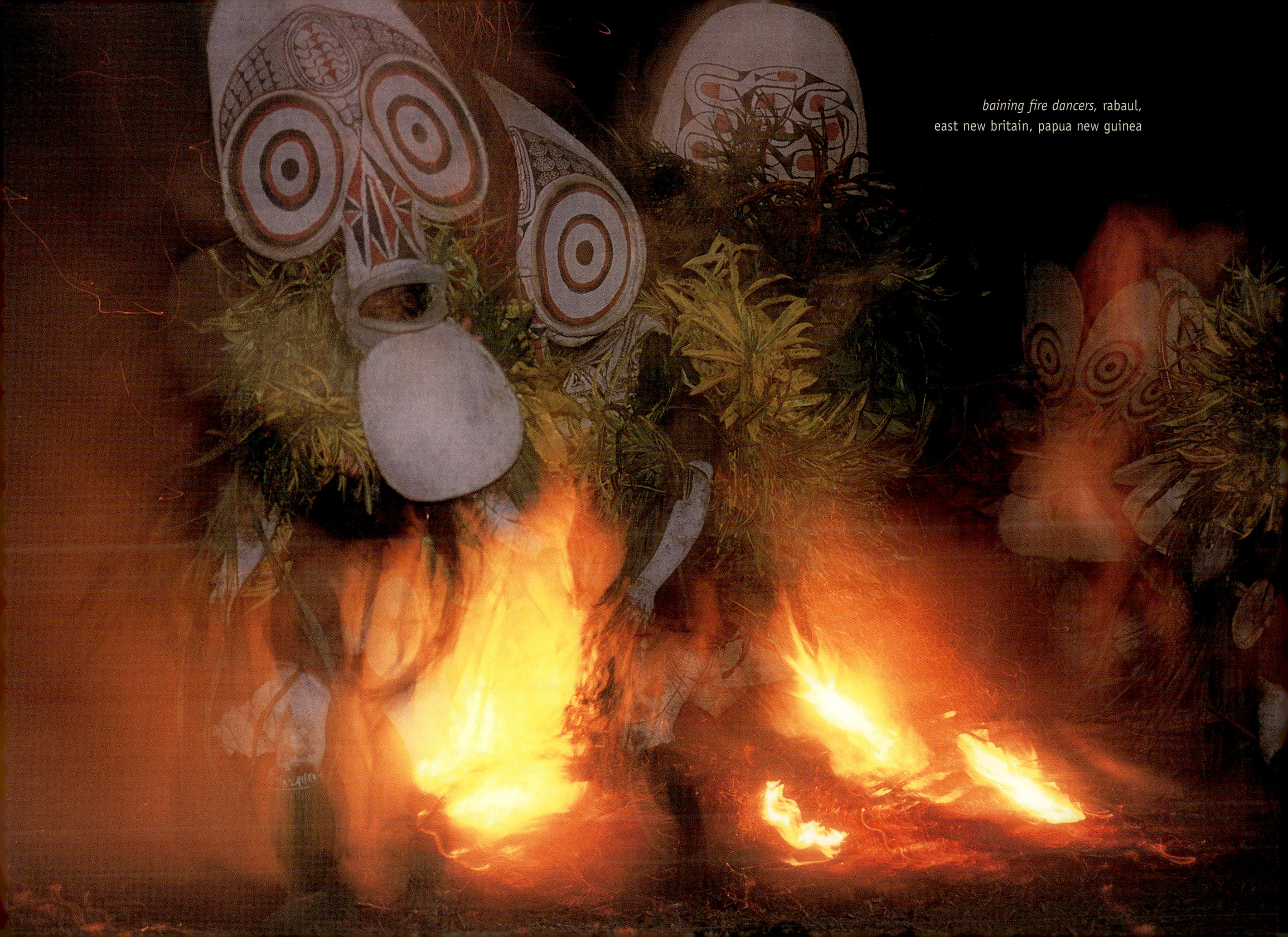

baining fire dancers, rabaul,
east new britain, papua new guinea

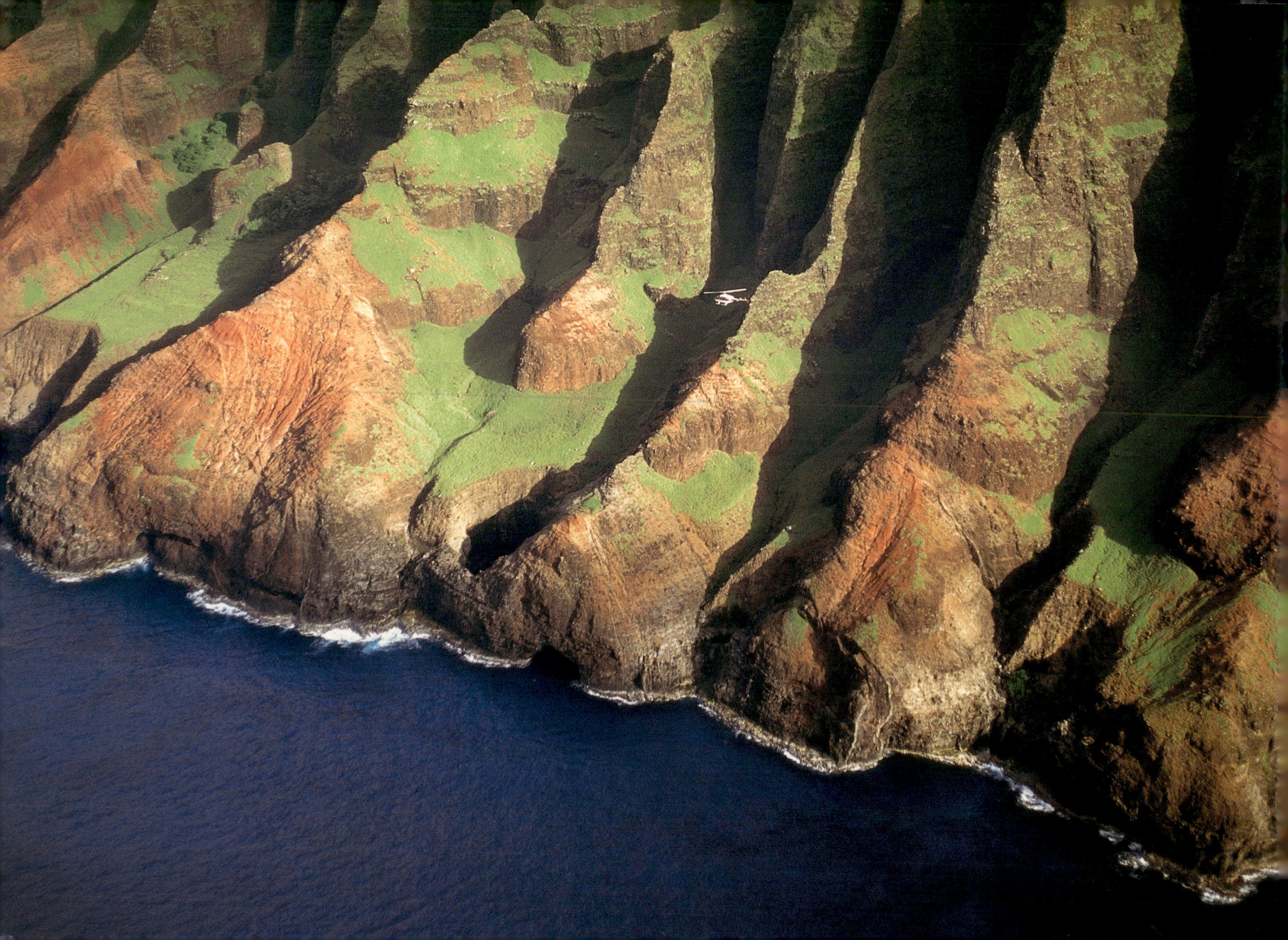

Introduction

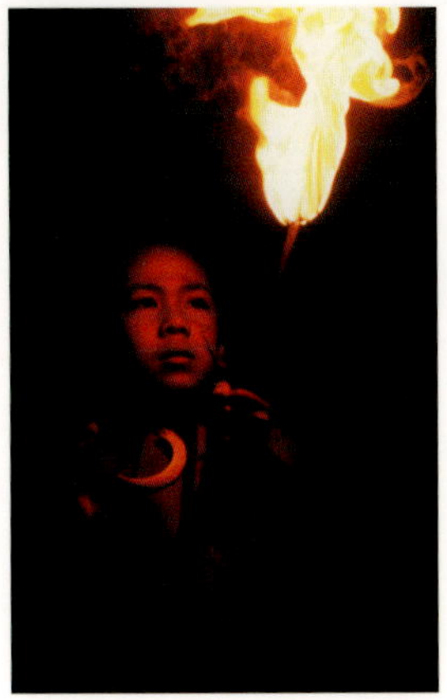

THE PACIFIC : AN OCEAN OF ISLANDS

by Professor Brij V. Lal
Professor of History and Director of the Centre for the Contemporary Pacific, Australian National University

THE PACIFIC OCEAN, the globe's largest single feature, covers a third of the earth's surface. It is 16 700 km wide at the equator, and the distance between the Bering Straits in the north and Antarctica in the south is 14 800 km. The Pacific is the deepest of all the oceans and home to the world's largest collection of islands. These islands range in size from tiny specks of coral atolls in the north, to large, mist-draped, sky-piercing volcanic formations in the west. Its southern stretches, cold, forbidding and empty, run for nearly six and a half thousand kilometers.

The islands and peoples of the Pacific have fascinated human beings for centuries and are invested with alluring images of romance and tranquillity. Tradition, recently backed by archaeological, botanical and linguistic research, has it that the first settlers of the Pacific Ocean came from the west, in a region now known as the Southeast Asian archipelago. New Guinea, settled perhaps as early as thirty-five thousand years ago, was their immediate homeland. From there, in waves upon successive waves, forced by adversity, the quest for adventure or conquest, accident or quirk of fate, the settlers travelled eastwards, to the Solomon Islands, the New Hebrides (Vanuatu), New Caledonia and Fiji which they reached about three thousand five hundred years ago. From there, Tonga and Samoa followed, and onward east they went to Tahiti, Hawai'i and New Zealand.

These voyages of discovery and settlement across a vast expanse of water through countless uncharted reefs and shoals, guided only by stars, cloud formations, homing birds and ocean currents, using traditional skills of navigation now vanished beyond recollection, remain among the greatest feats of man's achievements. The bravery, courage and skill of the early navigators continue to inspire wonder and amazement among the descendants of the original settlers who are keen to preserve the navigational heritage of their forebears. They also put in perspective the well-known and much-publicised achievements of later European explorers and discoverers.

The cultural and social systems the settlers founded varied in complexity and scale across the Pacific. In the islands of western Pacific we now call Melanesia (black islands) emerged countless small scale societies, fiercely independent, socially egalitarian, honouring individual achievement of inherited status, and speaking a variety of tongues. Papua New Guinea alone has over eight hundred languages spoken today. Across the east in the islands of Polynesia (many islands) emerged larger scale ranked societies, in Tahiti, Hawai'i and Tonga extending to vast kingdoms with intricate patterns of settled agriculture sustaining a culturally homogenous population of thousands. Micronesian (small) islands, much smaller in size honoured both rank

[**LEFT**] *helicopter over the na pali coast*, kauai, hawaiian islands [**ABOVE**] *fire dancer*, upolu island, samoa

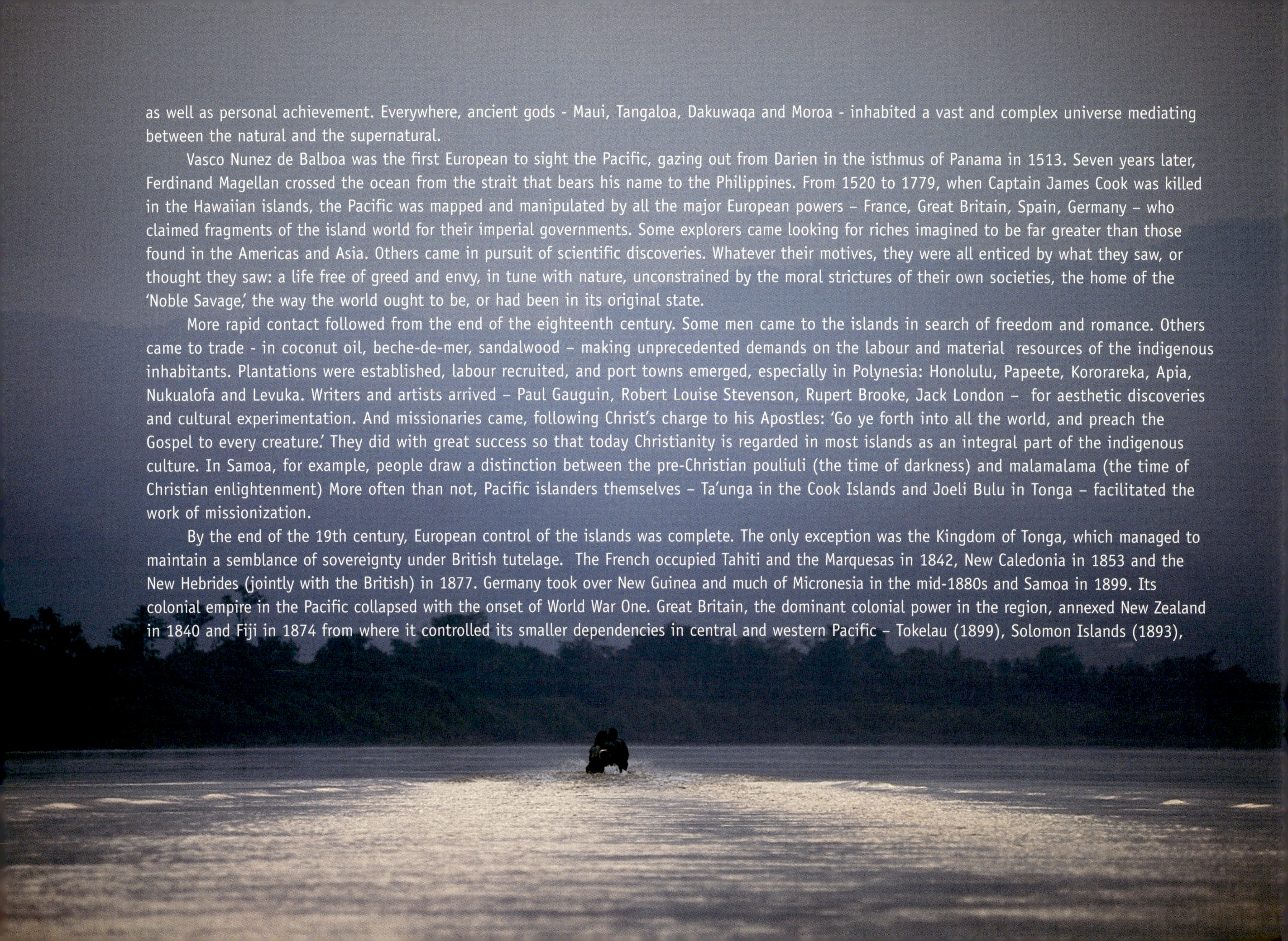

as well as personal achievement. Everywhere, ancient gods - Maui, Tangaloa, Dakuwaqa and Moroa - inhabited a vast and complex universe mediating between the natural and the supernatural.

Vasco Nunez de Balboa was the first European to sight the Pacific, gazing out from Darien in the isthmus of Panama in 1513. Seven years later, Ferdinand Magellan crossed the ocean from the strait that bears his name to the Philippines. From 1520 to 1779, when Captain James Cook was killed in the Hawaiian islands, the Pacific was mapped and manipulated by all the major European powers – France, Great Britain, Spain, Germany – who claimed fragments of the island world for their imperial governments. Some explorers came looking for riches imagined to be far greater than those found in the Americas and Asia. Others came in pursuit of scientific discoveries. Whatever their motives, they were all enticed by what they saw, or thought they saw: a life free of greed and envy, in tune with nature, unconstrained by the moral strictures of their own societies, the home of the 'Noble Savage,' the way the world ought to be, or had been in its original state.

More rapid contact followed from the end of the eighteenth century. Some men came to the islands in search of freedom and romance. Others came to trade - in coconut oil, beche-de-mer, sandalwood – making unprecedented demands on the labour and material resources of the indigenous inhabitants. Plantations were established, labour recruited, and port towns emerged, especially in Polynesia: Honolulu, Papeete, Kororareka, Apia, Nukualofa and Levuka. Writers and artists arrived – Paul Gauguin, Robert Louise Stevenson, Rupert Brooke, Jack London – for aesthetic discoveries and cultural experimentation. And missionaries came, following Christ's charge to his Apostles: 'Go ye forth into all the world, and preach the Gospel to every creature.' They did with great success so that today Christianity is regarded in most islands as an integral part of the indigenous culture. In Samoa, for example, people draw a distinction between the pre-Christian pouliuli (the time of darkness) and malamalama (the time of Christian enlightenment) More often than not, Pacific islanders themselves – Ta'unga in the Cook Islands and Joeli Bulu in Tonga – facilitated the work of missionization.

By the end of the 19th century, European control of the islands was complete. The only exception was the Kingdom of Tonga, which managed to maintain a semblance of sovereignty under British tutelage. The French occupied Tahiti and the Marquesas in 1842, New Caledonia in 1853 and the New Hebrides (jointly with the British) in 1877. Germany took over New Guinea and much of Micronesia in the mid-1880s and Samoa in 1899. Its colonial empire in the Pacific collapsed with the onset of World War One. Great Britain, the dominant colonial power in the region, annexed New Zealand in 1840 and Fiji in 1874 from where it controlled its smaller dependencies in central and western Pacific – Tokelau (1899), Solomon Islands (1893),

Gilbert and Ellice Islands (1892) and Niue (1900). In the 20th century, New Zealand joined the rank of colonial powers in Western Samoa and Cook Islands, along with Japan in Micronesia and Australia in Papua and New Guinea. The United States administered Micronesia under United Nation's Trusteeship after the Second World War.

Colonialism partitioned the Pacific, created states out of diverse societies and introduced western notions of law and order and political governance. Customs and practices deemed offensive to Christian notions of decent moral behaviour or threatening to the power of the colonial state – head hunting, witchcraft and sorcery, tribal warfare – were abolished through relentless campaigns of pacification, especially in island Melanesia. Groups which embraced the new order out of necessity or expediency were patronised and promoted, thus upsetting the balance of power in the islands and freezing fluid political dynamics. Resources were exploited by expatriate companies – phosphate on Ocean Island, Nauru, Angaur in Belau and Makatea in French Polynesia, nickel in New Caledonia, gold in Fiji and Papua New Guinea, copper in Bougainville and cash crops such as copra and sugar in Fiji and other places. These enterprises brought the first wave of globalization to the islands of the Pacific in unexpected and unprecedented ways.

The 'winds of change' which had ended colonial empires in Asia and Africa in the late 1940s and 1950s reached the Pacific in the early 1960s. Samoa became independent in 1962, Cook Islands in 1965, Nauru in 1968, Fiji in 1970, Niue in 1974, Papua New Guinea in 1975, Tuvalu and Solomon Islands in 1978, Kiribati in 1979 and Vanuatu in 1980. Everywhere, independence came through peaceful negotiation rather than through a protracted, violent struggle. In most cases those who assumed the reins of power at independence were themselves prepared for national leadership by the departing colonial powers. Of the original colonial powers, only France remains, and is likely to remain in the region in the foreseeable future. Unceasing political turbulence in the Solomon Islands, on Bougainville and in many parts of Papua New Guinea, makes the French presence attractive, sporadic demands for independence from an assortment of indigenous groups and censure from sections of the non-francophone community notwithstanding. And French prestige, a factor in its foreign policy, is at stake, too. North of the equator, the United States maintains its strategic presence in the islands of Micronesia through a variety of political and diplomatic arrangements.

By world standards, the Pacific Islands have fared well. Except in Fiji, with its coups in 1987 and again in 2000, the verdict of the ballot box has been respected. Elections take place, governments change, life goes on. Western institutions, suitably indigenised, continue to exist though they now face the threat of being undermined by emergent forces of tribalism, provincialism and sub-nationalism. Global forces of change – market economy, urbanisation, western education, rapid electronic communication: the e-mail, the internet – impinge on the islands with increasing force, creating internal economic disparities and destabilising societies. Traditional cultural values of rank, hierarchy and ascribed status clash with forces of modernity which emphasise individual initiative and enterprise. The best and the brightest are leaving island shores for greener pastures in metropolitan centres, draining the islands of much needed skills and talents.

The Pacific Islands are thus vulnerable both to self-inflicted wounds as well as to far-reaching changes wrought by globalization. In this, they are not alone of course. But their predicament is exacerbated by their smallness, isolation and fragile economies vulnerable to both natural calamities and the vagaries of global trade. Nonetheless, Pacific Island peoples have, in the past, shown courage and resilience in coping with changes that have come to their shores. They have adapted, and triumphed. Its present leaders will need the vision and courage of their forebears to navigate the treacherous, uncharted waters ahead. That is their challenge, their opportunity at the dawn of a new century.

[**LEFT**] *canoe approaching the upper sepik river town of ambunti,* papua new guinea

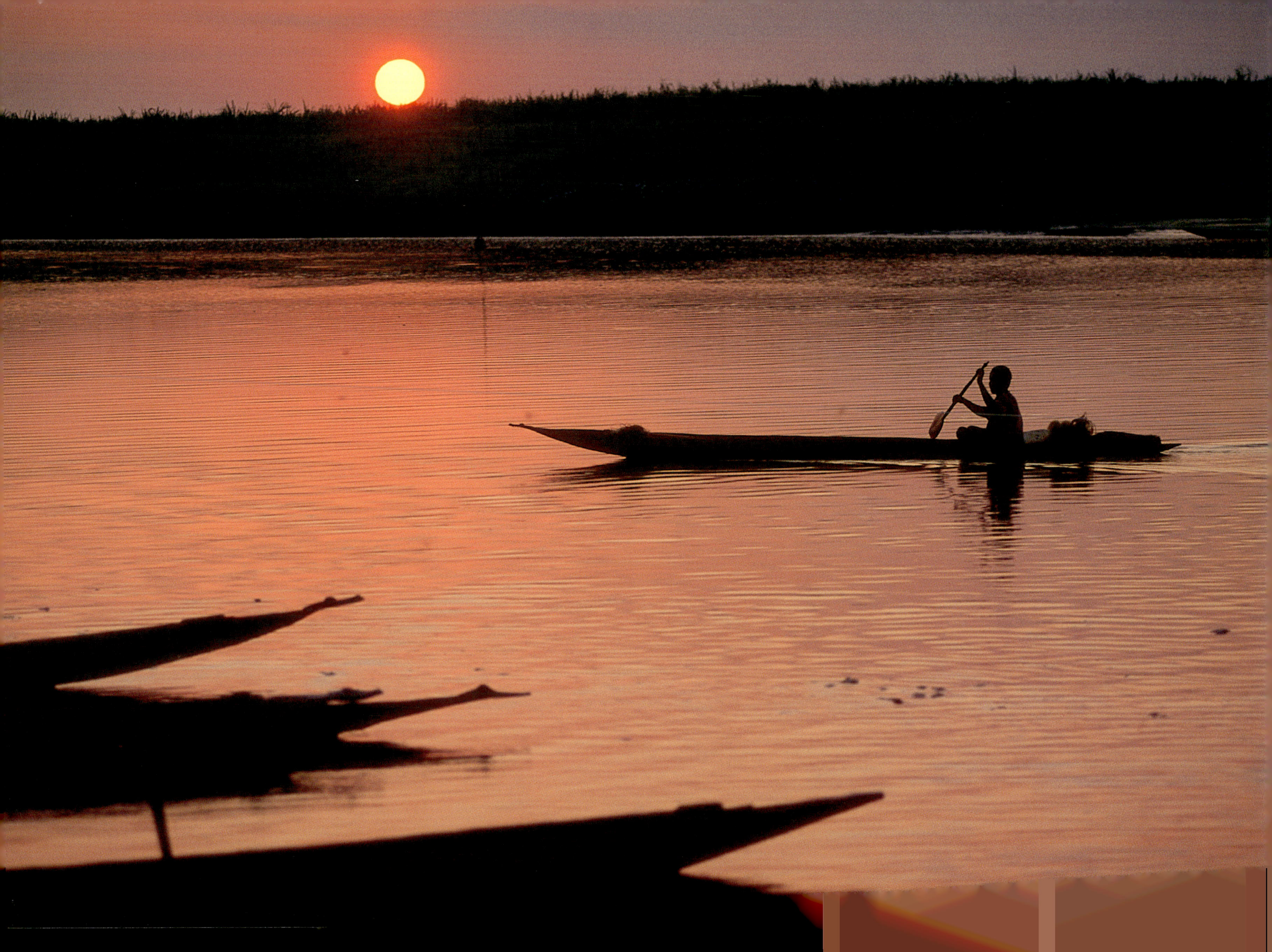

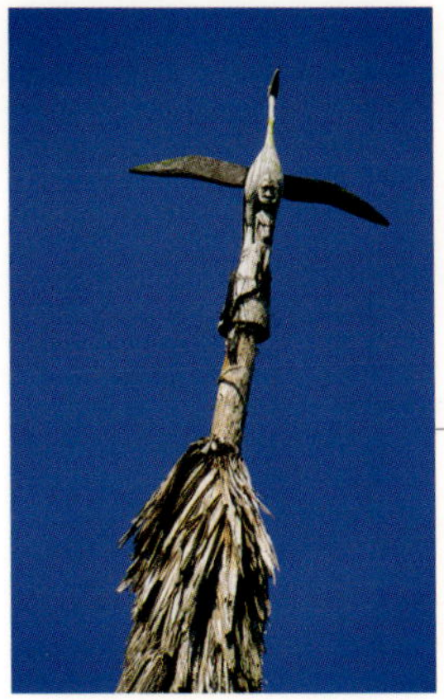

Papua New Guinea

THE INHABITANTS of Papua New Guinea probably migrated in several waves through the Indonesian archipelago about 35 thousand years ago. The rugged, mountainous terrain that they encountered isolated the different population groups, which developed into an extraordinarily diverse country of 700 different tribal and cultural groups speaking more than 800 languages in a population of just 4.5 million people.

Located a little south of the Equator with a tropical climate, the physical diversity ranges from snow-capped mountains with deep tropical rainforest-adorned valleys and active volcanic chains to the large river systems of the Sepik and Fly with their fertile plains. Numerous islands and reefs abound with an abundance of marine life.

The variety of animal and plant life is extraordinary with over 860 species of birds, 3000 varieties of orchids and 1400 species of fish and a wide range of reptiles, mammals and insects including the world's largest butterflies.

Papua New Guinea was known to the Europeans from the 16th century and colonised by the British and Germans who limited themselves to the accessible coastal regions in the late 19th century. It remained the last large landmass in the world to be fully explored and it wasn't until the discovery of gold in 1926 that the huge highland cultures were first known. Over a million people living in the hidden mountain valleys soon became a favourite subject for anthropologists from around the world. From the end of WWI, Australia under the League of Nations Mandate administered New Guinea, until it gained full independence in 1975 as the nation of Papua New Guinea.

The people can be divided into four ethnic groups: New Guineans (from the North of the main island), Papuans (from the South), Highlanders and Islanders.

Nearly all tribes in PNG have their distinctive forms of artistic expression. The peoples of the Sepik and Papuan gulf regions are famous for their wood carving, painting and pottery. These are prized by collectors and represented in the great museums around the world and have also had a significant influence on 20th century art. The people of the highlands, however, artistically express themselves in body and facial painting and adornments, using colourful feathers, shells, butterflies and skins for this purpose.

[LEFT] *canoes with carved crocodile bows,* wombun village, chambri [ABOVE] *bird carving atop a haus tambaran (spirit house),* middle sepik

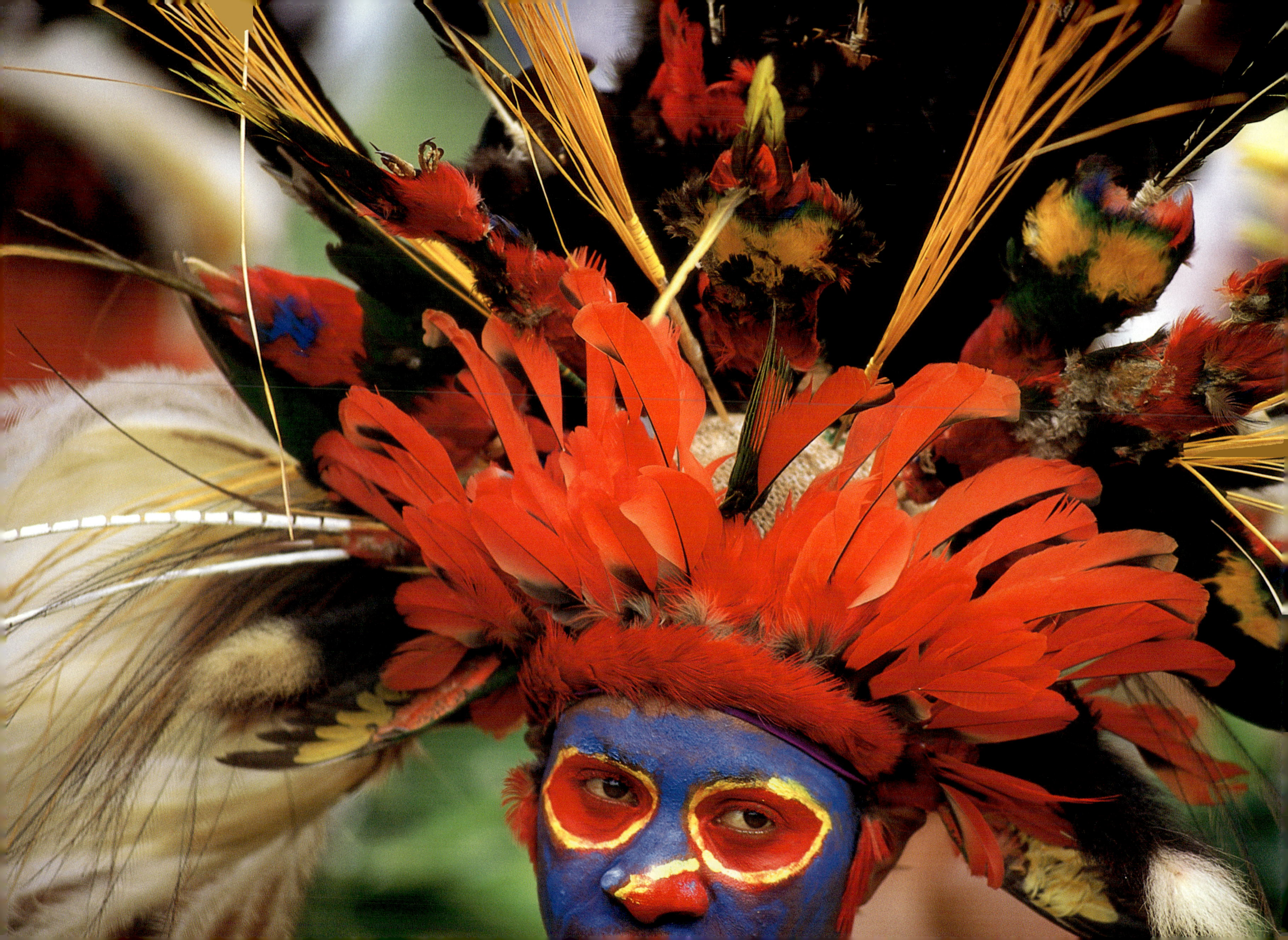

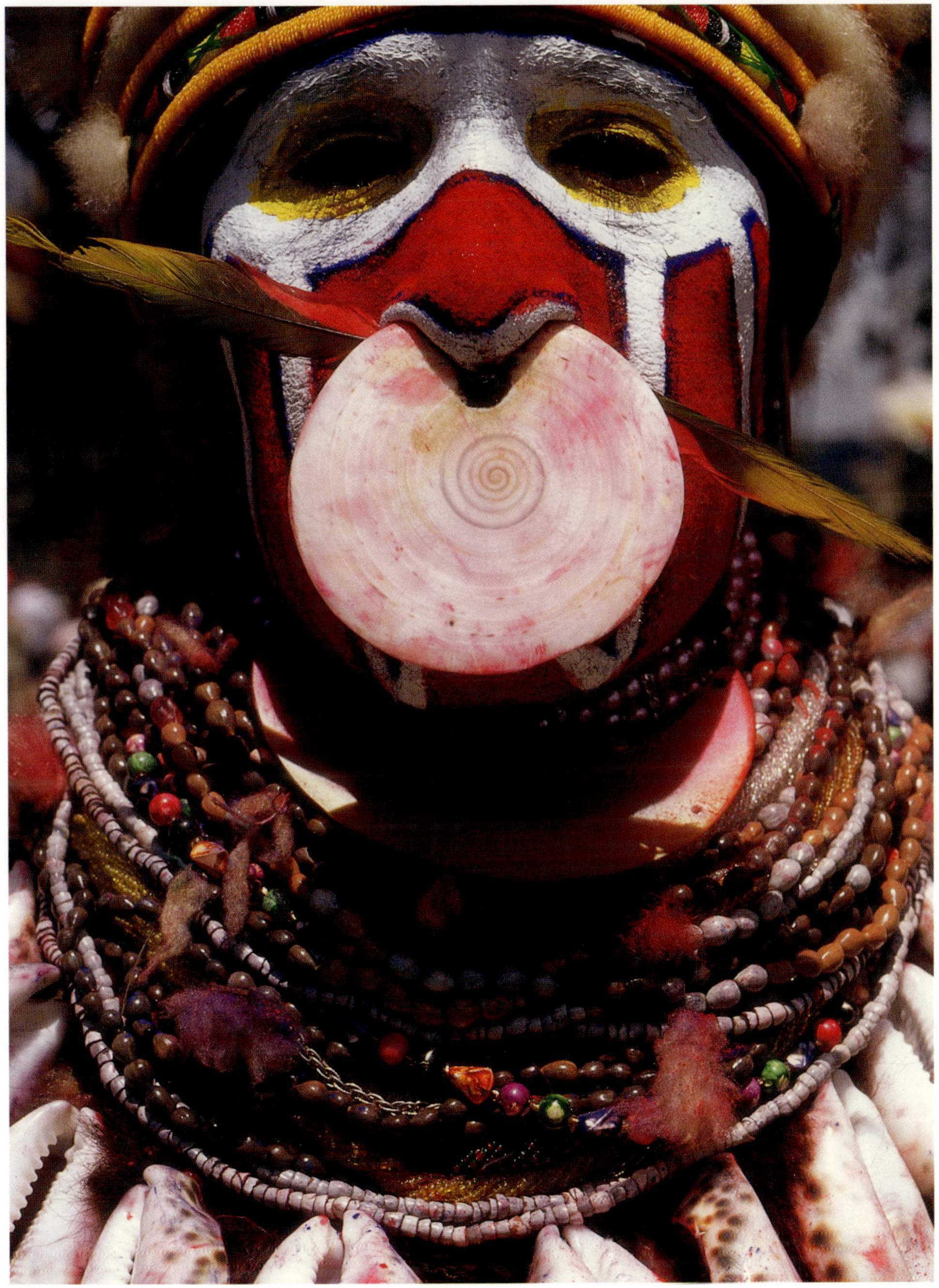

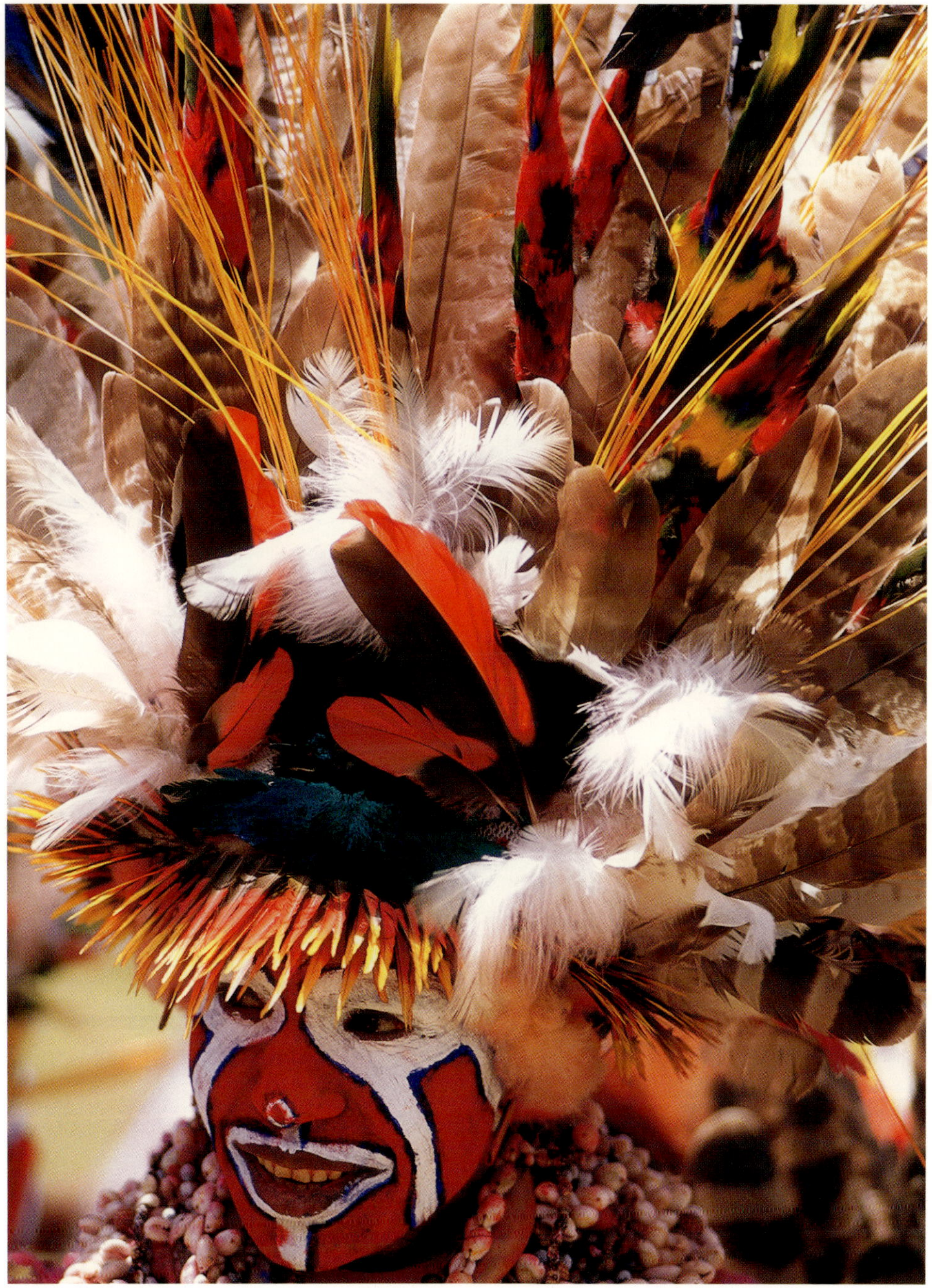

[LEFT] *golgoi dancer,* western highlands province [ABOVE LEFT] *kumdi amps woman,* western highlands province [ABOVE] *kui east woman,* western highlands province

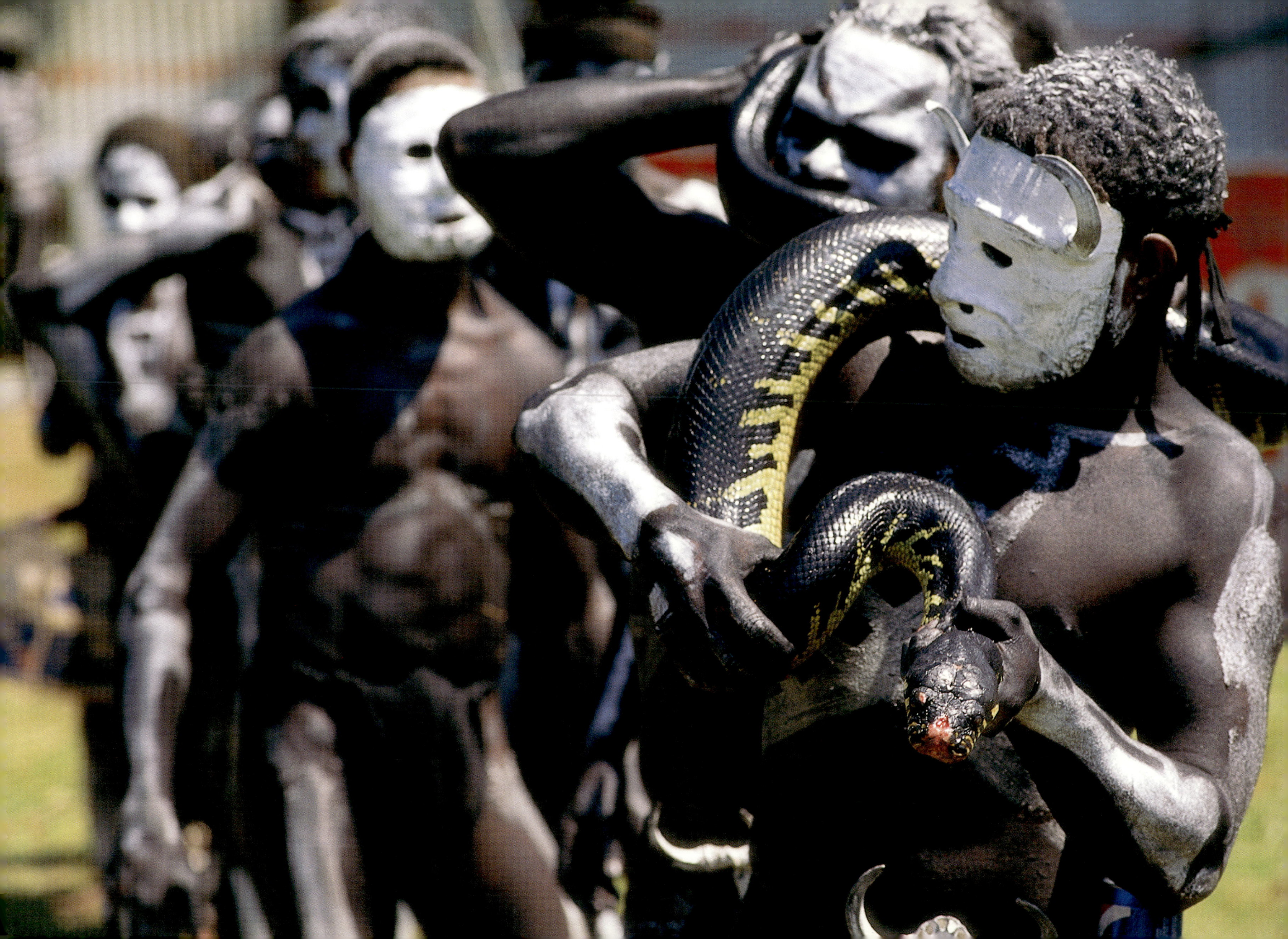

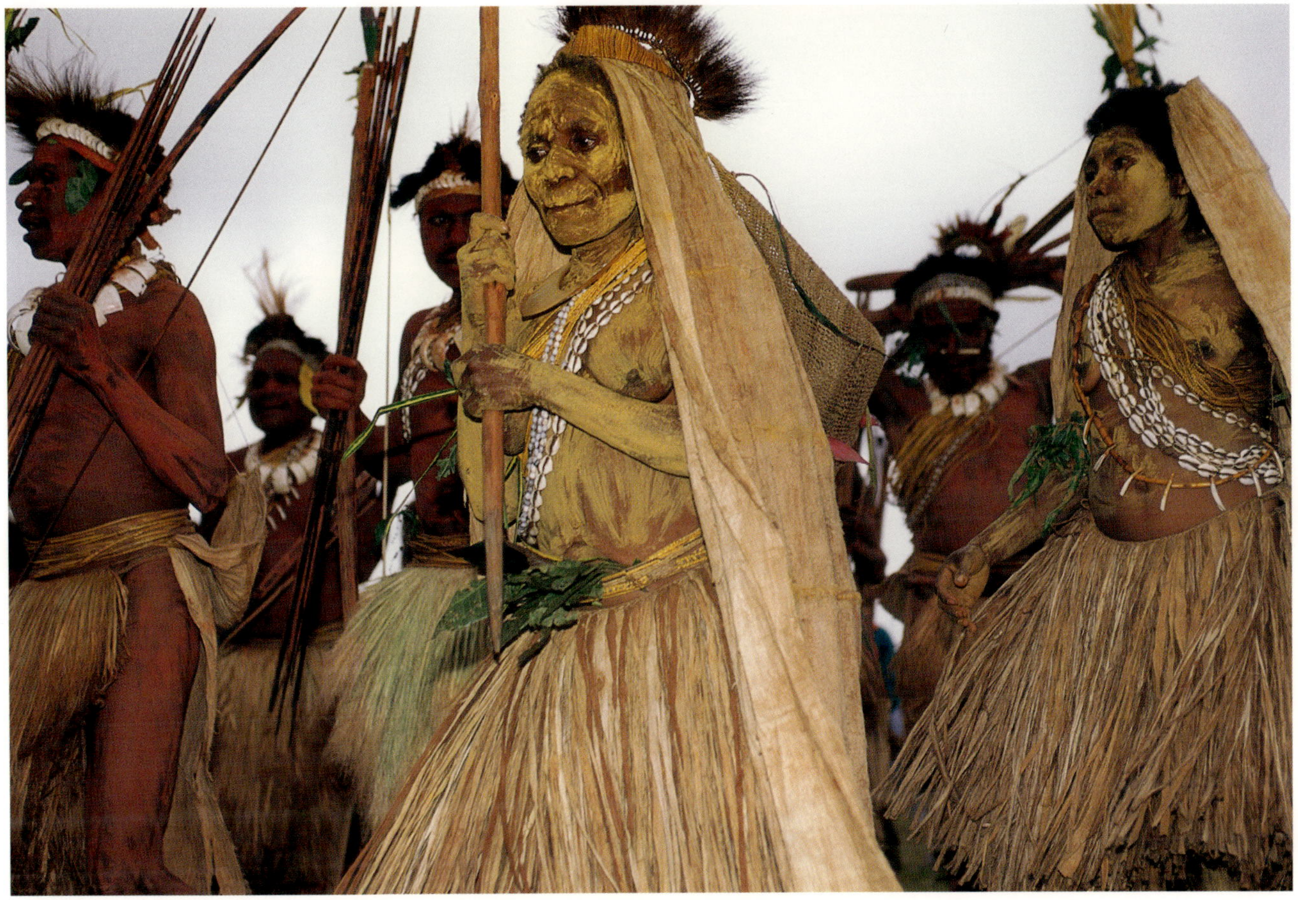

[ABOVE] *kaimanga dancers,* eastern highlands province

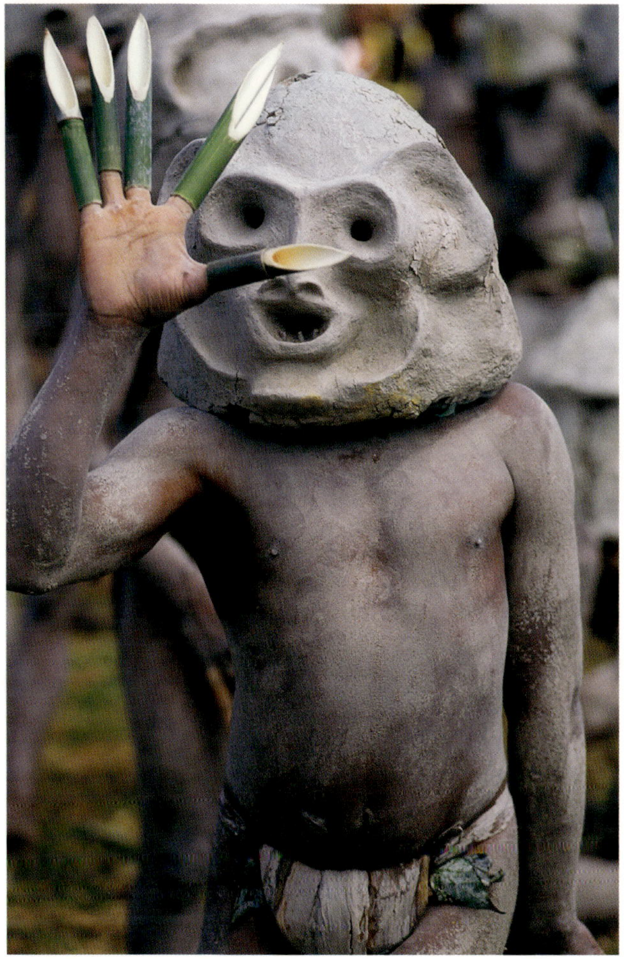

[RIGHT] *asaro mudman,* eastern highlands province

[LEFT] *omo masalai dancers,* chimbu province

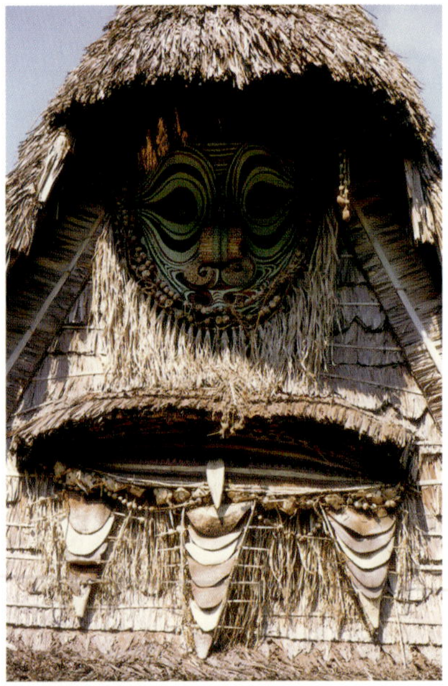

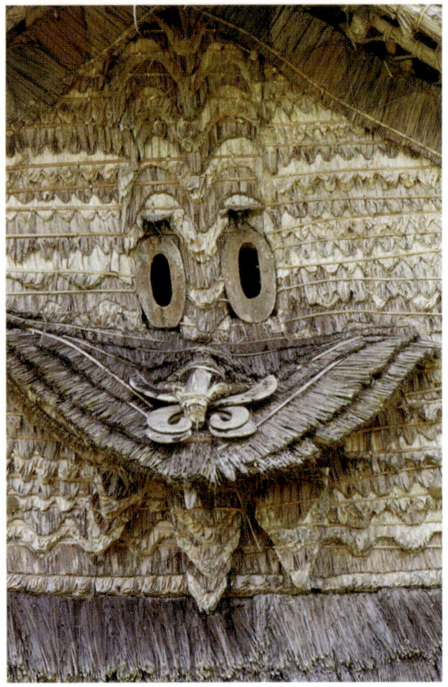

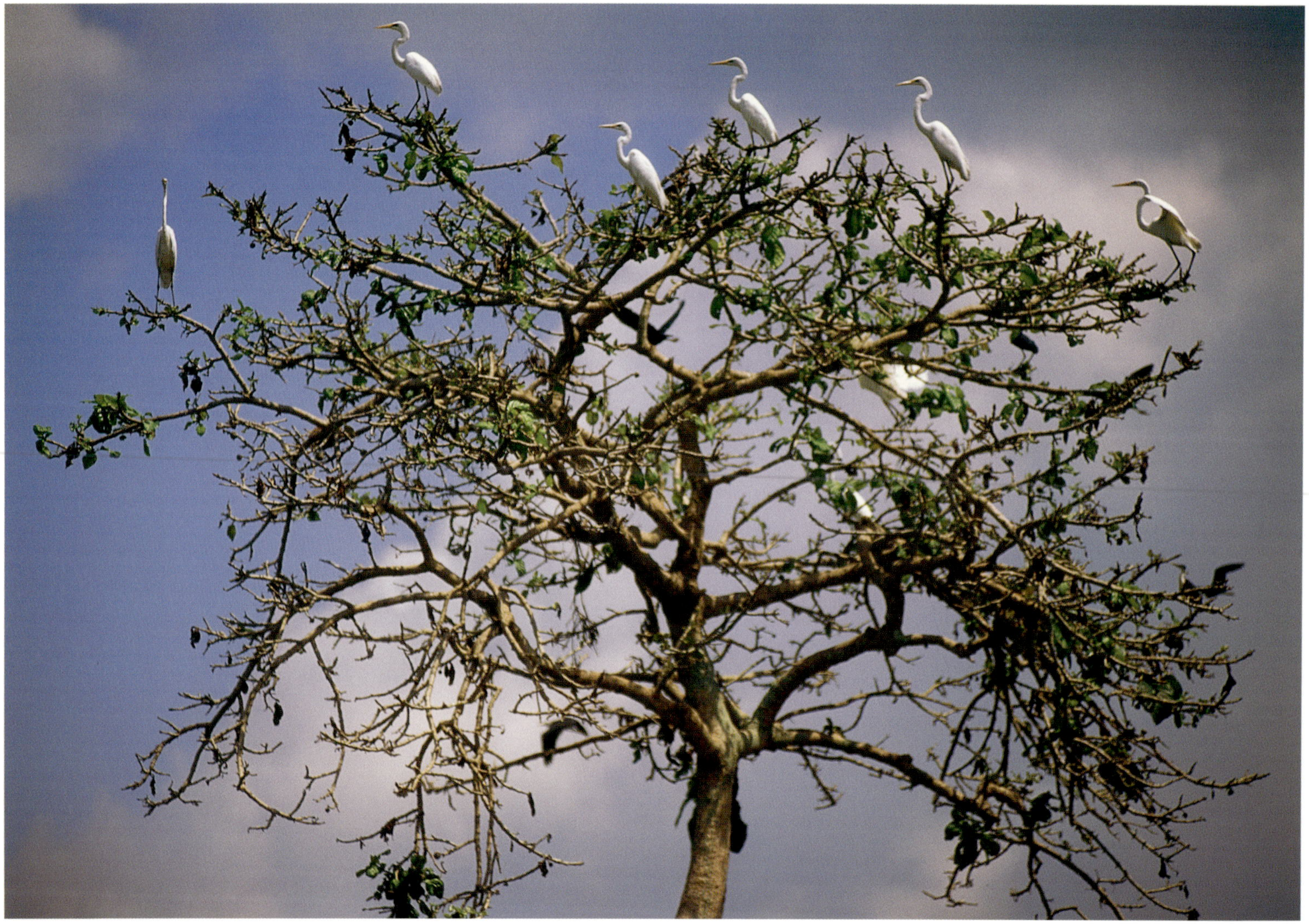

[**ABOVE**] *white egrets,* upper sepik region

[**ABOVE AND BELOW LEFT**] *spirit faces on haus tambaran (spirit house),* middle sepik

[**RIGHT**] *haus tambaran at yentchen village,* middle sepik

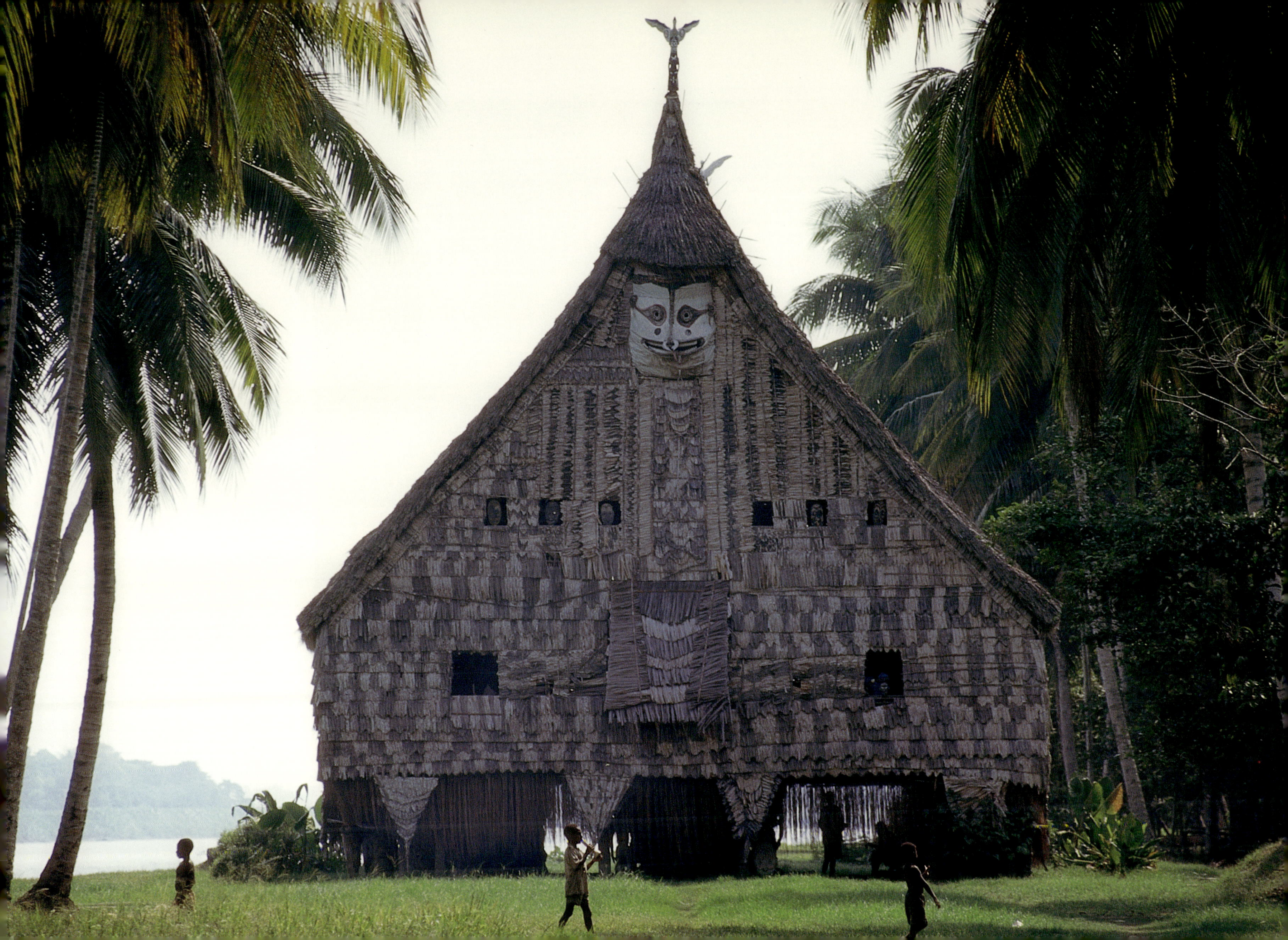

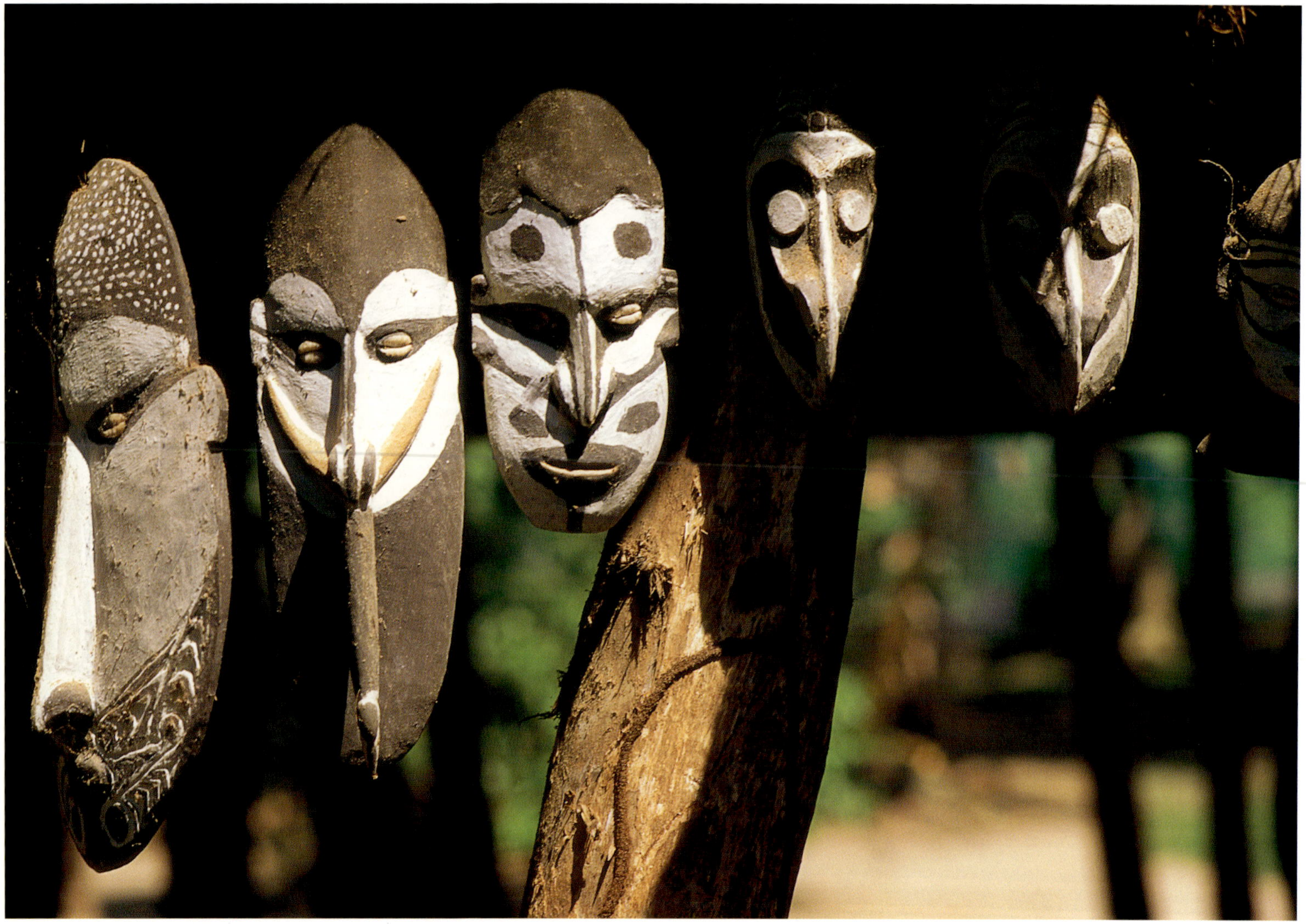

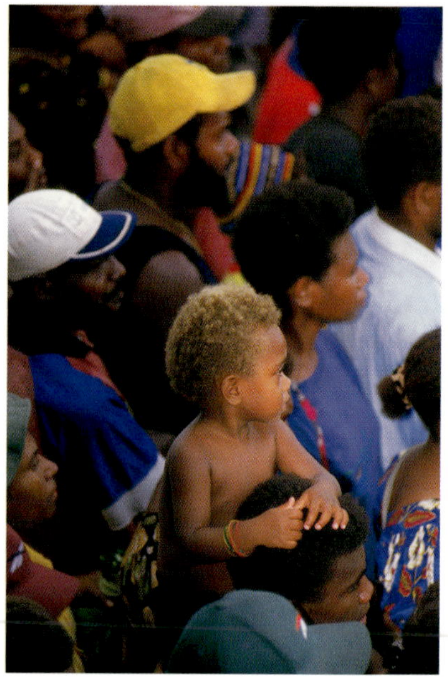

[ABOVE] *masks at tambanum village,* middle sepik [RIGHT] *spectators at the rabaul mask festival,* east new britain

[FAR RIGHT] *tambuan dancers,* tolai tribe, east new britain

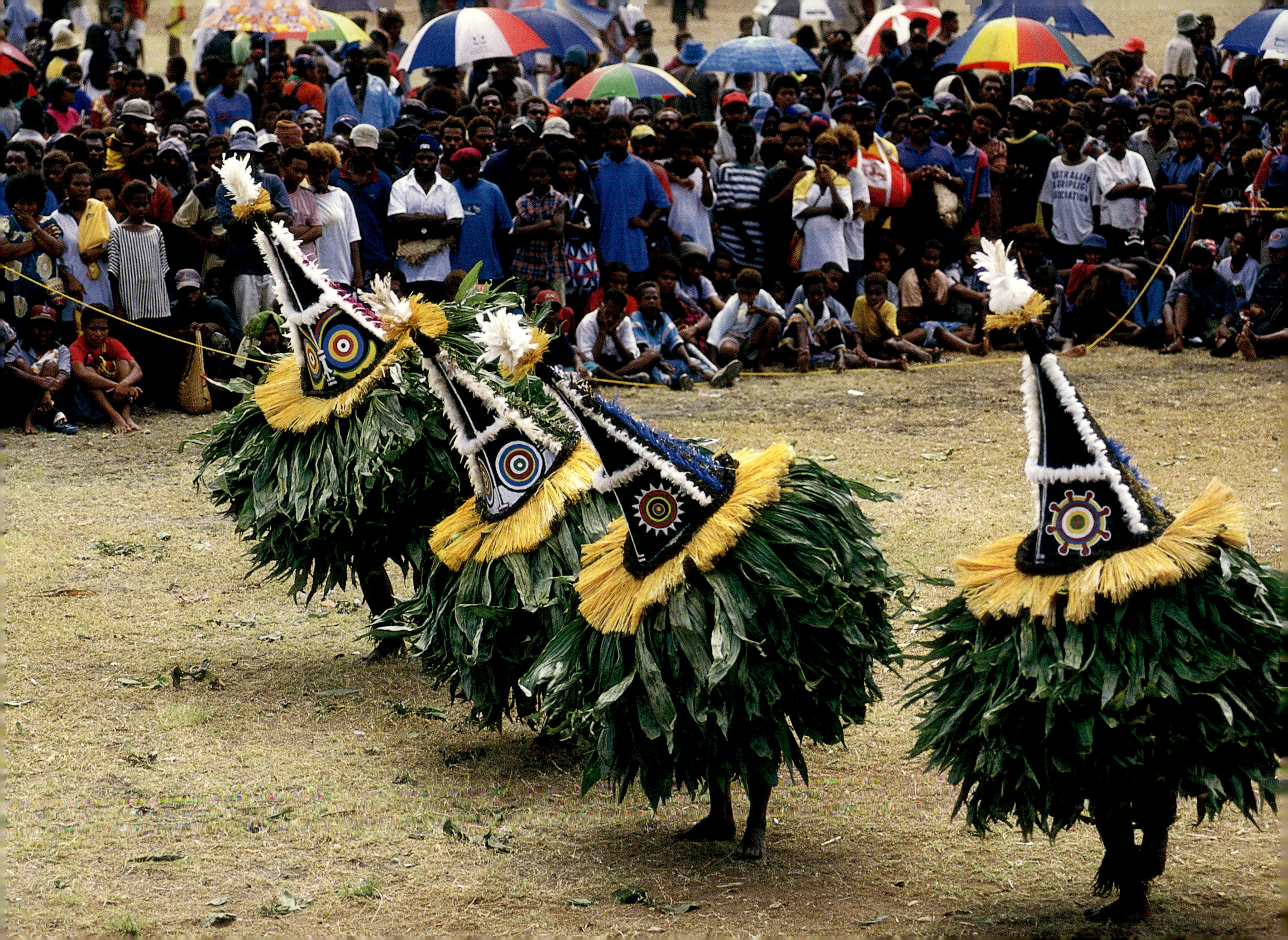

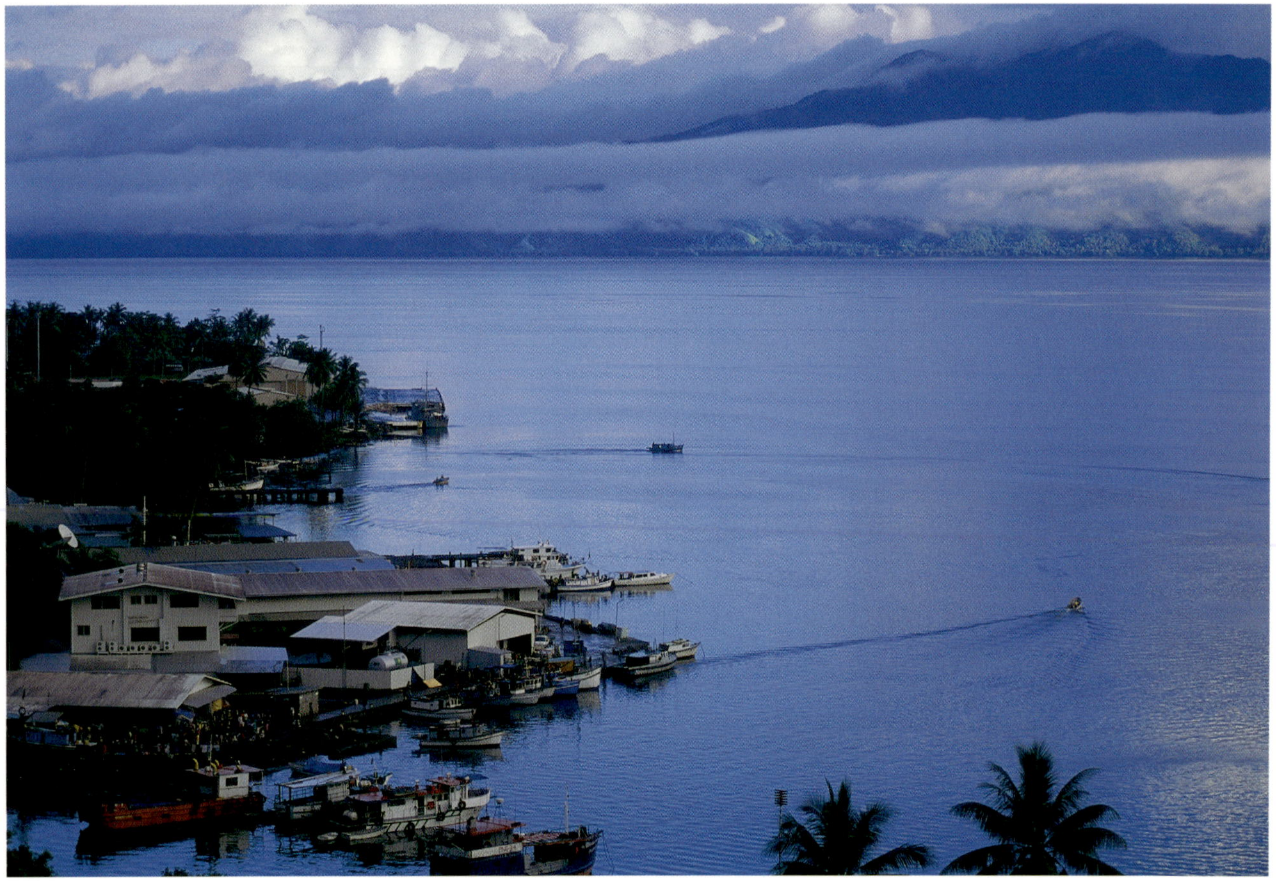

[**ABOVE**] *alotau,* milne bay province

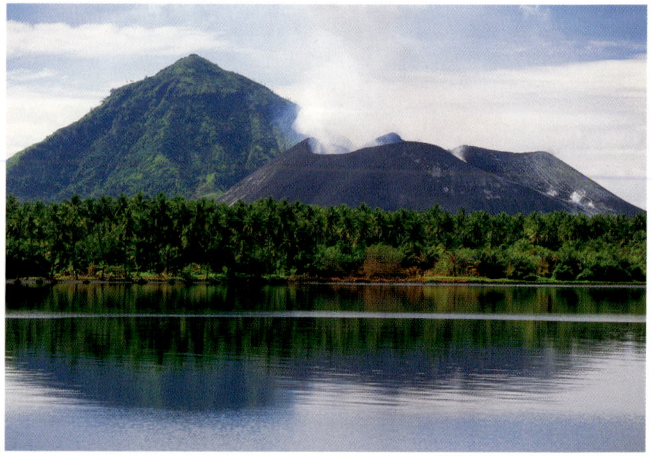

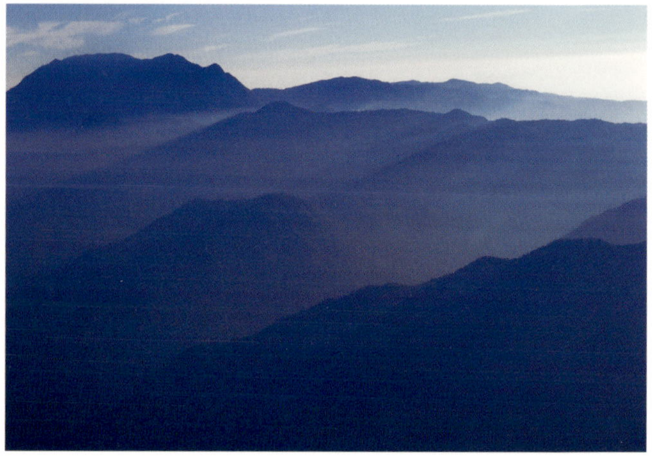

[**ABOVE RIGHT**] *tavurvur and turangunan volcanoes,* rabaul, east new britain

[**RIGHT**] *highlands in early morning mist*

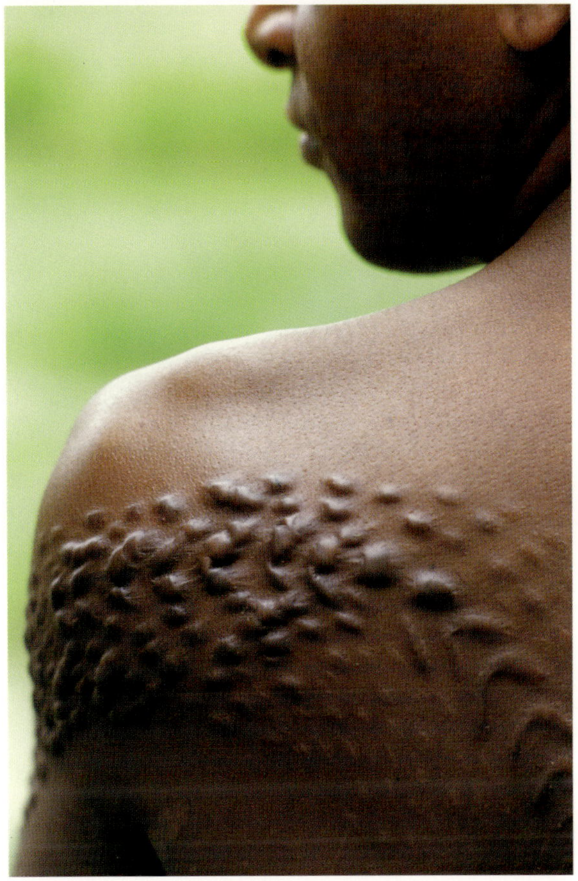

[ABOVE] *crocodile pattern scarification,* middle sepik

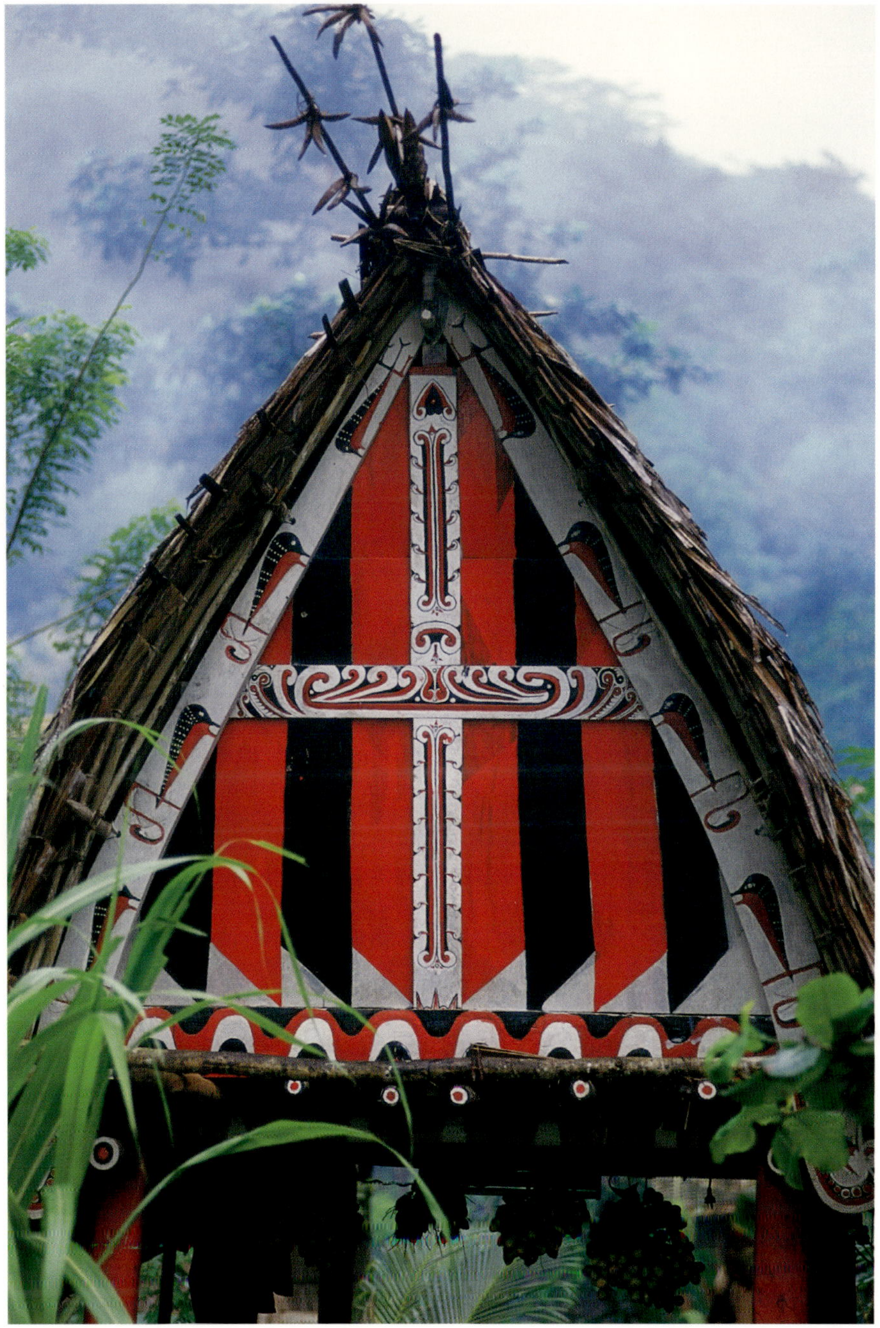

[RIGHT] *trobriand yam house with hanging bunches of betel nut,* milne bay province

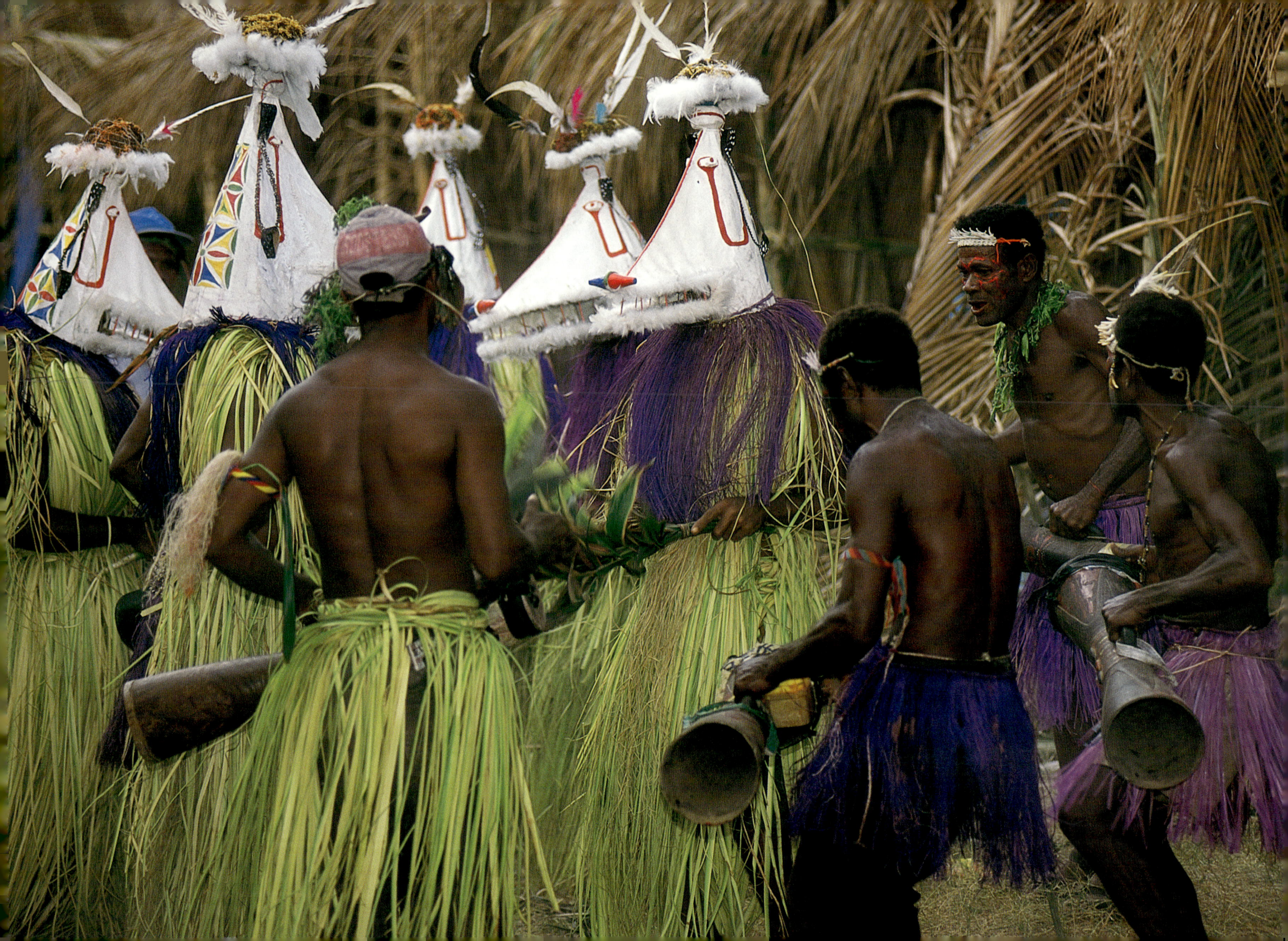

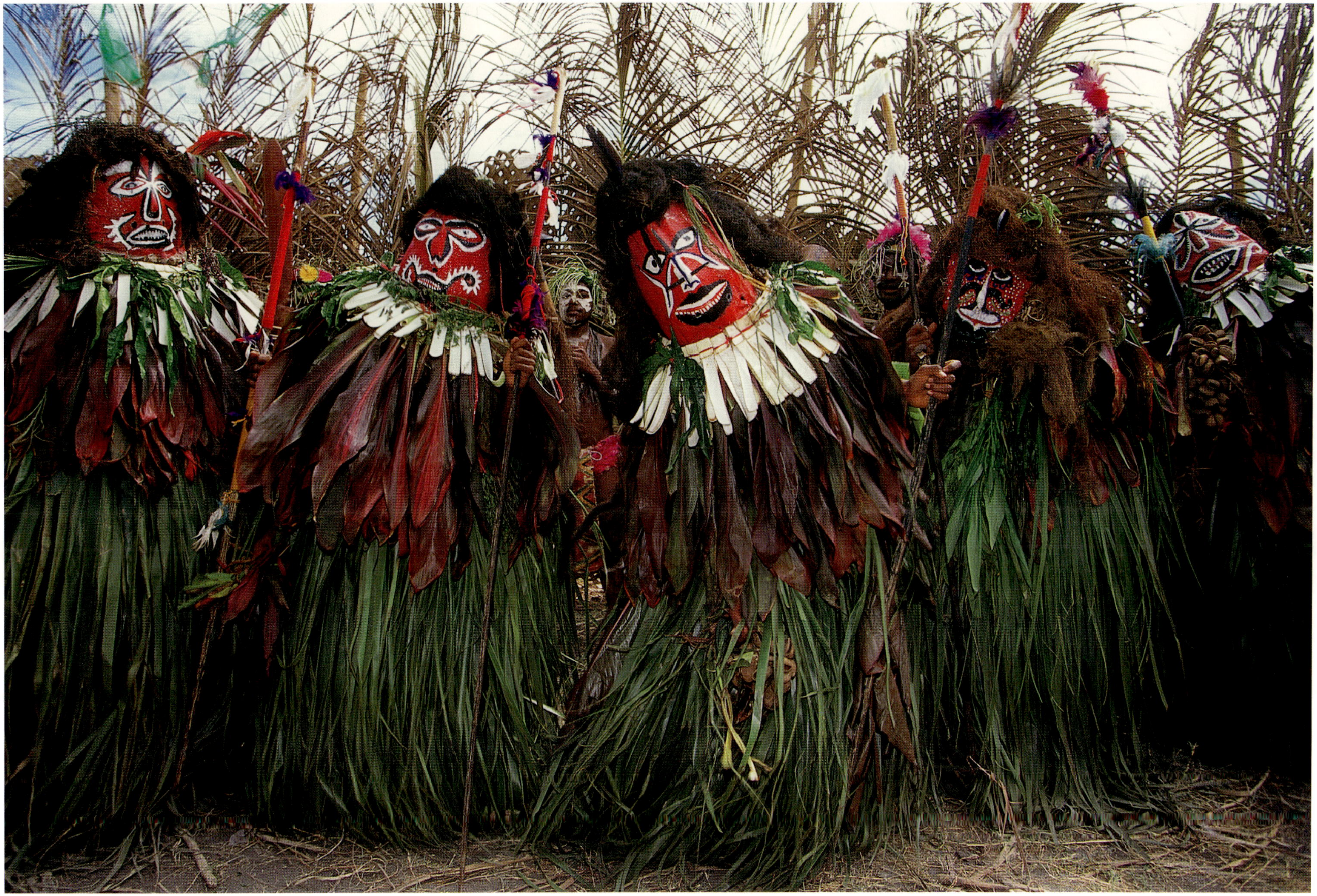

[**LEFT AND ABOVE**] *pomio dancers,* east new britain

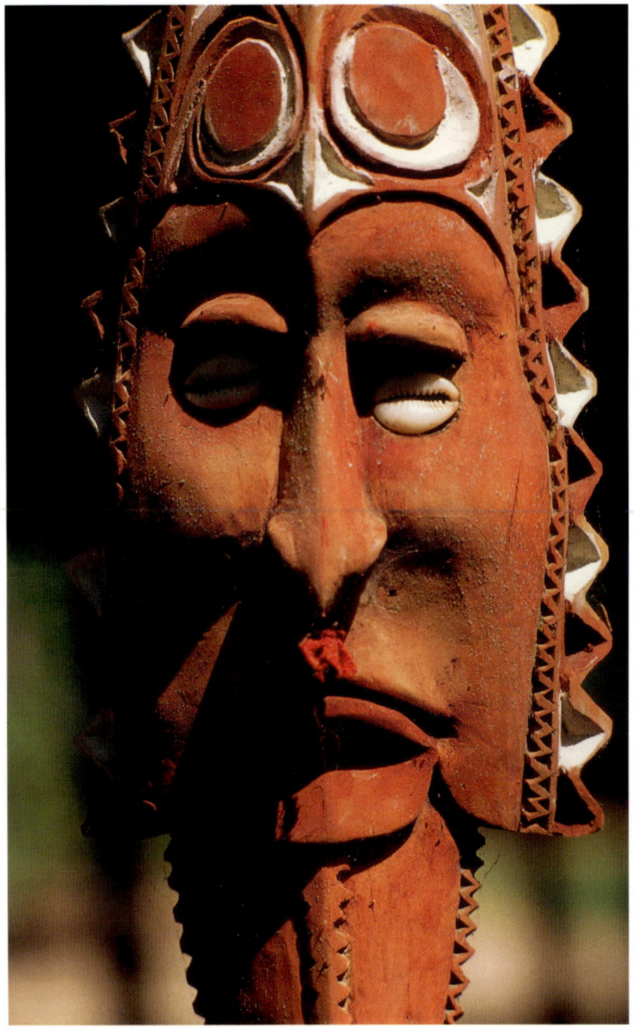

carving from tambanum village, middle sepik

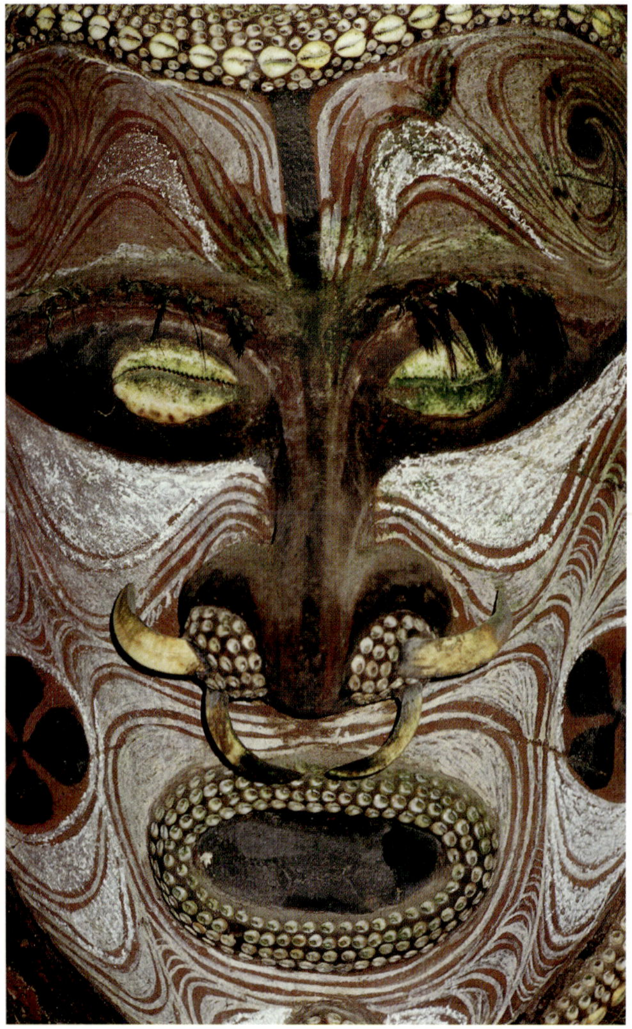

latmul mask, middle sepik

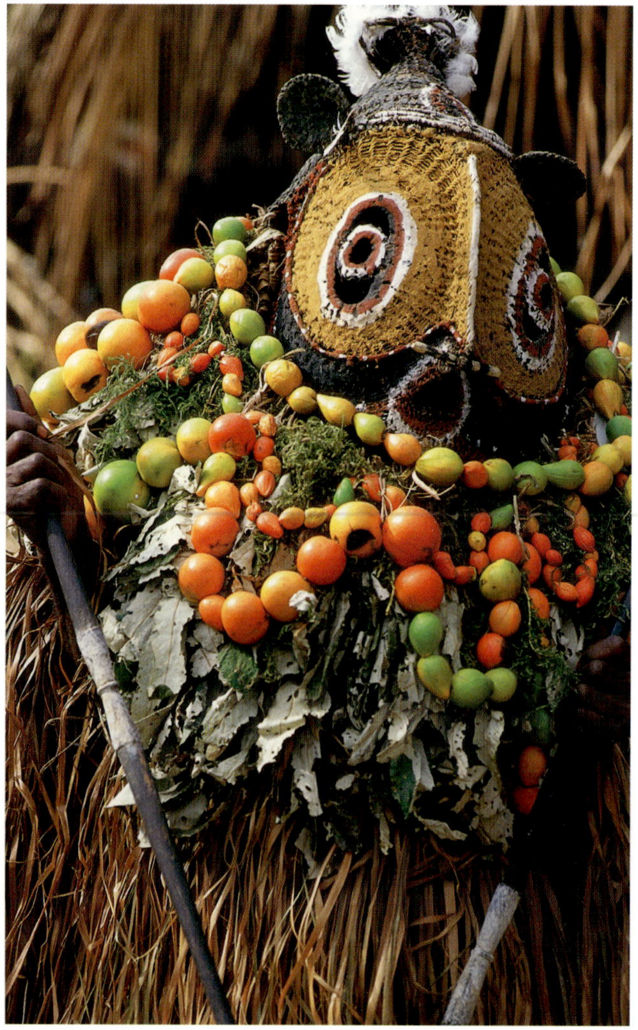

sepik wara dancer, east new britain

[RIGHT] *pomio dancers,* east new britain

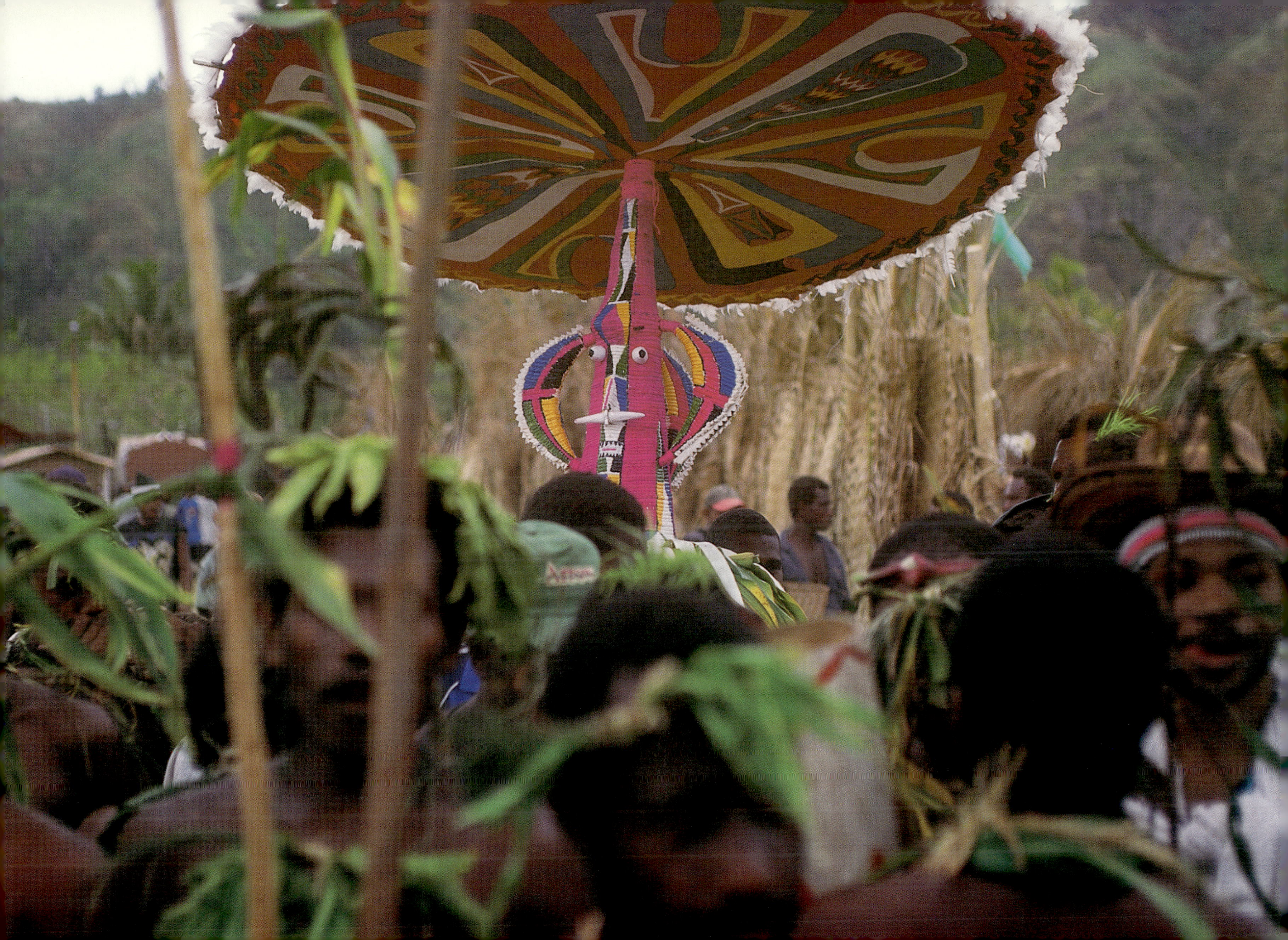

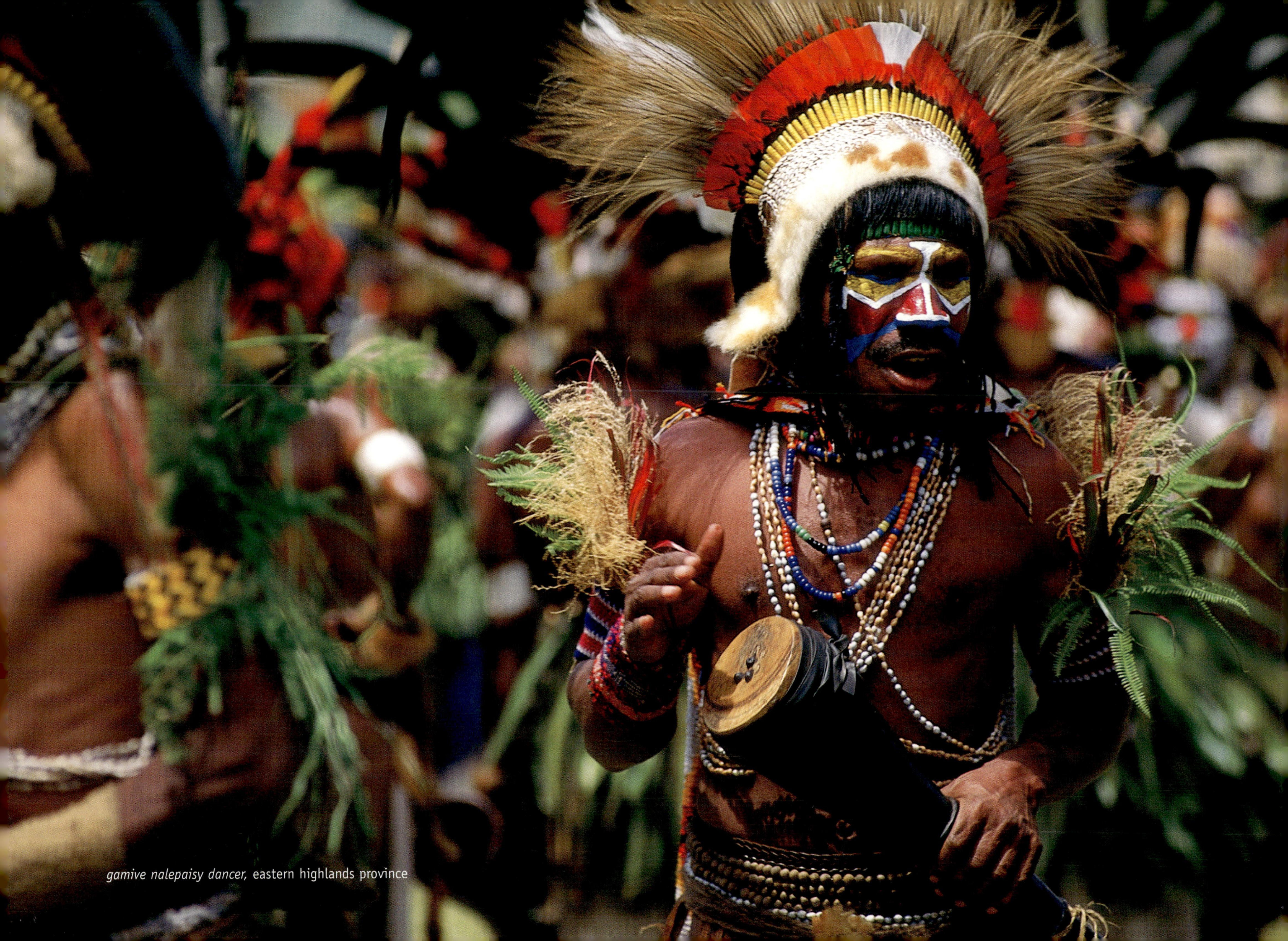

gamive nalepaisy dancer, eastern highlands province

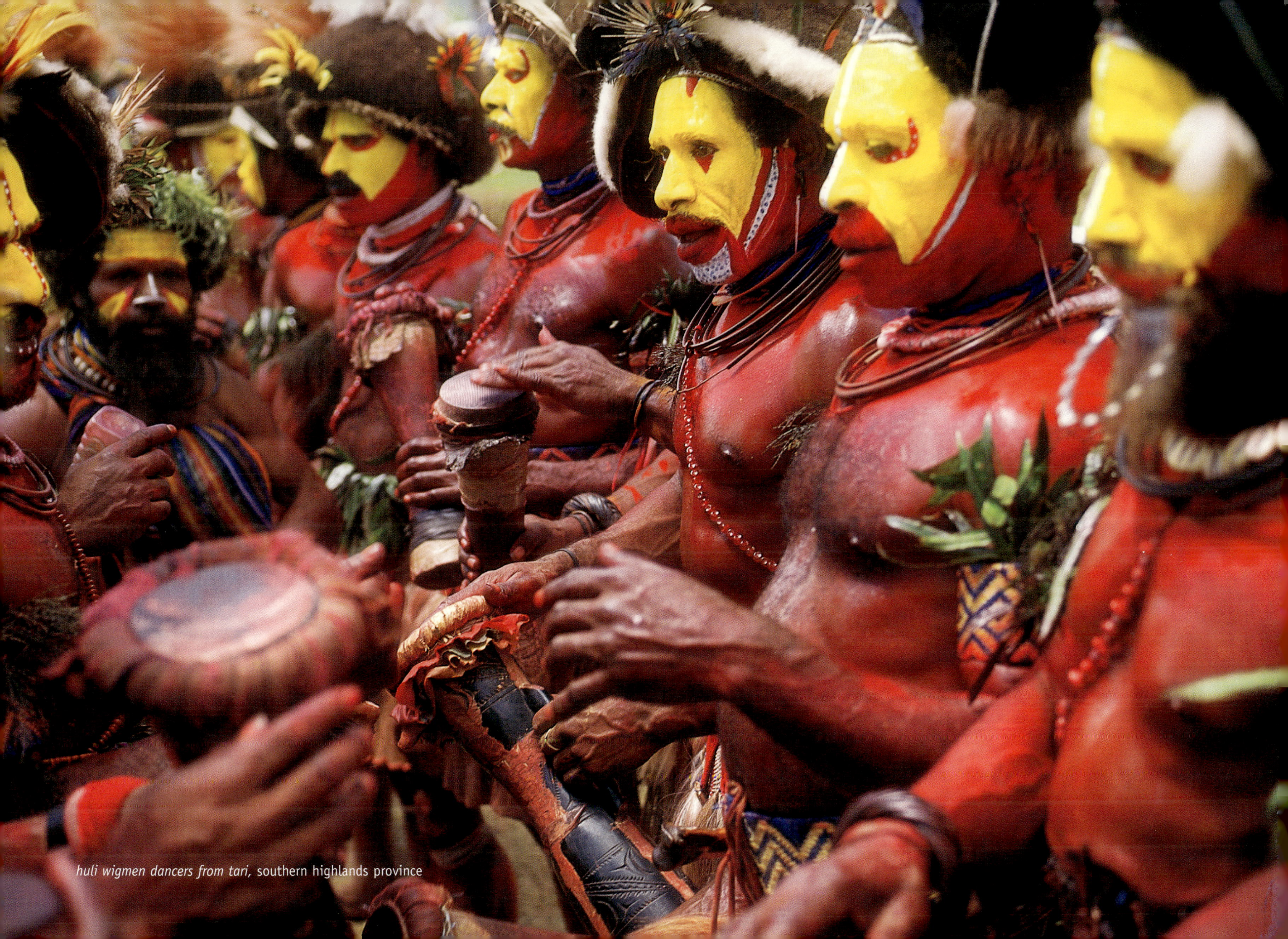

huli wigmen dancers from tari, southern highlands province

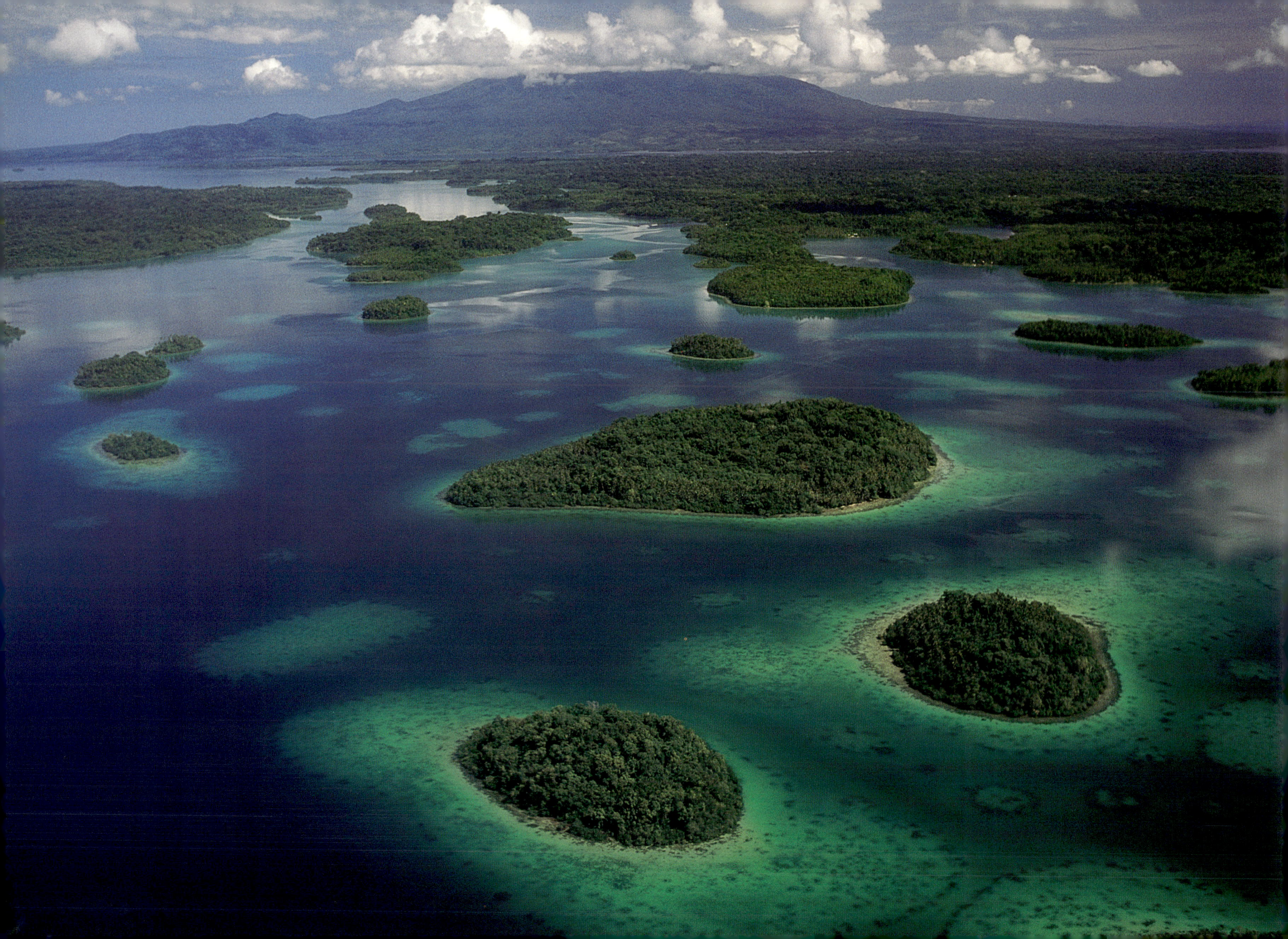

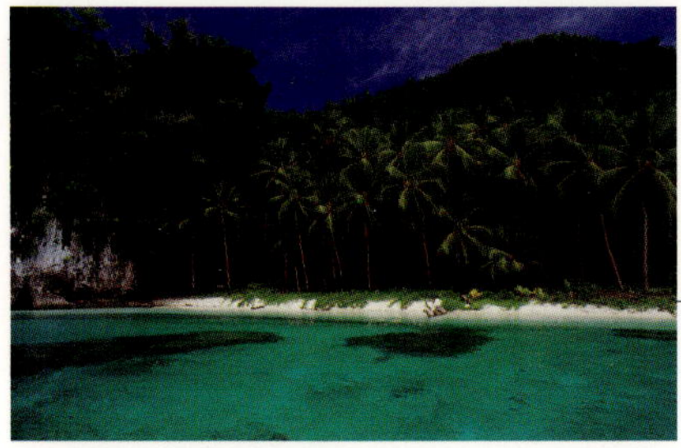

Solomon Islands

NAMED BY Alvaro de Mendaña after the biblical King Solomon, this island group of 28,000sq.km remains one of the Pacific's least known and travelled destinations.

There are 6 large mountainous islands with fertile coastal plains and nearly 1,000 other islands. These range from small volcanic islands and tiny coral atolls with lagoons to uplifted coral reefs such as Rennell Island and are mainly covered with lush tropical rainforest with mangrove swamps along the coasts and around the river mouths. The main islands are rich in undeveloped mineral resources such as gold, nickel, lead, zinc and have extensive areas of tropical hardwood forests.

The islands were first settled over 10,000 years ago when the sea levels were much lower and many of the islands were joined. The original hunter-gatherers would be followed by later migrations of seafaring agriculturalists who brought with them food plants, pigs and chickens.

From the 19th century on, increased contact by whalers, traders, missionaries and labour recruiters led to the islands becoming a British protectorate in 1896, gaining full independence in 1978. Between the years 1870 – 1910, about 30,000 islanders were taken to Australia and Fiji as labourers on pastoral properties in the sugar industry. The practice known as 'black-birding' inflicted cruelty and dislocation on the labourers, many of whom would never be returned to their homes. During the colonial period, large plantations were established for the production of copra.

Some of the fiercest fighting in the Pacific during World War II was around the current Capital of Honiara on Guadalcanal at places such as Bloody Ridge and Red Beach. In this malaria-infested environment, casualties were extremely high on both sides of the conflict, as well as for the indigenous population. In the surrounding seas there are the remains of 67 sunken warships and transports from American, Australian and Japanese navies.

There are at least 65 different languages spoken amongst the predominantly Melanesian population, with sizeable communities of Polynesians and Micronesians. Family and clan ties remain strong with the population of 500,000, who predominantly make their livelihood from agriculture and fishing. The people range physically from coal black through dark tan to light copper toned complexions and blonde, curly hair.

With areas where shark calling and sorcery is still practised and the majority of people follow traditional lifestyles and beliefs, the Solomon Islands are one of the least developed wilderness areas left in the Pacific.

[**LEFT**] *vona vona lagoon,* west new georgia [**ABOVE**] *kanggava bay,* rennell island

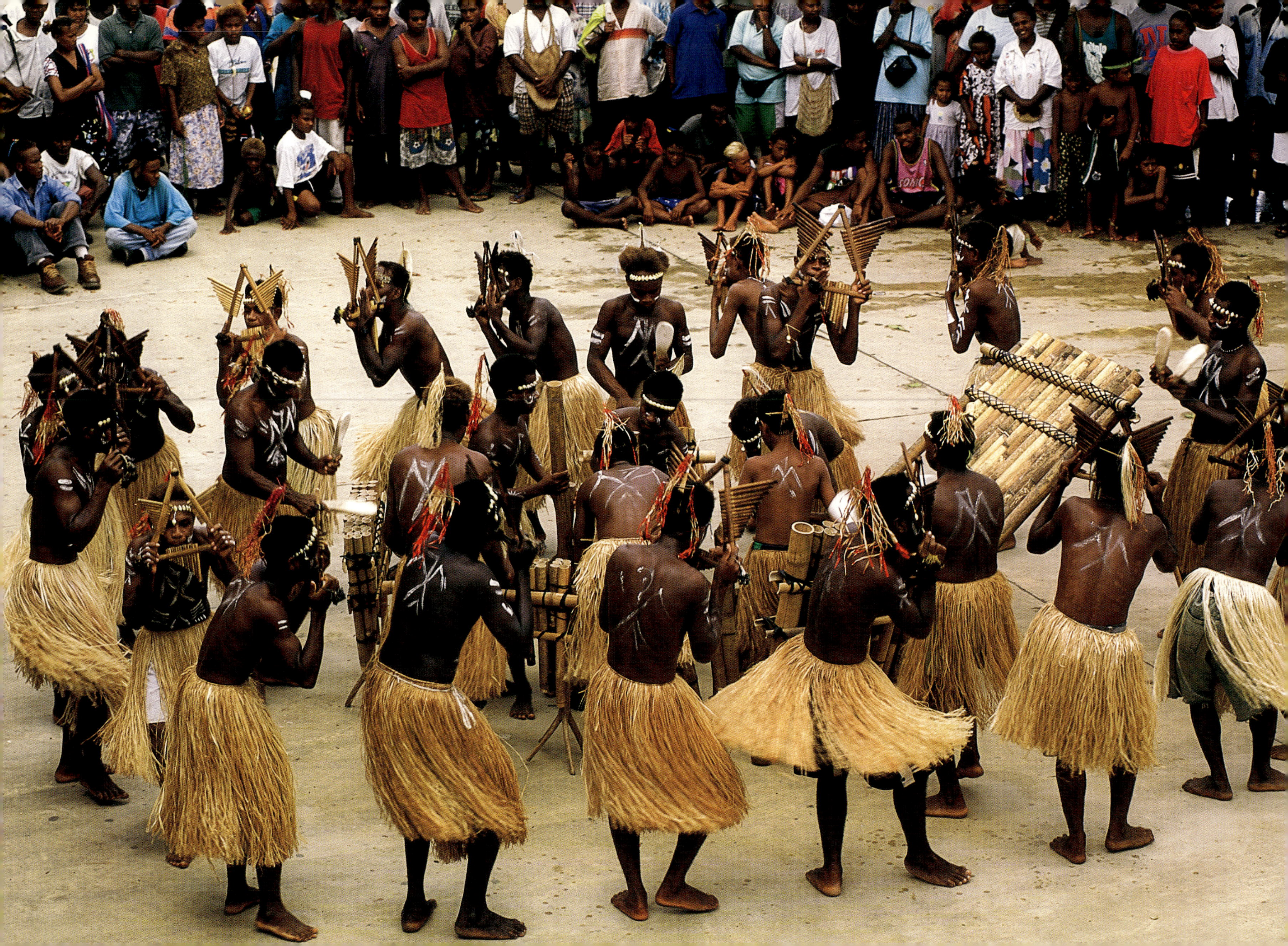

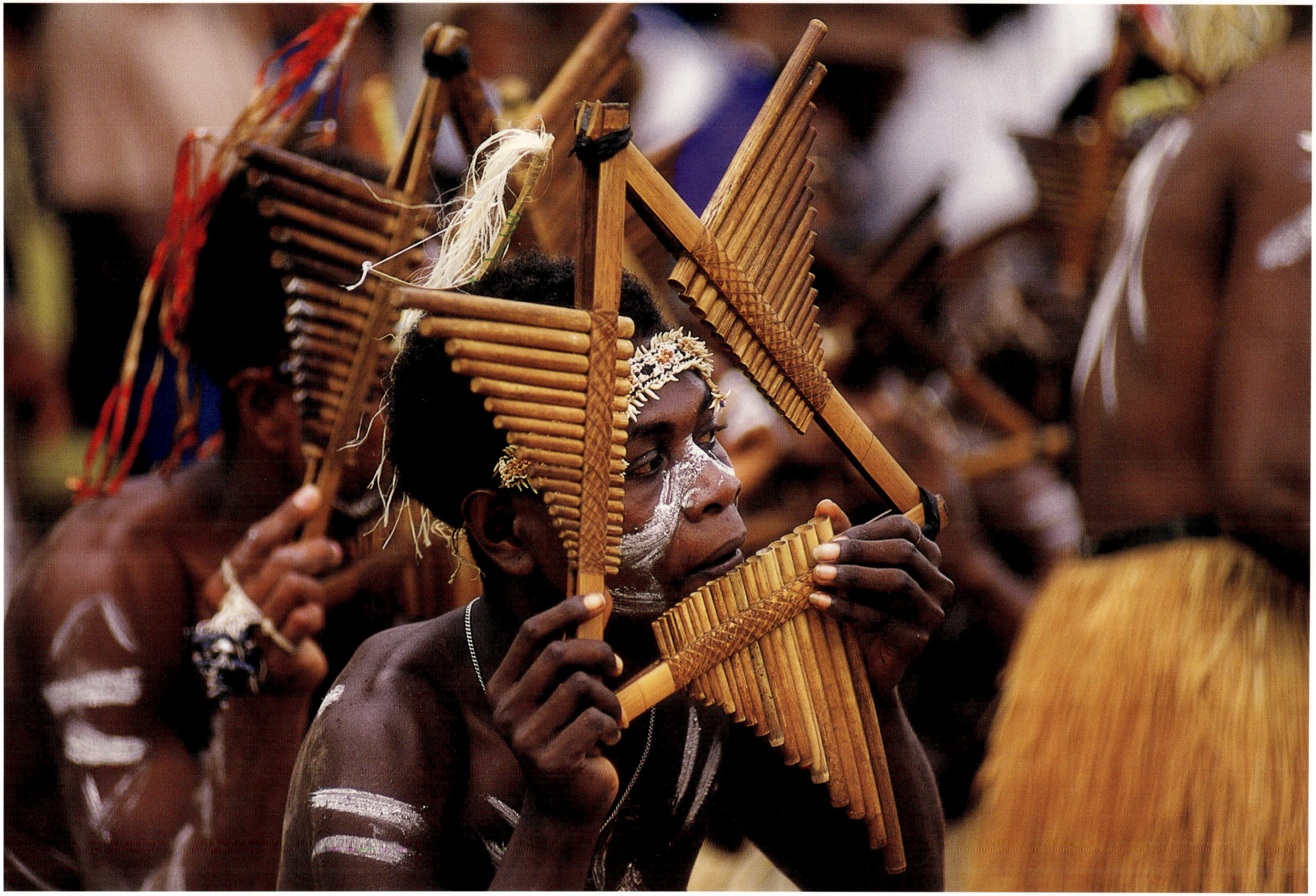

[**LEFT AND ABOVE**] *malaitan pan pipers,* honiara market

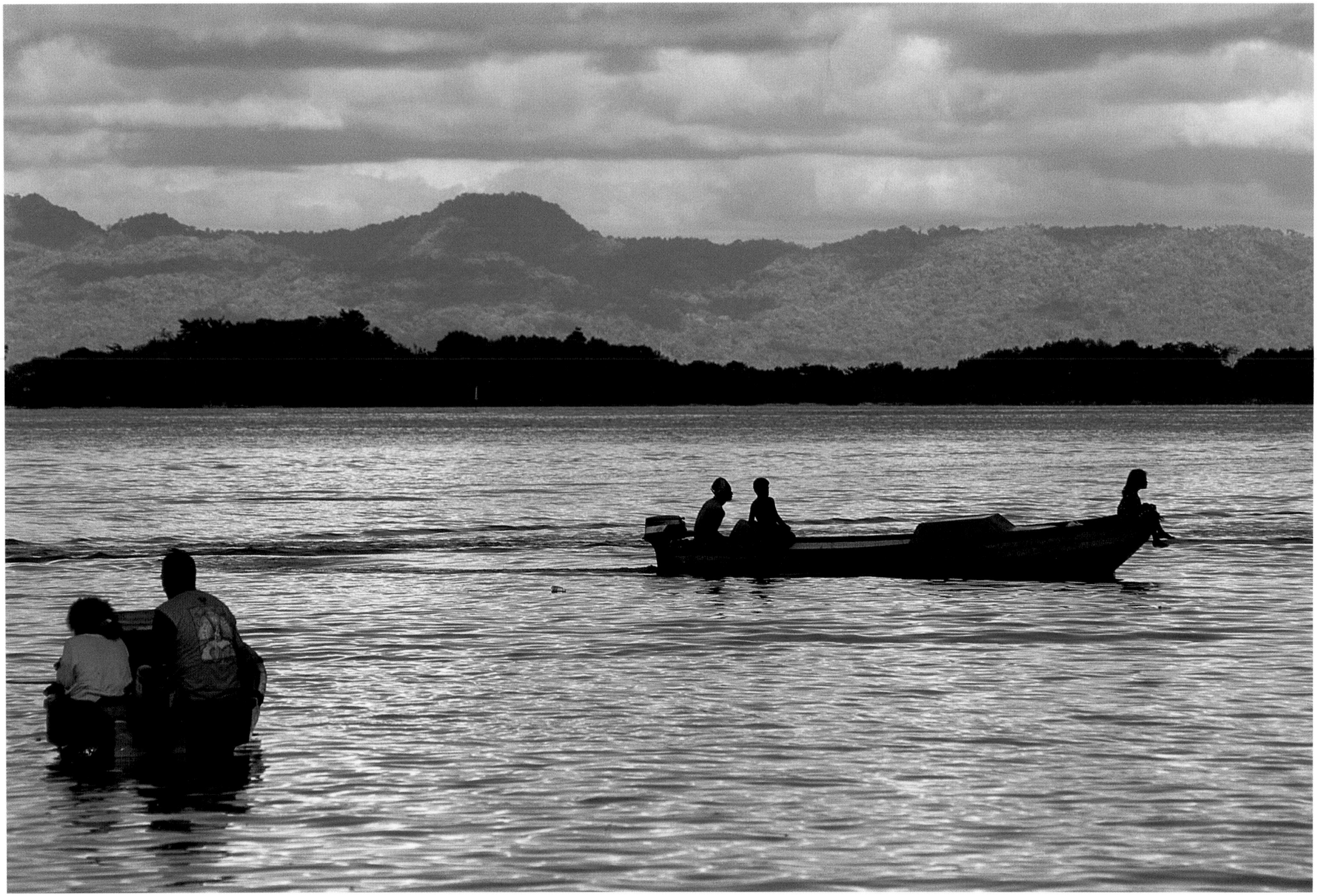

homeward bound, gizo lagoon, western province

[RIGHT] *west ghizo island,* western province

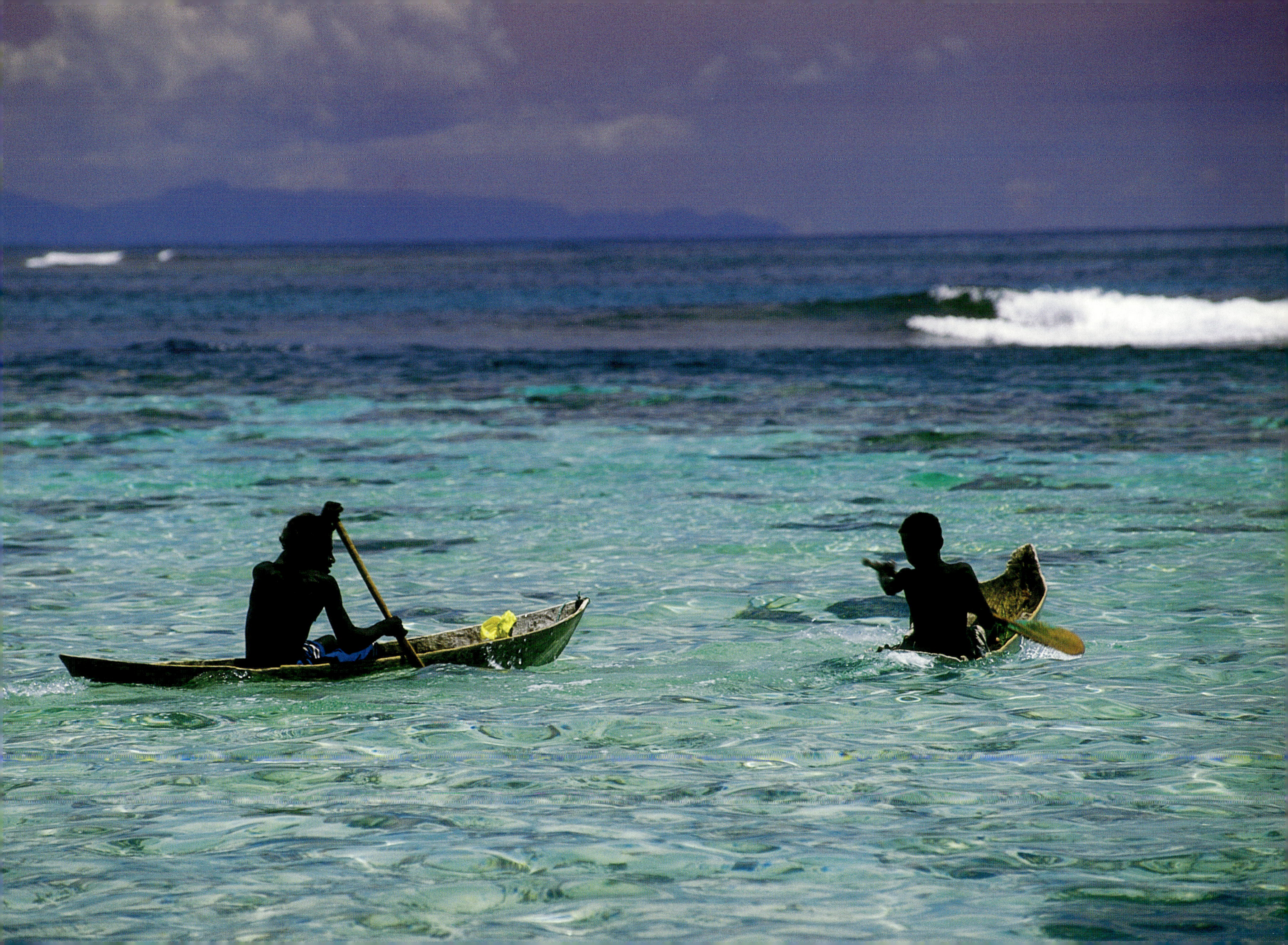

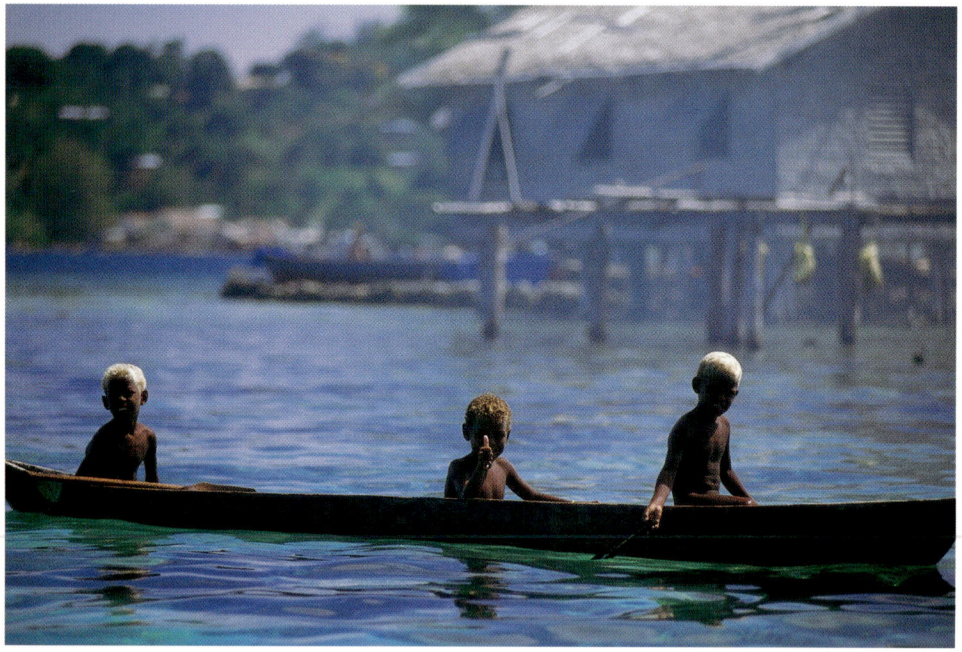

malaitan village, gizo lagoon, western province

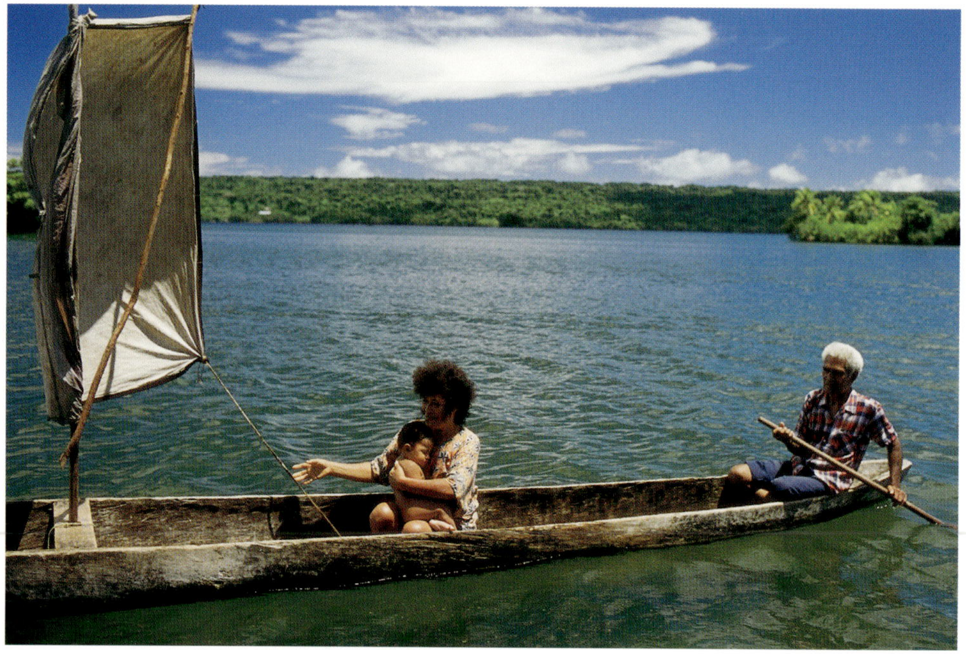

family on lake te'nggano, rennell island

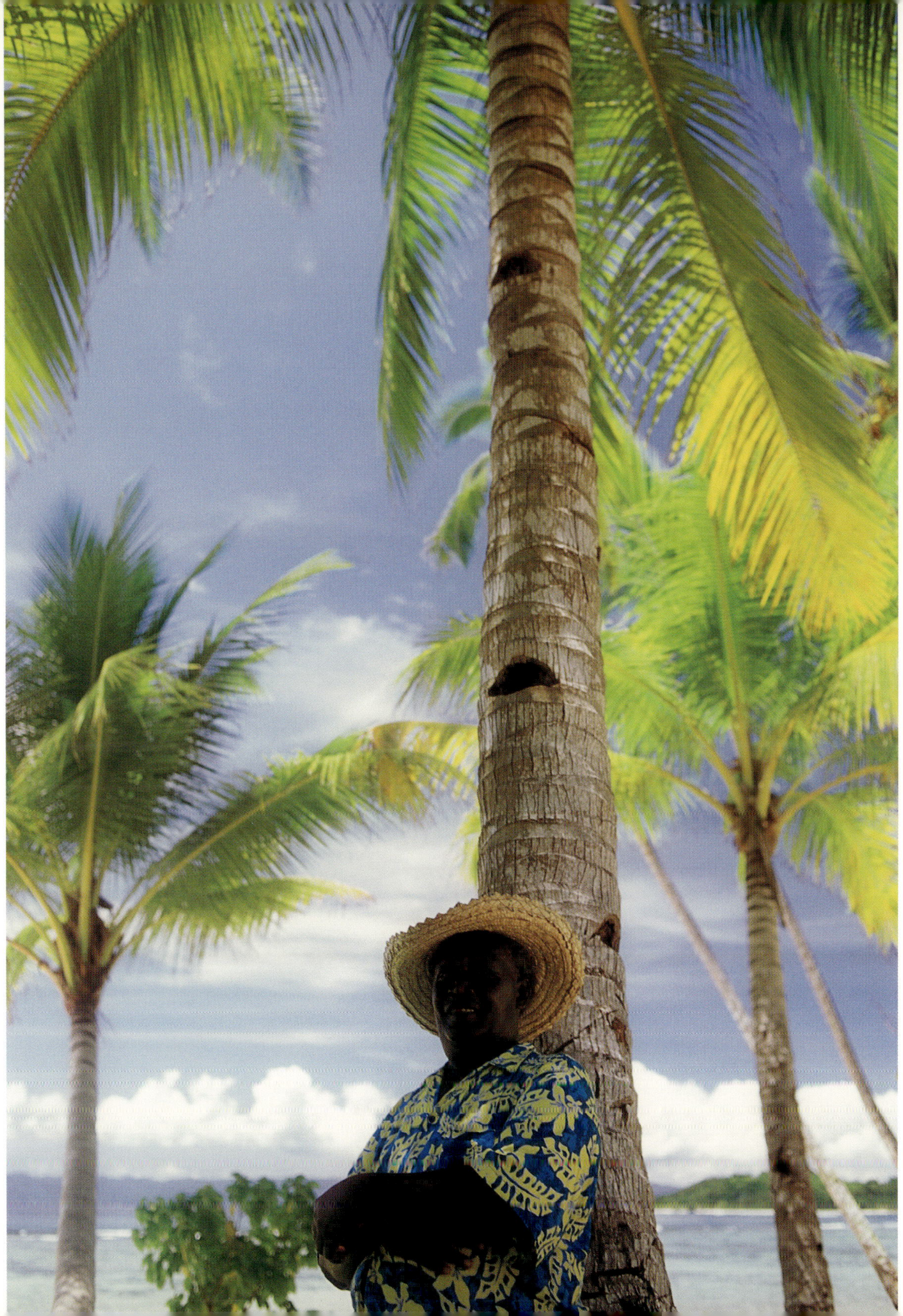

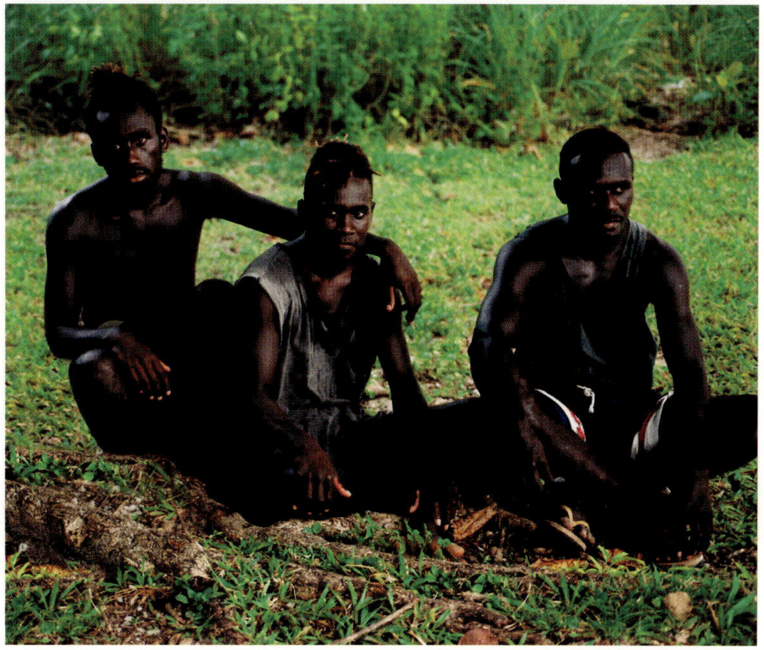

resting at seghe airstrip, new georgia island

local identity wilson hisu, west ghizo island

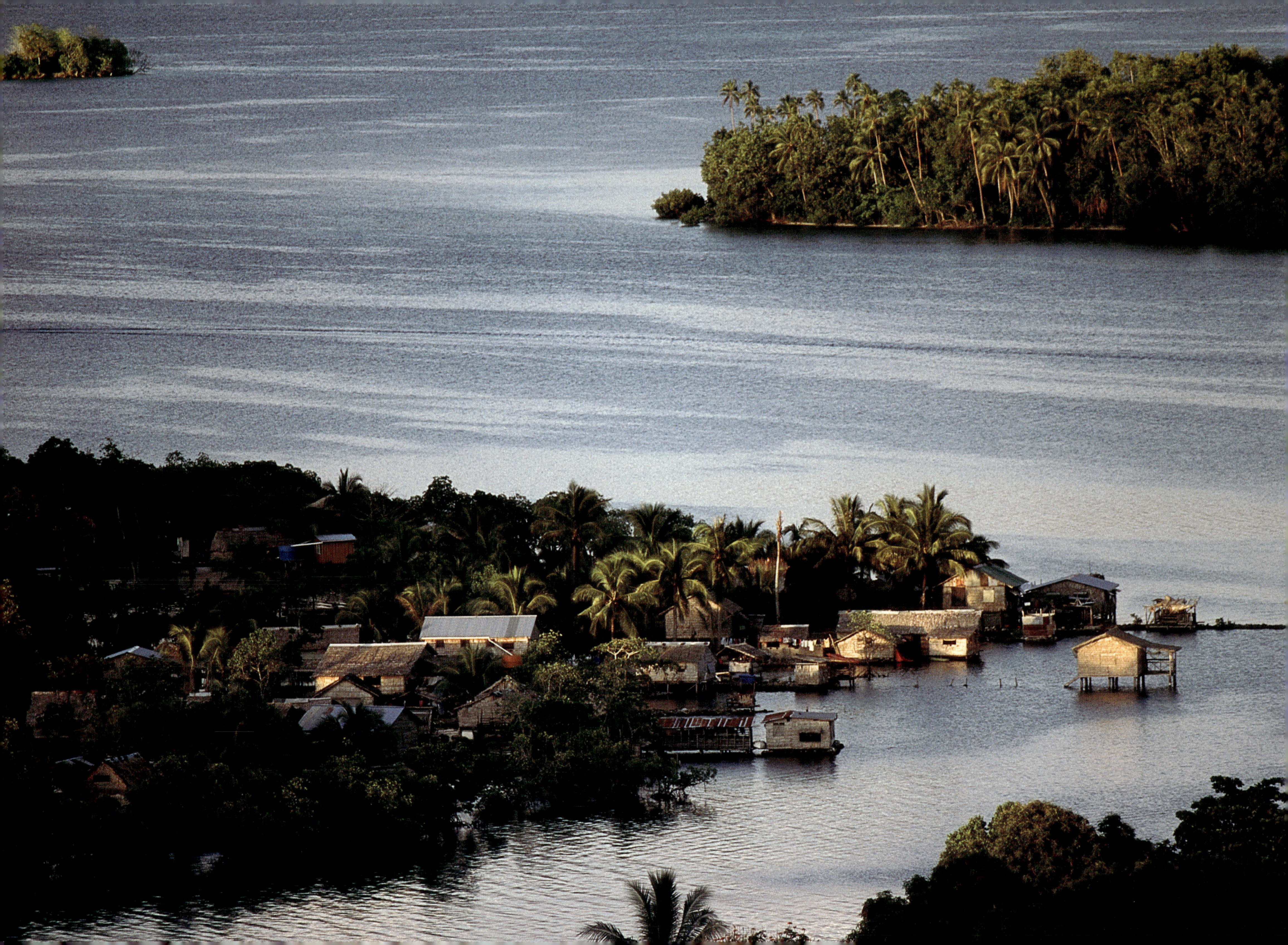

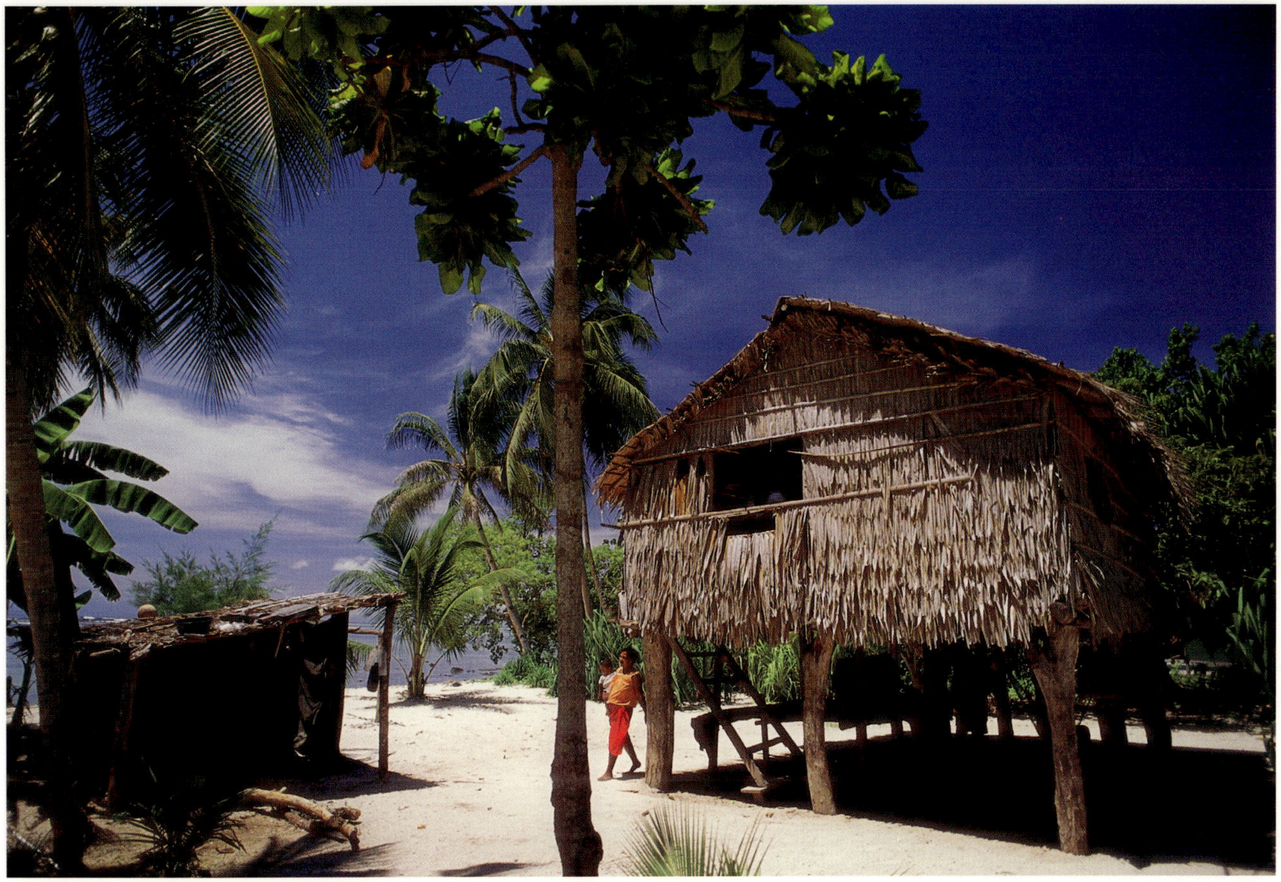

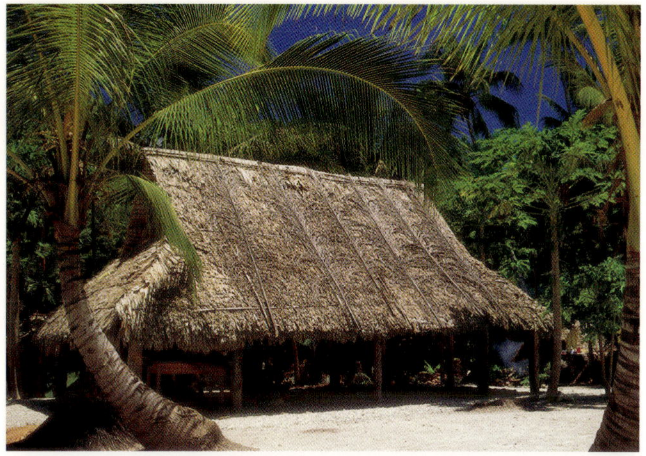

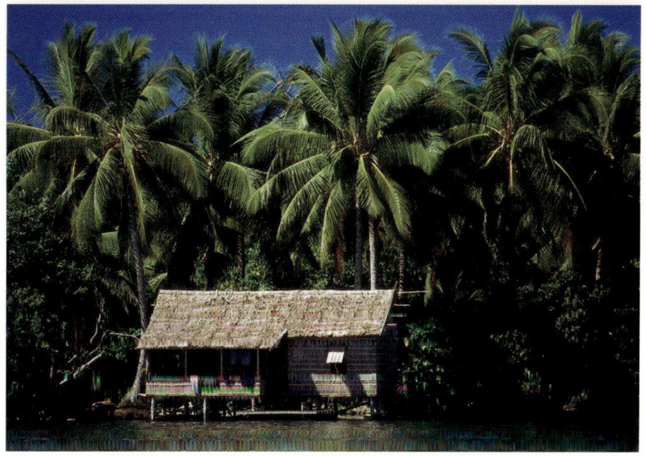

[ABOVE] *traditional house,* south west coast village, ghizo island

[ABOVE RIGHT] *traditional house,* gilbert islanders' village, ghizo island

[RIGHT] *rest house,* lake te'nggano, rennell island

[LEFT] *malaitan fishing village,* gizo lagoon, western province

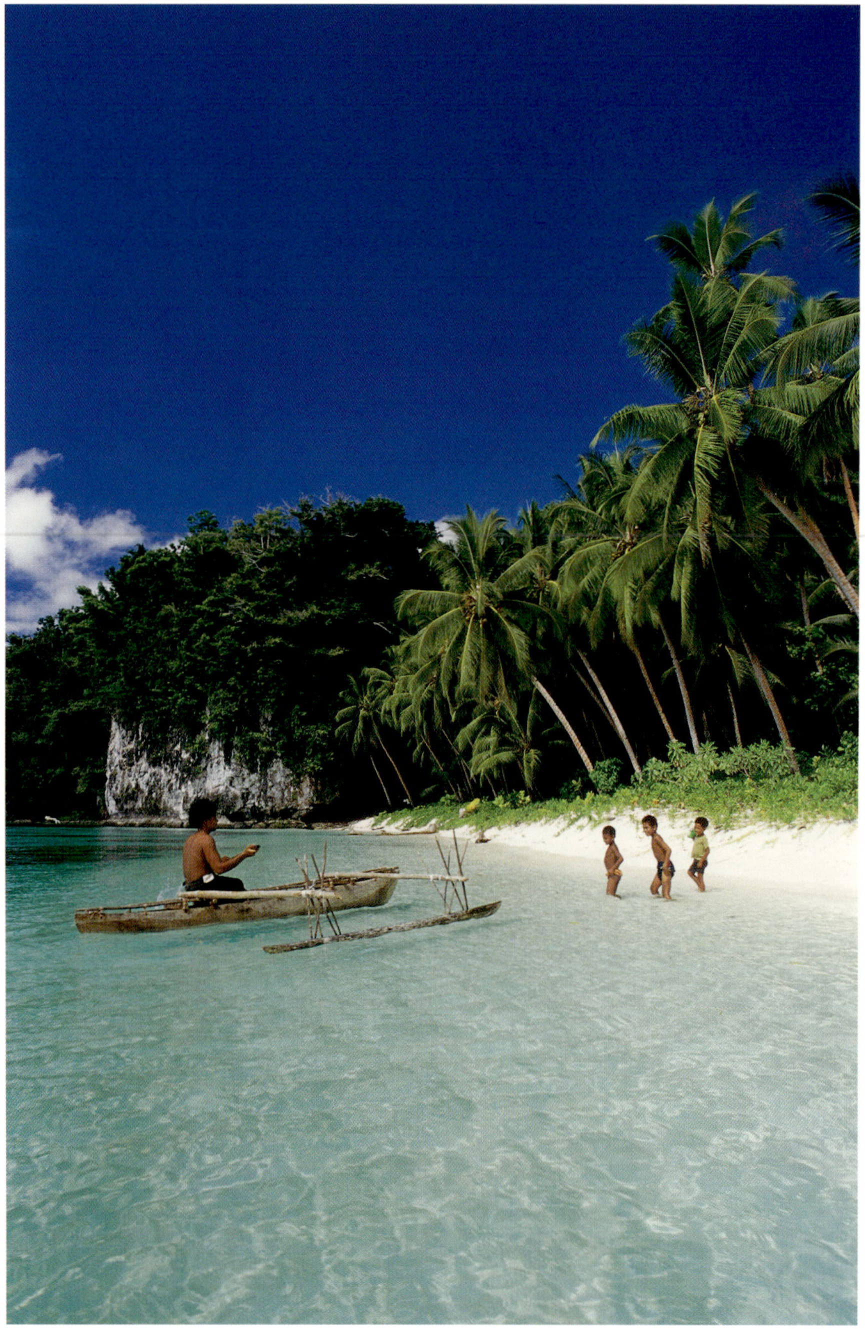

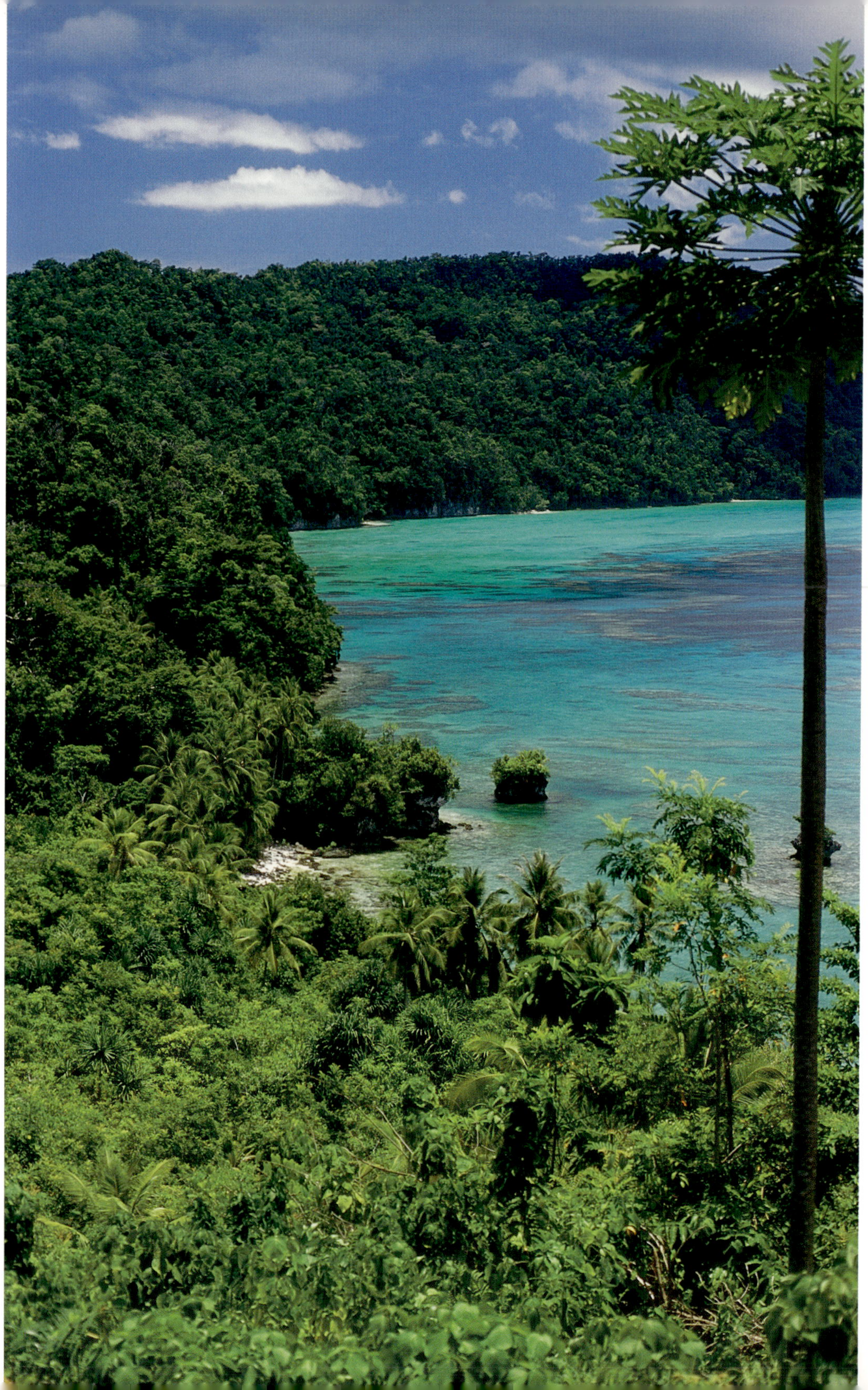

[**ABOVE AND RIGHT**] *kanggava bay,* rennell island

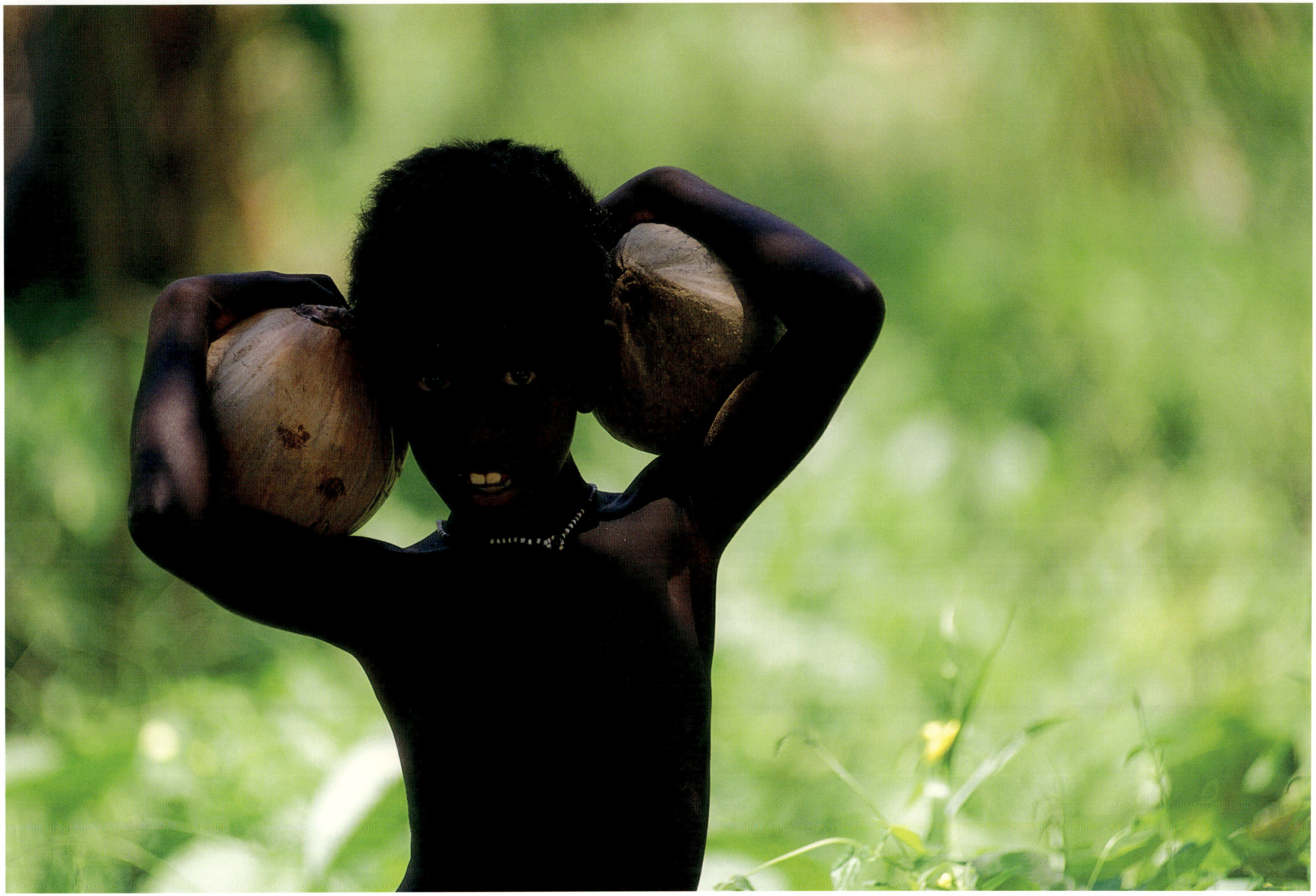

titiana village, ghizo island, western province

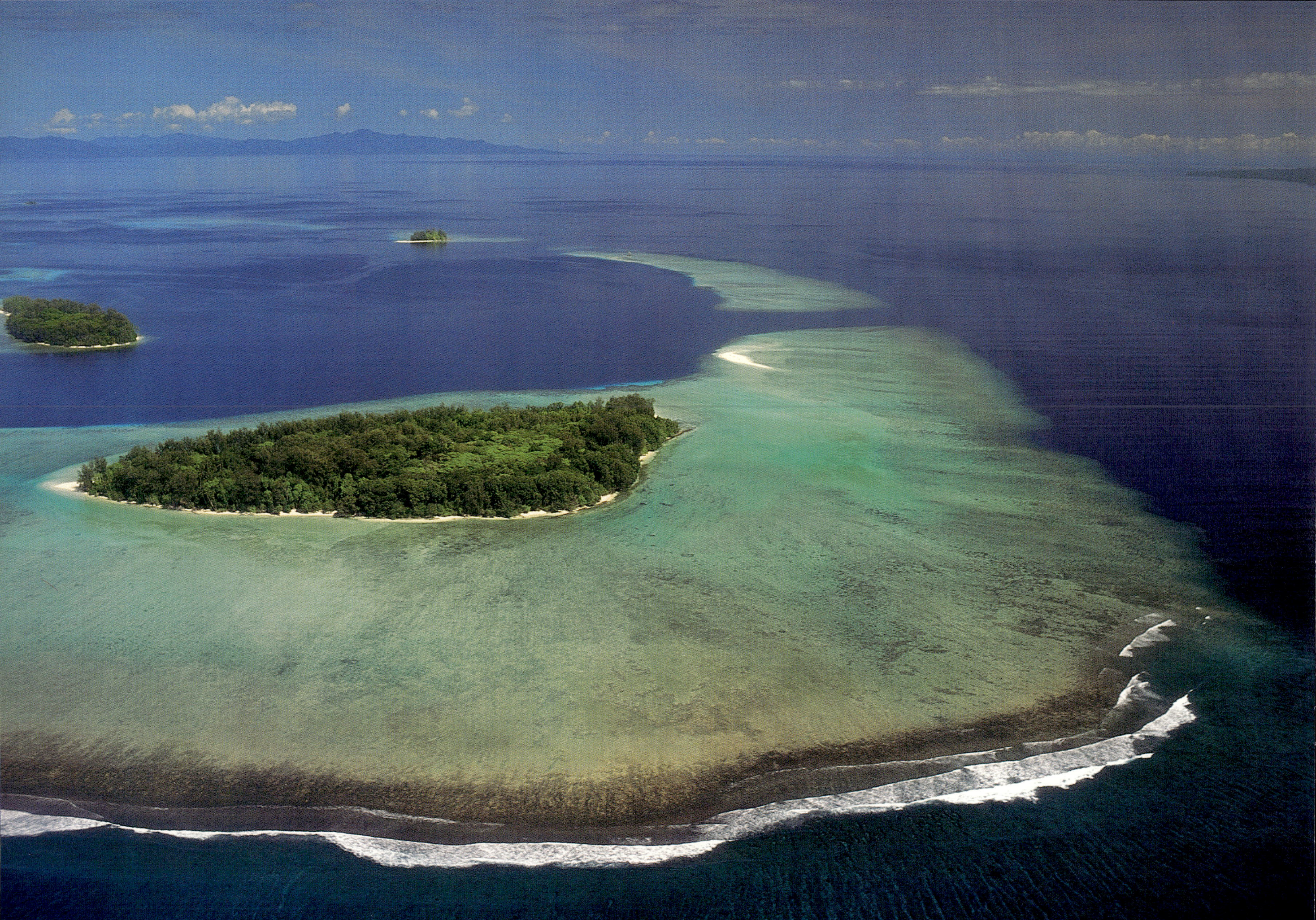

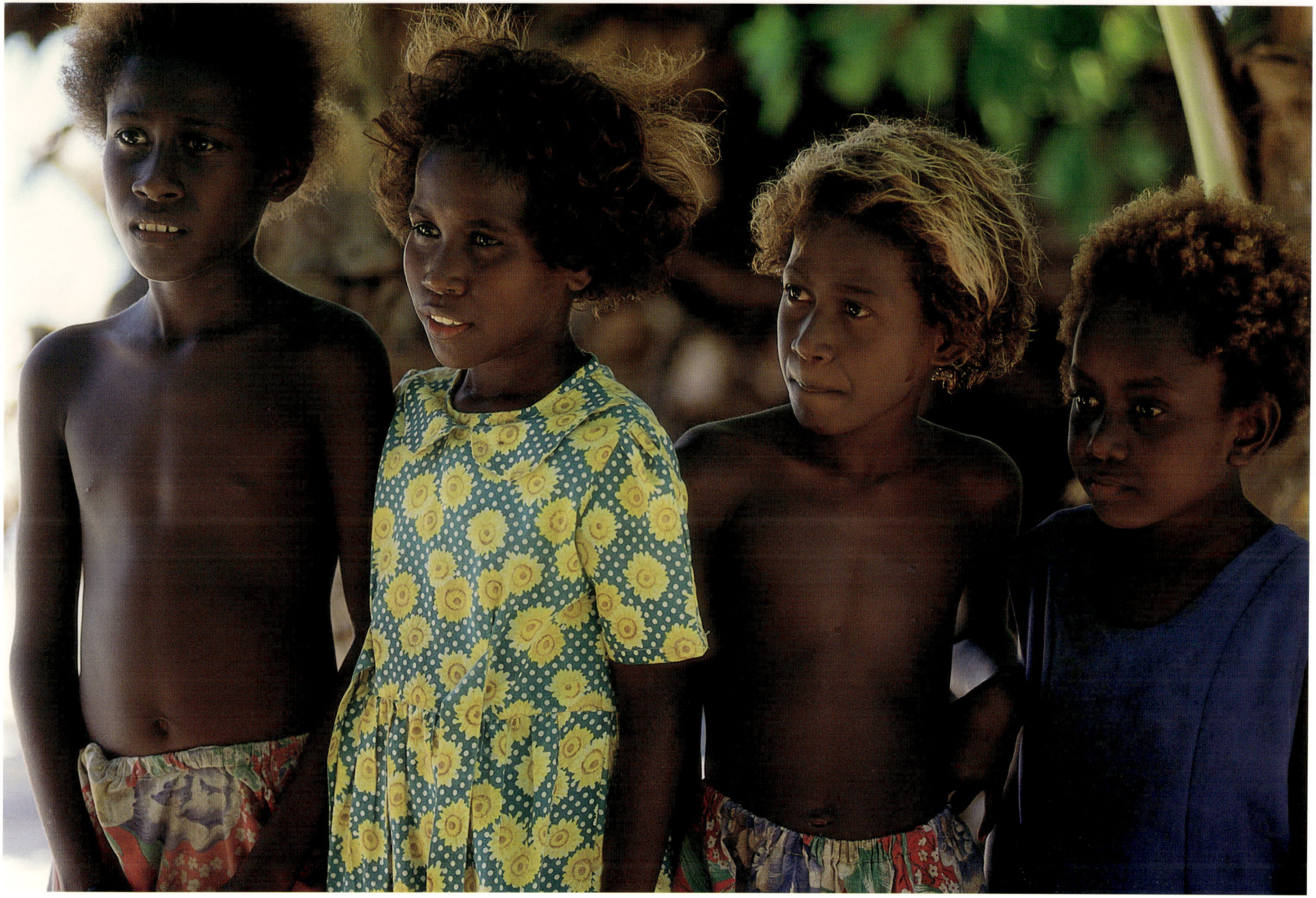

[LEFT] *island in the blackett strait,* western province

pailongge village, ghizo island, western province

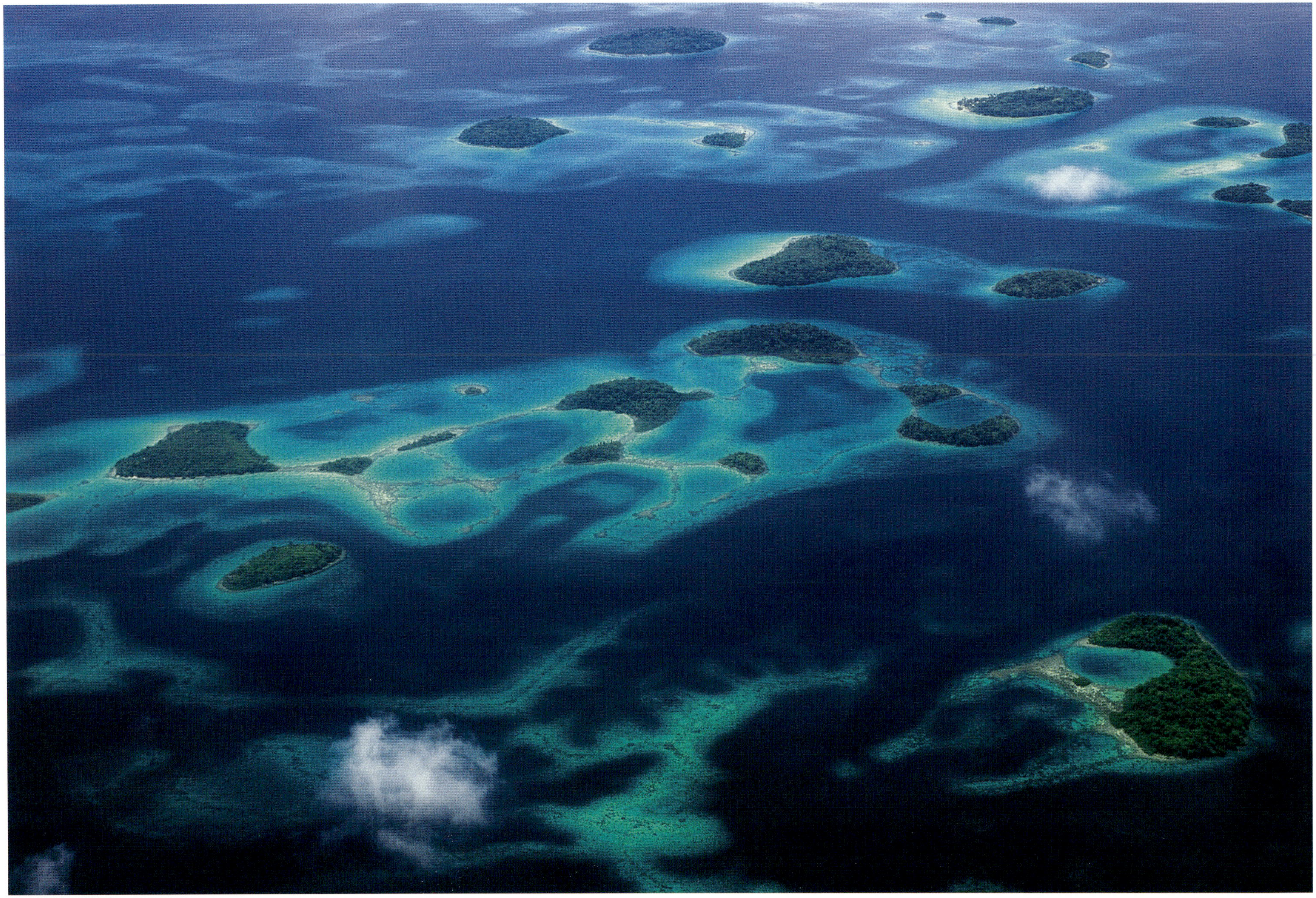

morovo lagoon, new georgia island

[RIGHT] *morovo lagoon from uepi island*

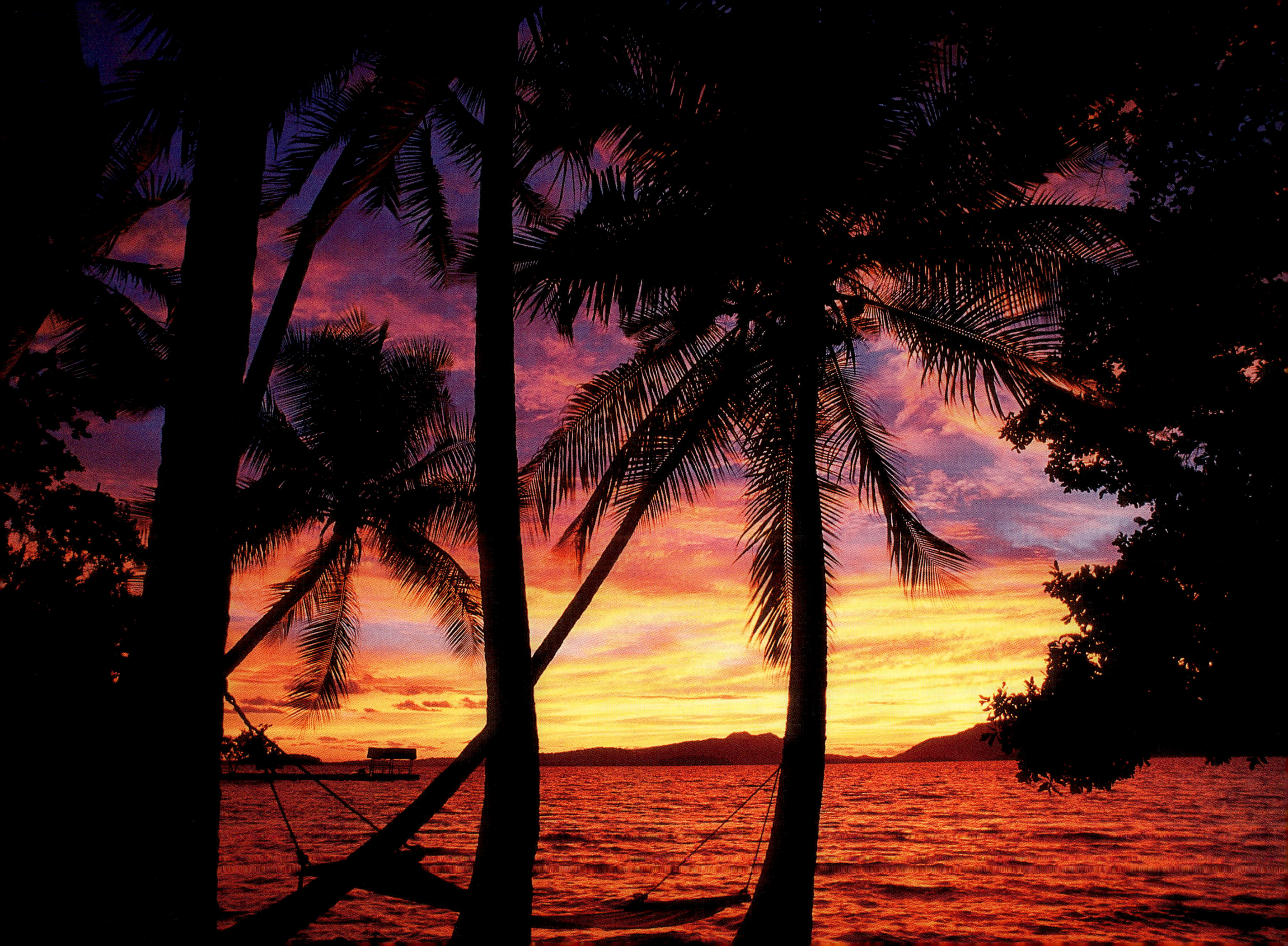

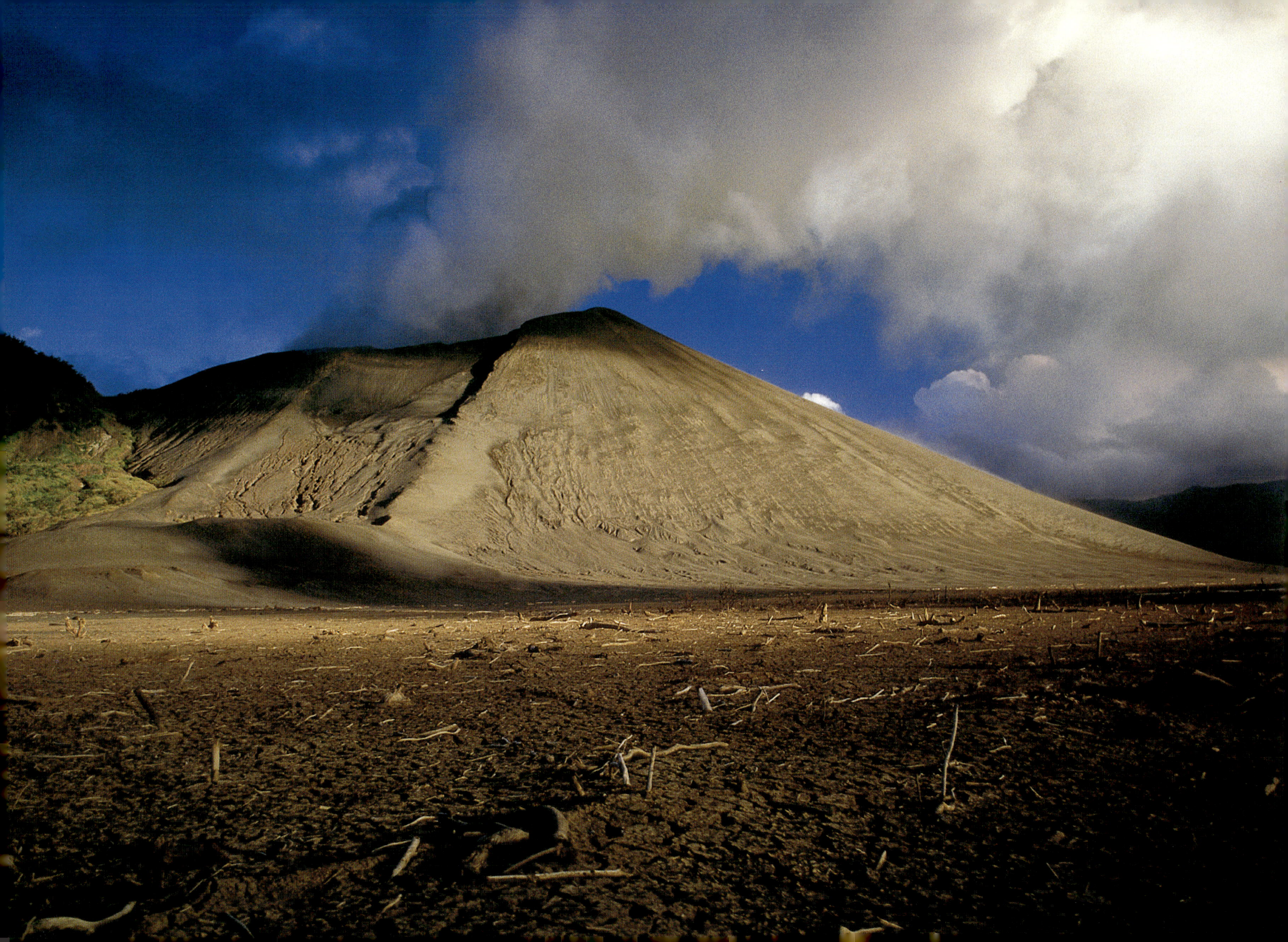

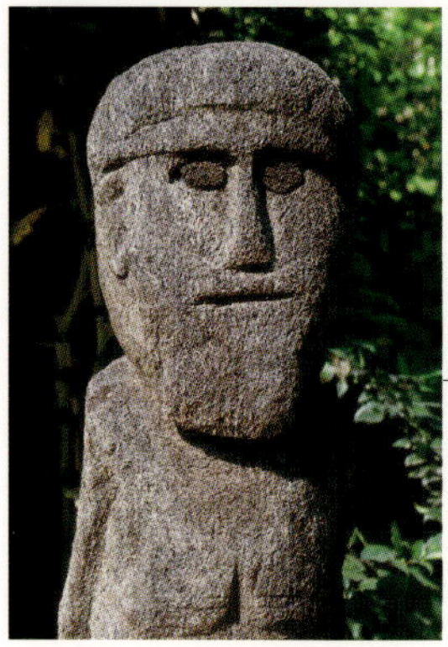

Vanuatu

A CHAIN of some 80 islands extending north-south in the South West Pacific, Vanuatu still has many active volcanoes which form part of the 'Pacific Ring of Fire' stretching from New Zealand up through to Papua New Guinea.

The land area is 12,000sq.km and the largest islands are Espiritu Santo, Malekula, Erromango and Efate. With extremely fertile soil, Vanuatu has one of the highest per hectare output of agricultural crops in the Pacific.

Settled first about 5,000 years ago, the islands have experienced waves upon waves of migrant peoples slowly making their way down through the islands, intermarrying and continuing on their journey eastward. The Lapita peoples (the ancestors of the present day Polynesians) passed through between two and three thousand years ago.

People lived in small clans with ceremonial gift-giving relationships between them. Big men attained rank and status by amassing wealth in the form of pigs and other valuables. Victims of inter-clan fighting were often eaten to acquire the power of their spirits. The early missionaries had great difficulty in trying to convert the indigenous people to their faith.

The first European to reach the islands was the Portuguese explorer Fernandez de Quiros in 1606. He named the largest island 'Espiritu Santo.' He was followed by Captain James Cook who named the islands 'New Hebrides' after the islands off the coast of Scotland.

In the 19th century, the New Hebrides became the site of extensive trading especially in sandalwood, with profound implications for social and cultural change in the islanders' lifestyle. European settlers arrived from the middle of the 19th century onwards and France and Britain administered the islands through a joint commission complete with separate languages, educational systems and police forces.

A haphazard movement for independence started in the 1960's and 70's and the New Hebrides gained independence in 1980 as the 'Ripablik Blong Vanuatu.'

Vanuatu has abundant marine life with excellent dive sites and fishing. It is also famous for its many varied cultures from Pentecost 'Bungy Jumpers' to the 'Cargo Cult' followers on Tanna Island.

[**LEFT**] *yasu volcano,* tanna island [**ABOVE**] *carved tree-fern figure*

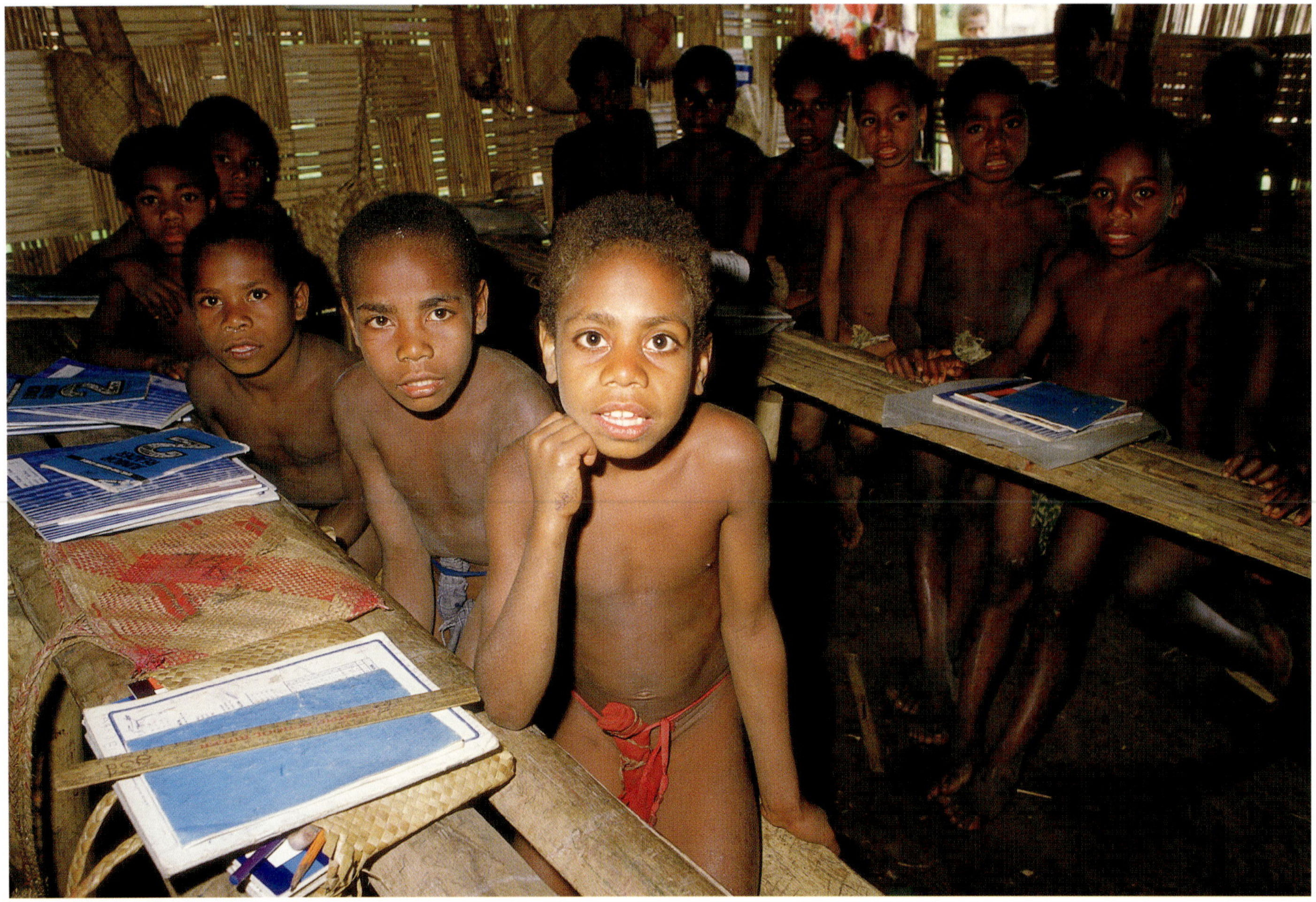

classroom in village school, tanna island

village boys, tanna island

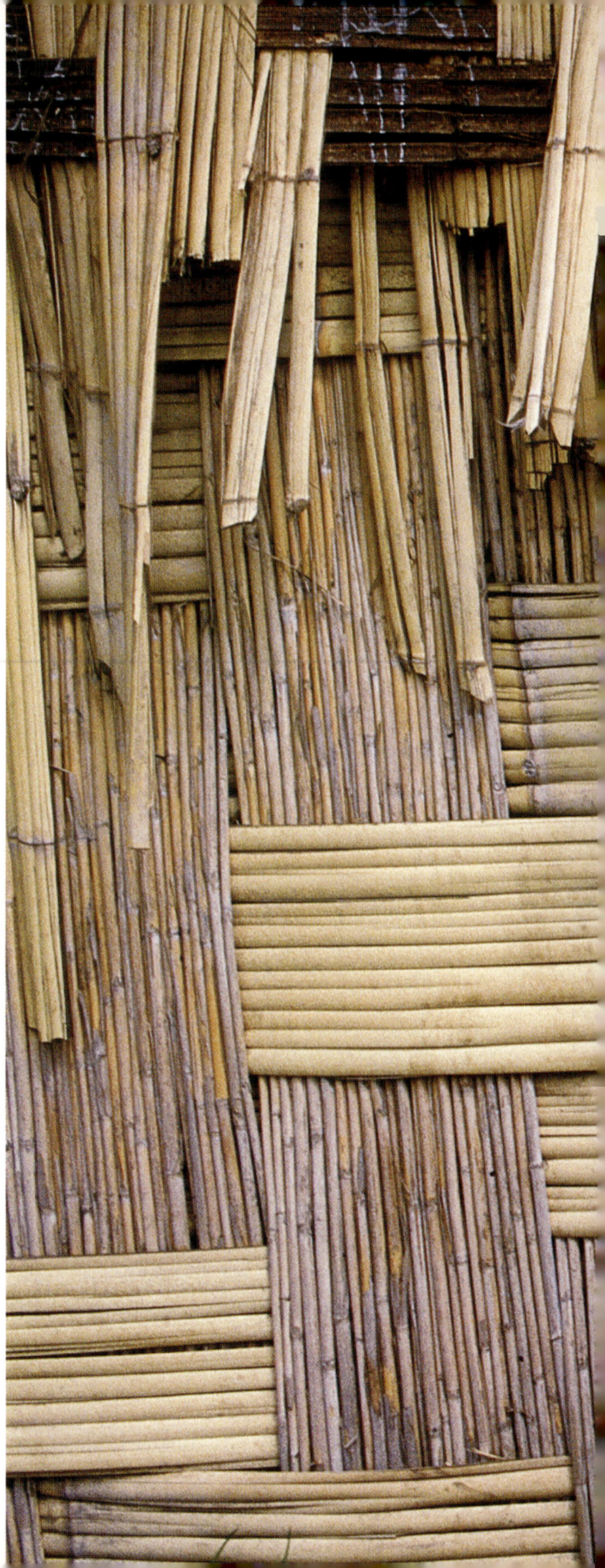

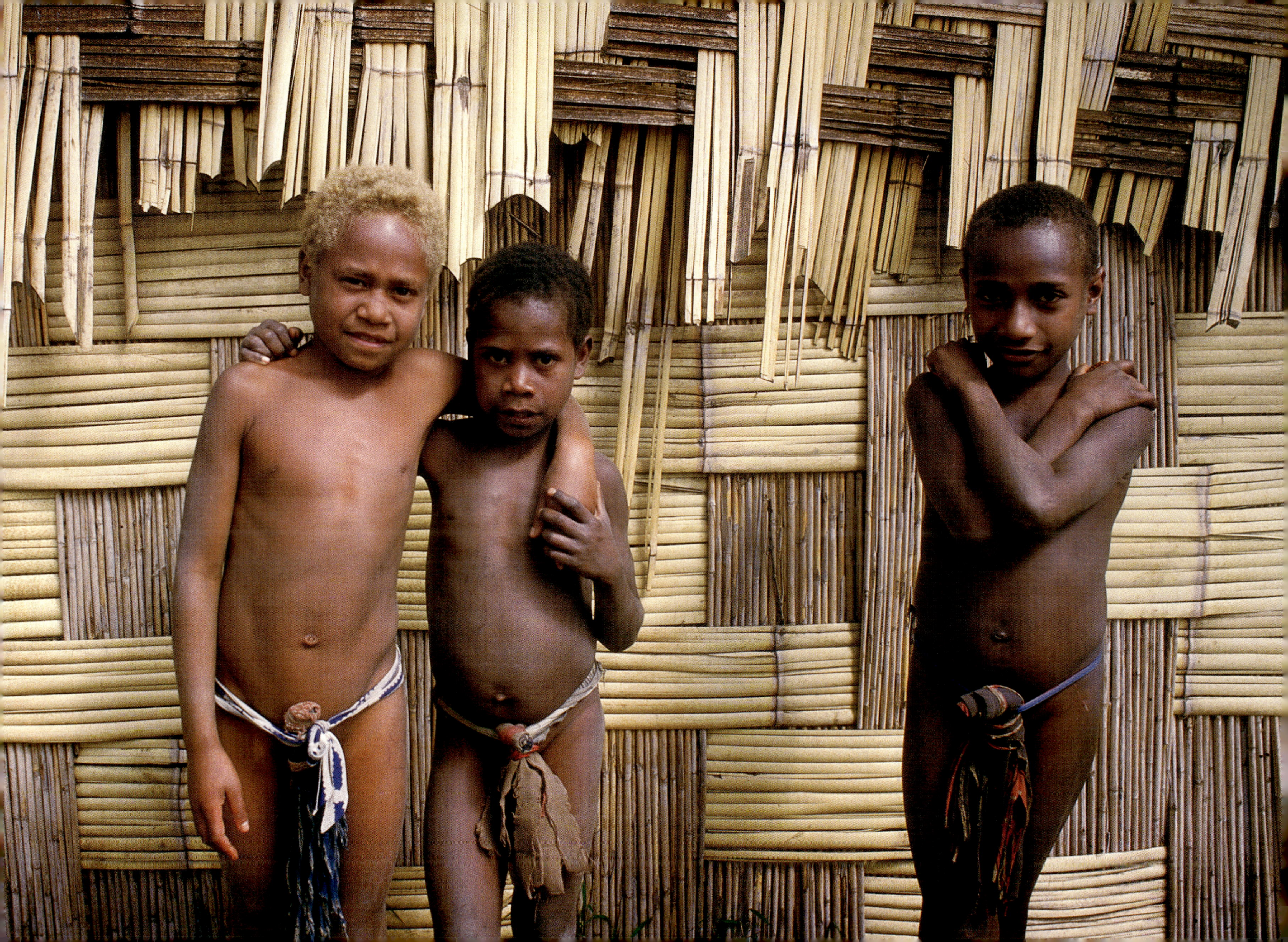

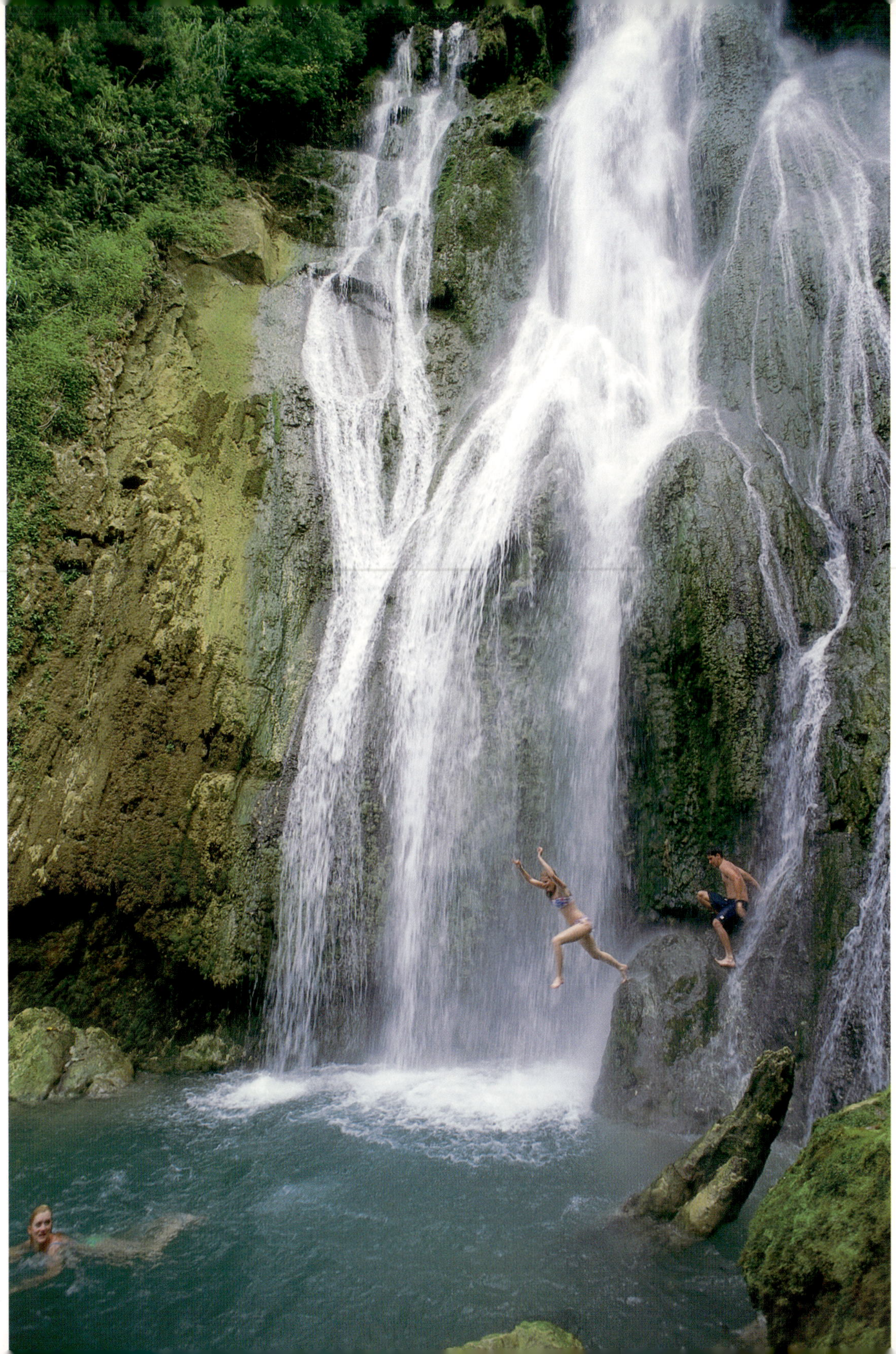

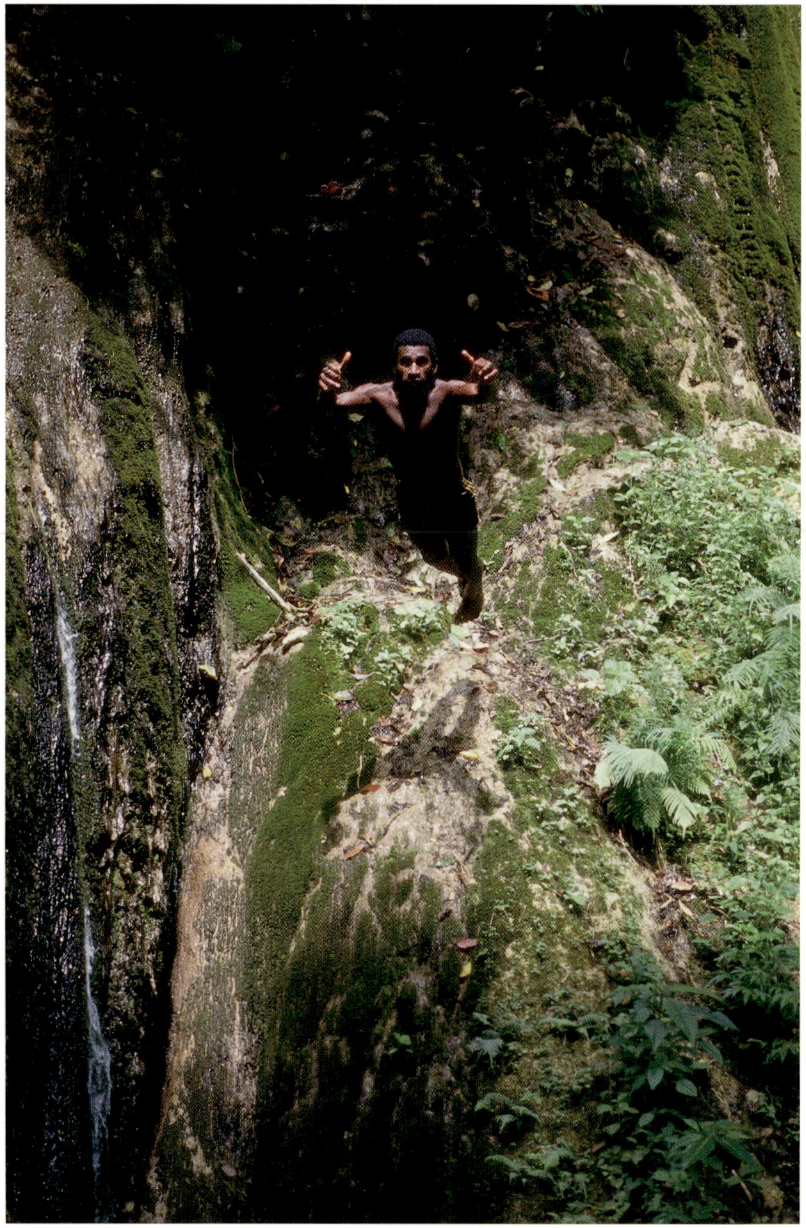

[**LEFT AND ABOVE**] *mele-maat cascades,* efate

[**RIGHT**] *port vila harbour,* efate

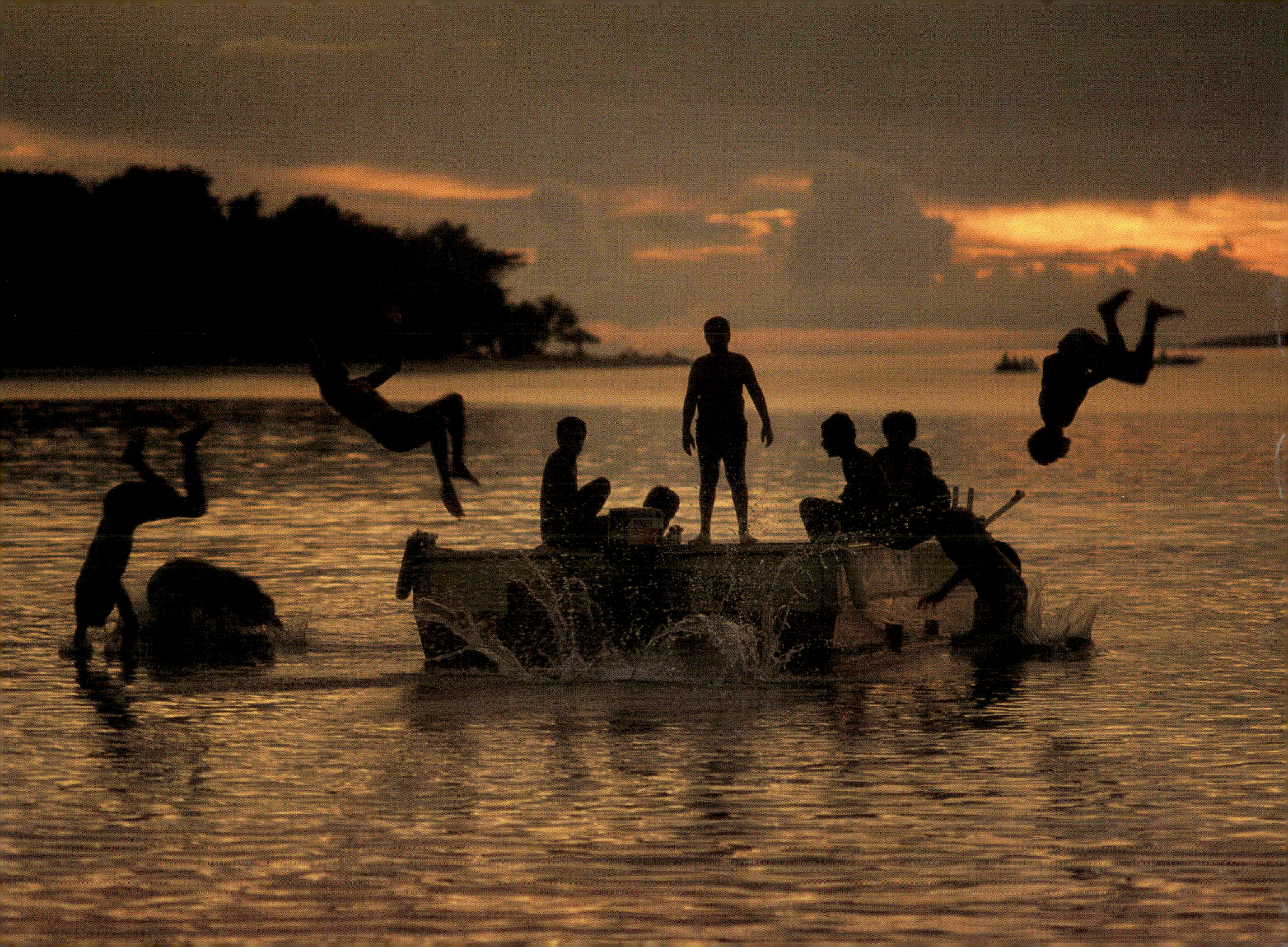

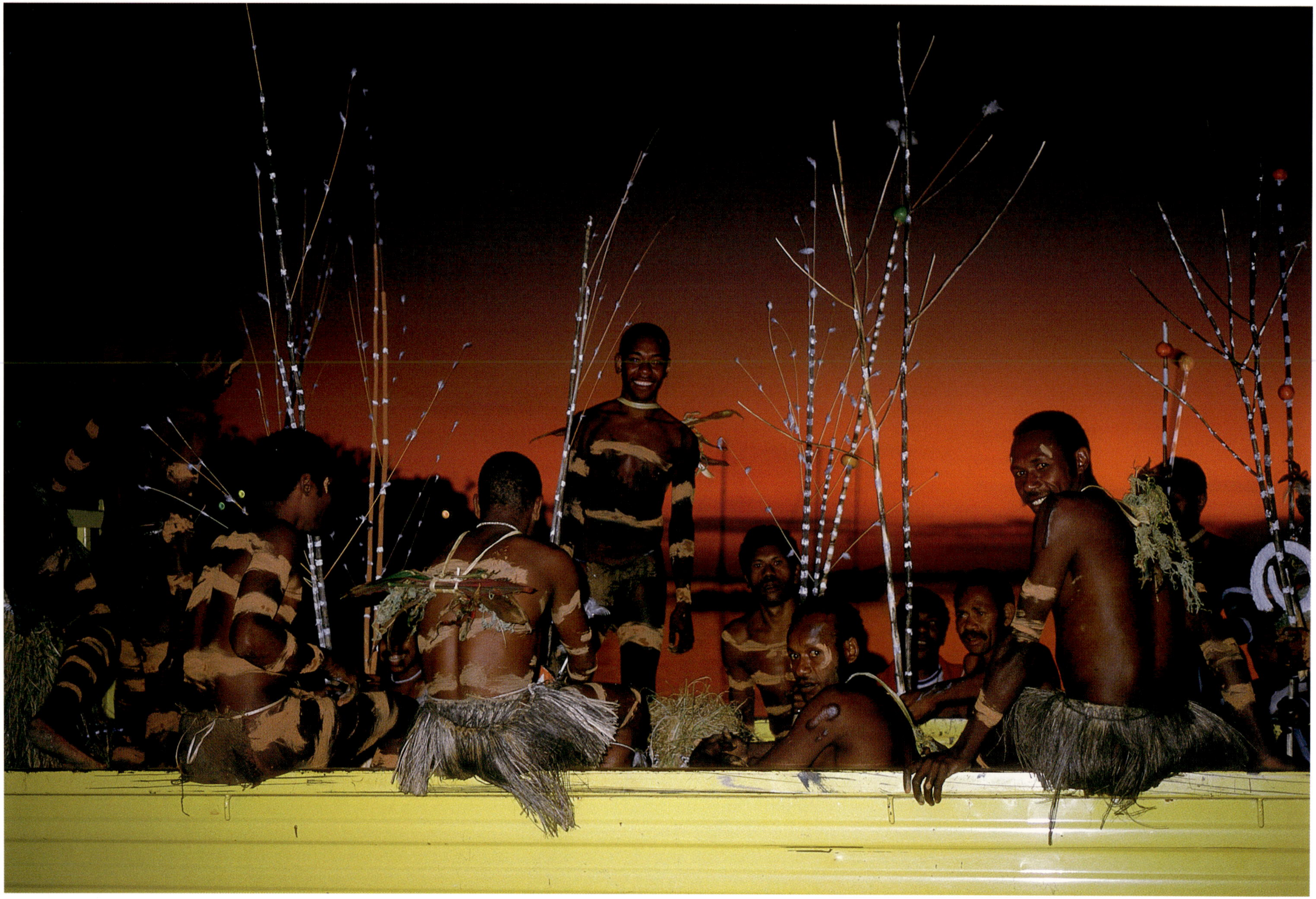

banks islands dancers

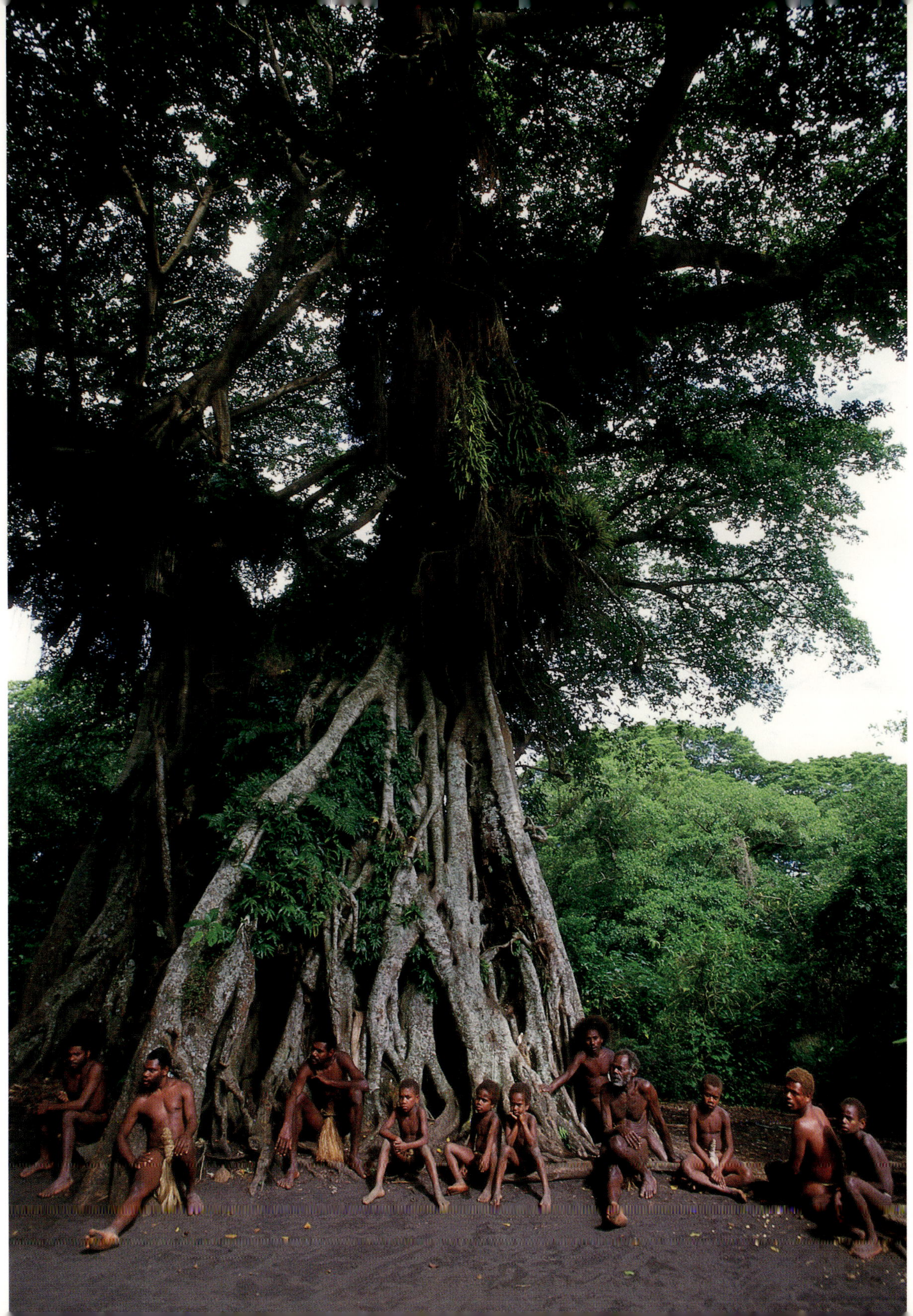

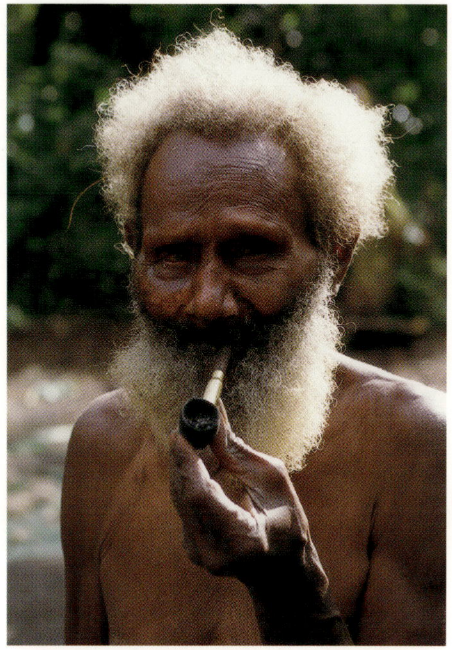

village elders,
yankel custom village

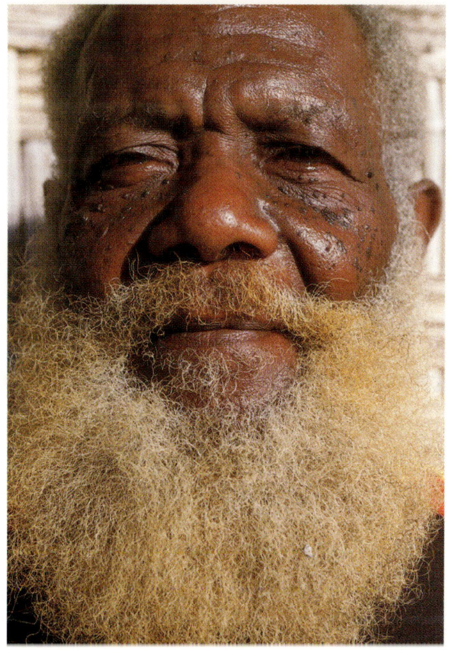

yankel custom village, tanna island

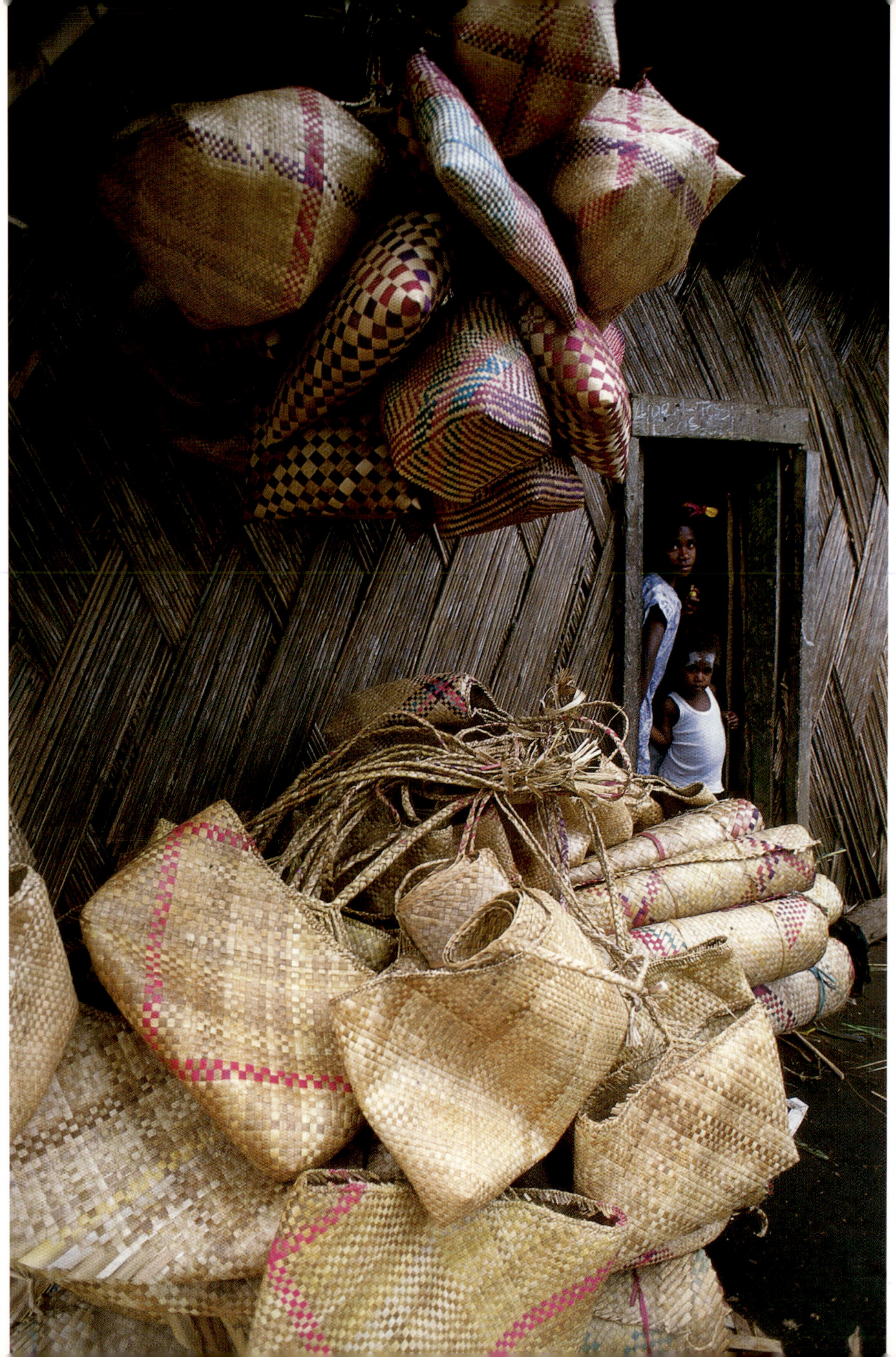

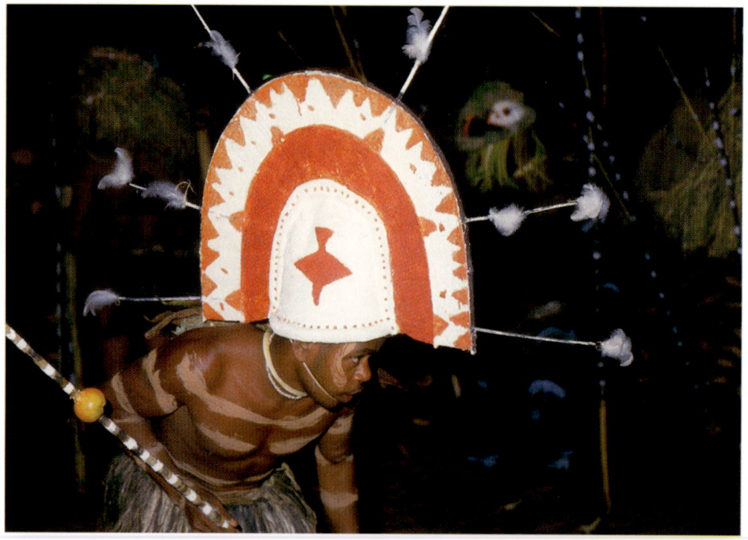

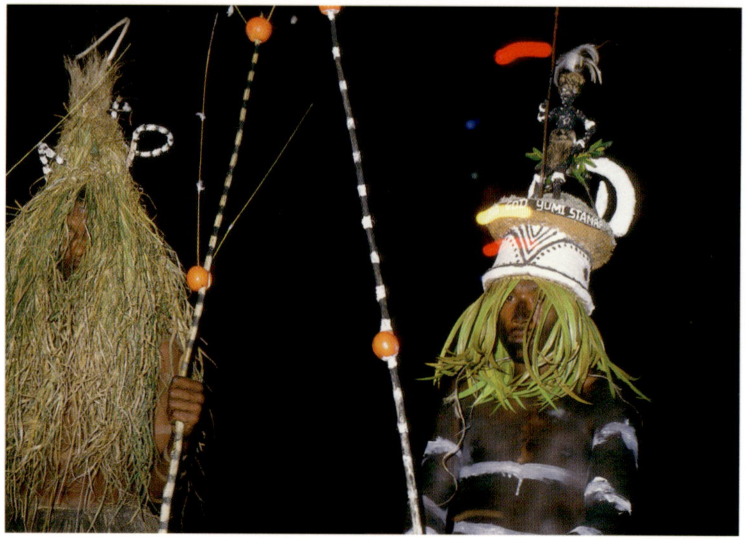

[ABOVE] *banks islands dancers*

[LEFT] *baskets made for circumcision festival,* tanna island

[RIGHT] *custom dance performed by young males,* tanna island

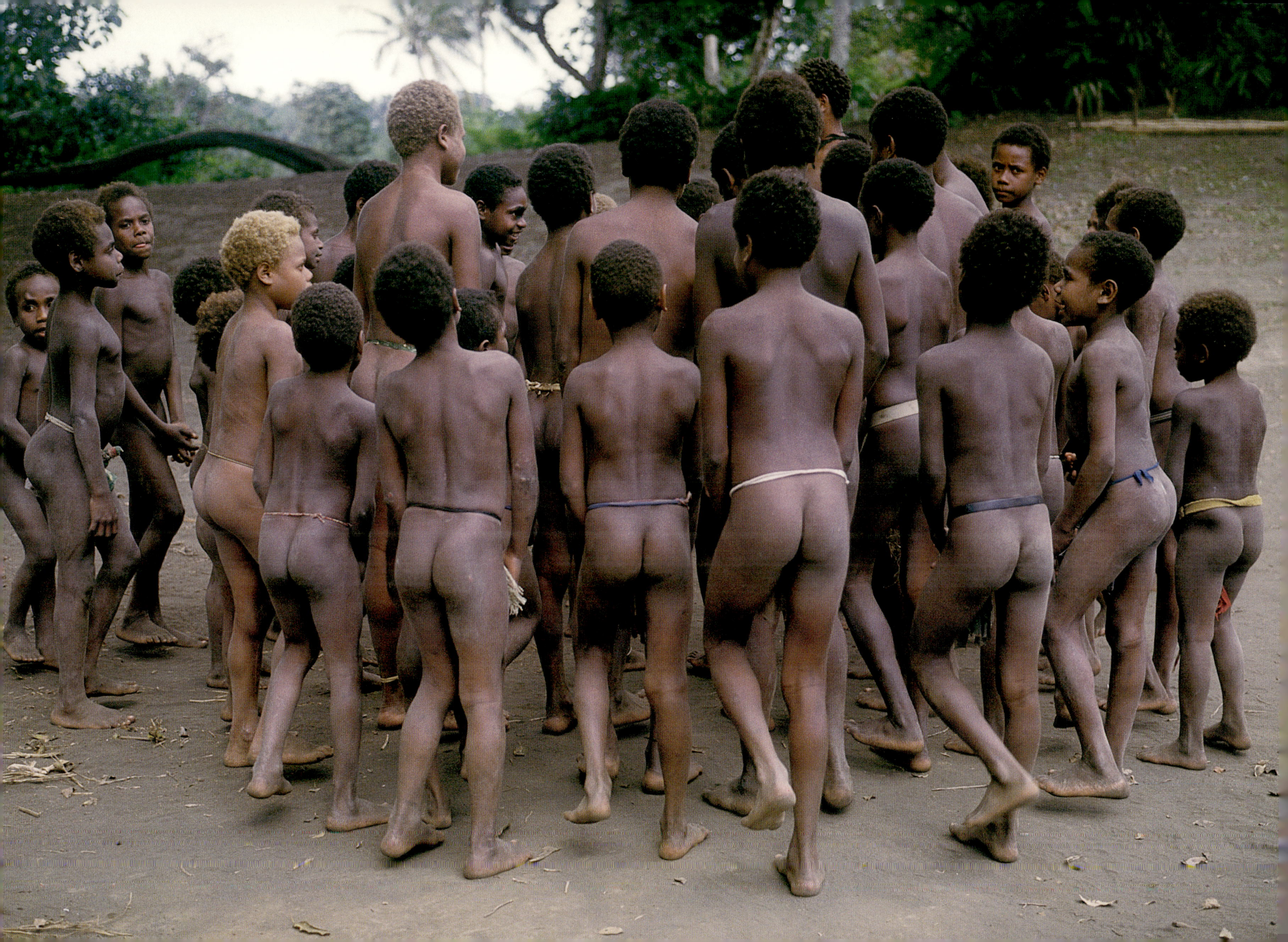

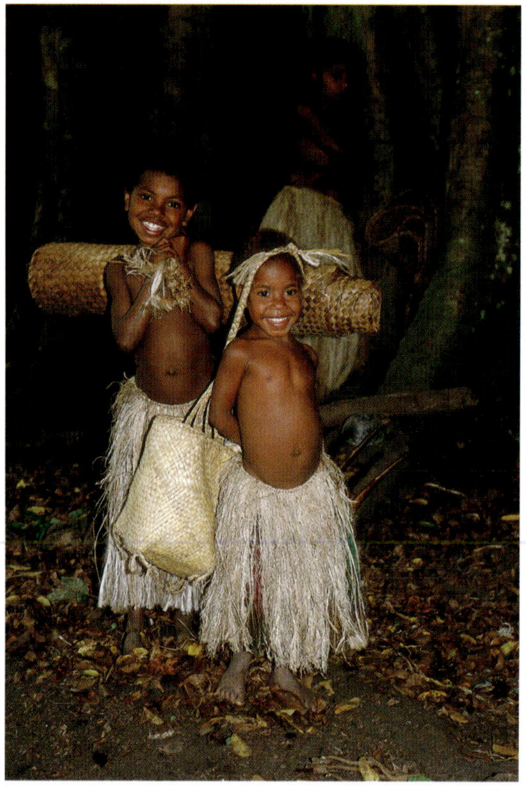

girls in custom dress, tanna island

champagne beach, espiritu santo island

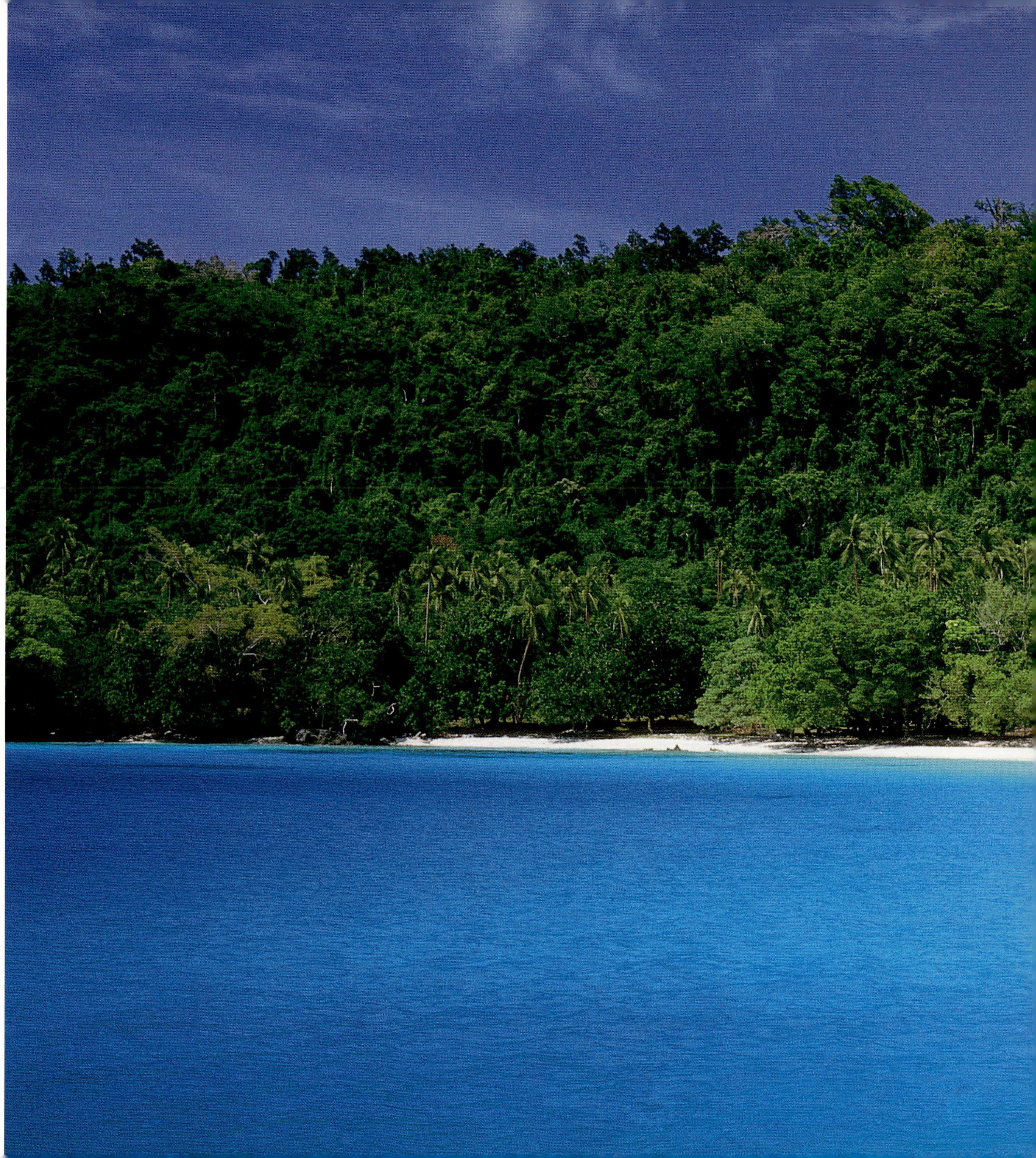

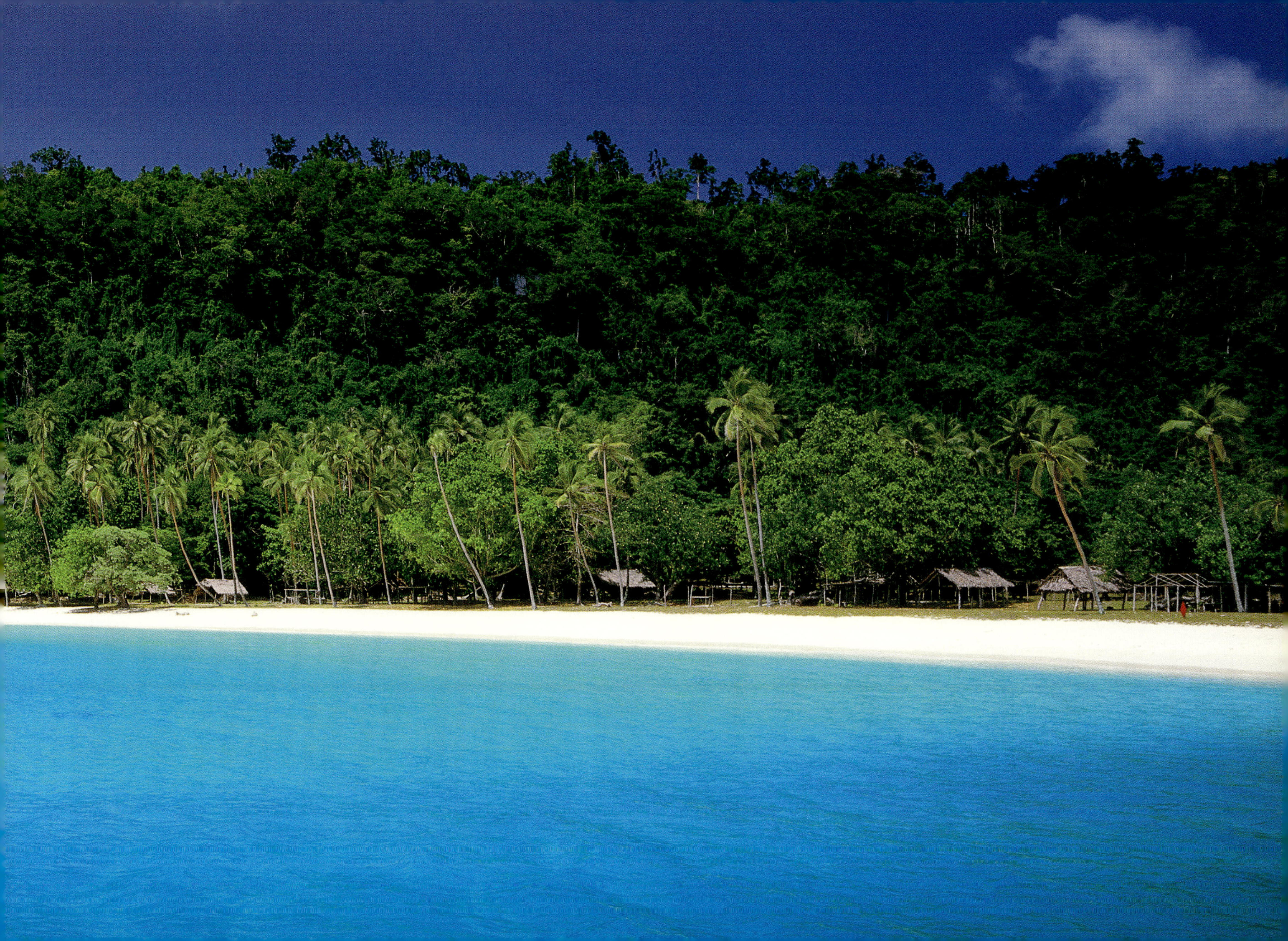

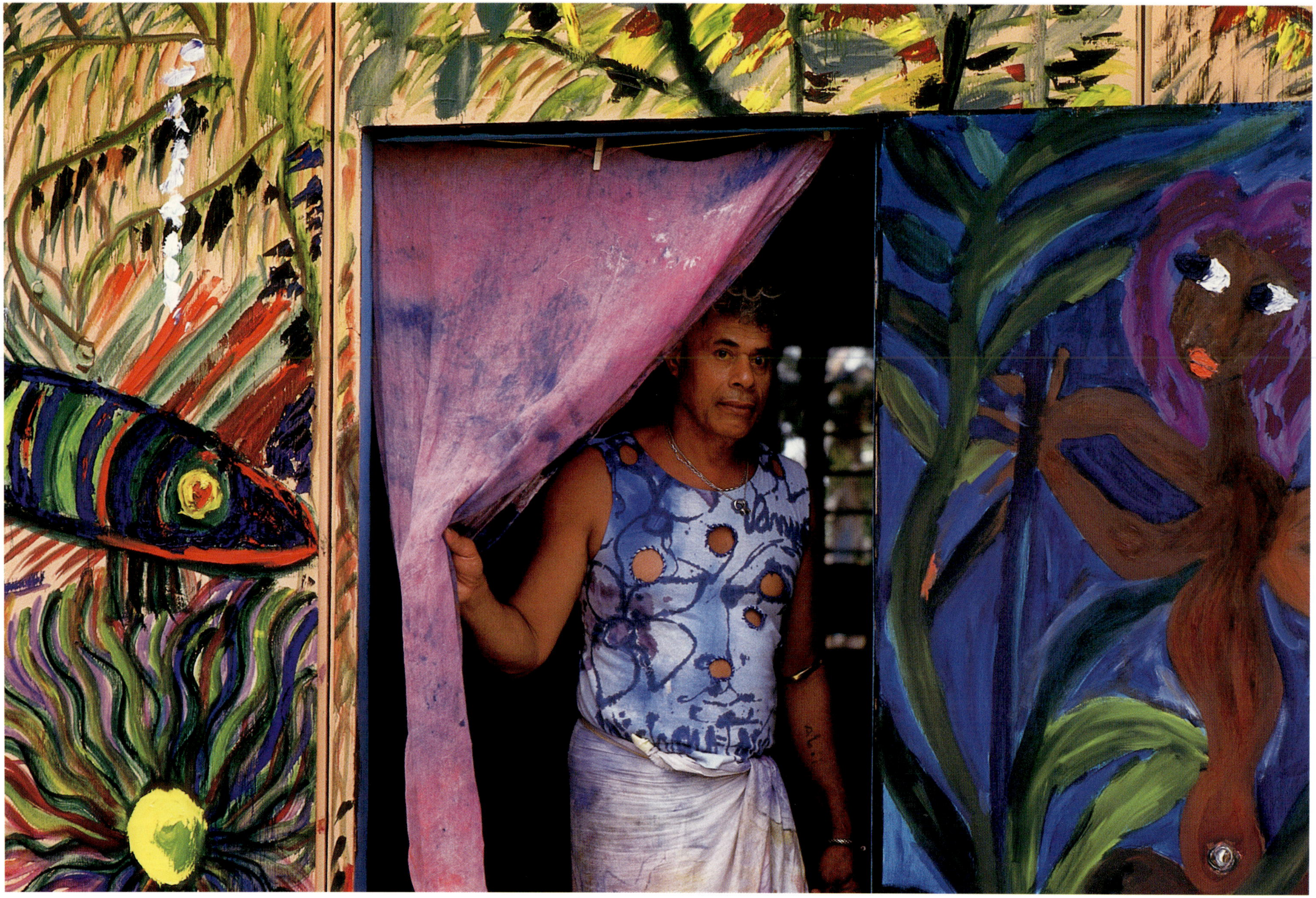

the wallasian artist alio pilioko, a long time resident of vanuatu at his port vila studio

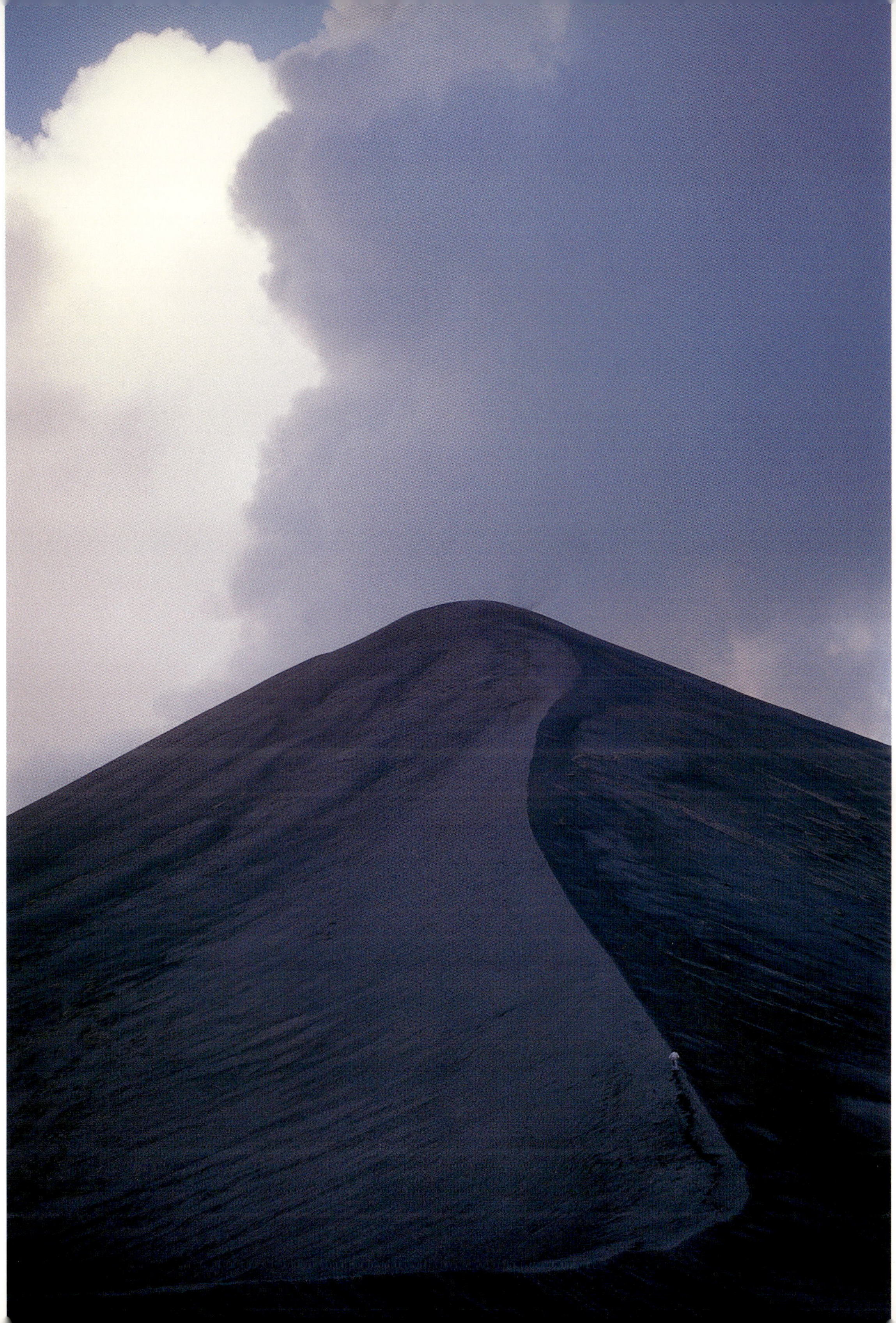

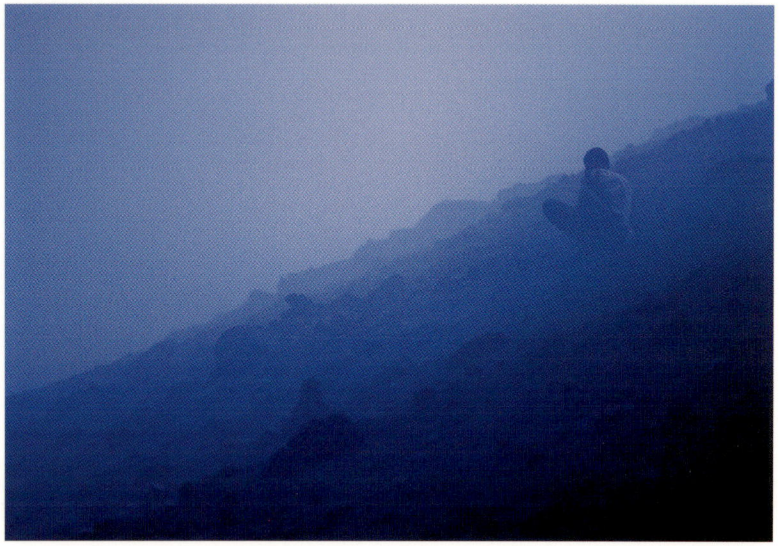

[**LEFT AND ABOVE**] *yasu volcano,* tanna island

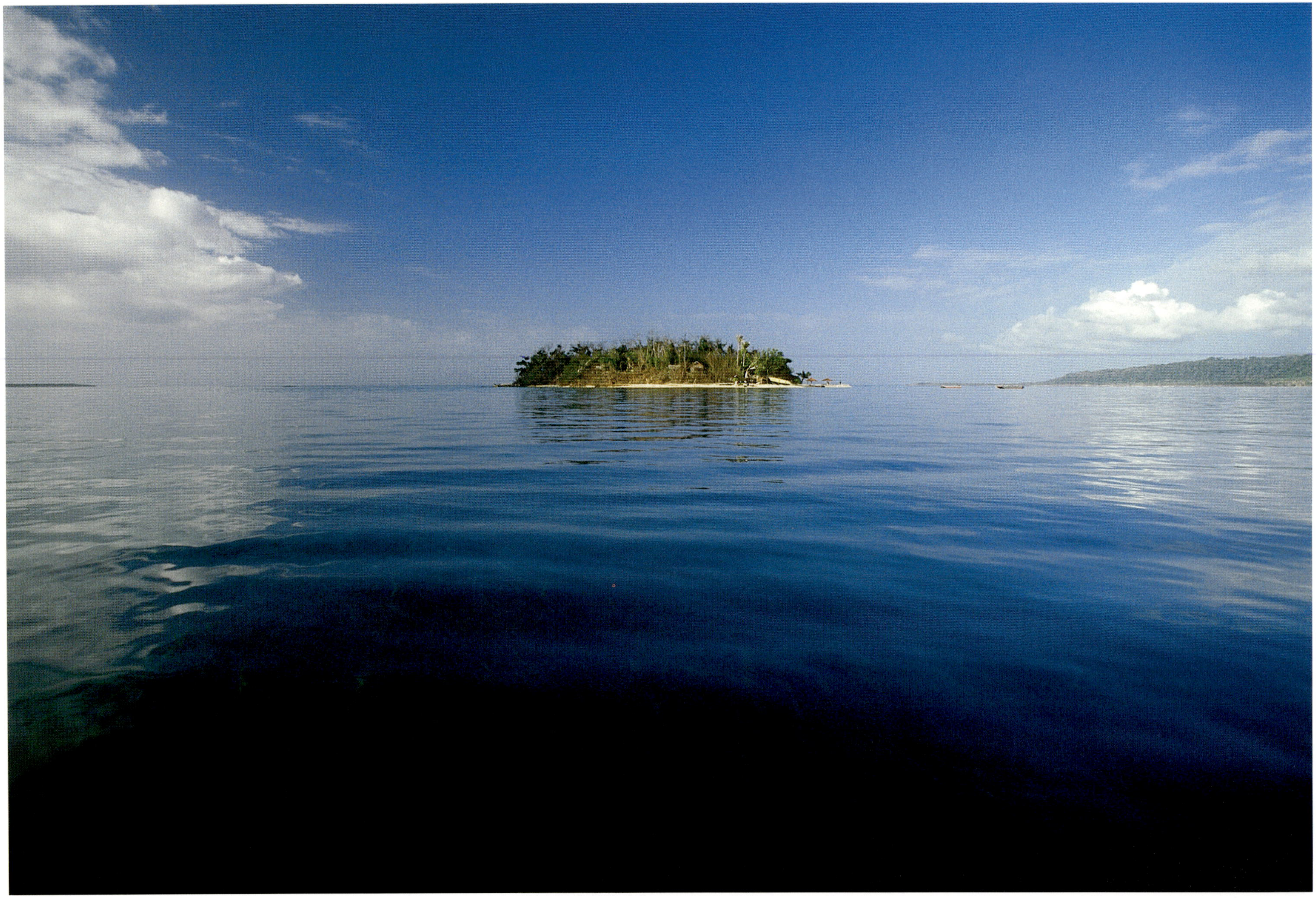

hideaway island, mele bay, efate island

[RIGHT] *yasu volcano,* tanna island

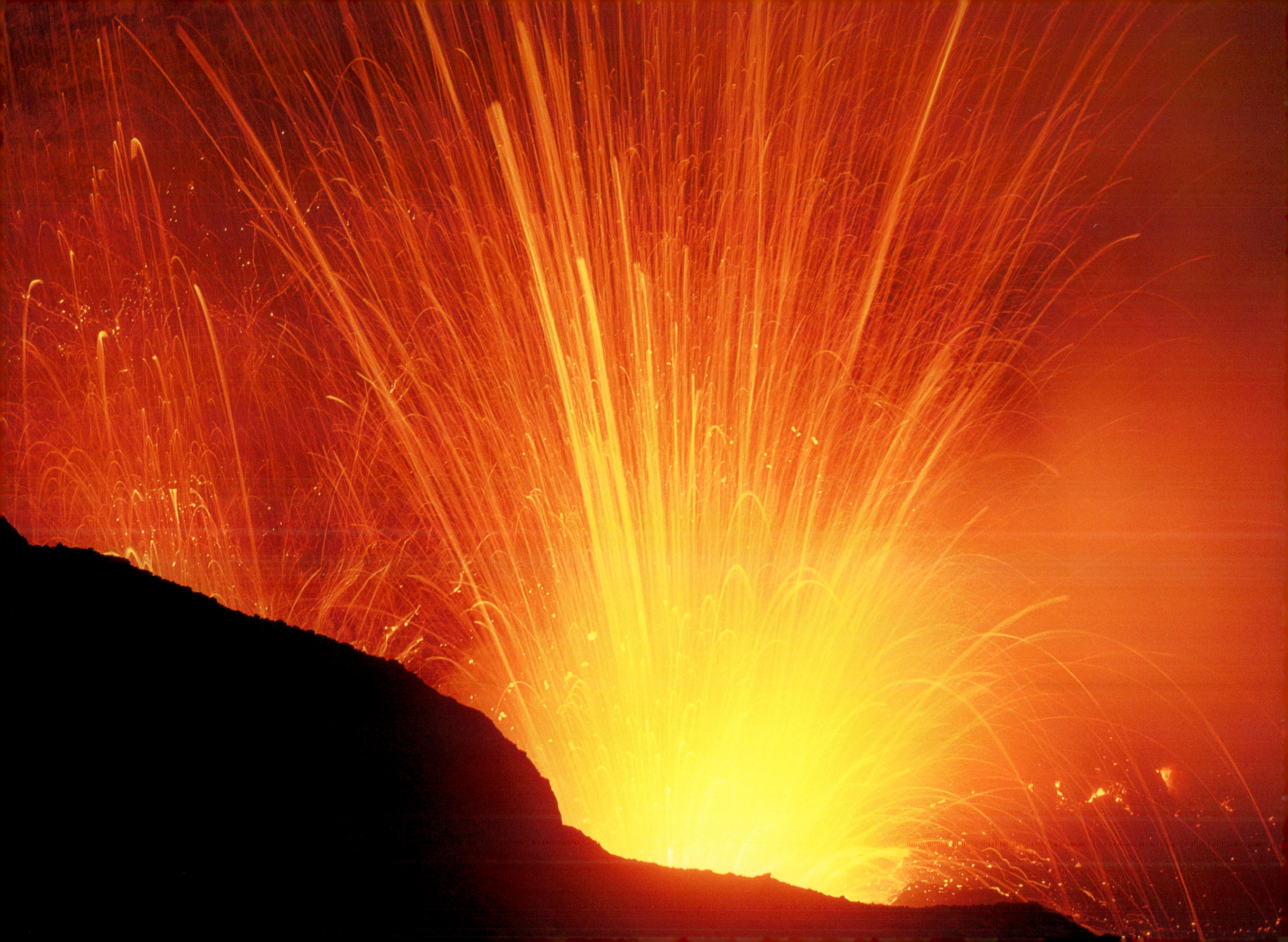

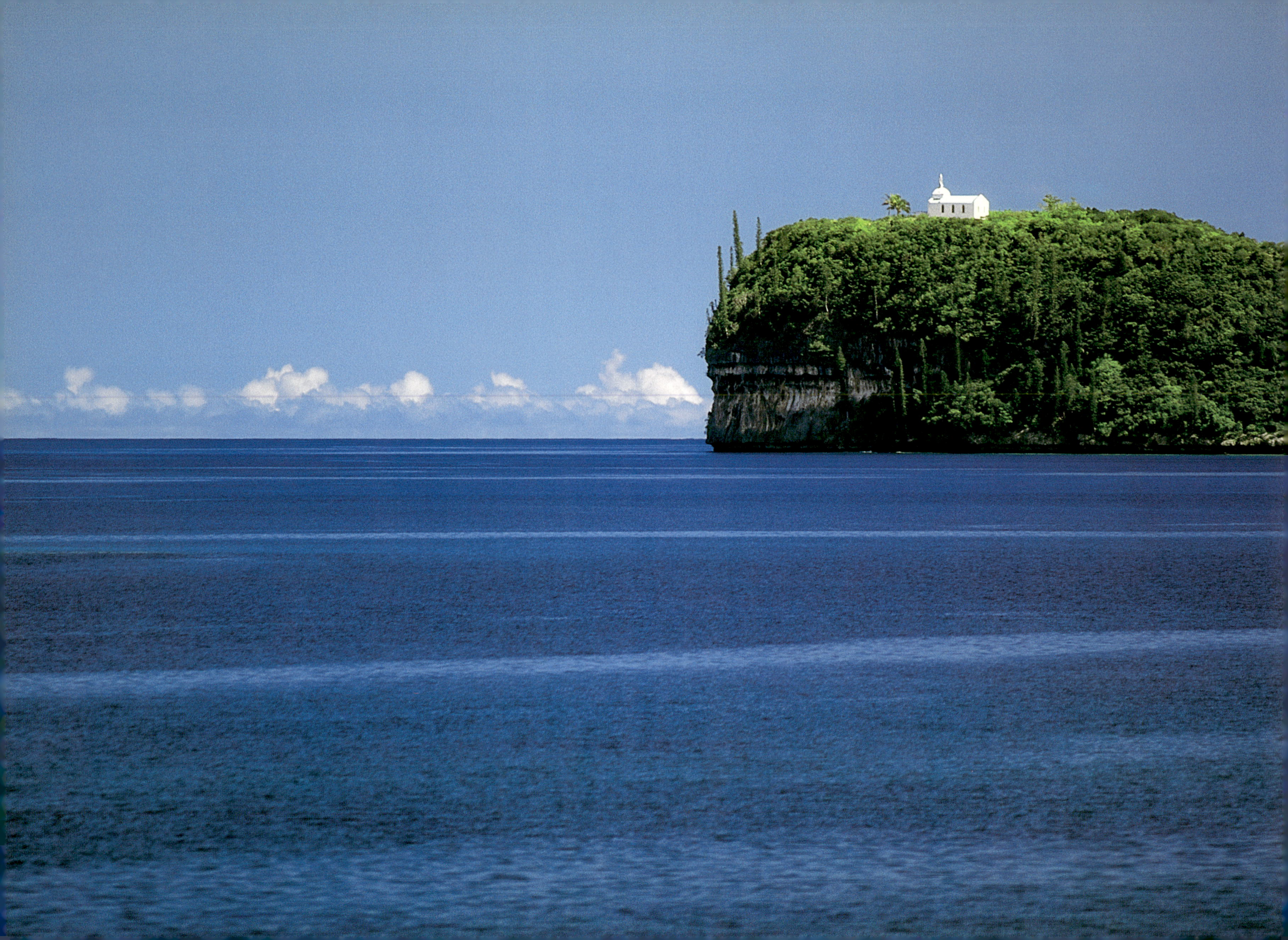

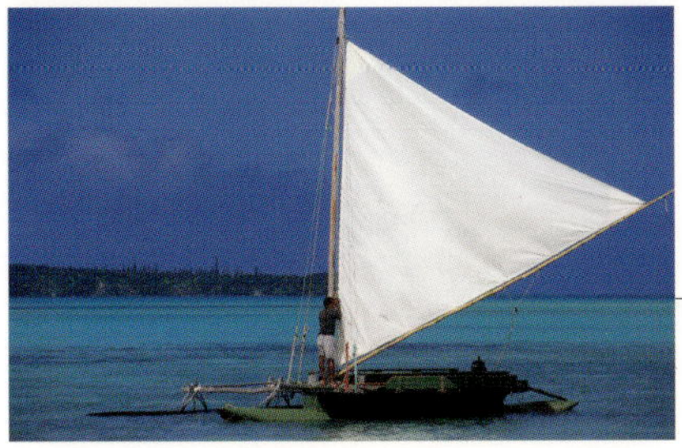

New Caledonia

NEW CALEDONIA, sometimes also known by its traditional name of Kanaky, is an Overseas Territory of France.

The main island of Grande Terre that comprises over 4/5ths of total land area has a central mountain range separating the wetter eastern side that has tropical rainforests and numerous rivers from the drier, sparser coastal plains on the west. Although Grande Terre has many species of plants and animals, it has at times a remarkable similarity to Australia to which it was joined in the ancient super continent of Gondwanaland. The Barrier Reef surrounding it is the 2nd longest in the world after Australia's Great Barrier Reef.

Settled around four thousand years ago by voyagers from Vanuatu and Papua New Guinea, the culture that the people developed was based on subsistence agriculture with the root crop yam having a major symbolic significance in the islanders' cultural and ritual life. The Kanaks lived in small villages and owned their land collectively.

The British navigator James Cook was the first European to visit the island in 1774 and it was he who named it New Caledonia after the Roman name for his birthplace of Scotland. Annexed by France in 1853, it became a French penal colony from 1864 until 1897 during which time over 20,000 convicts, many of them political prisoners, were transported.

Noumea, the capital with over 40% of the total population, reminds the visitor of the south of France. Surrounded by numerous bays and backed by hills, the city has a bustling restaurant and water sports culture with one of the highest boat ownership to population ratio in the Pacific. The economy is based on mineral production – especially nickel, of which it has 30% of total world reserves and also deposits of chrome, iron, gold and cobalt. The population of over 200,000 comprises 43% Melanesian, 37% European with sizeable Tahitian, Wallisian, Indonesian and Vietnamese. The Noumea Accord of 1998 provides the framework for the island's self-determination and independence in the future.

The uplifted coral atolls of Lifou, Mare and Ouvea comprise the Loyalty Islands with their beautiful palm tree-lined beaches and lagoons. Traditional lifestyles have remained stronger and Kanak culture more preserved on these less developed islands. The Isle of Pines, a small volcanic island a short distance from Noumea, is a popular tourist destination with many stunning beaches and bays and its distinctive Araucaria trees for which it was named.

[LEFT] *chapel notre dame,* easo peninsula, lifou, loyalty islands [ABOVE] *pirogue sailing canoe,* isle of pines

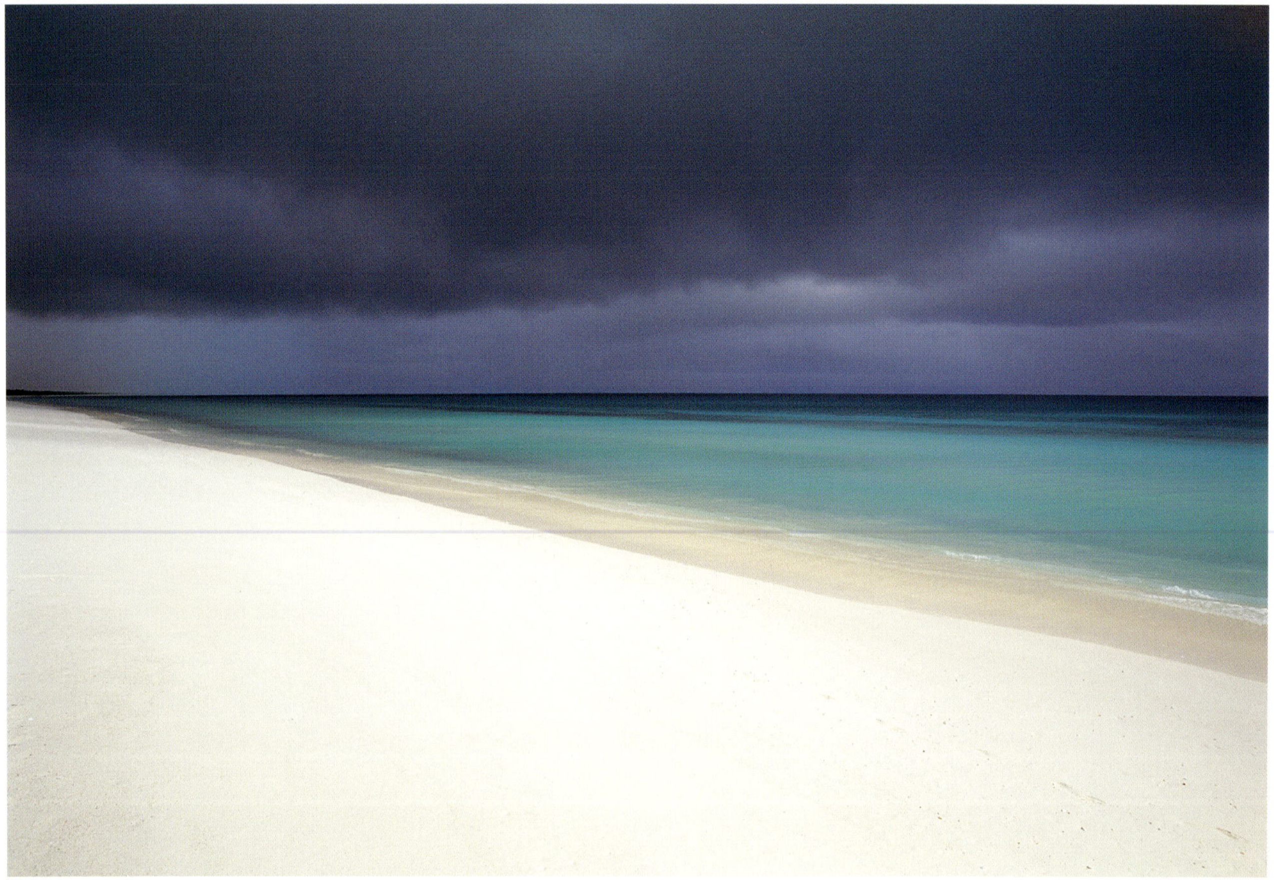

[**ABOVE**] *lagoon beach,* ouvéa, loyalty islands

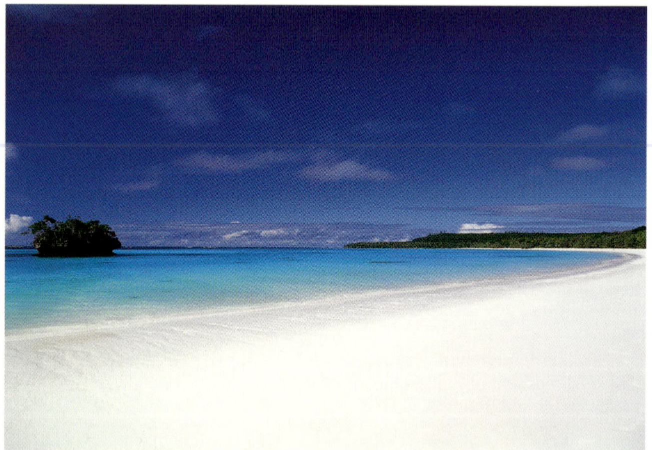

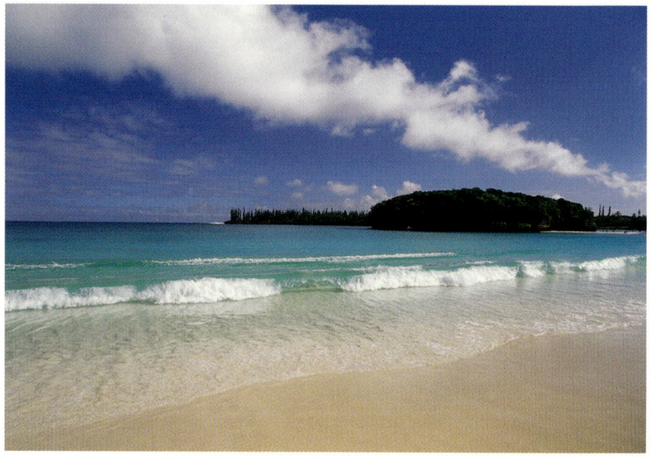

[**ABOVE RIGHT**] *bay of luengoni,* lifou, loyalty islands

[**RIGHT**] *bay of kanumera,* isle of pines

[**FAR RIGHT**] *peng beach on the bay of santal, lifou, loyalty islands*

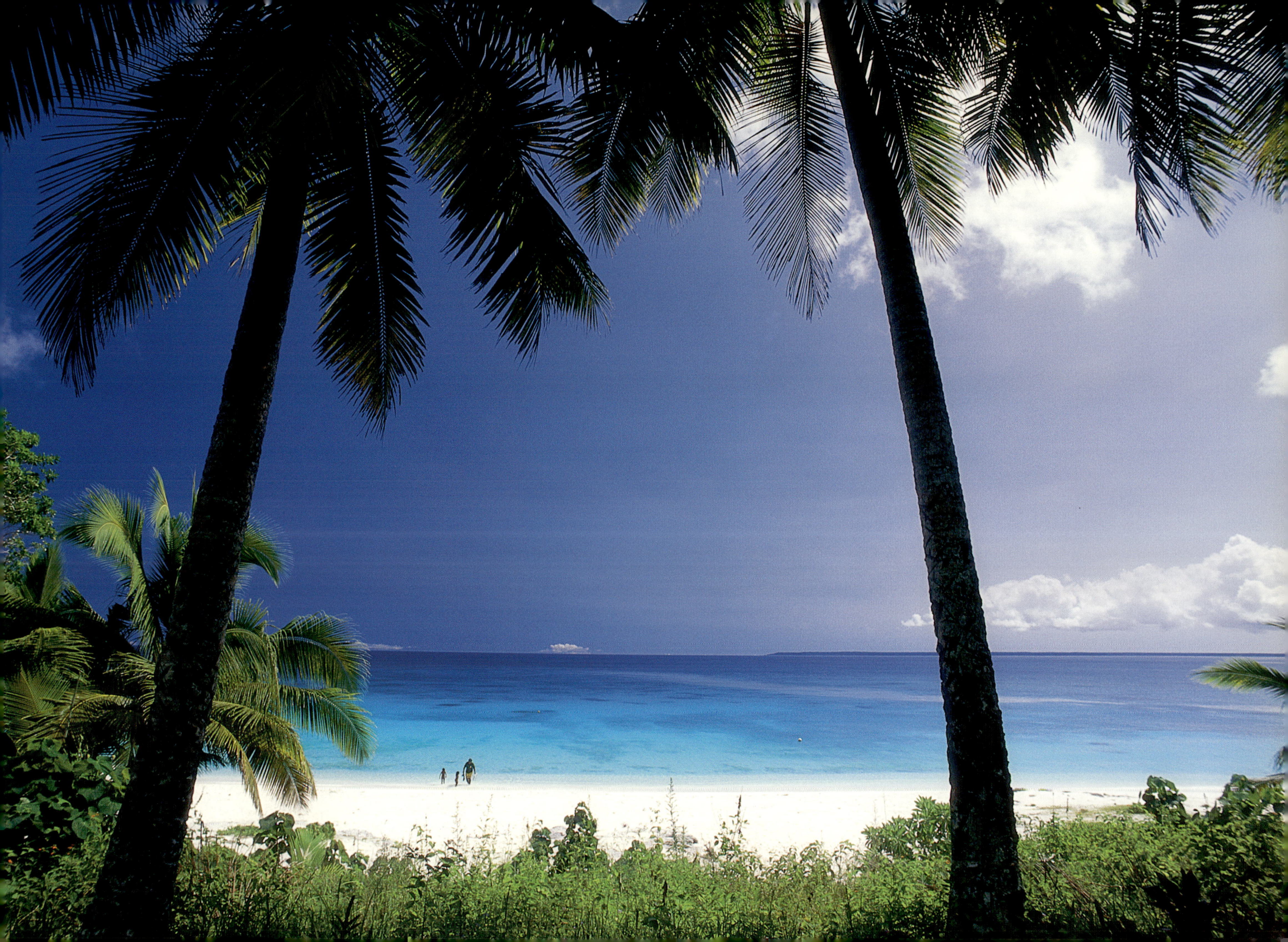

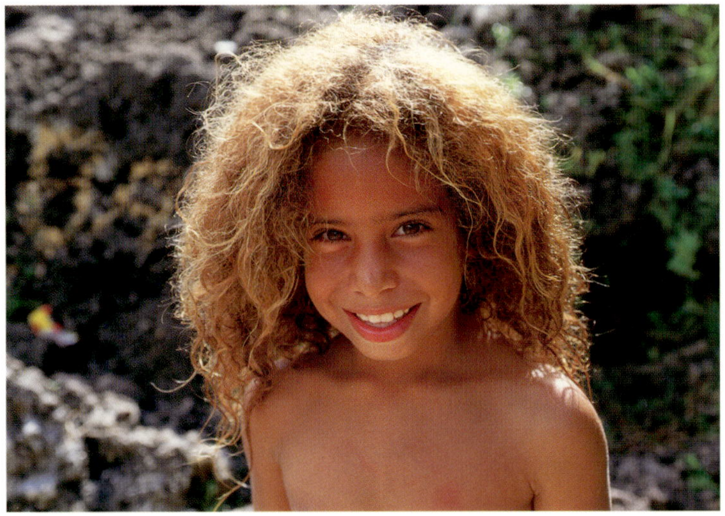

bay of joking, lifou, loyalty islands

kanak elder, noumea

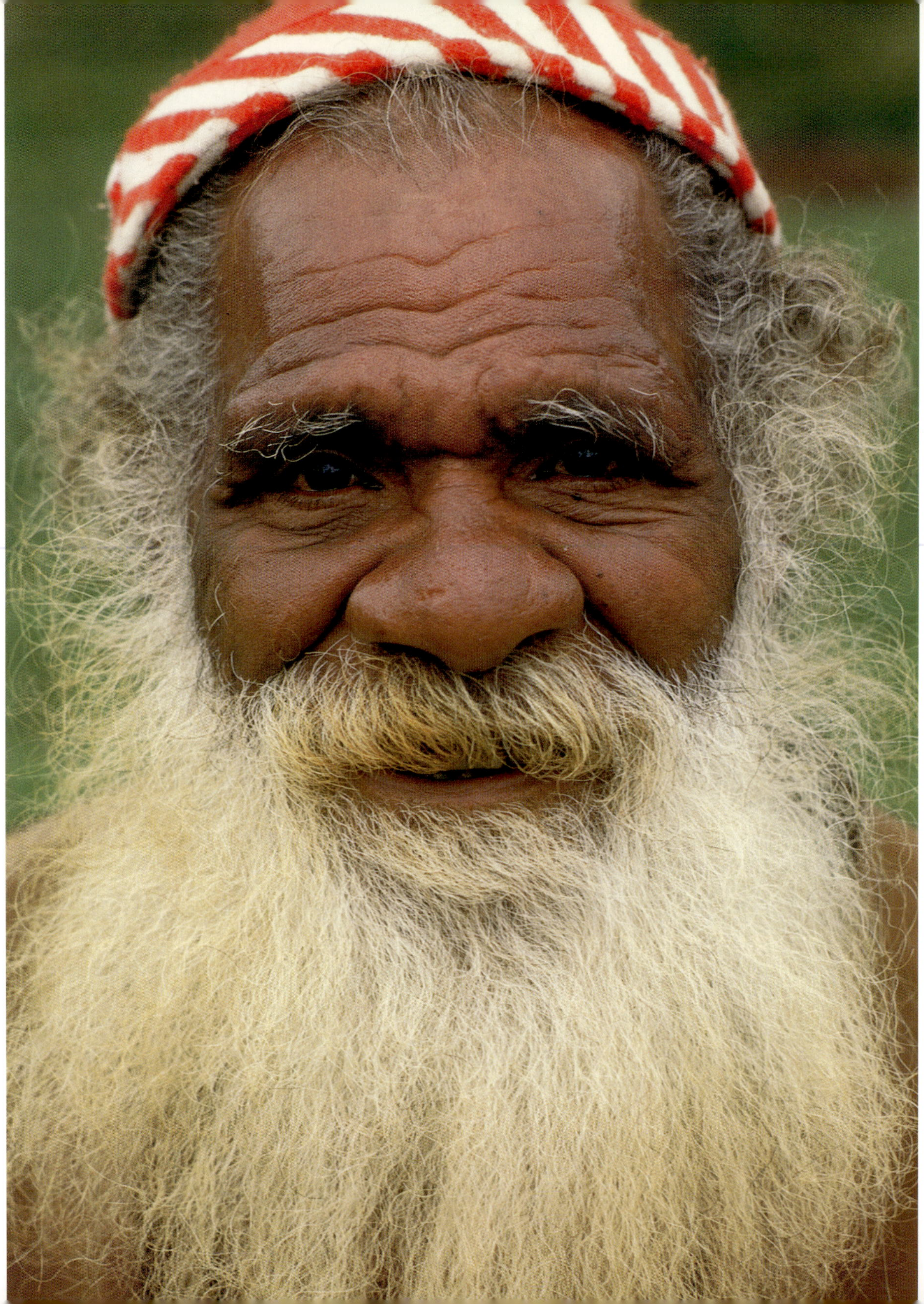

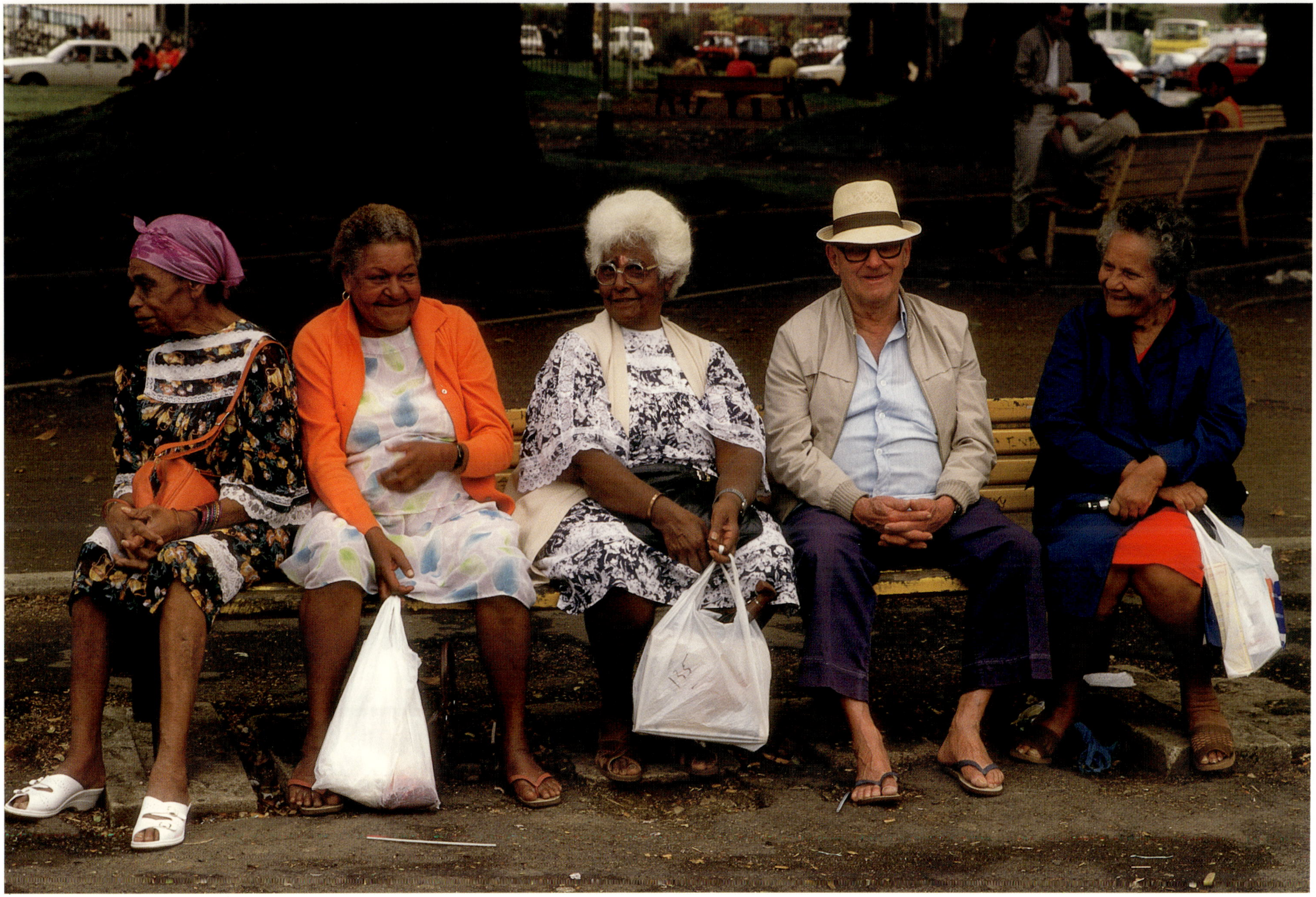

seniors sitting in park, noumea

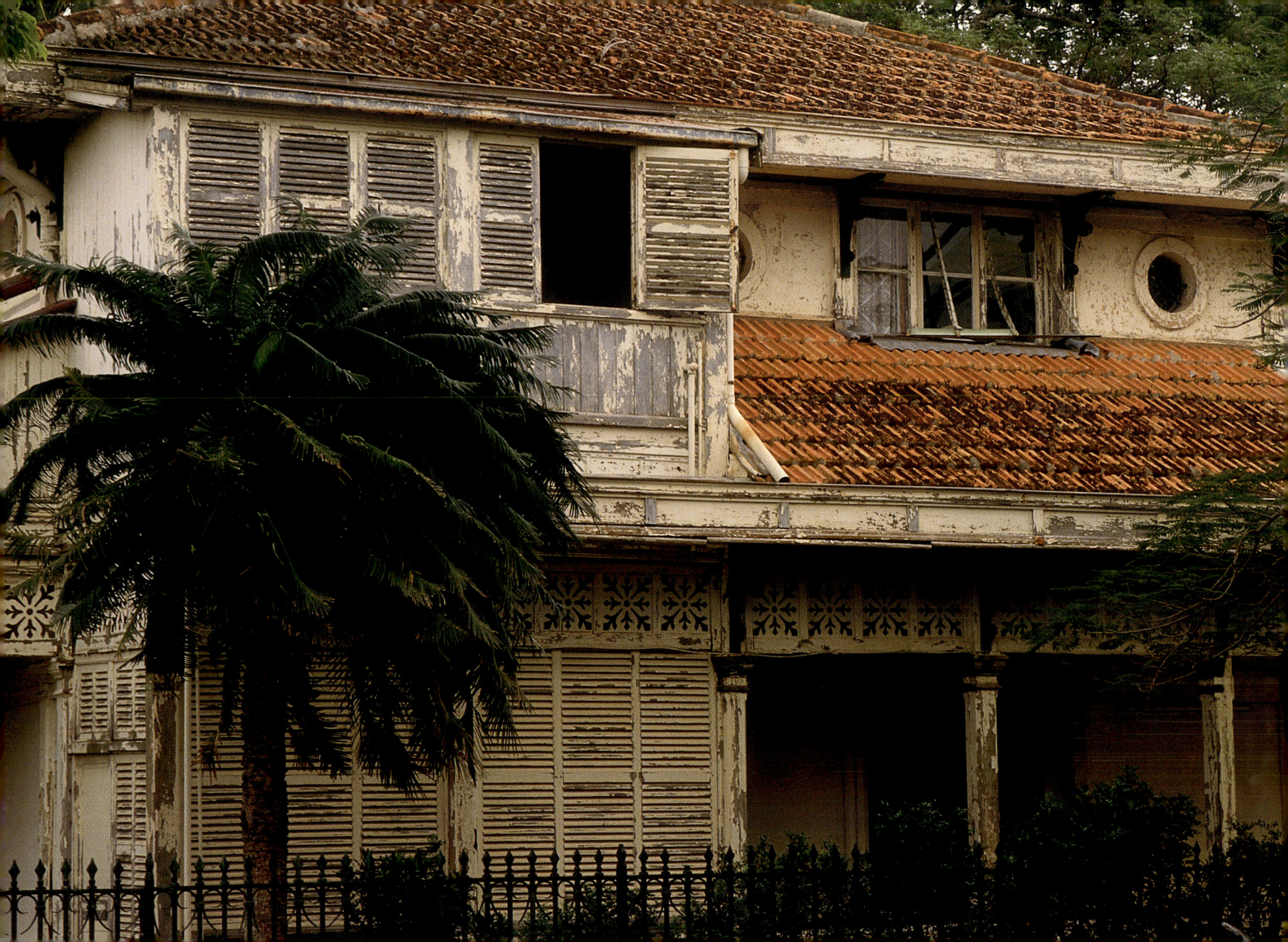

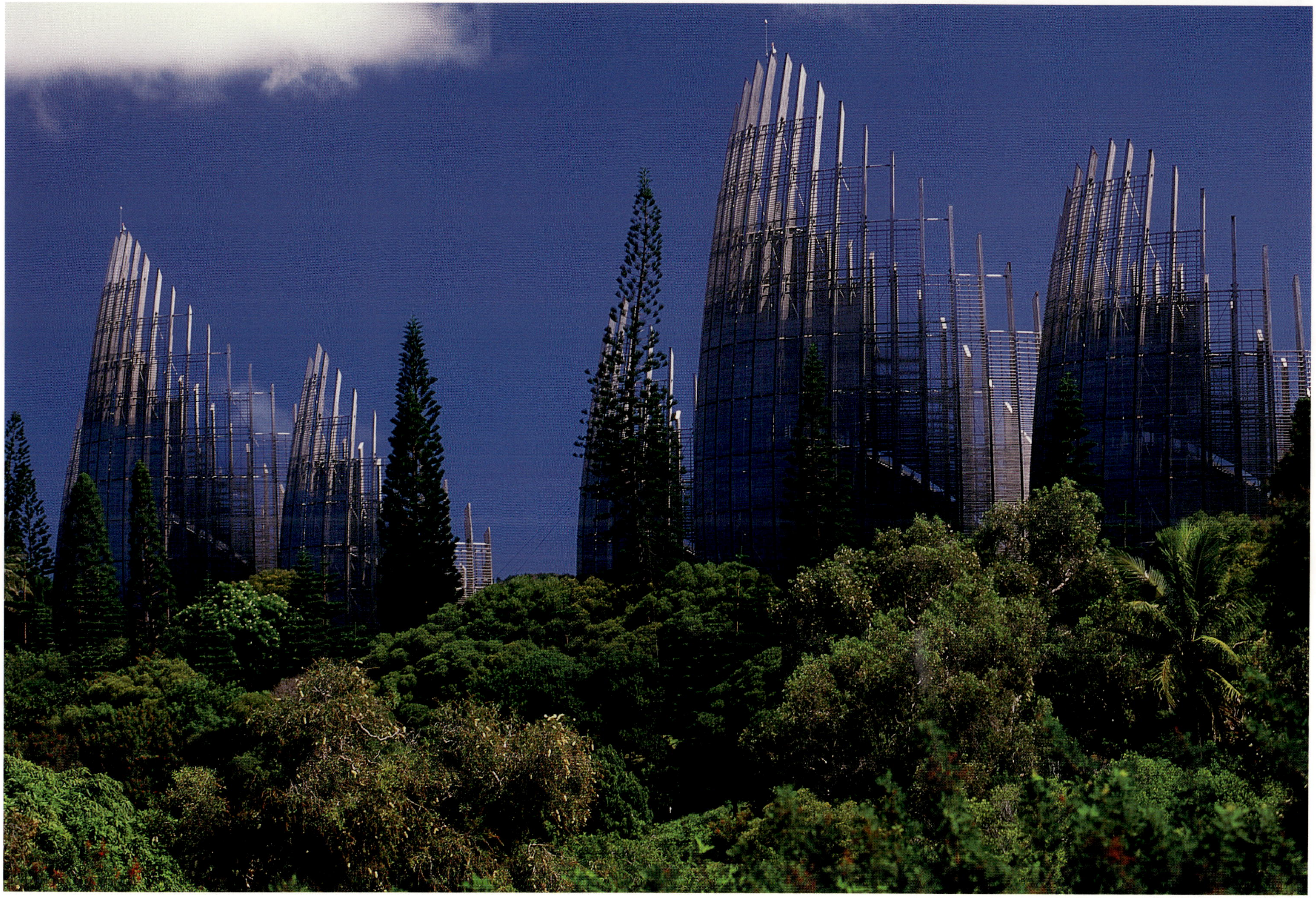

[LEFT] *colonial architecture,* noumea

tijbaou arts and cultural centre, noumea

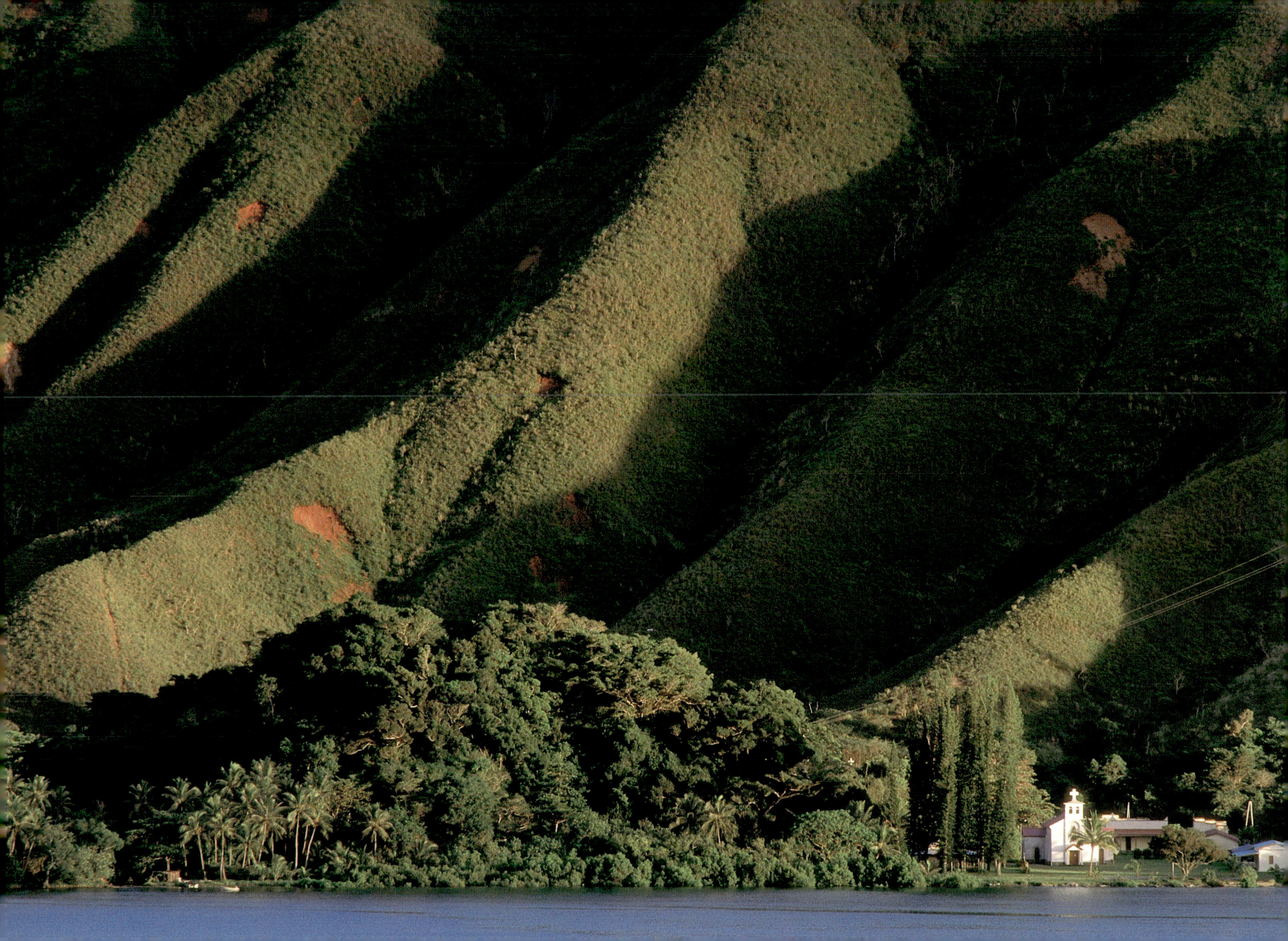

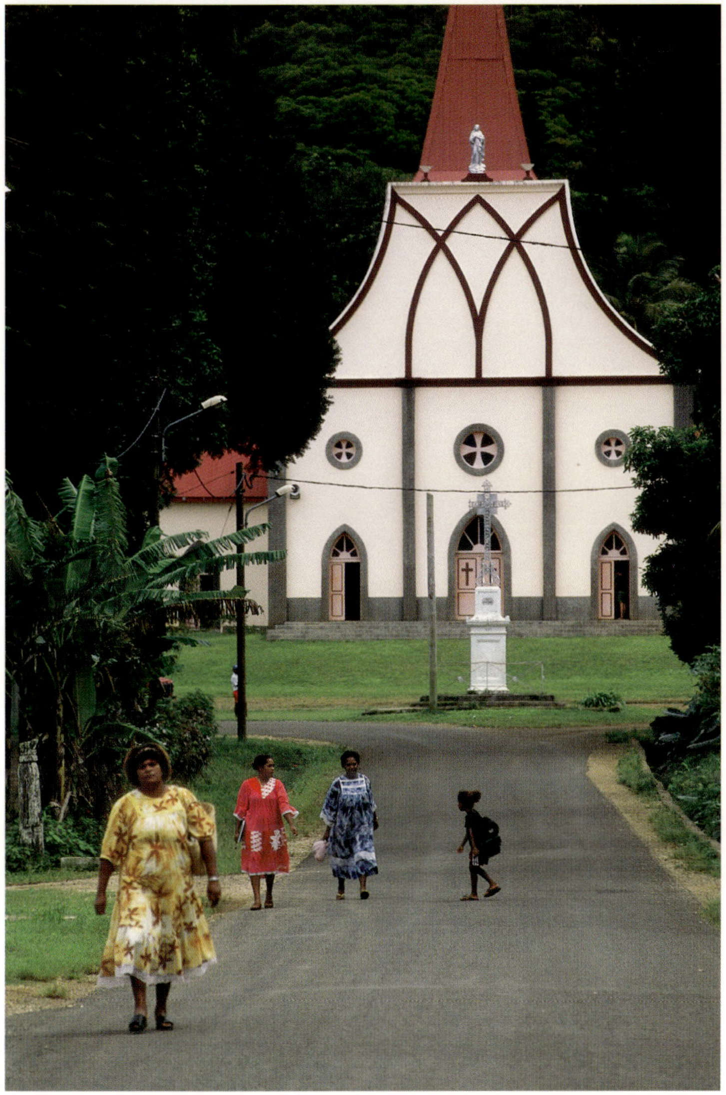

church of vao, isle of pines

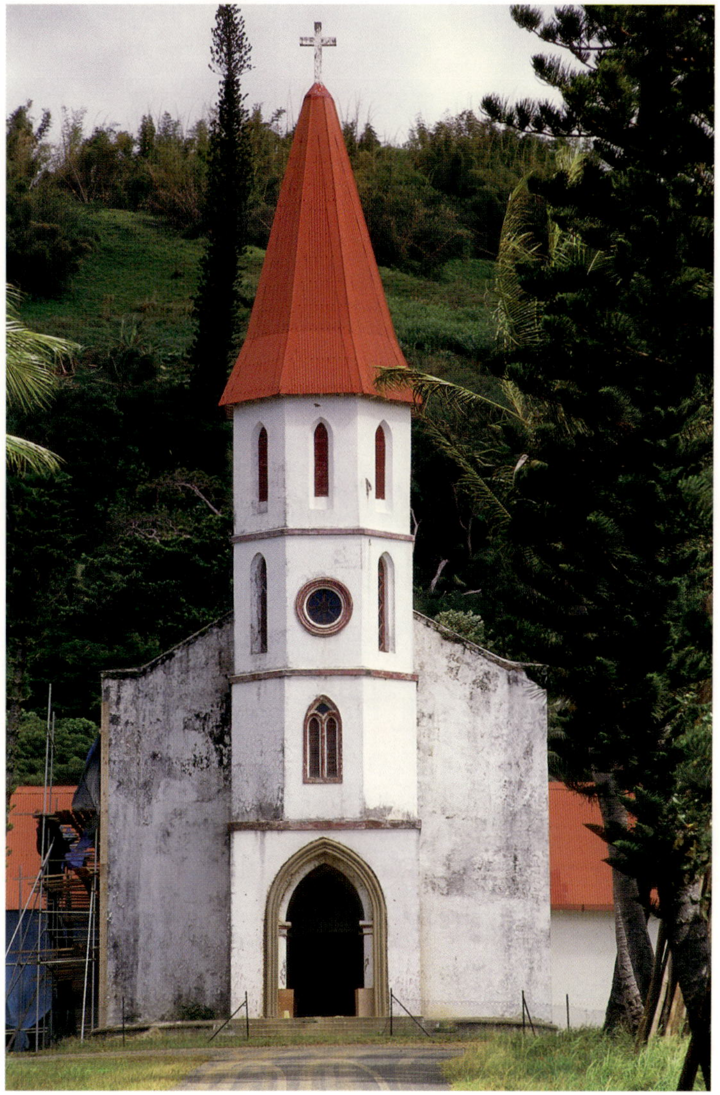

island church styles, grande terre

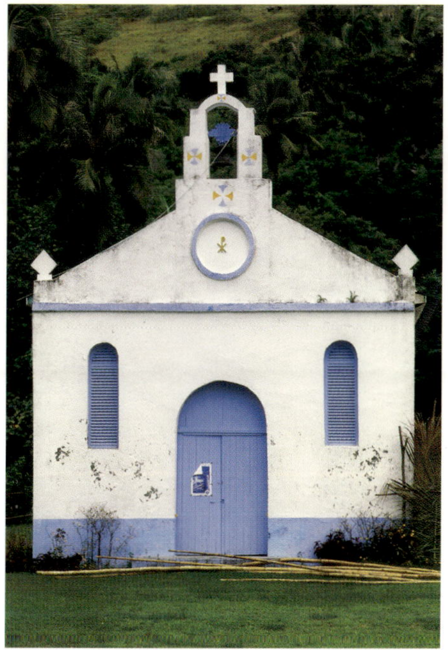

[LEFT] *ouaré chapel,* hienghène, grande terre

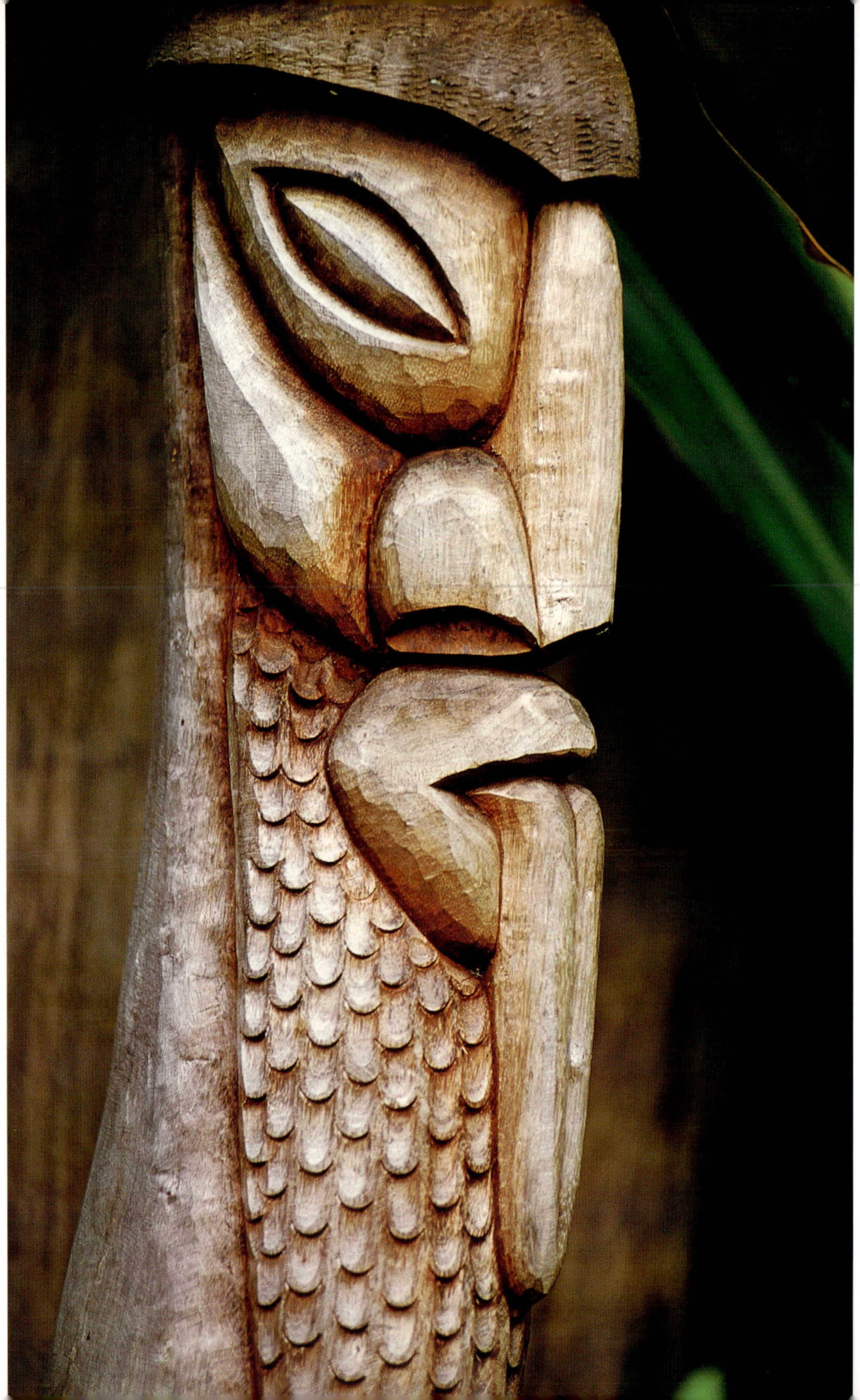

carvings representing protective ancestral spirits
by mr koitche chanel from the touéte tribal village,
le meridien hotel, isle of pines

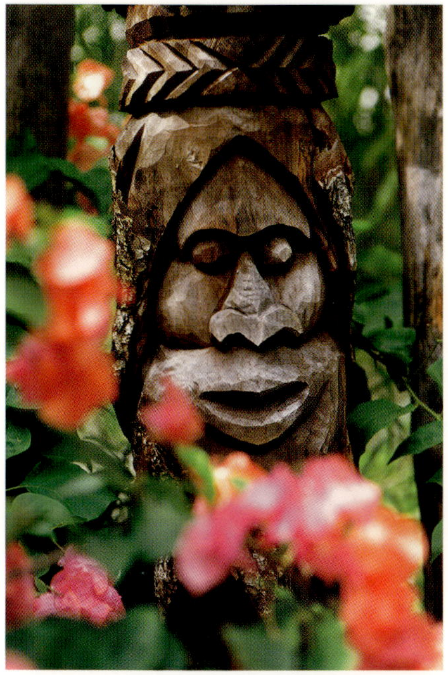

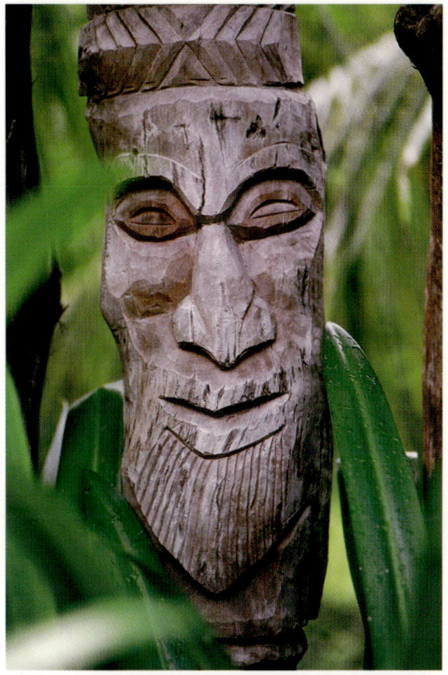

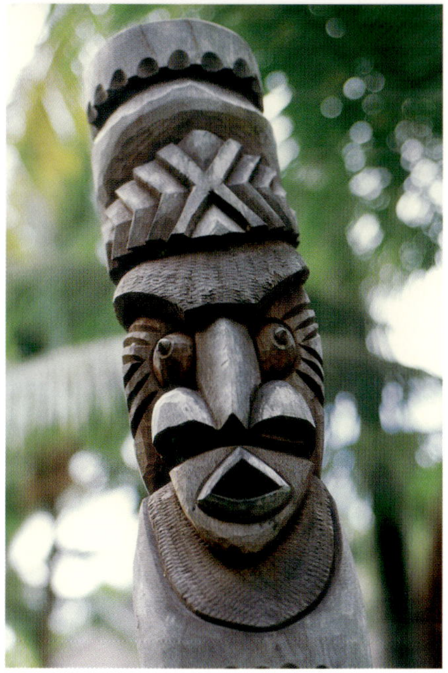

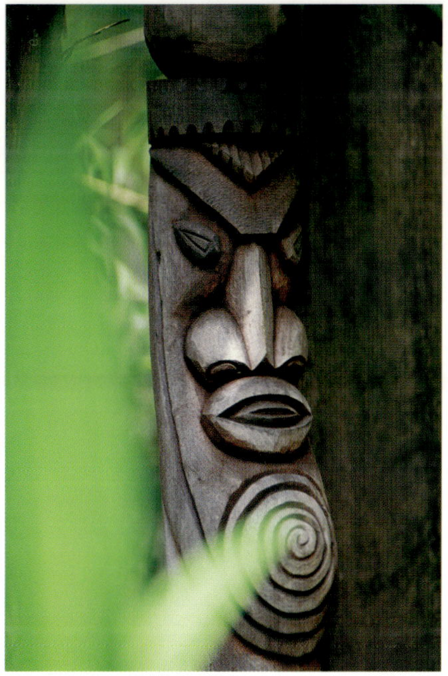

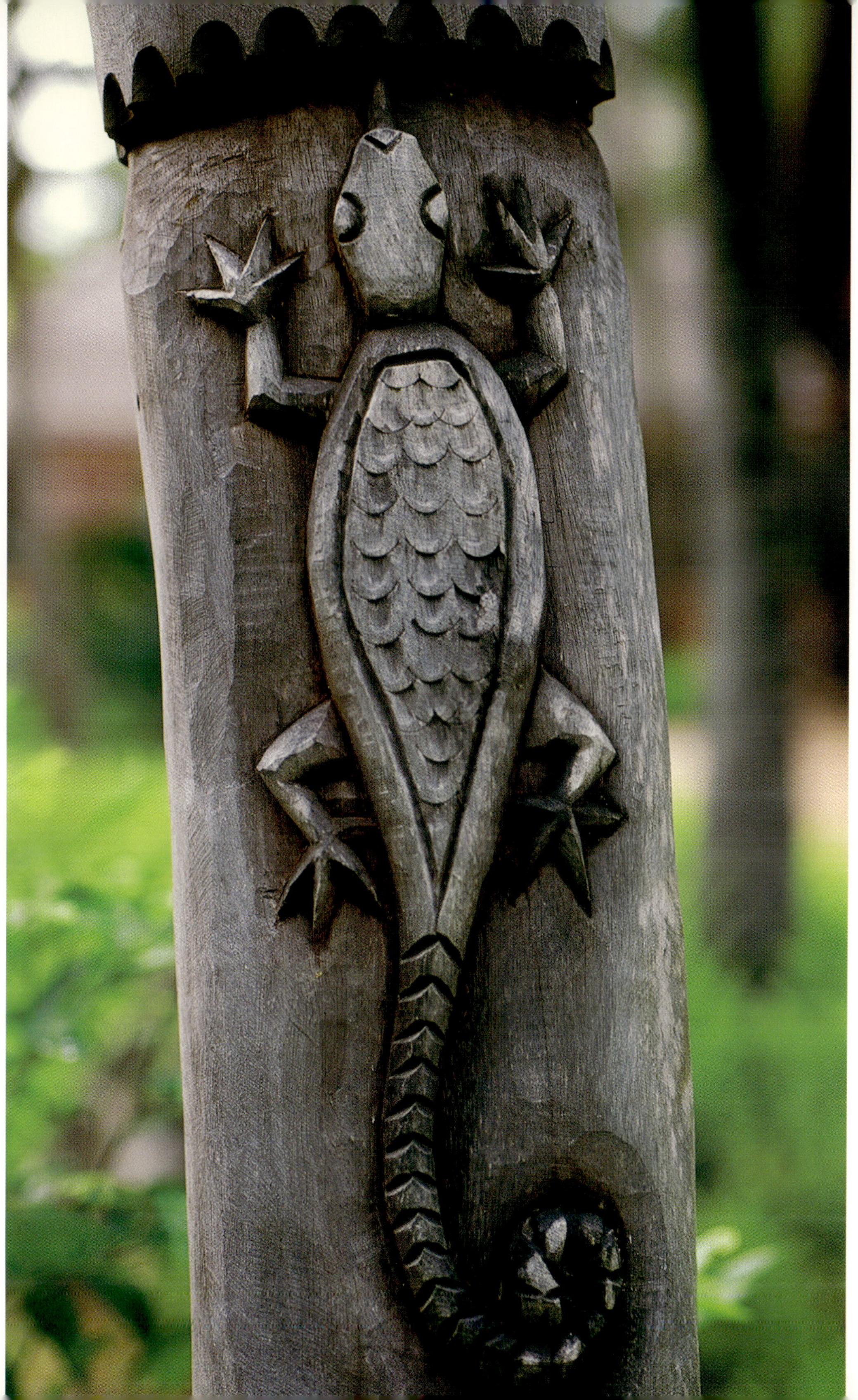

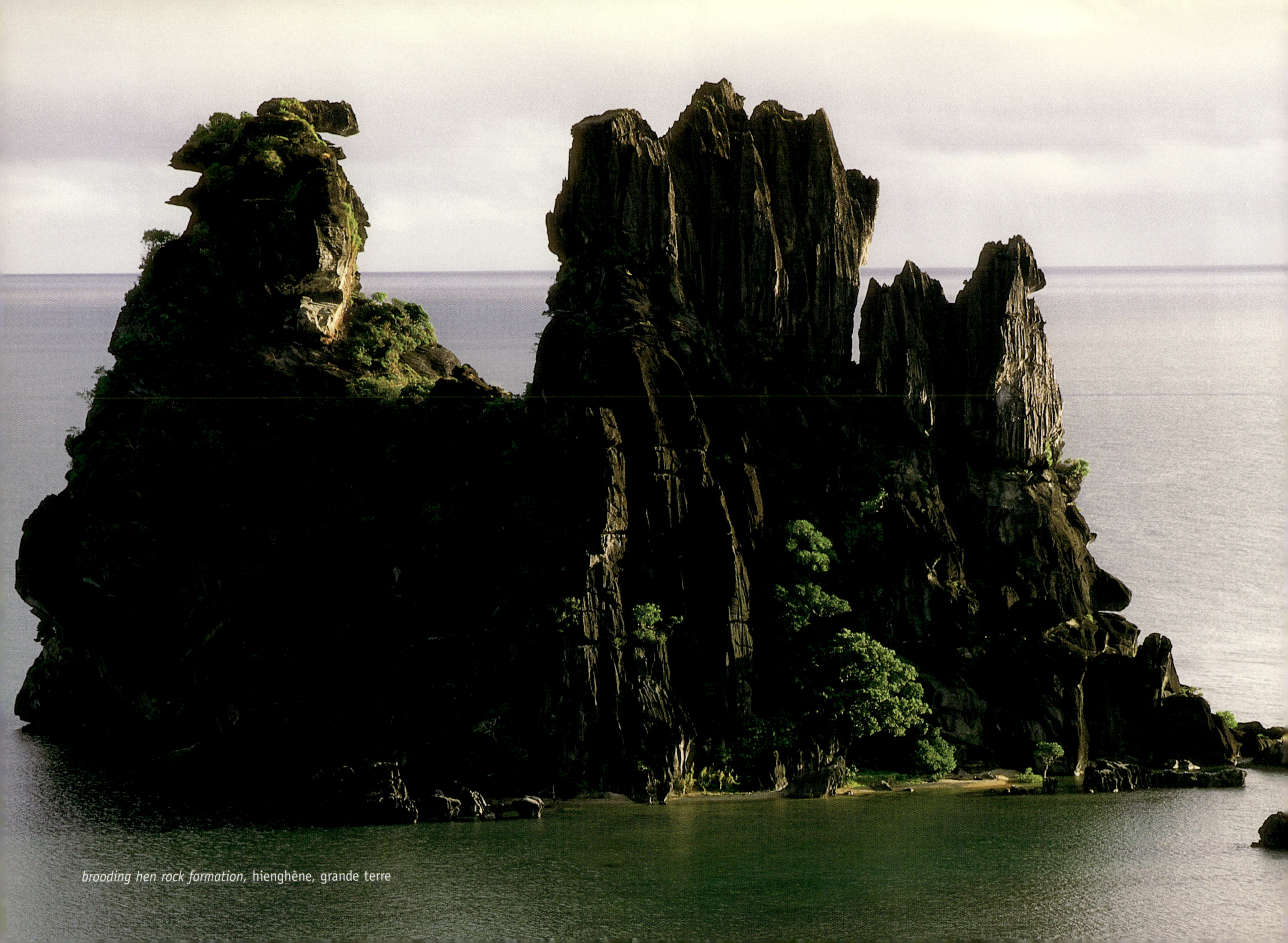

brooding hen rock formation, hienghène, grande terre

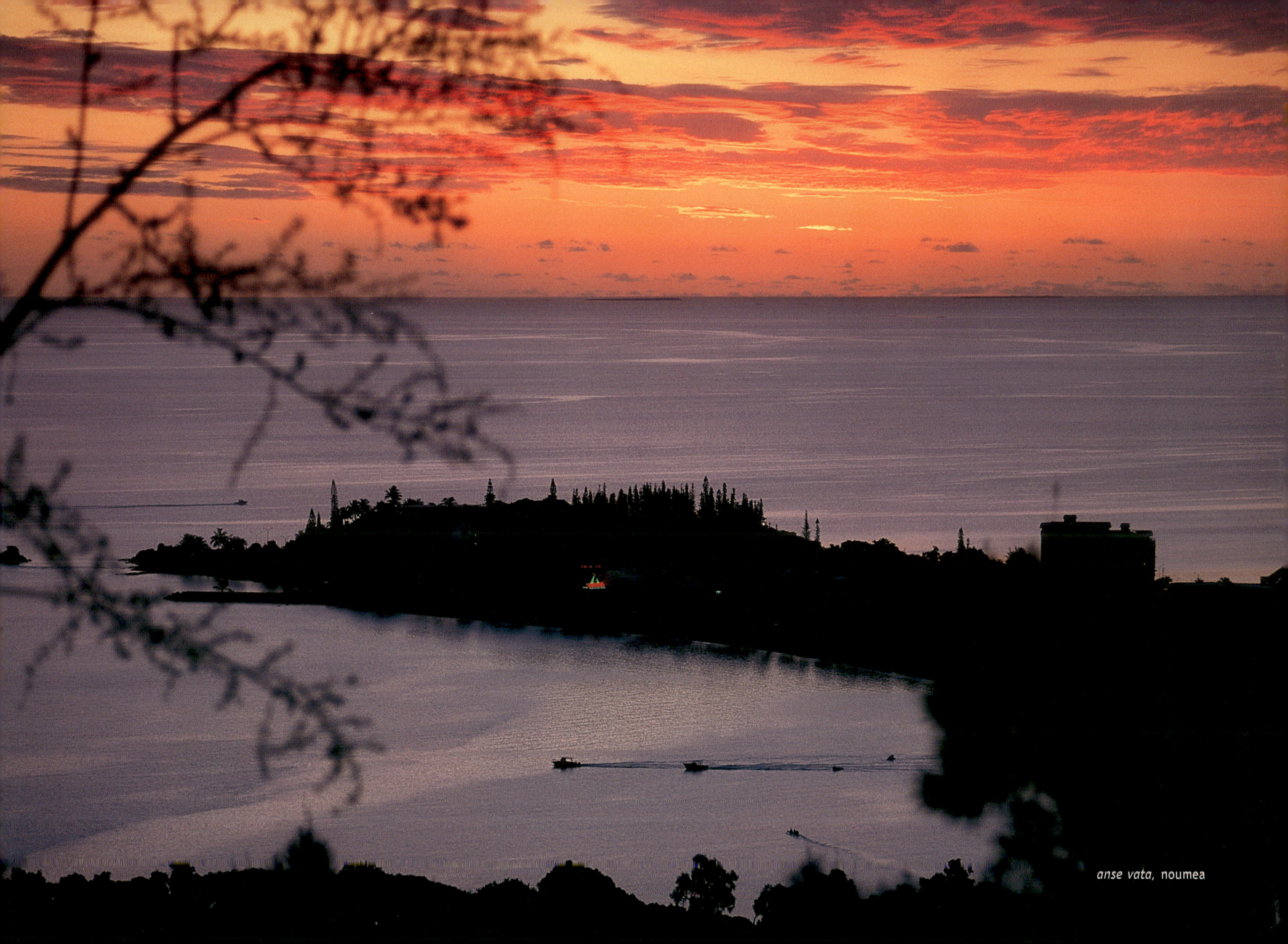

anse vata, noumea

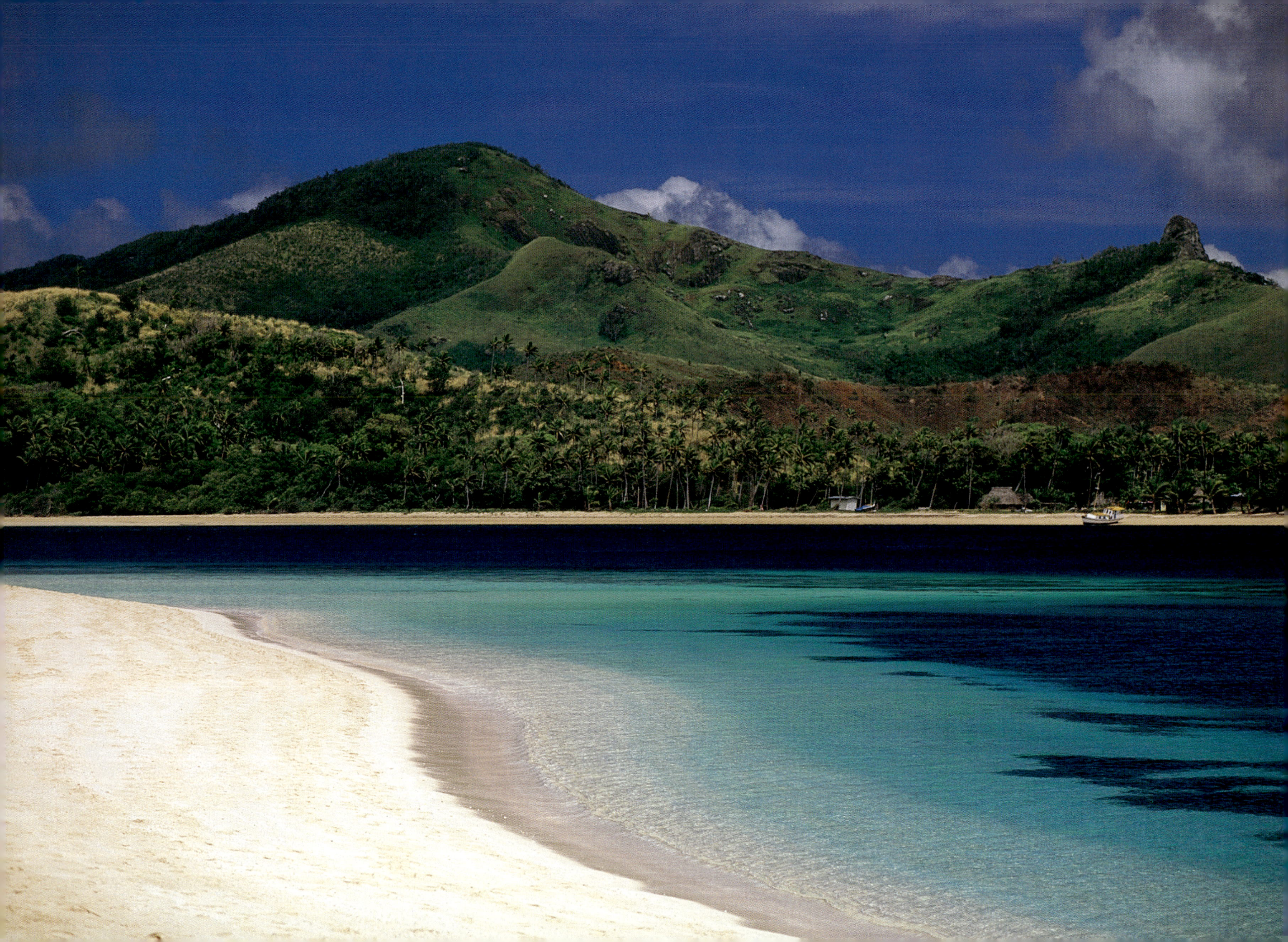

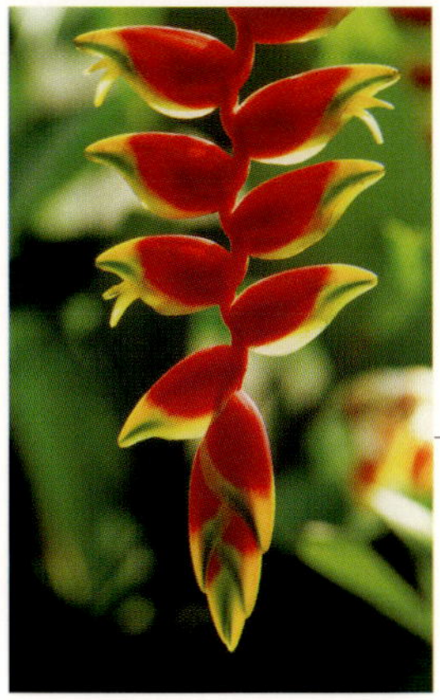

Fiji

AN ARCHIPELAGO of more than 320 islands, Fiji was settled about 3500 years ago in successive waves of migration by a great seafaring people from Western Melanesia. Melanesian social and physical characteristics are more notable in the hinterlands of the two major islands, while the islands in the eastern part exhibit more Polynesian characteristics through contact with Tonga and Samoa.

The two main volcanic islands of Viti Levu and Vanua Levu contain most of the people, land area and economic activity although a wide range of tourist resorts are scattered throughout the other islands. The Fijians have a natural friendliness, a relaxed and cheerful attitude to life. Their greeting 'Bula', meaning hello, is expressed enthusiastically.

Many traditional crafts and customs are still practised especially Tapa cloth making, weaving, pottery and carving. The drinking of Yagona, a mild narcotic prepared from the roots of a type of pepper plant, is both highly ritualised and common throughout the islands. The island of Bega, about 7km off the south coast of Viti Levu, is the home of Fiji's renowned firewalkers who walk barefoot on white-hot stones without being burned. Firewalking is also practised by Indo-Fijians as part of Hindu festivals.

The Dutch navigator Abel Tasman was the first European to sail the Fijian waters in 1643. Followed 130 years later by James Cook and then in 1789 by William Bligh who had been cast adrift in a small row boat by the 'Bounty' mutineers. By this time Fiji had become known as the Cannibal Islands. This had deterred all but the most desperate, so escaped convicts from the British penal colonies in Australia and shipwrecked sailors were amongst the first Europeans to settle in Fiji.

European mercenaries and firearms were in great demand by politically ambitious chiefs. Sandalwood and Bêche-de Mer, the principal trading items in the islands in the 19th century, were highly valued by the Europeans. European trading and competition destabilised a society already under stress.

In 1874, Fiji became a British colony and in 1879 Indian indentured labourers arrived to work on Colonial Sugar Refining Company plantations. Many Indo-Fijians who are mostly Hindu, Muslim or Sikh, have through hard work and business ability become successful as shopkeepers, traders and professionals, although most of the land remains in indigenous ownership.

The country's 800,000 population of indigenous Fijians (51%) and Indo-Fijians (42%) live warily side by side as they contemplate a troubled future ahead.

[LEFT] *blue lagoon from nanuya lailai island, yasawa islands* [ABOVE] *hanging heliconia*

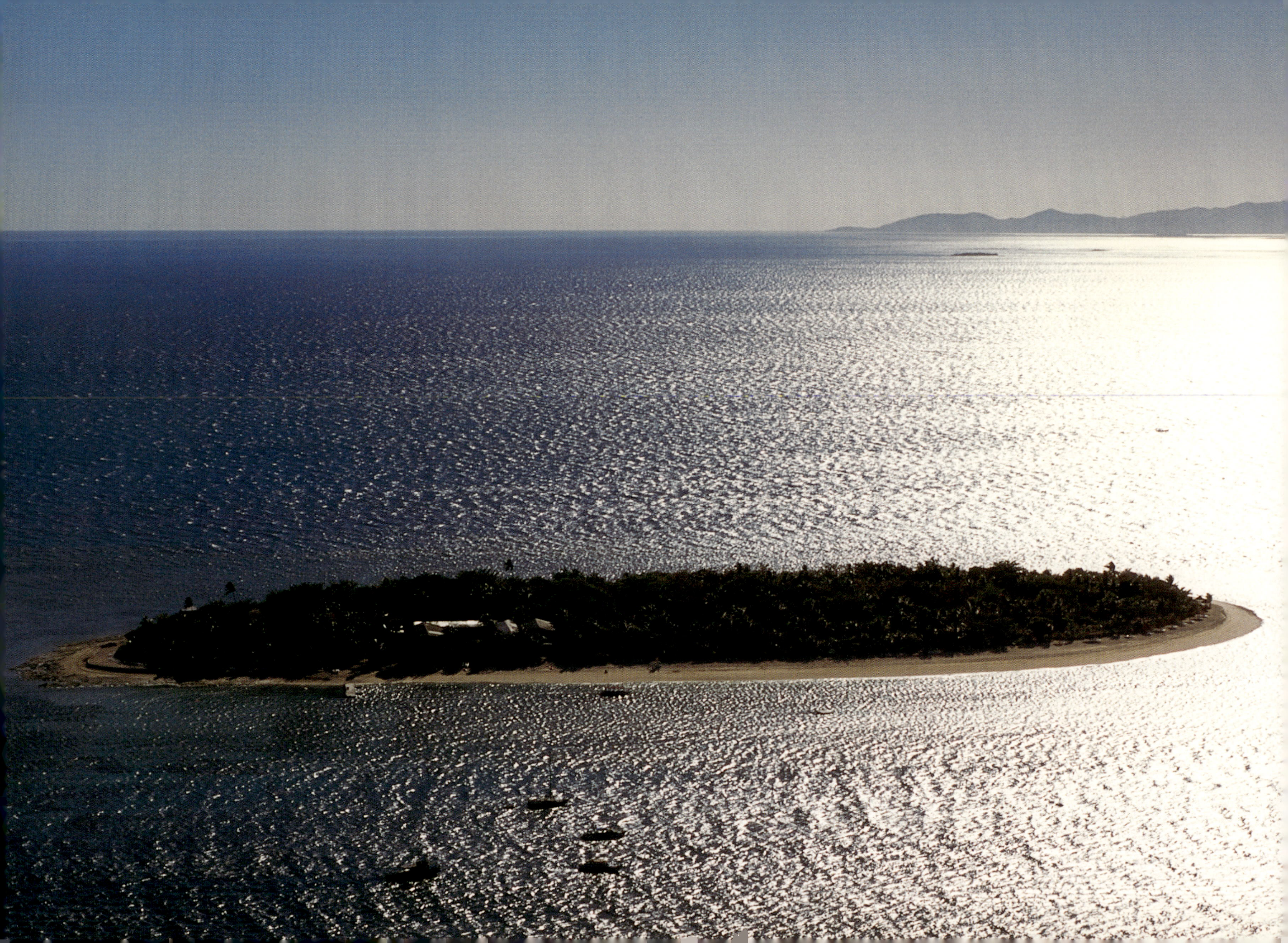

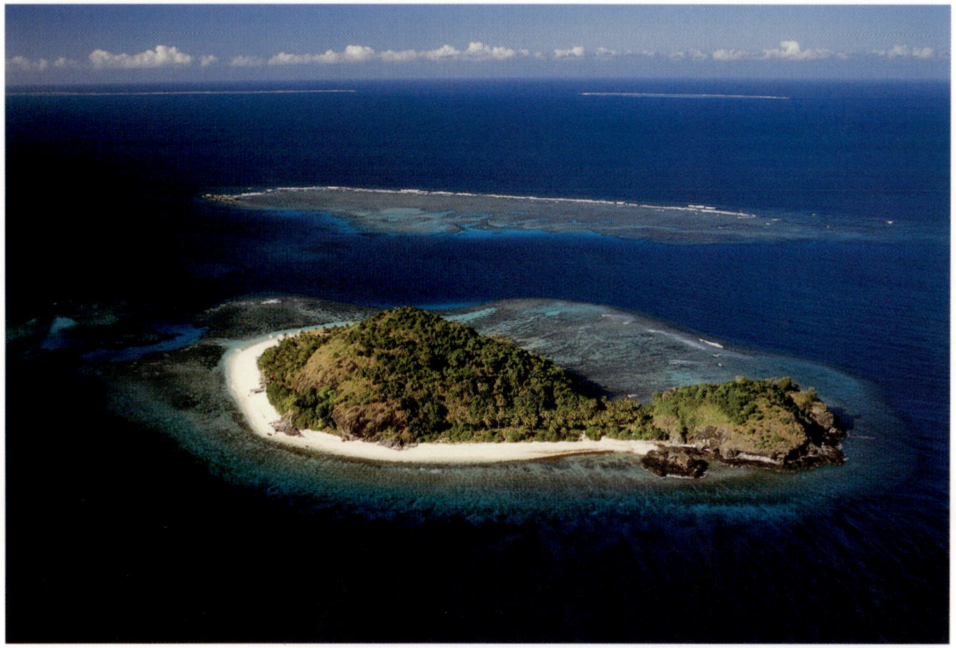

matamanoa island,
mamanuca group

traditional sailing canoe

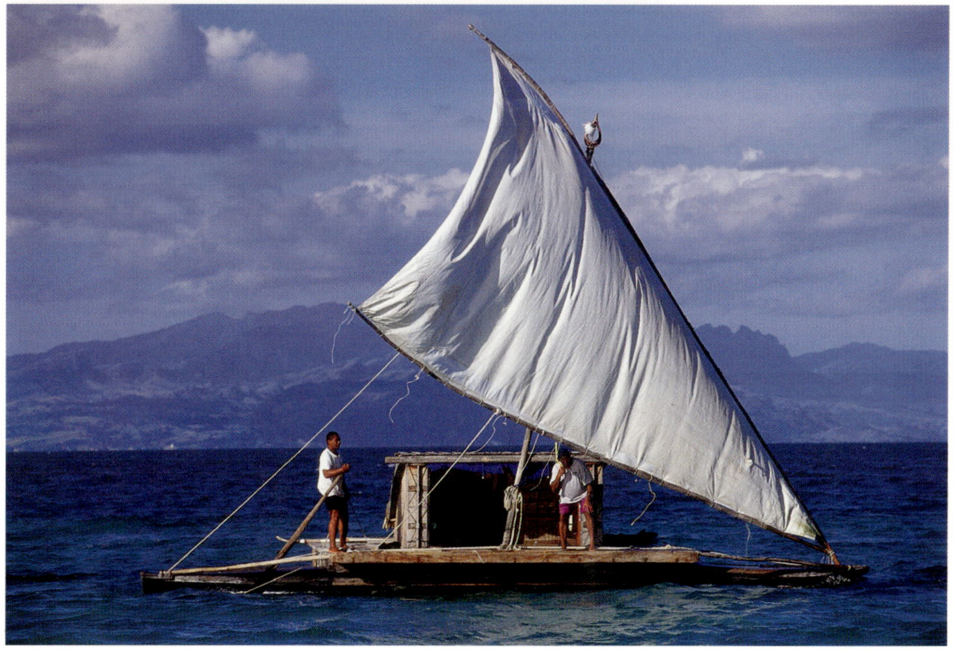

treasure island, mamanuca group

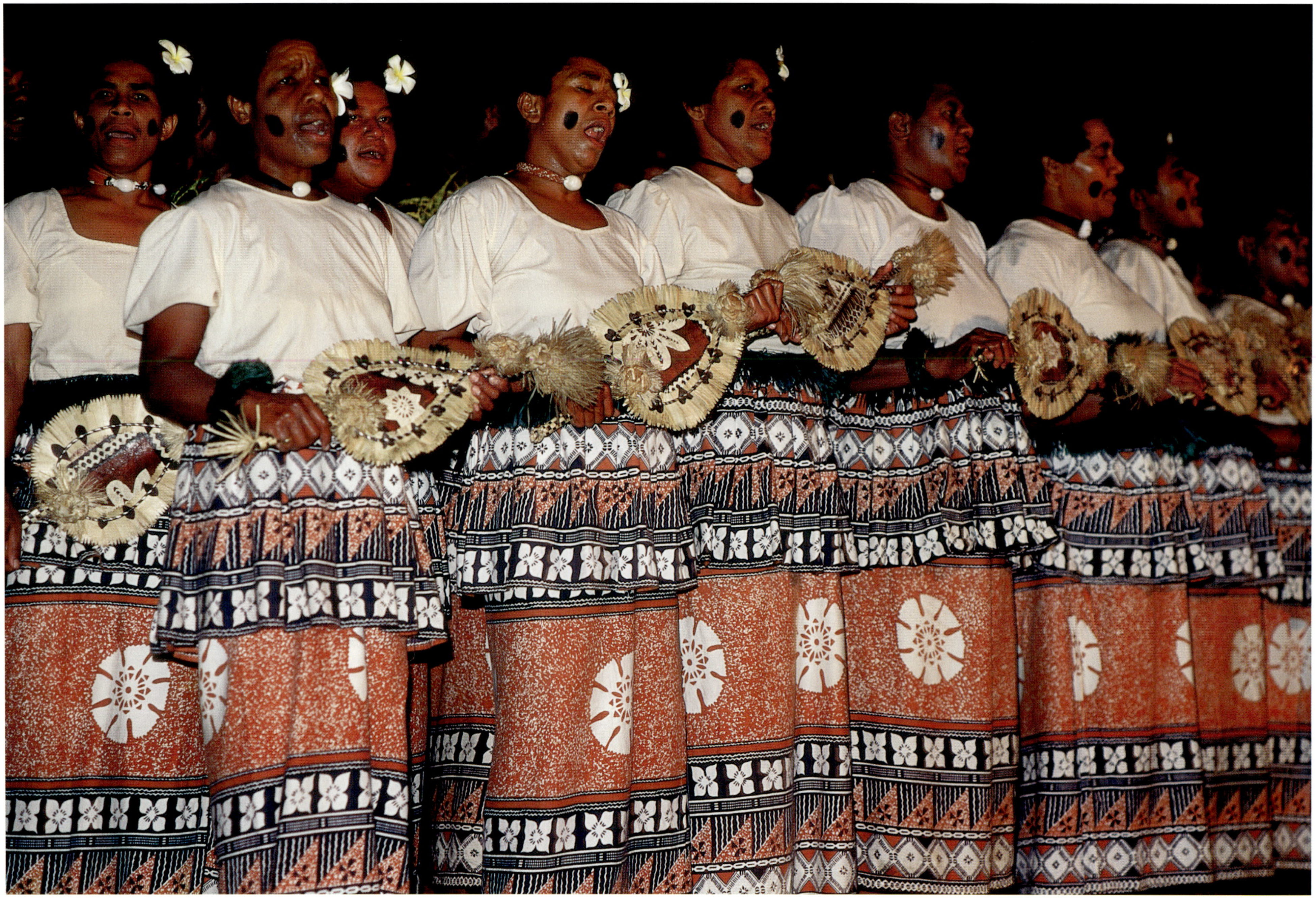

choir, denarau island

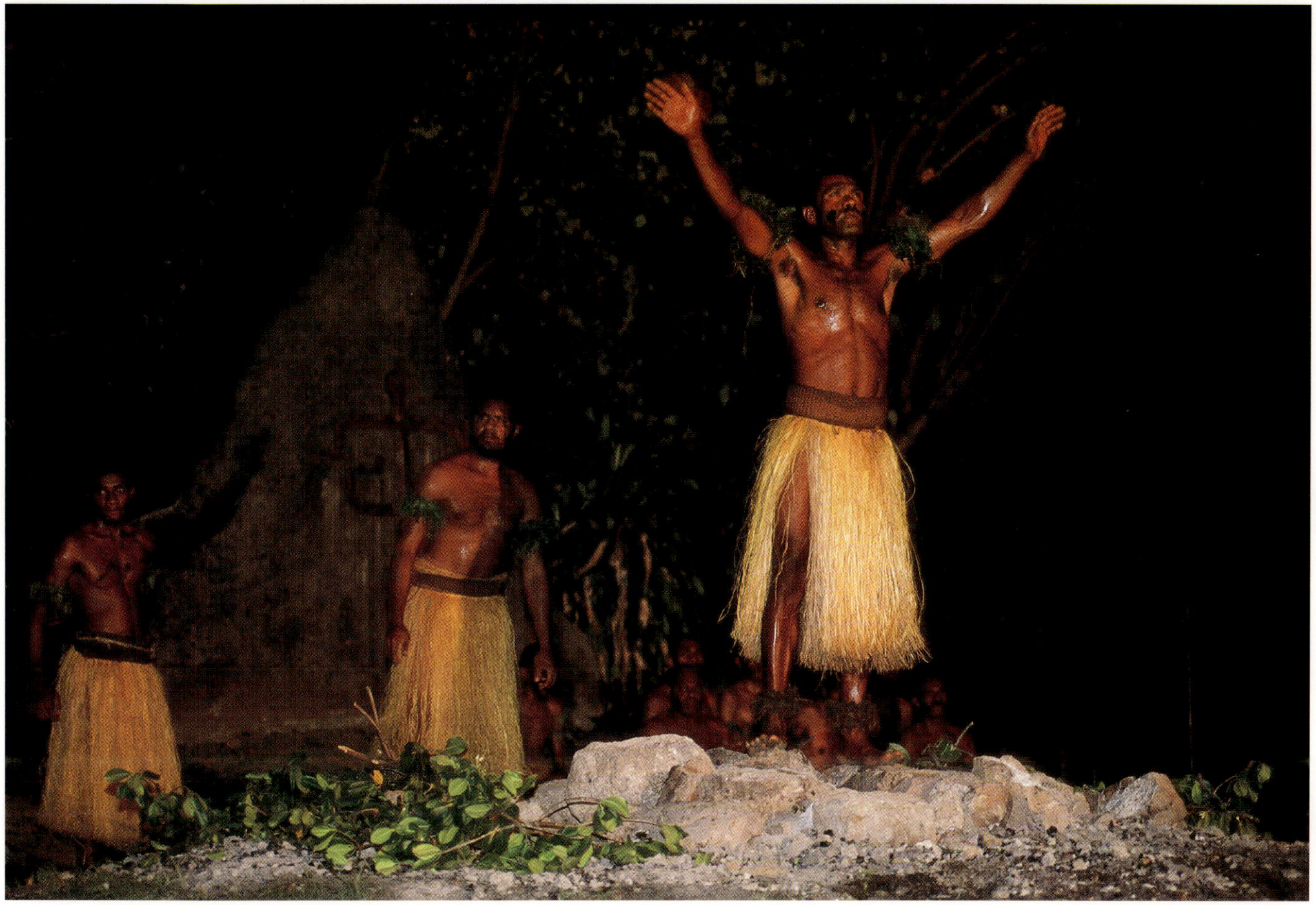

fire walker, denarau island, viti levu

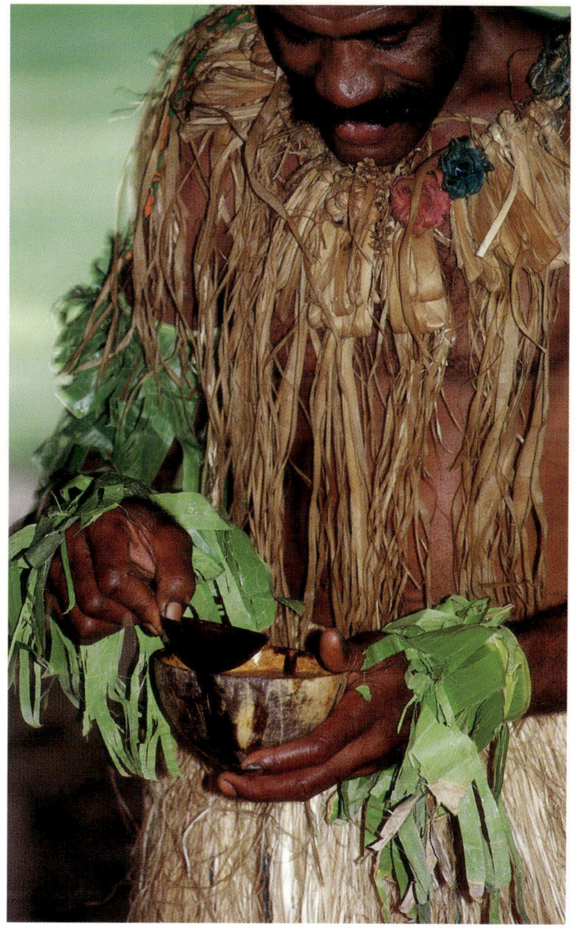

kava ceremony, yasawa island

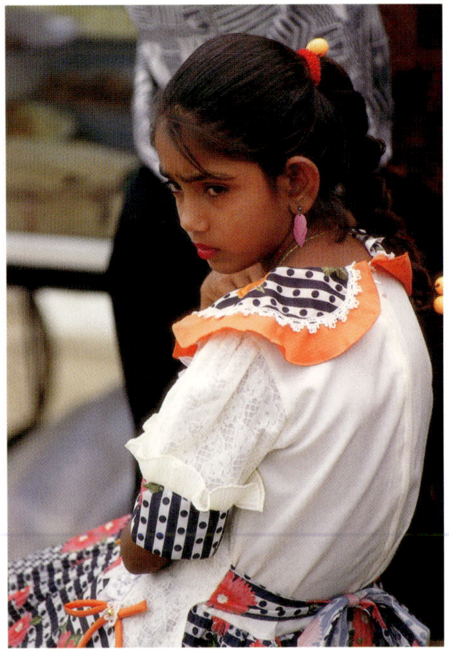

indo-fijian girl, nadi

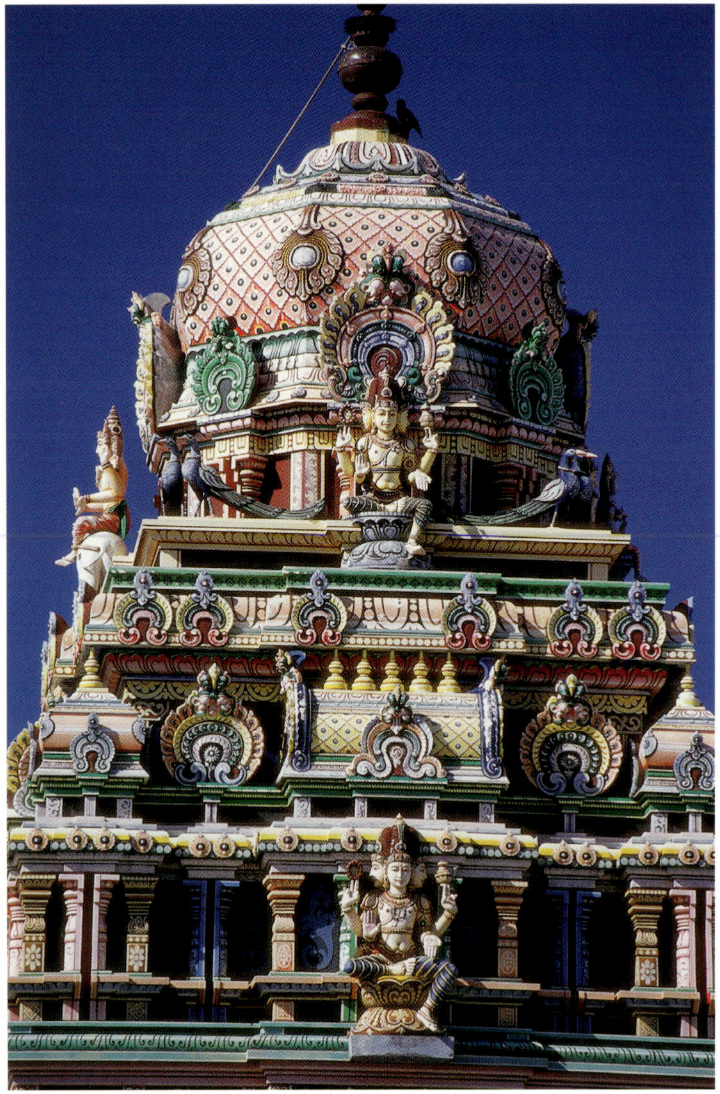

sri siva subramaniya temple, nadi

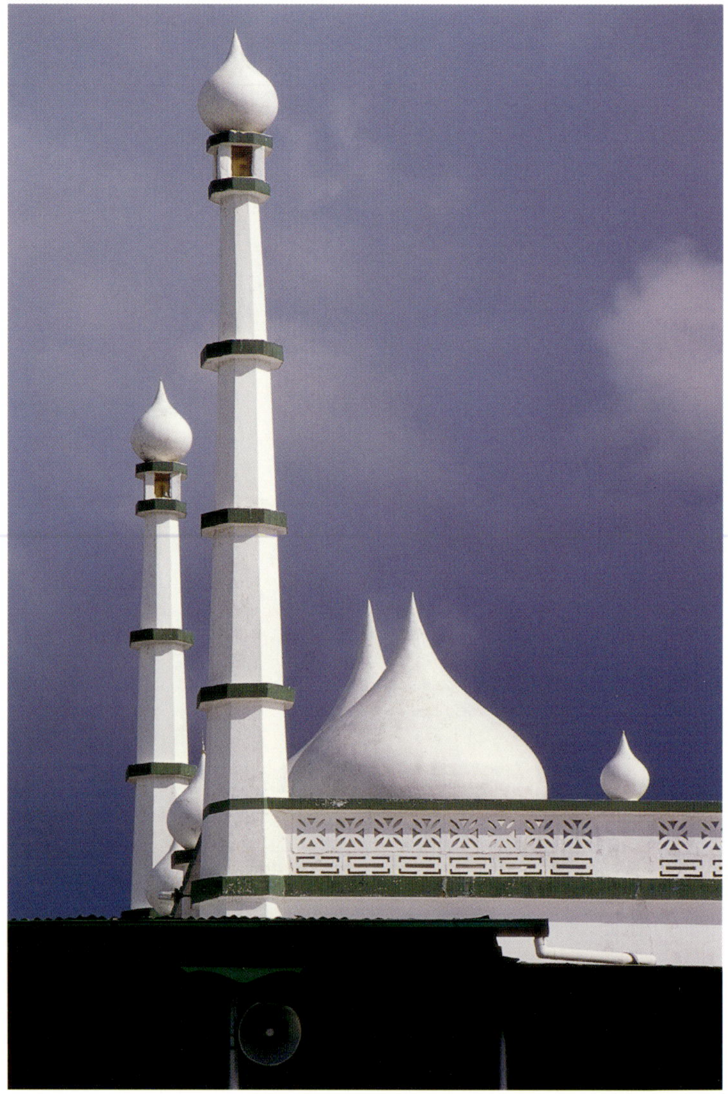

mosque, nadi, viti levu

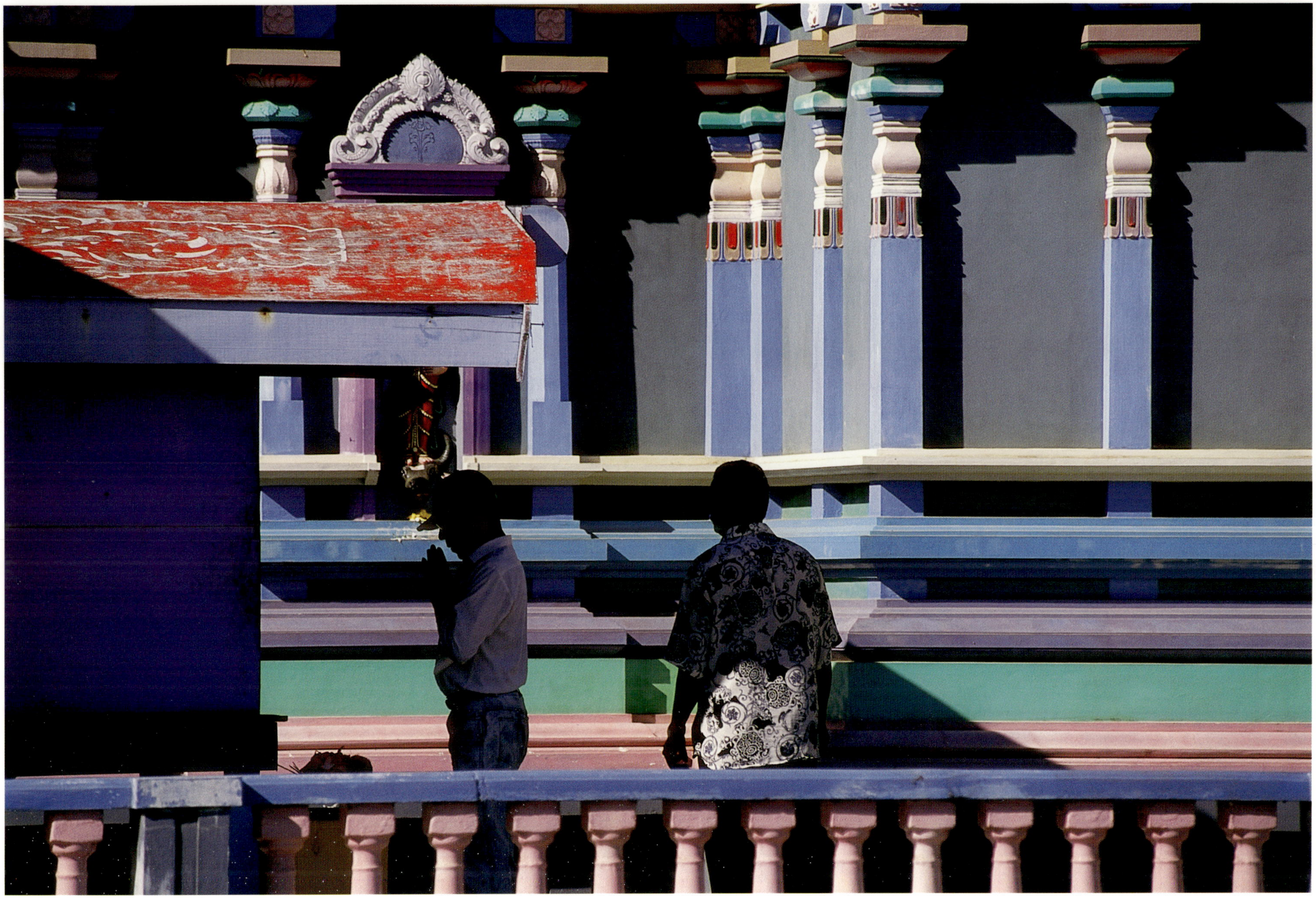

sri siva subramaniya temple, nadi

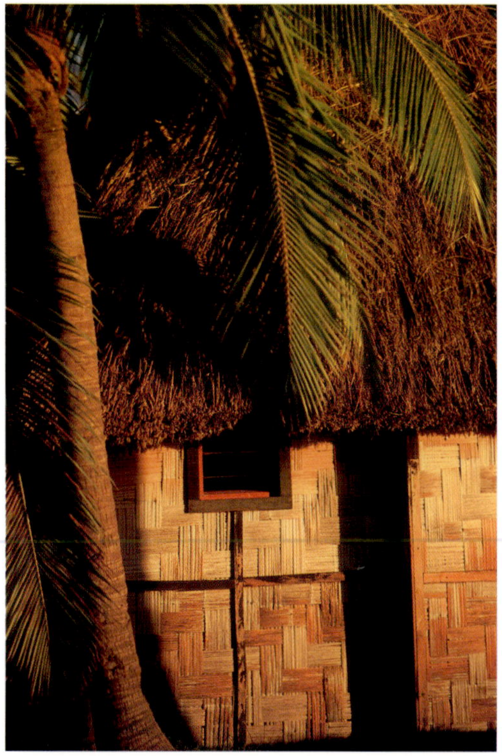

traditional hut, savu savu, vanua levu

sugarcane farm, sariyara, vitu levu

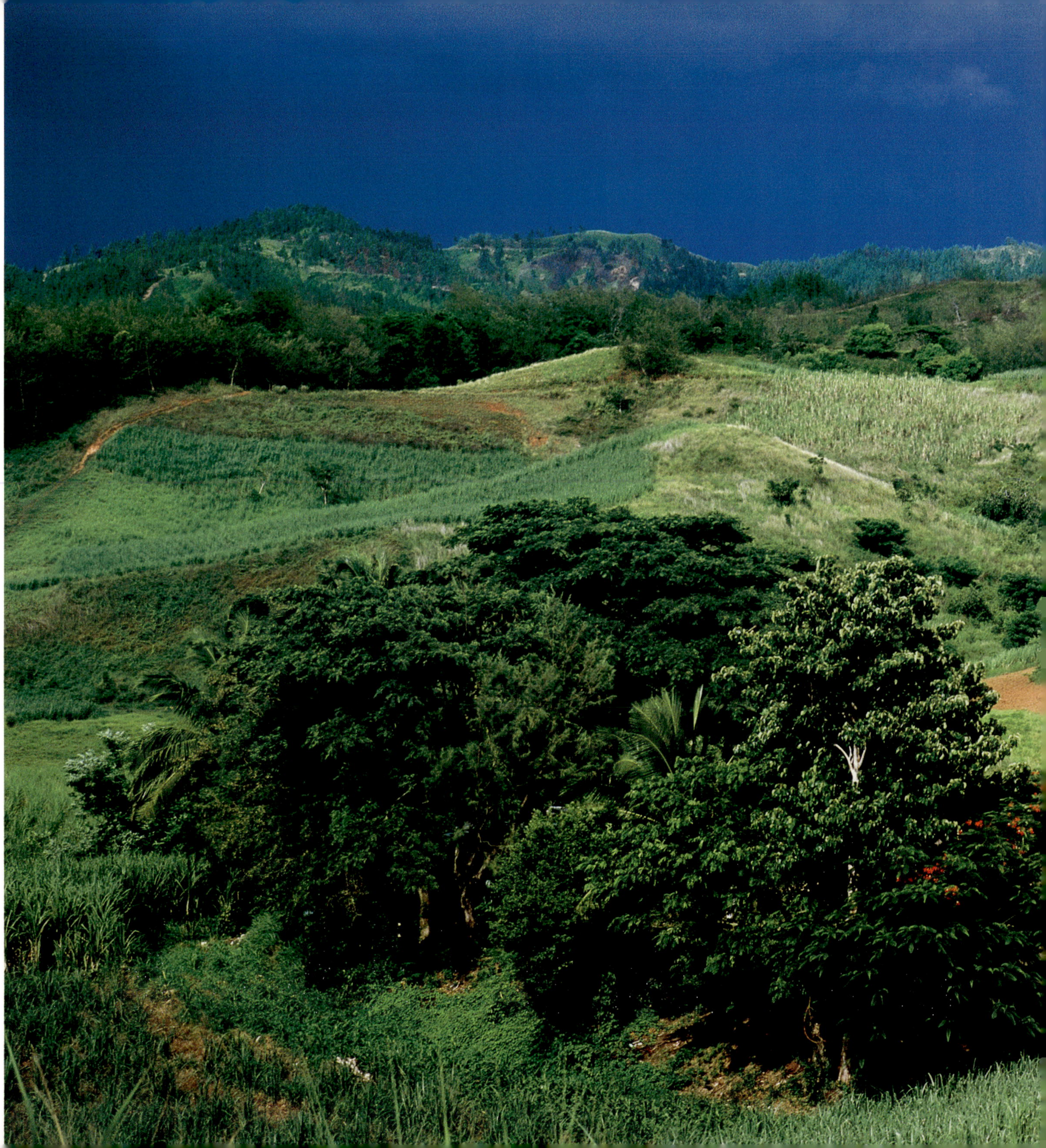

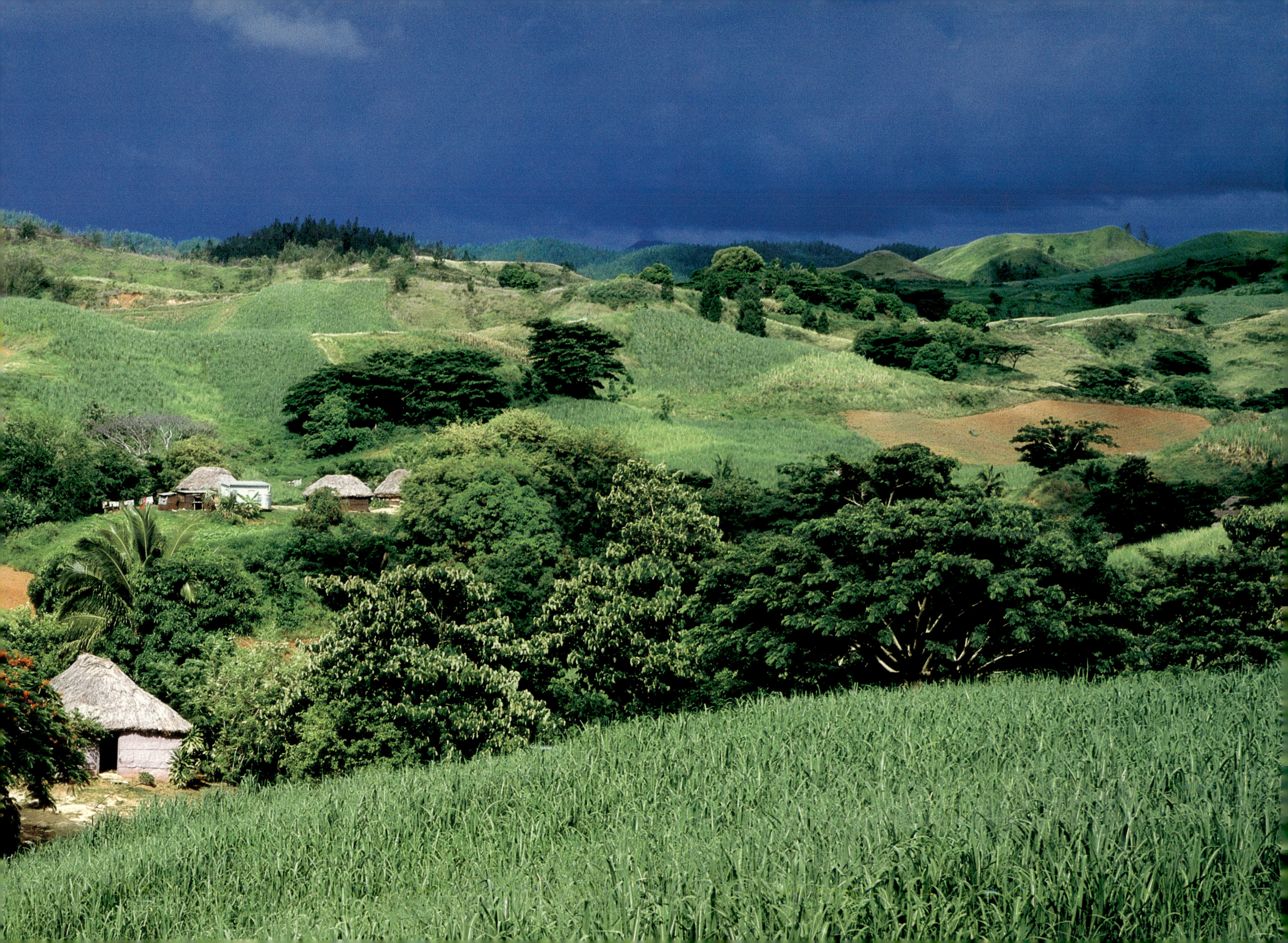

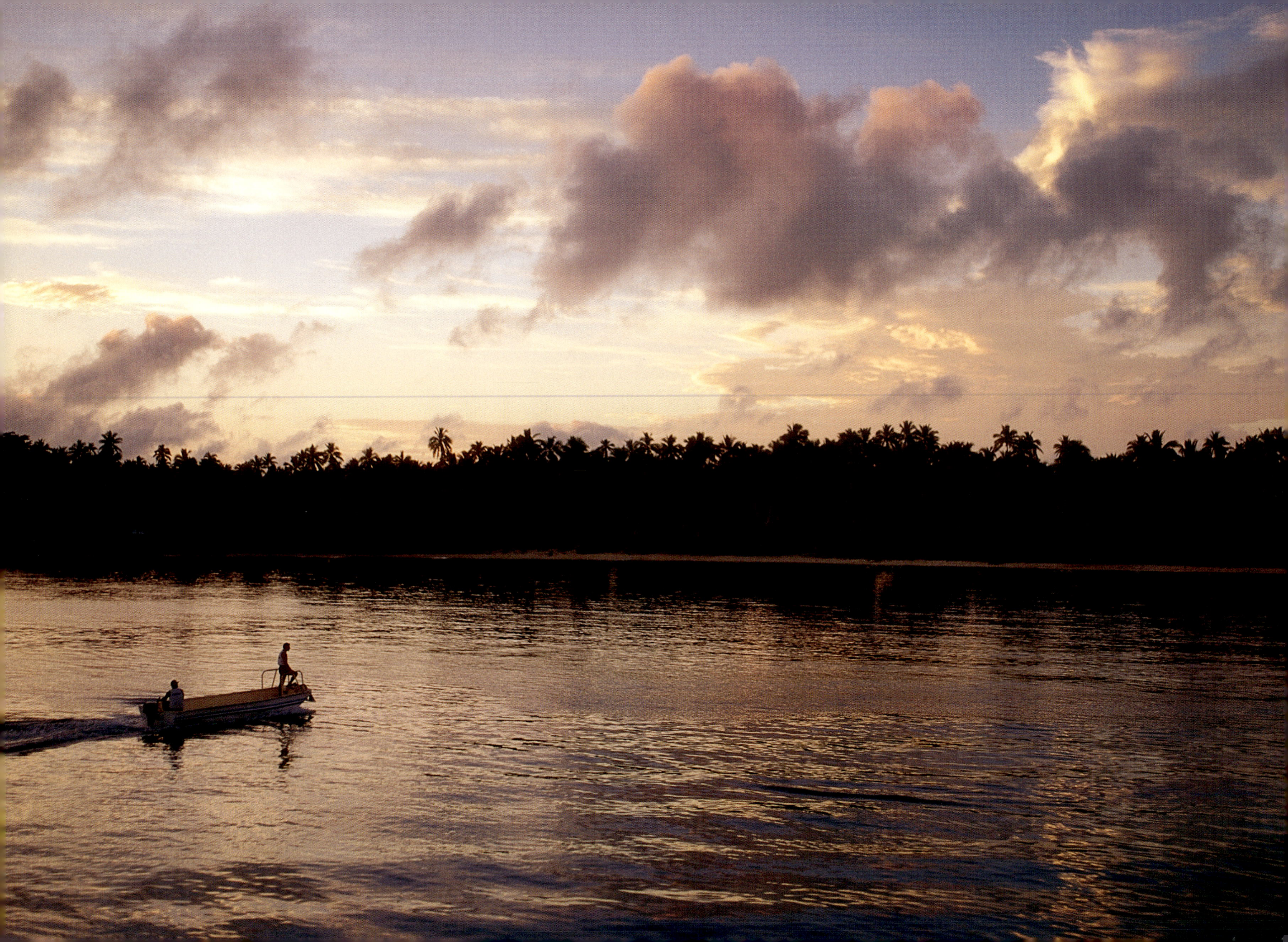

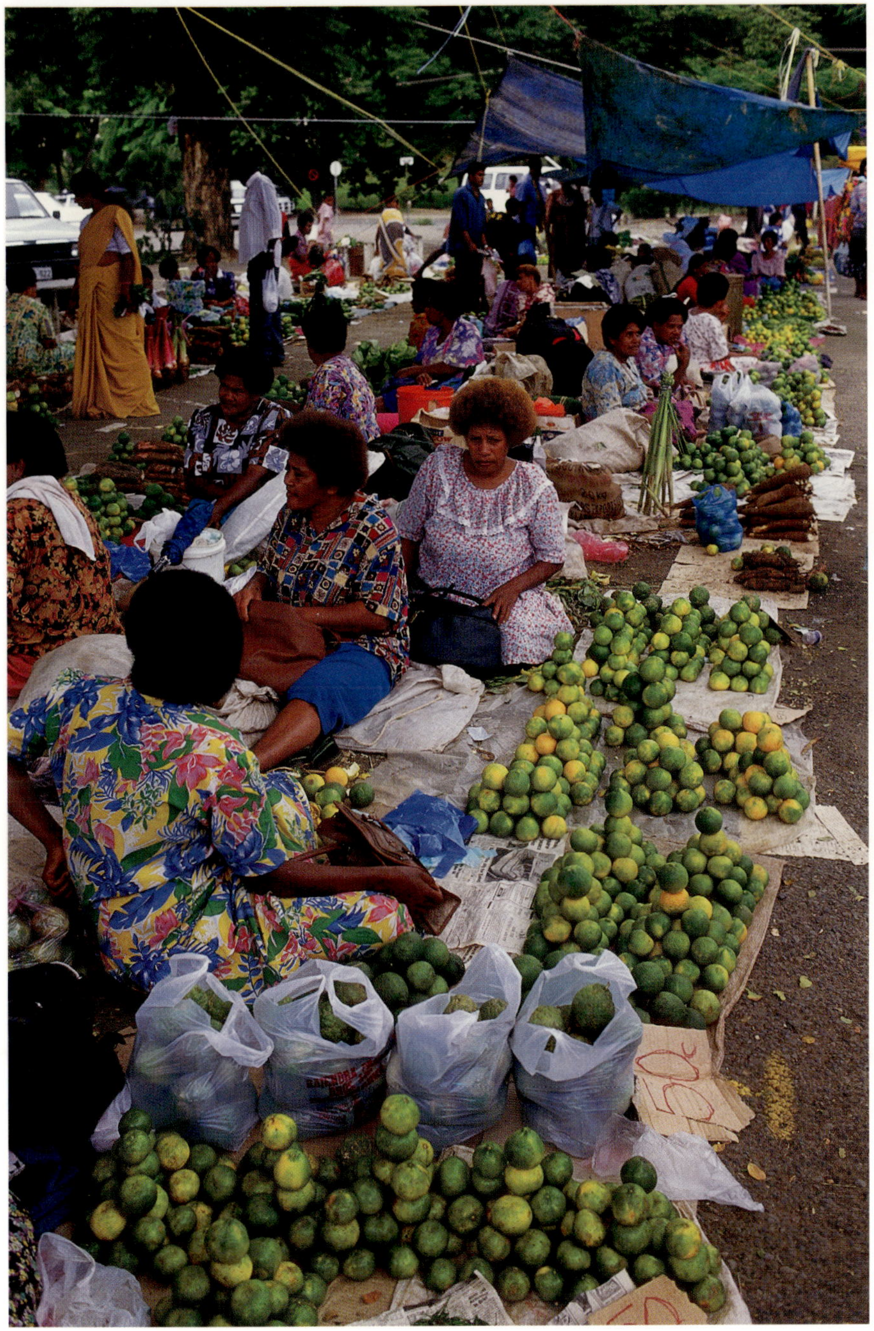

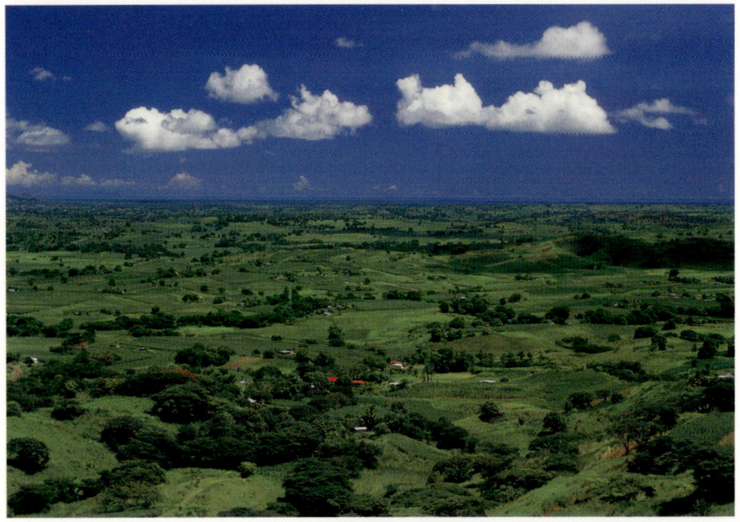

cane farms from namau, north viti levu

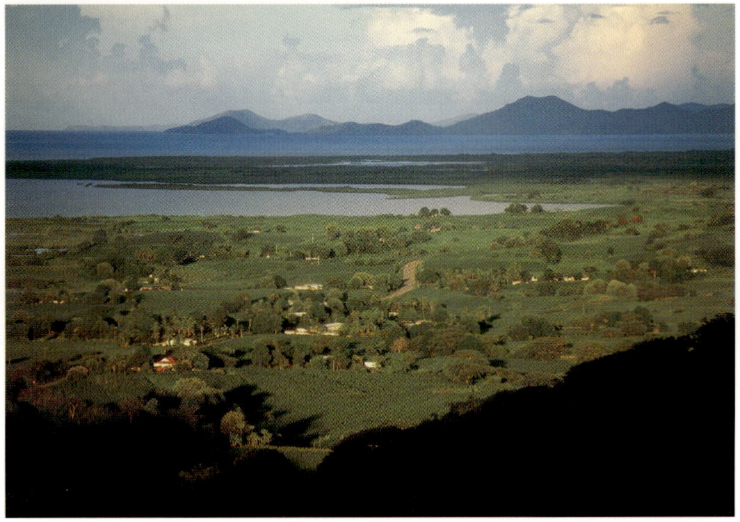

cane farms and coastline from qalela, north viti levu

nadi market

[LEFT] *dawn,* yasawa islands

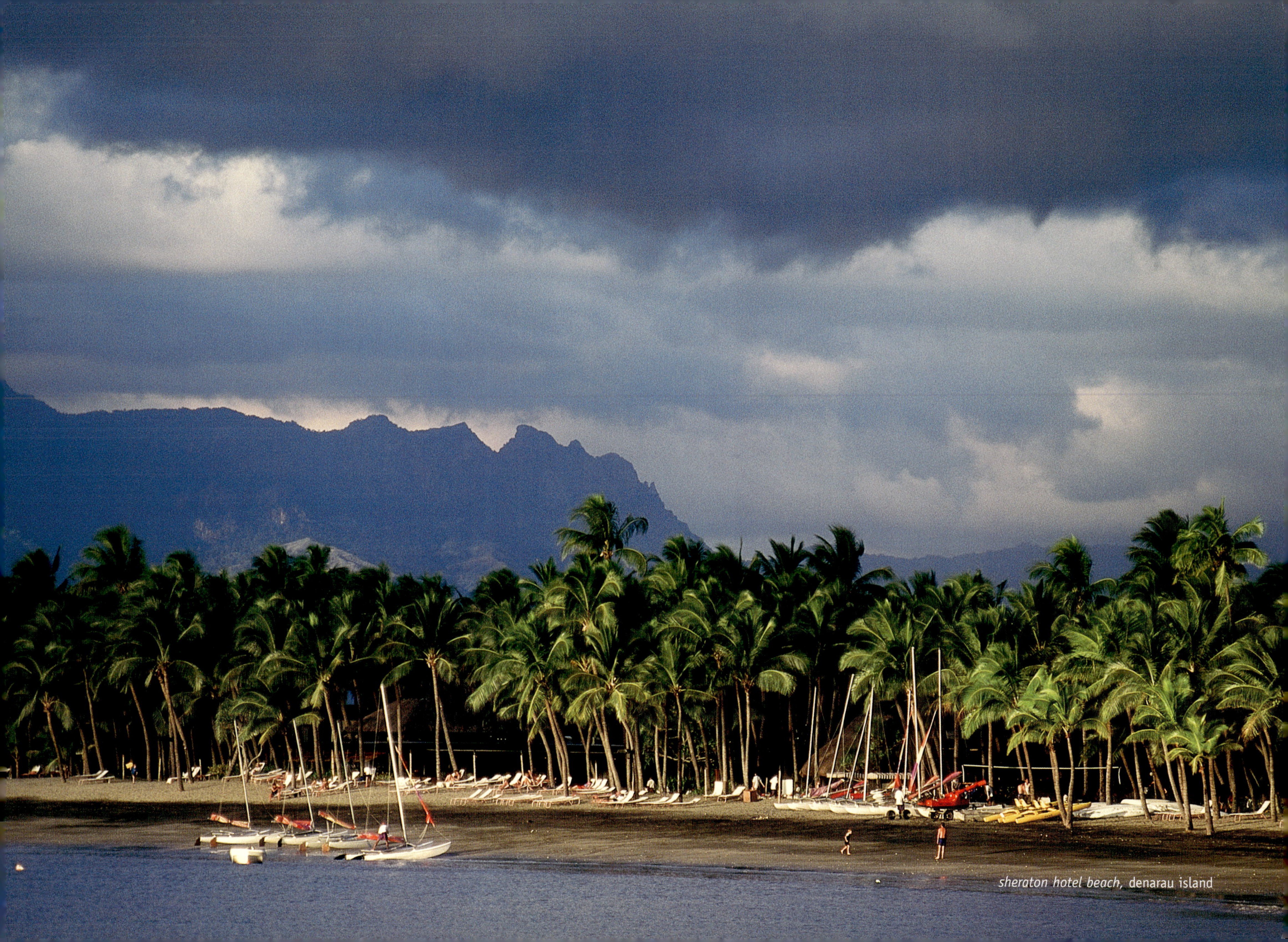

sheraton hotel beach, denarau island

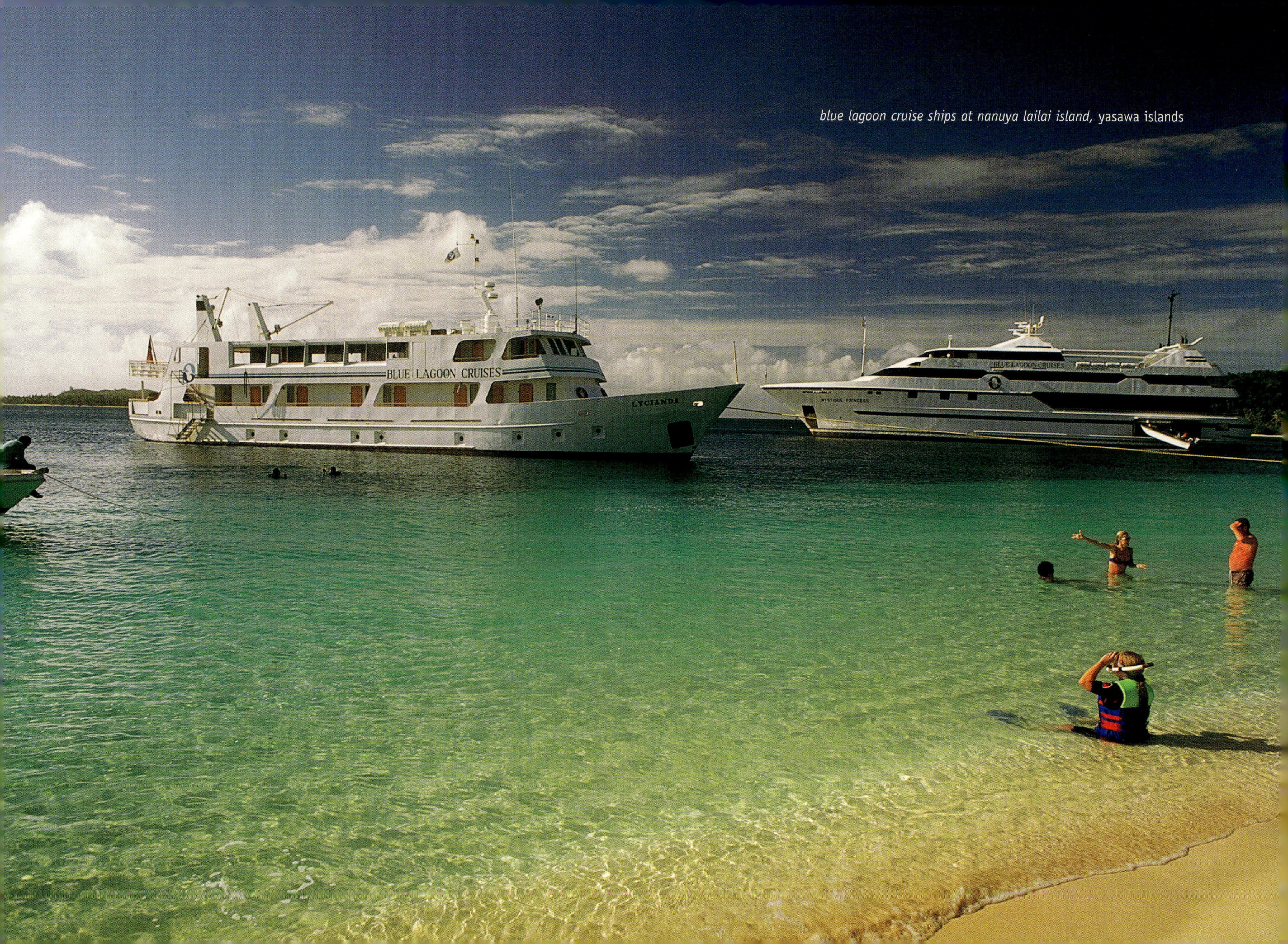

blue lagoon cruise ships at nanuya lailai island, yasawa islands

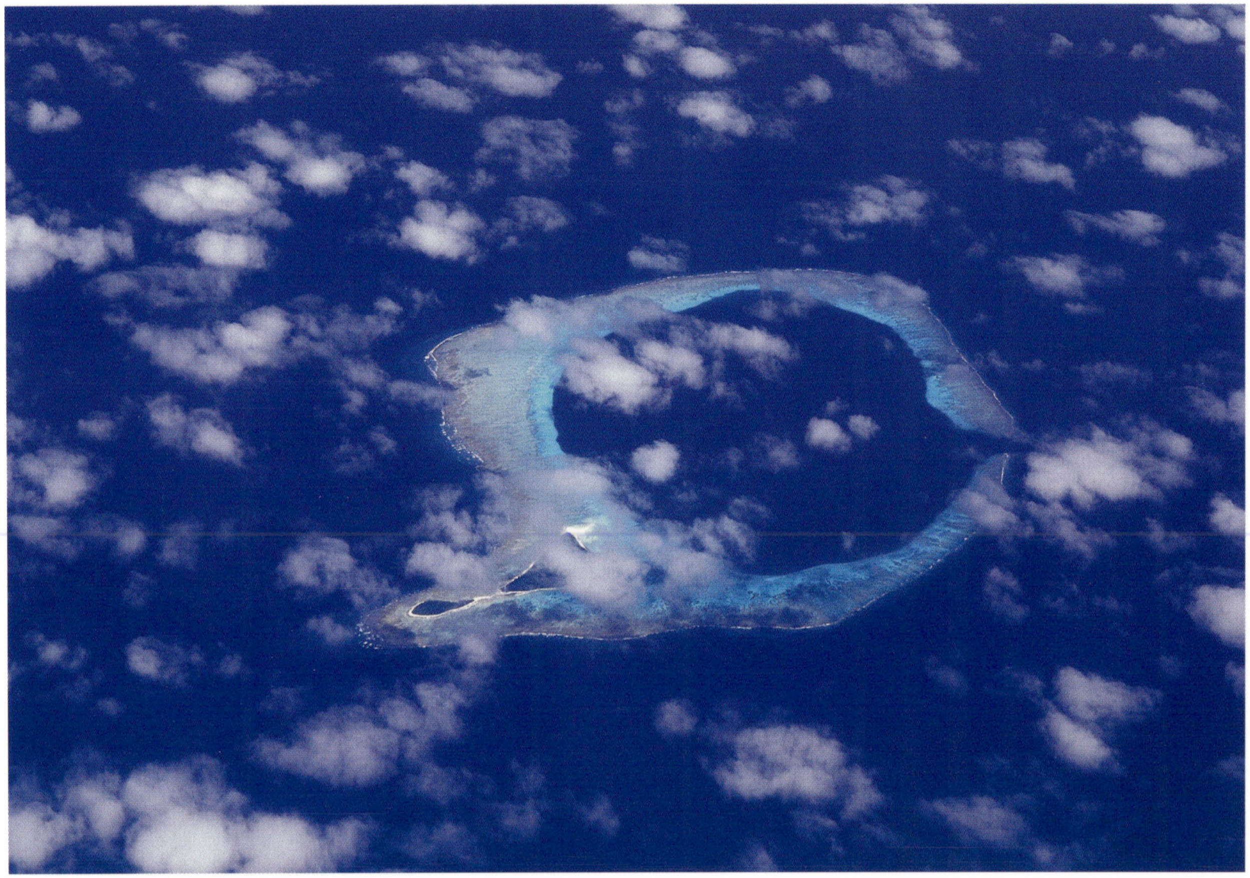

island and lagoon in the lau group

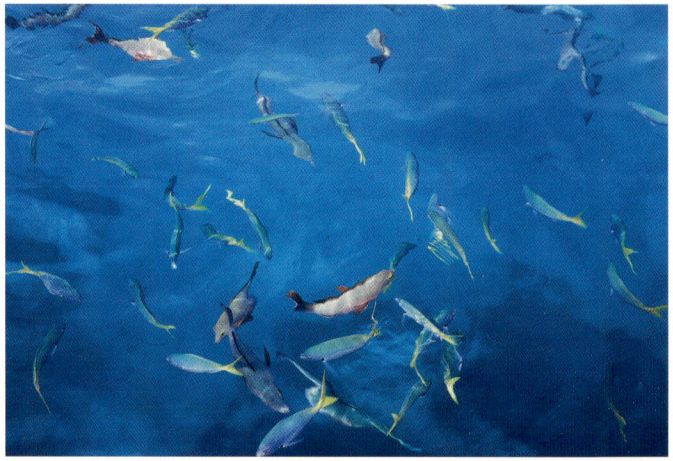

[RIGHT] *reef fish,* yasawa islands **[FAR RIGHT]** *seaplane,* mamanuca island

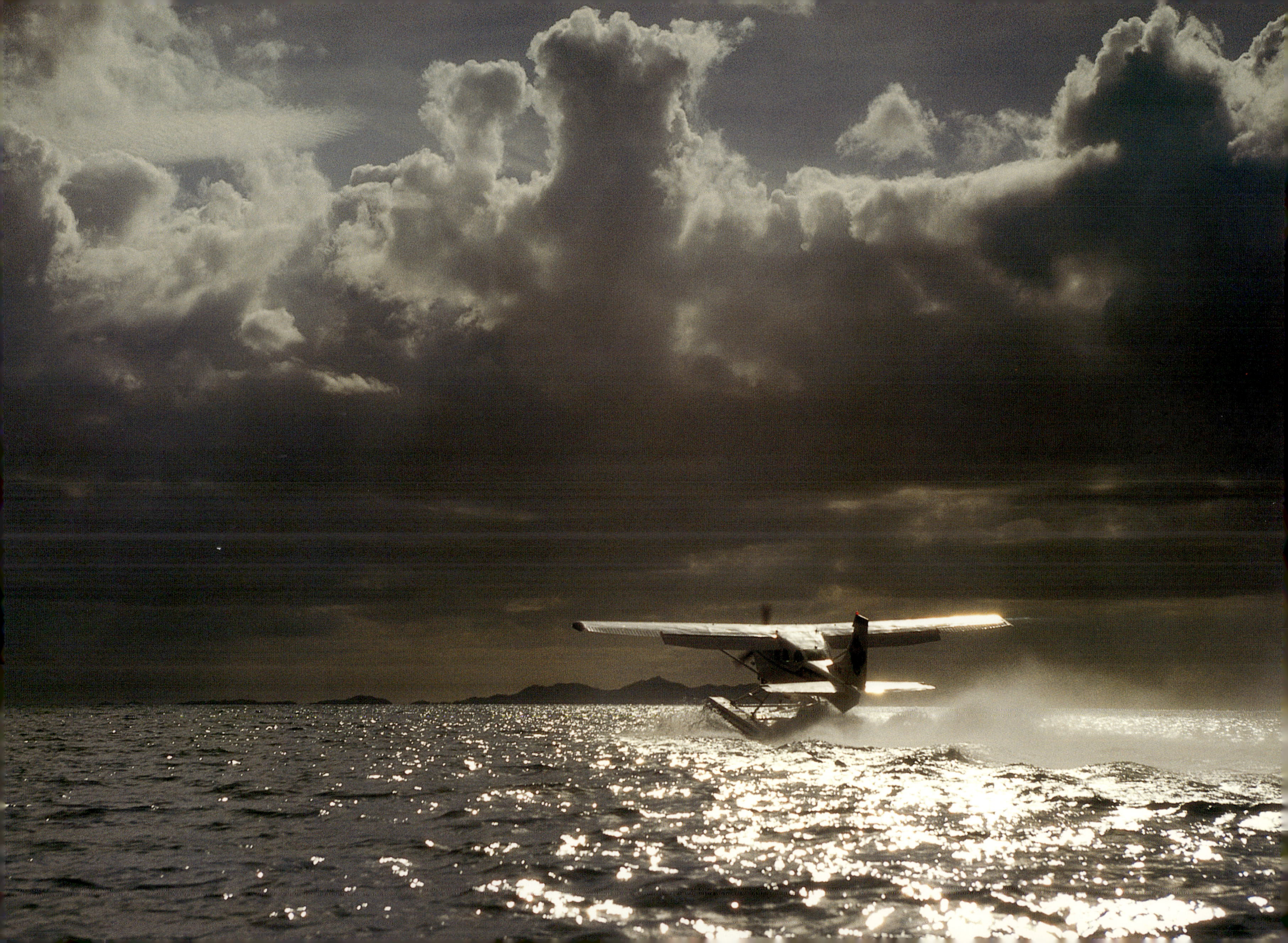

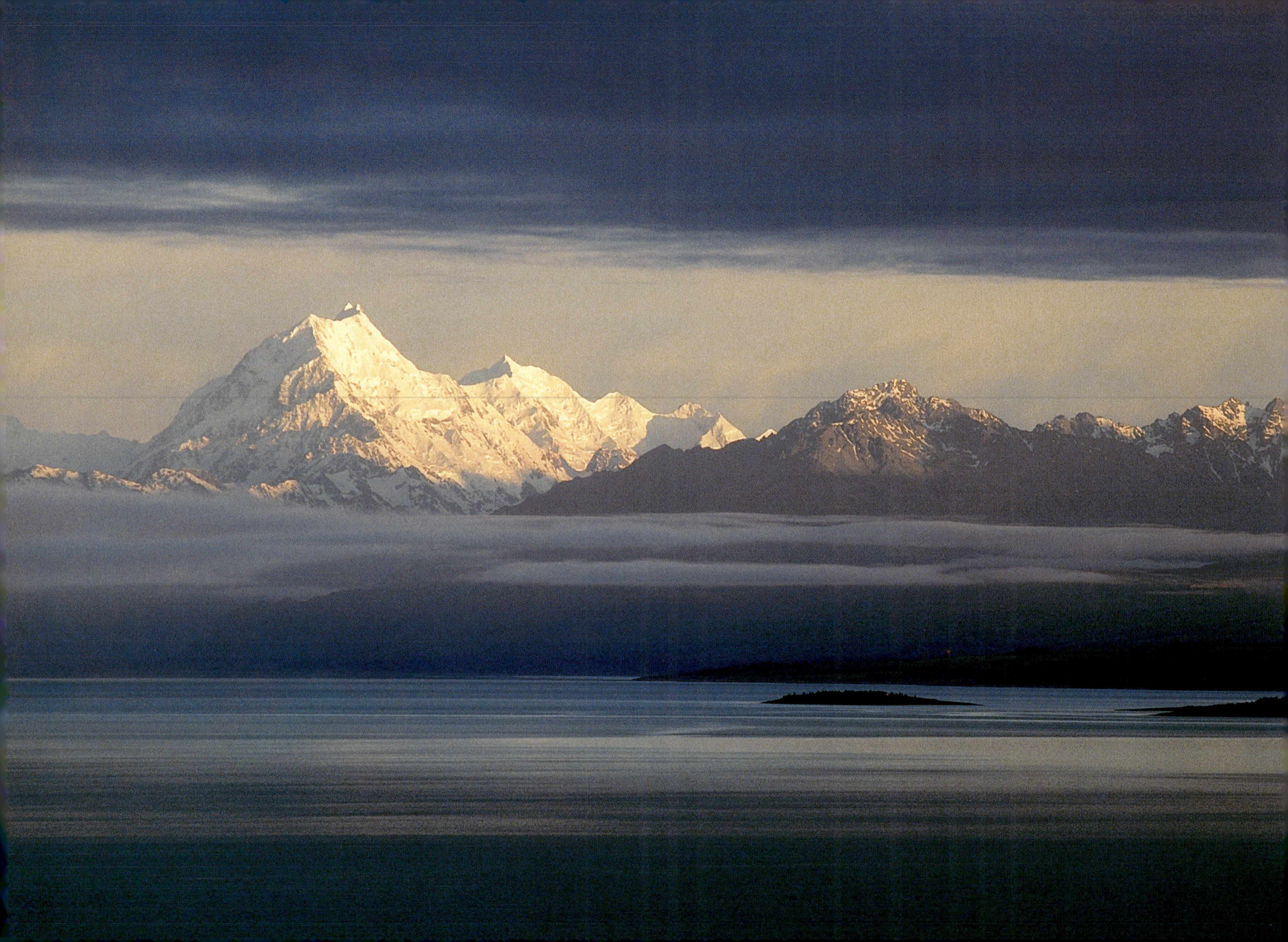

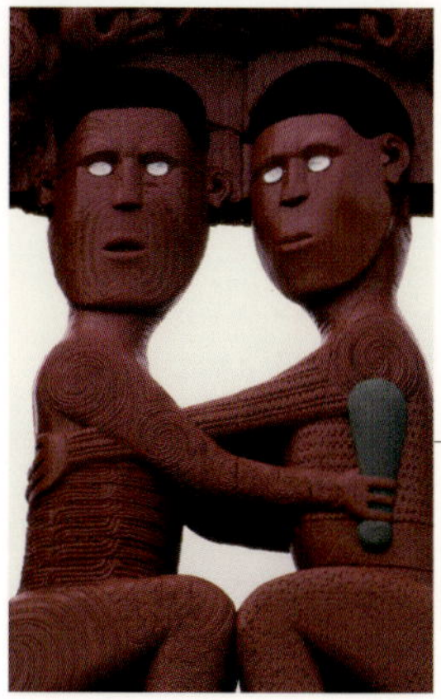

New Zealand

NEW ZEALAND or *Aotearoa – The Land of the Long White Cloud*, is an independent country comprising of 2 main islands with a total land area of 286,000sqkm. It was the largest landmass the Polynesians had ever colonised, larger than all that of Polynesia combined and very different from the tropical islands that they had been used to. With a cooler climate, many of the tropical food crops such as yams, taro and coconuts did not grow well, with the exception of the sweet potato, which became the staple food.

This primeval land broke off from the ancient continent of Gondwanaland long before Australia and Africa did, before mammals had evolved and plants had developed colourful flowers. The land drifted, isolated with its unique flora and fauna. The Polynesians encountered a land with active volcanoes, geysers and thermal lakes, snow-capped mountain ranges and long inland rivers. They also found the Moa, a flightless bird of which there were several species ranging from the size of a chicken to 3.5 meters. These birds had lost the ability to fly as there were no predators and became extinct centuries before European contact. Recent evidence seems to suggest that there were enormous numbers of these birds inhabiting the temperate forests of the North Island and the eastern parts of the South Island.

The Polynesians developed a culture rich in mythology, with a wide range of gods. Courage was valued above all else. It was a fiercely tribal warrior culture where the defeated became slaves or were eaten in ritualistic cannibal feasts.

The Maori produced beautifully carved war canoes and meeting houses and exquisite woven cloaks made of bird feathers. Their tattoos or Moko were fine intricate designs covering the face, buttocks and thighs of men and the lips and chins of women. Moko has seen a revival in recent years.

The Dutch explorer Abel Tasman was the first European to visit Aotearoa in 1642, followed by Cook in 1769. In the early nineteenth century, whalers, traders and seal hunters settled in the Bay of Islands and other areas. Russell developed a reputation as a dangerous place of firearms and alcohol. The Maori suffered greatly from the introduced diseases and muskets (that were also used in inter-tribal warfare).

In 1840 the Treaty of Waitangi was signed between the British Monarchy and powerful Maori chiefs. Although still disputed, the Treaty was the founding document for the new country of New Zealand.

[**LEFT**] *mount cook over lake pukaki,* south island [**ABOVE**] *maori carvings,* rotorua, north island

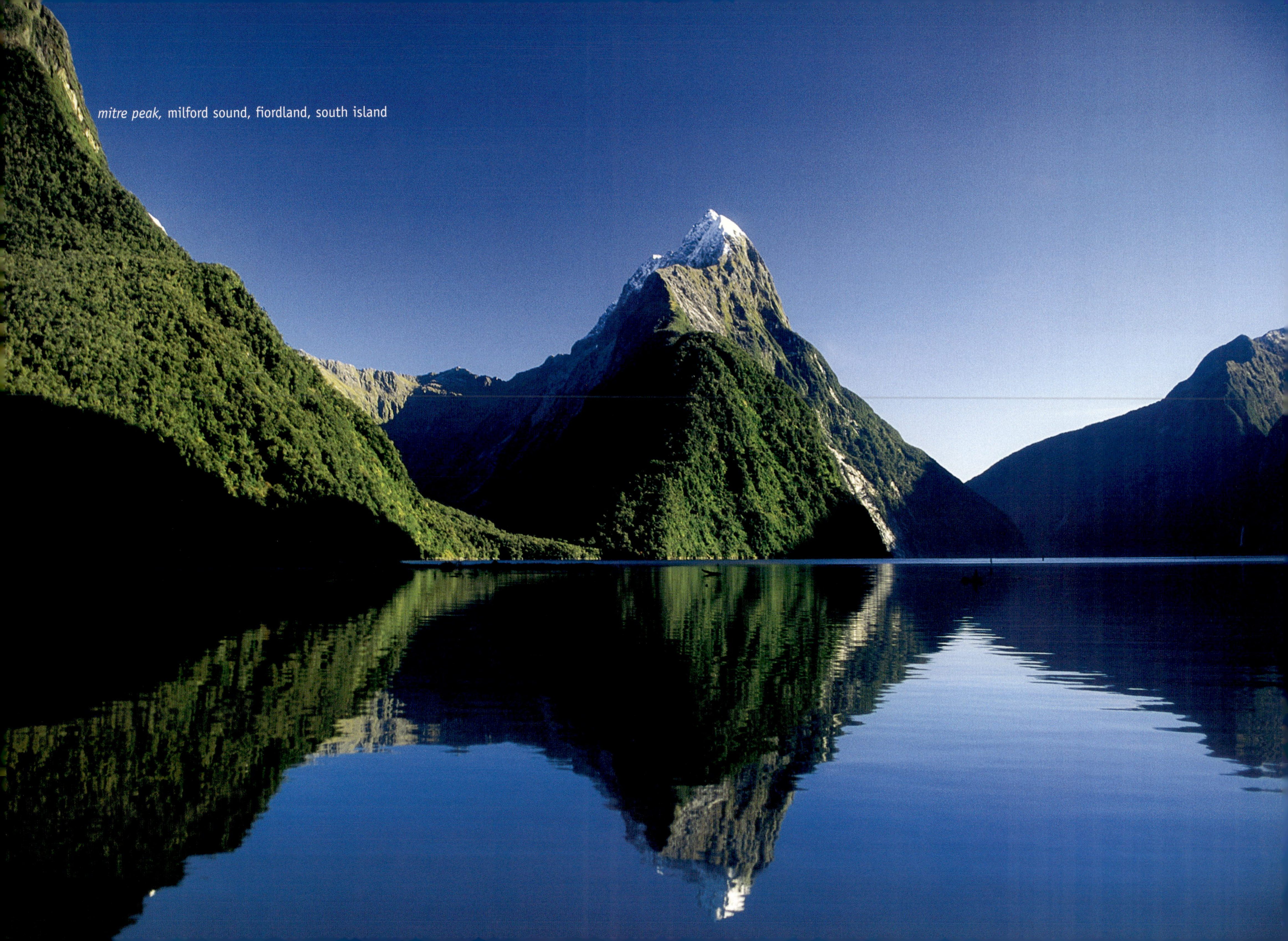

mitre peak, milford sound, fiordland, south island

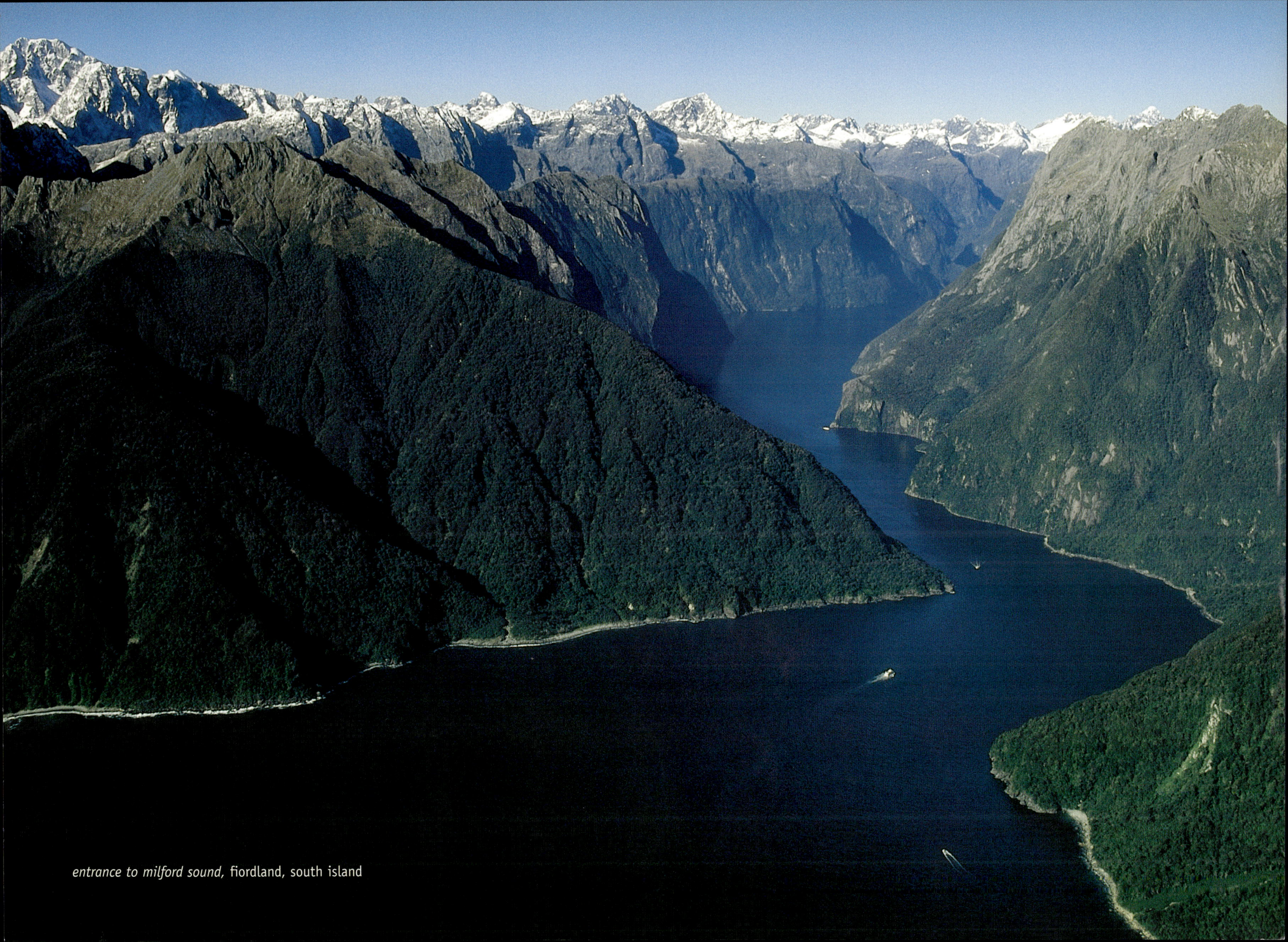

entrance to milford sound, fiordland, south island

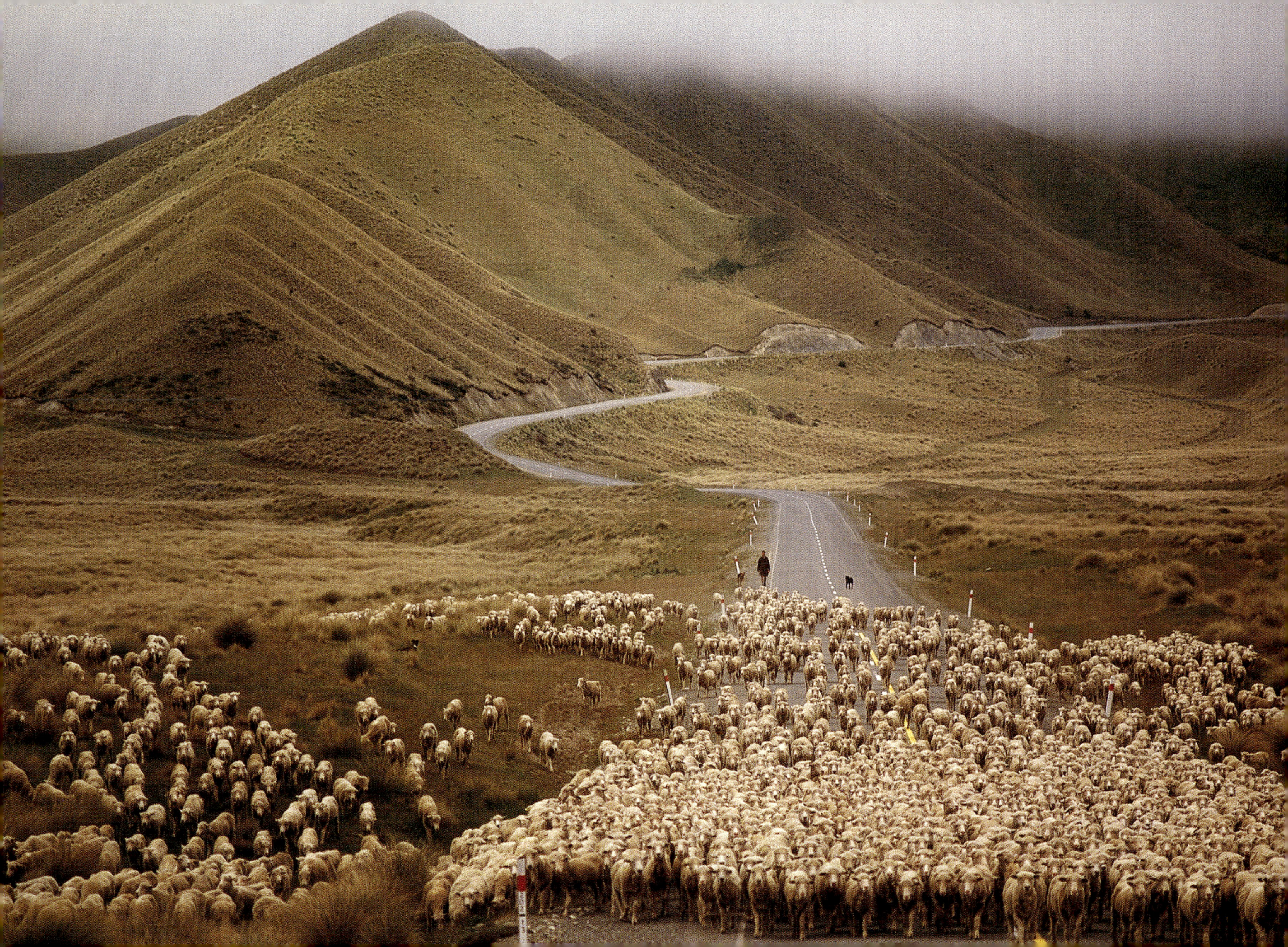

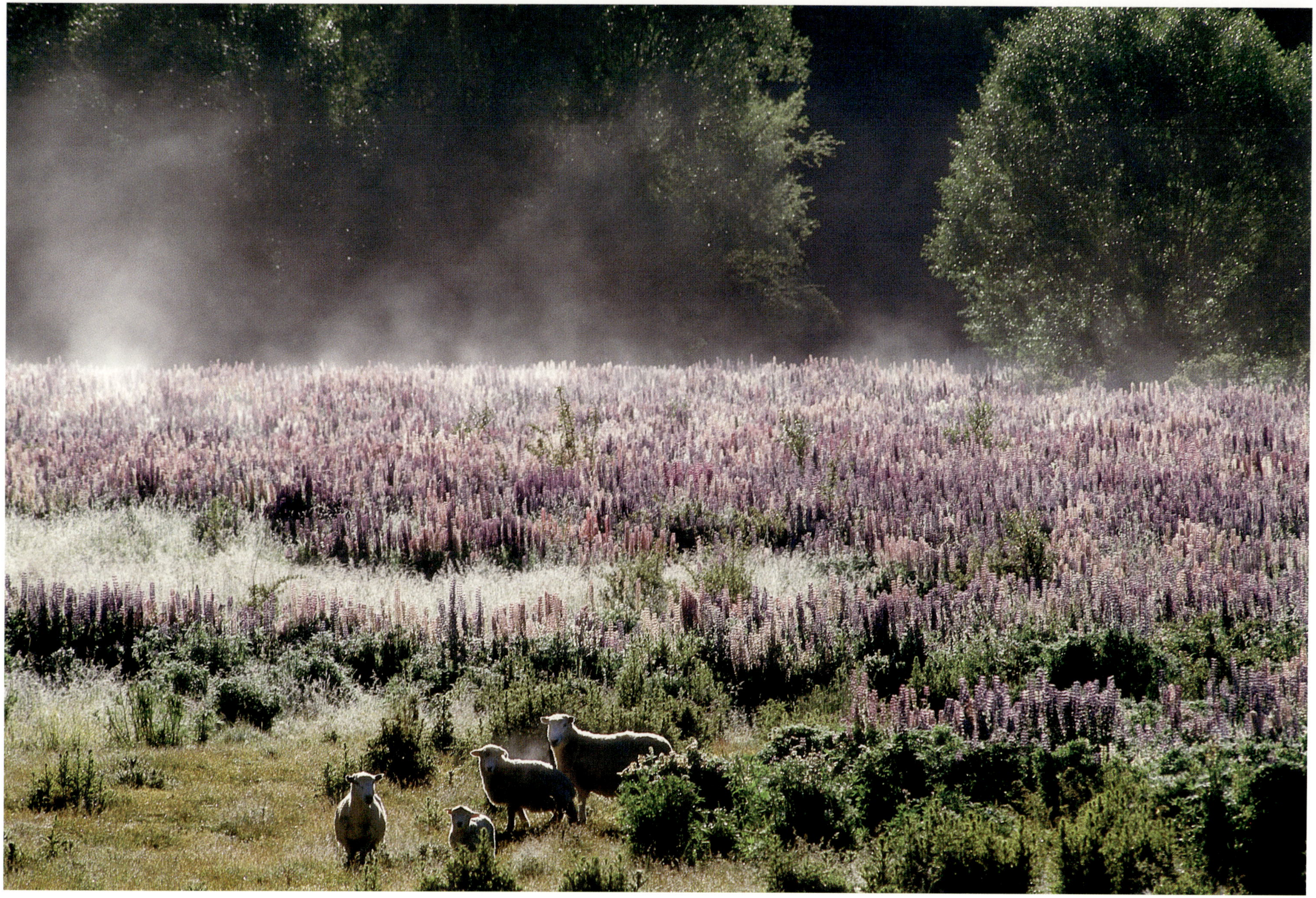

[LEFT] *otago,* south island

central otago, south island

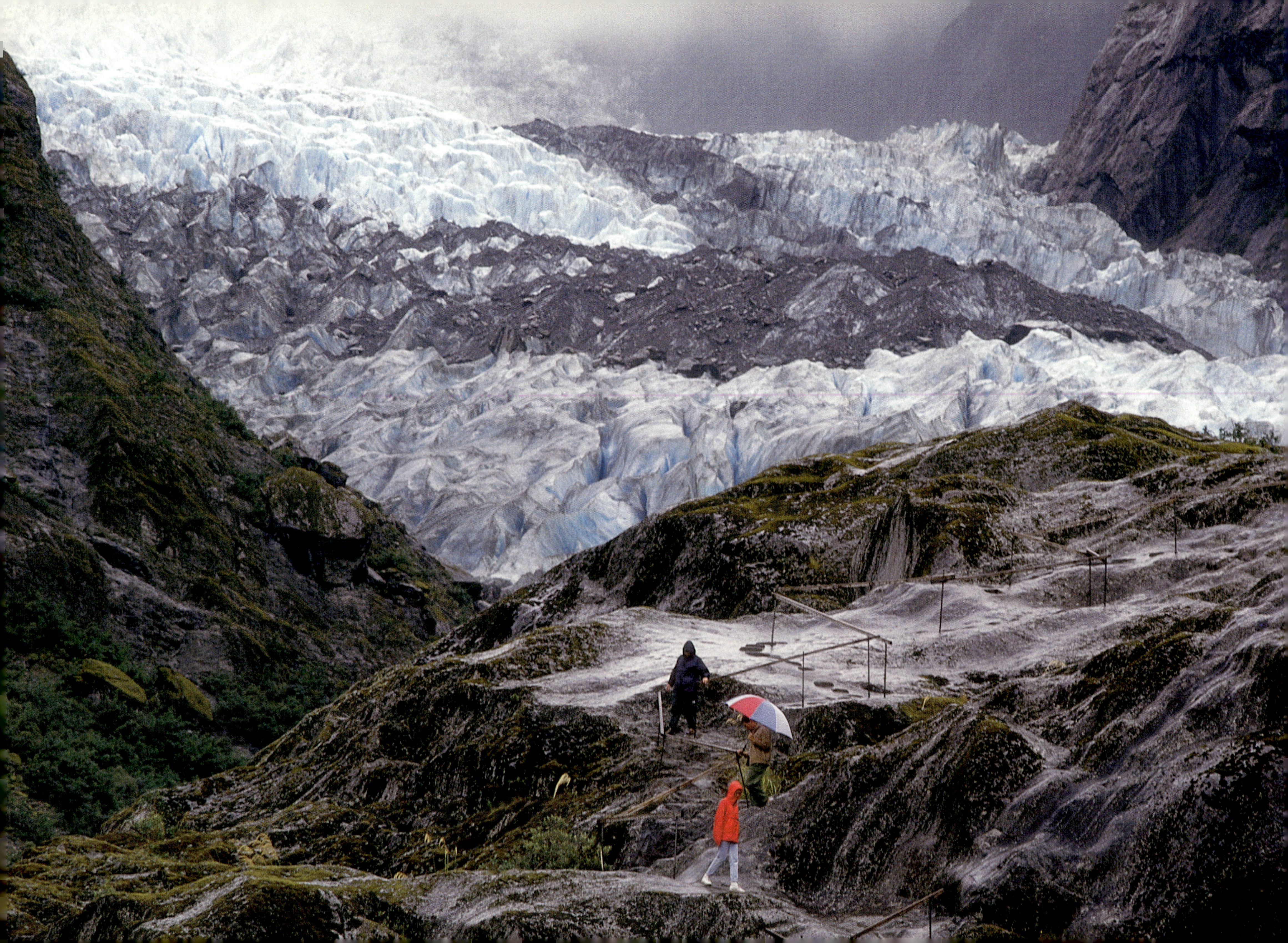

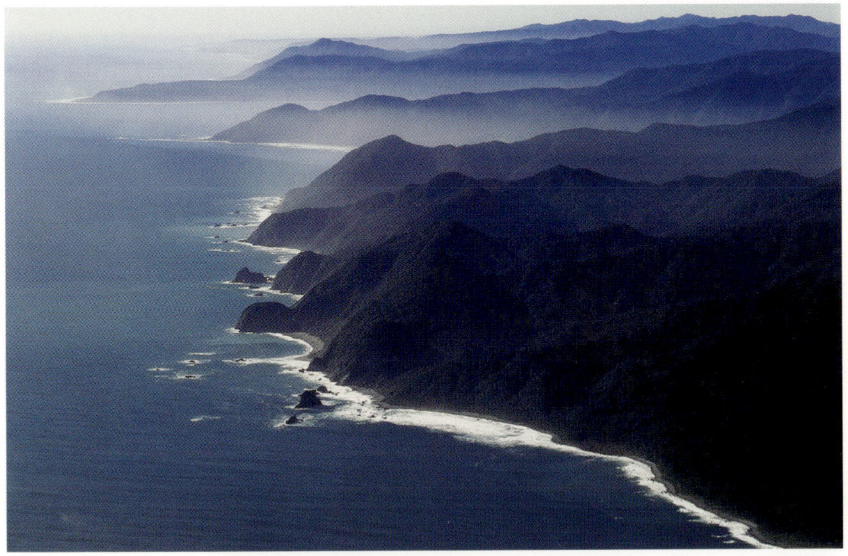

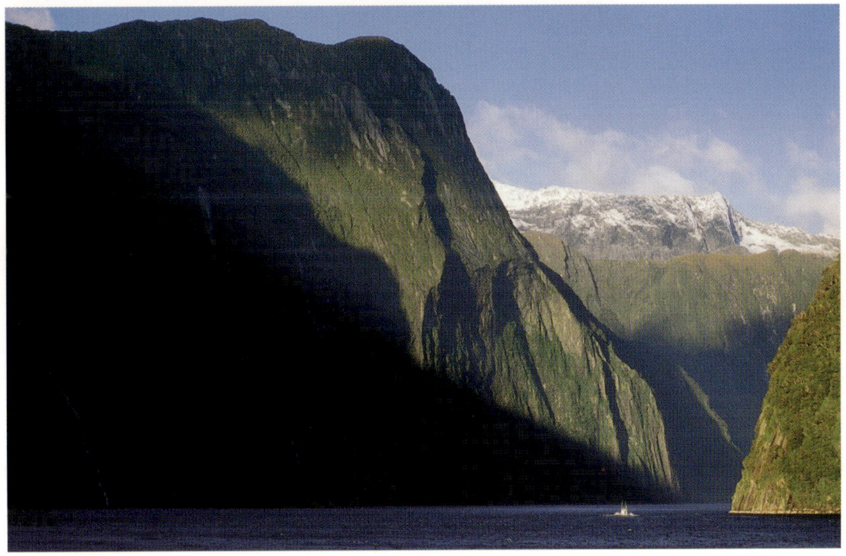

[ABOVE LEFT] *coastline north from milford sound,* south island

[ABOVE] *entrance to milford sound,* fiordland, south island

[RIGHT] *waterfalls,* west coast, south island

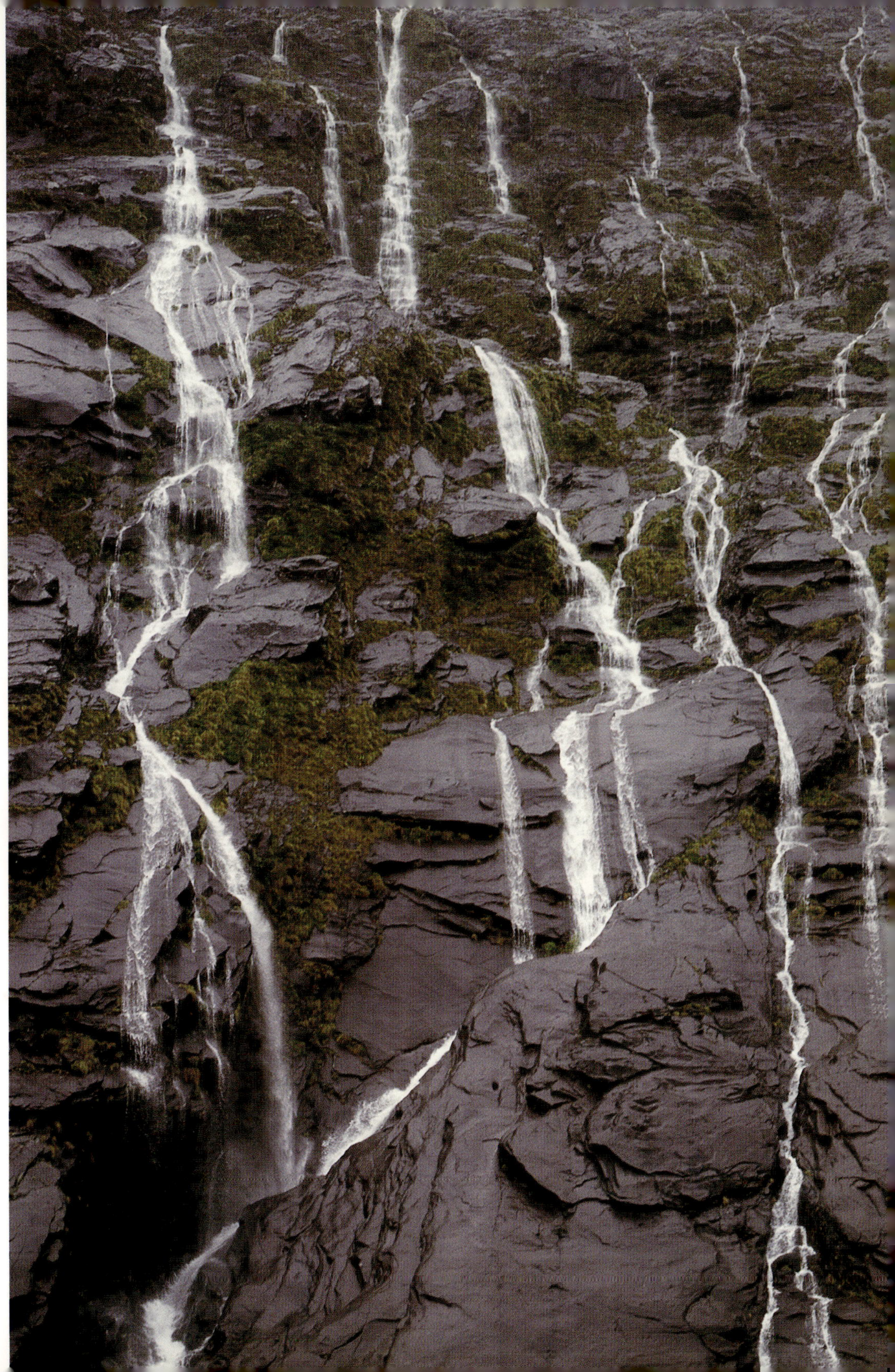

[LEFT] *franz josef glacier,* west coast, south island

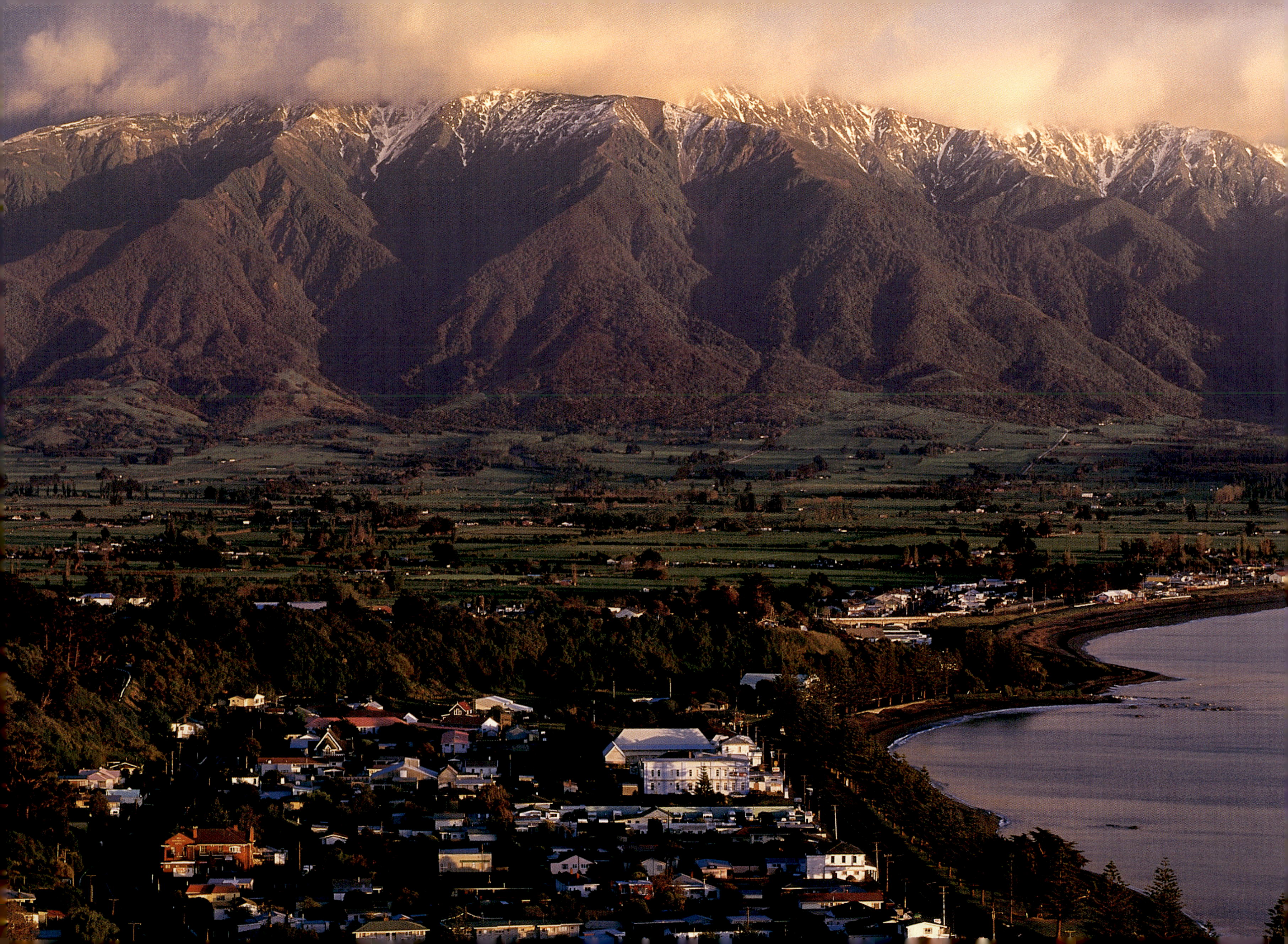

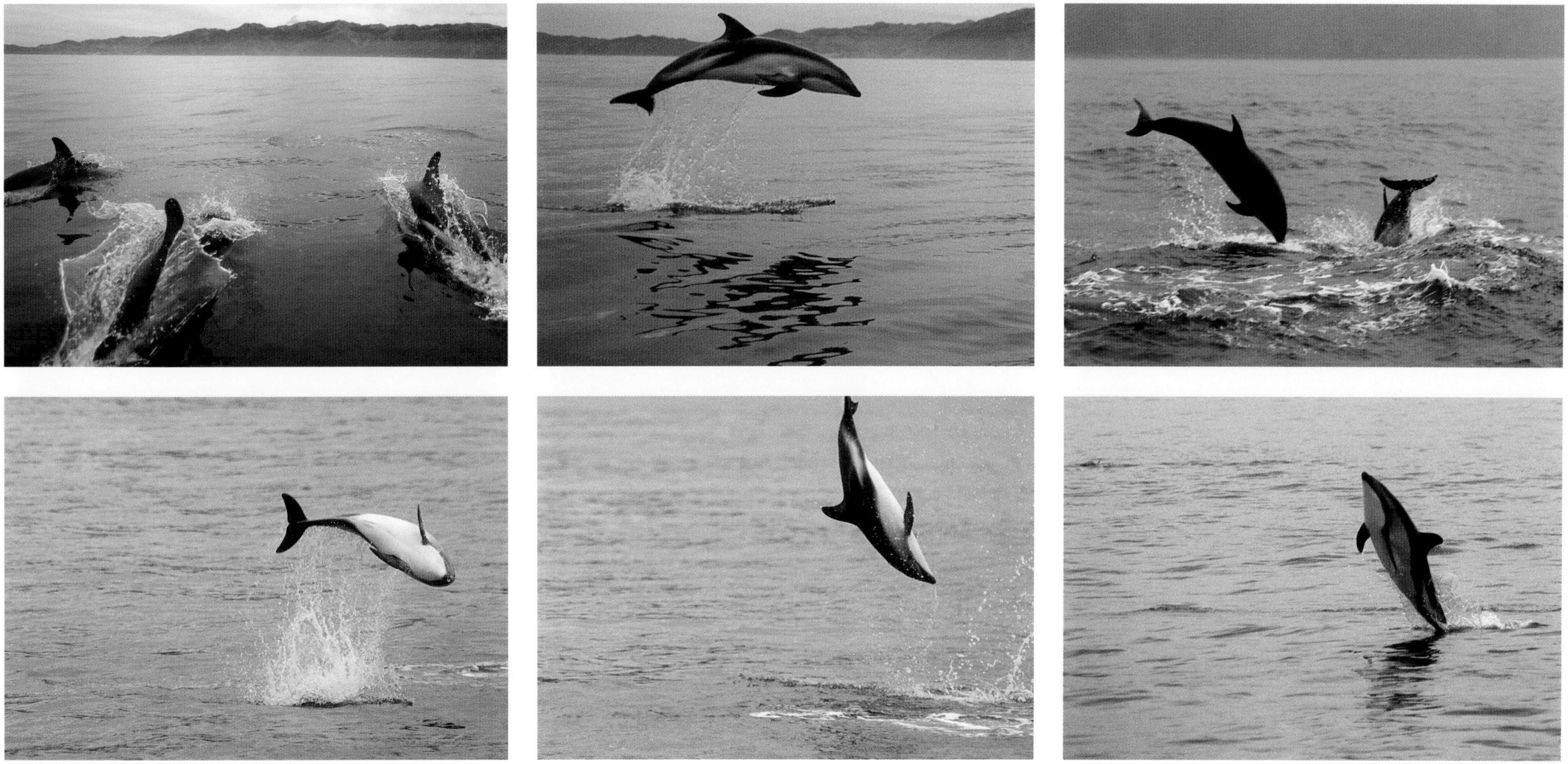

bottle nose and dusky dolphins at kaikoura and doubtful sound, south island

[LEFT] *kaikoura township,* south island

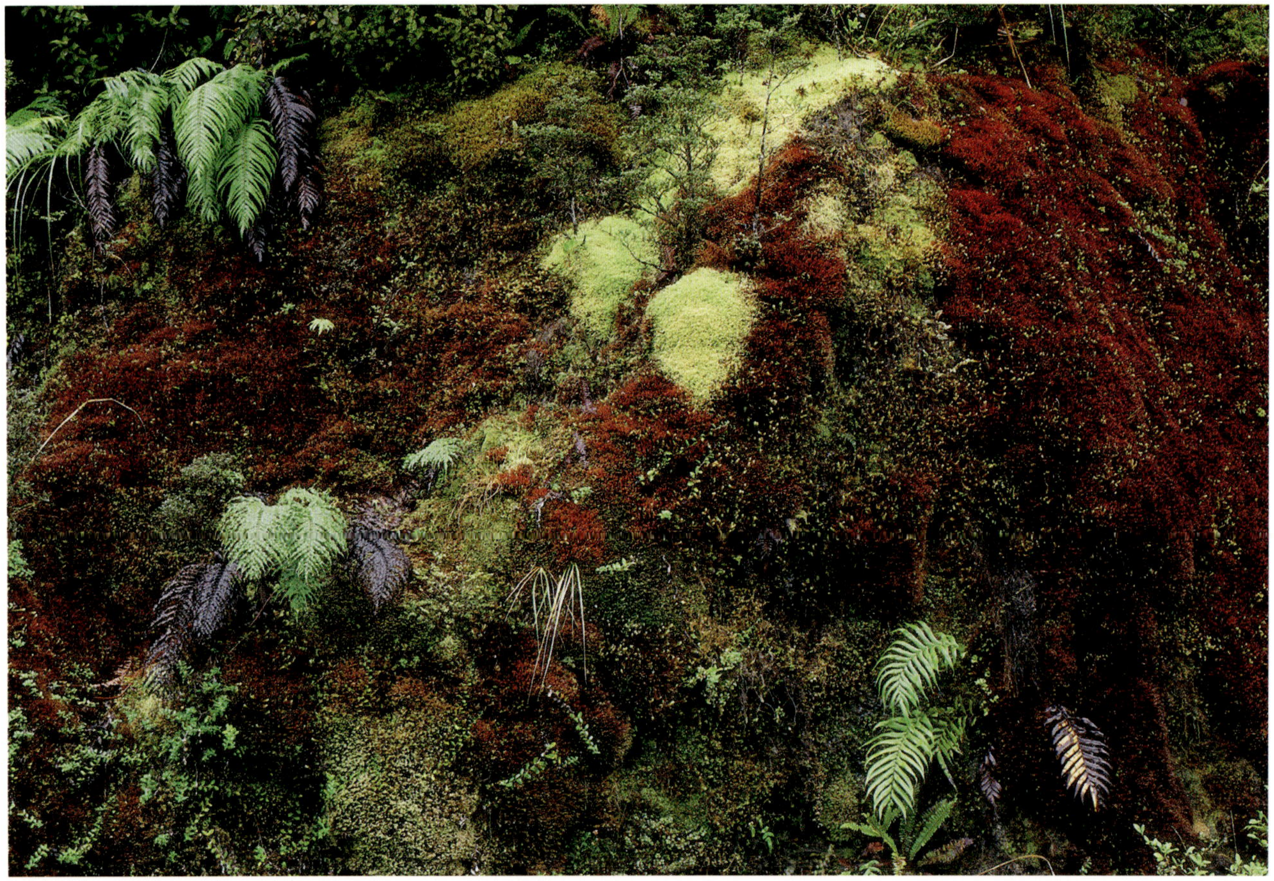

ferns, moss and lichens, cameron mountains, fiordland, south island

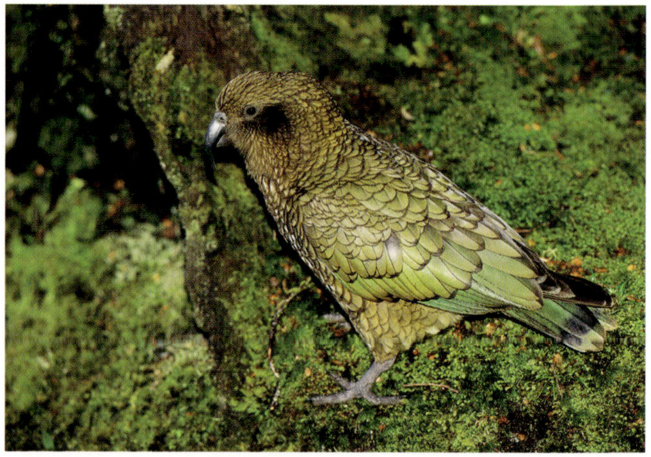

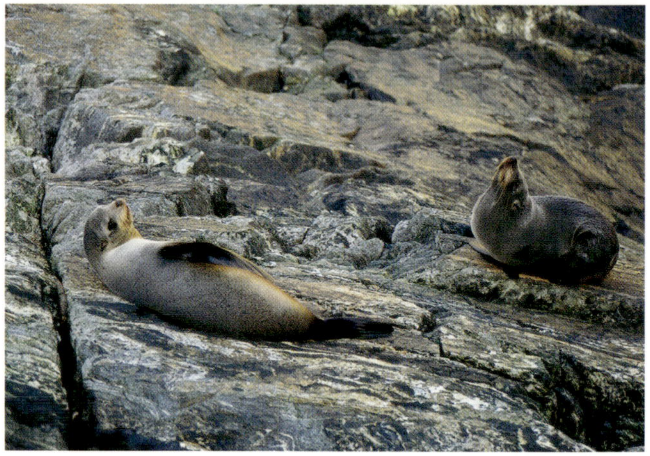

[**ABOVE RIGHT**] *kea parrot,* fiordland, south island

[**RIGHT**] *new zealand fur seals,* milford sound, south island

[**FAR RIGHT**] *moss covered beech tree, fiordland,* south island

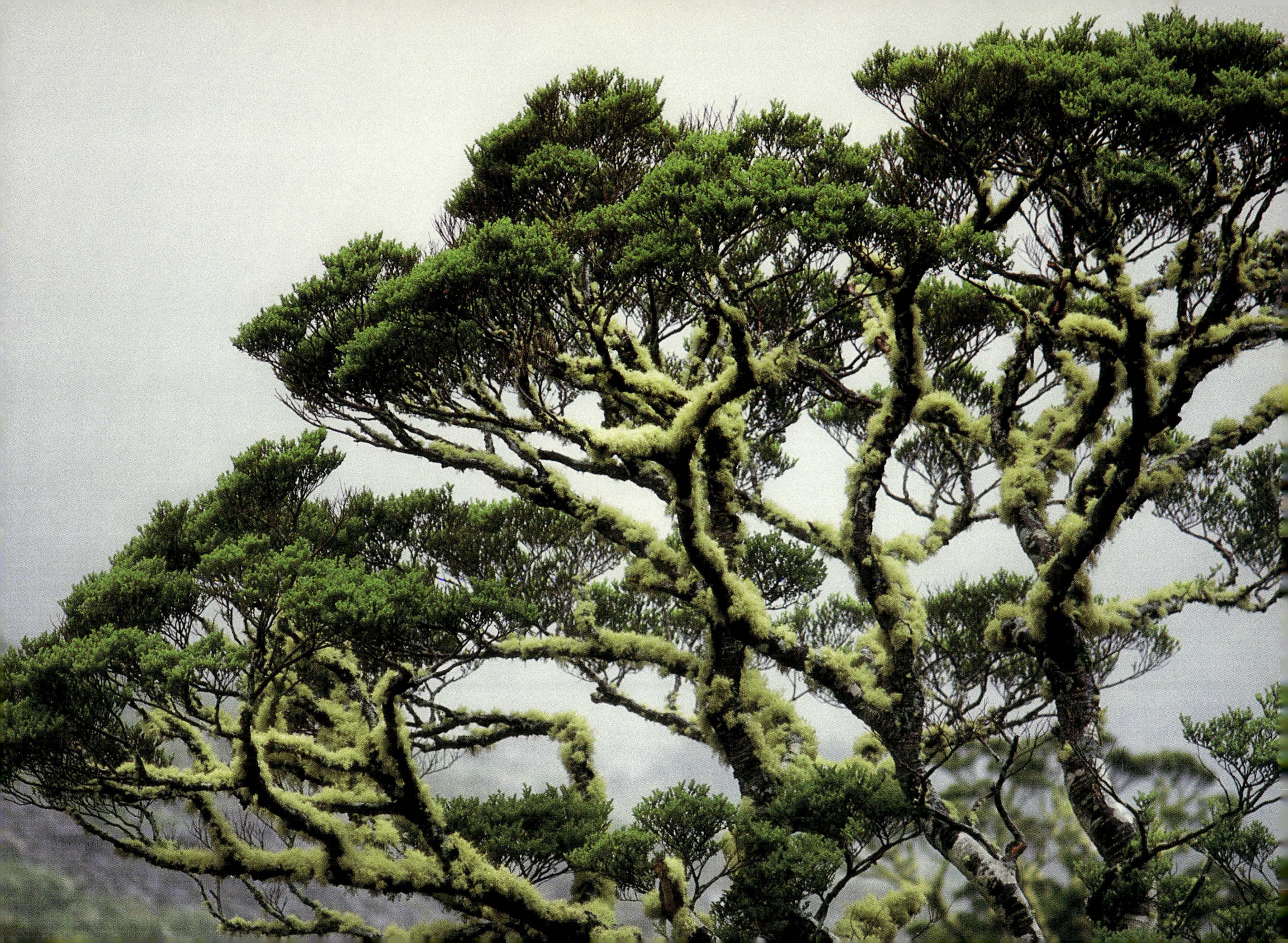

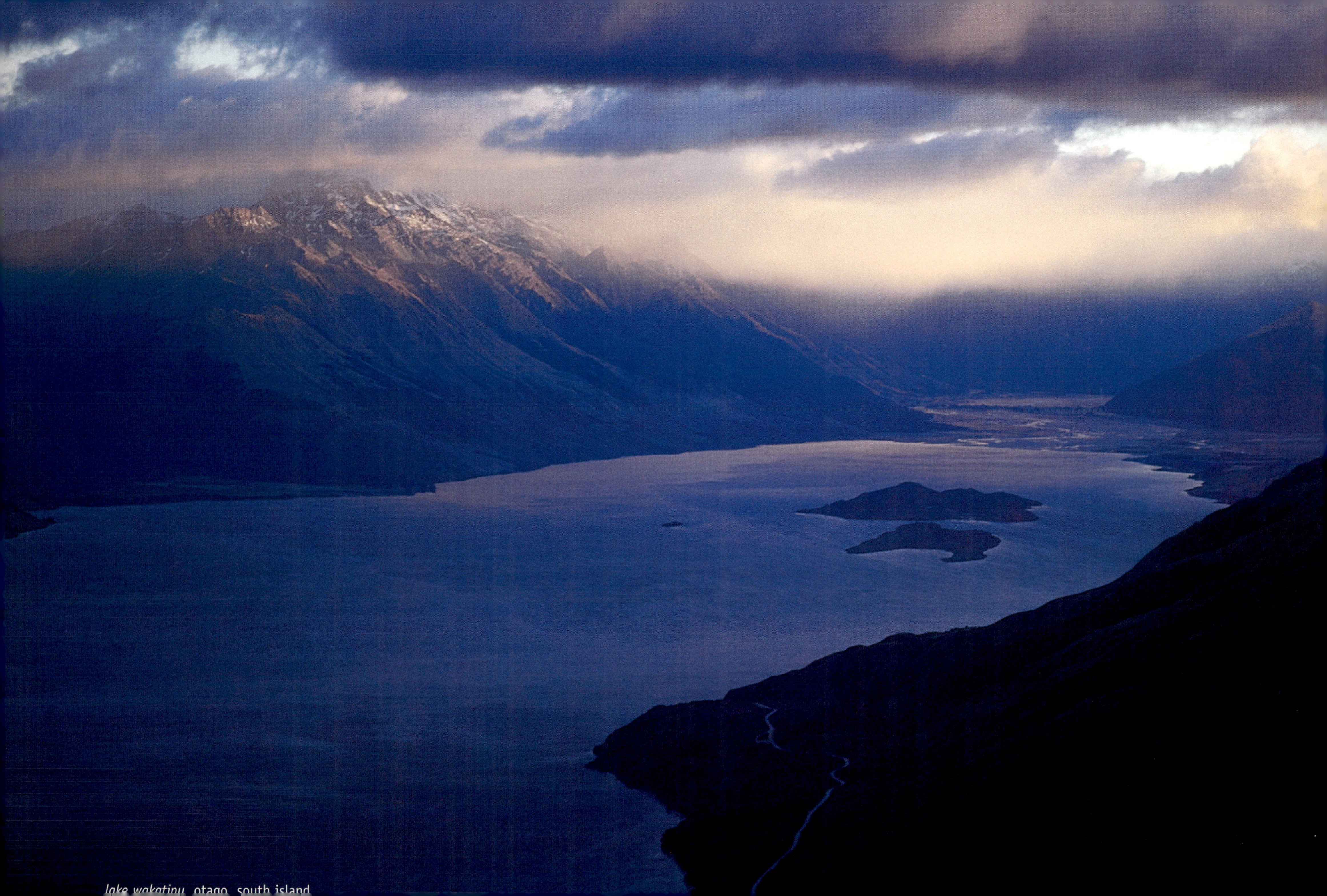

lake wakatipu, otago, south island

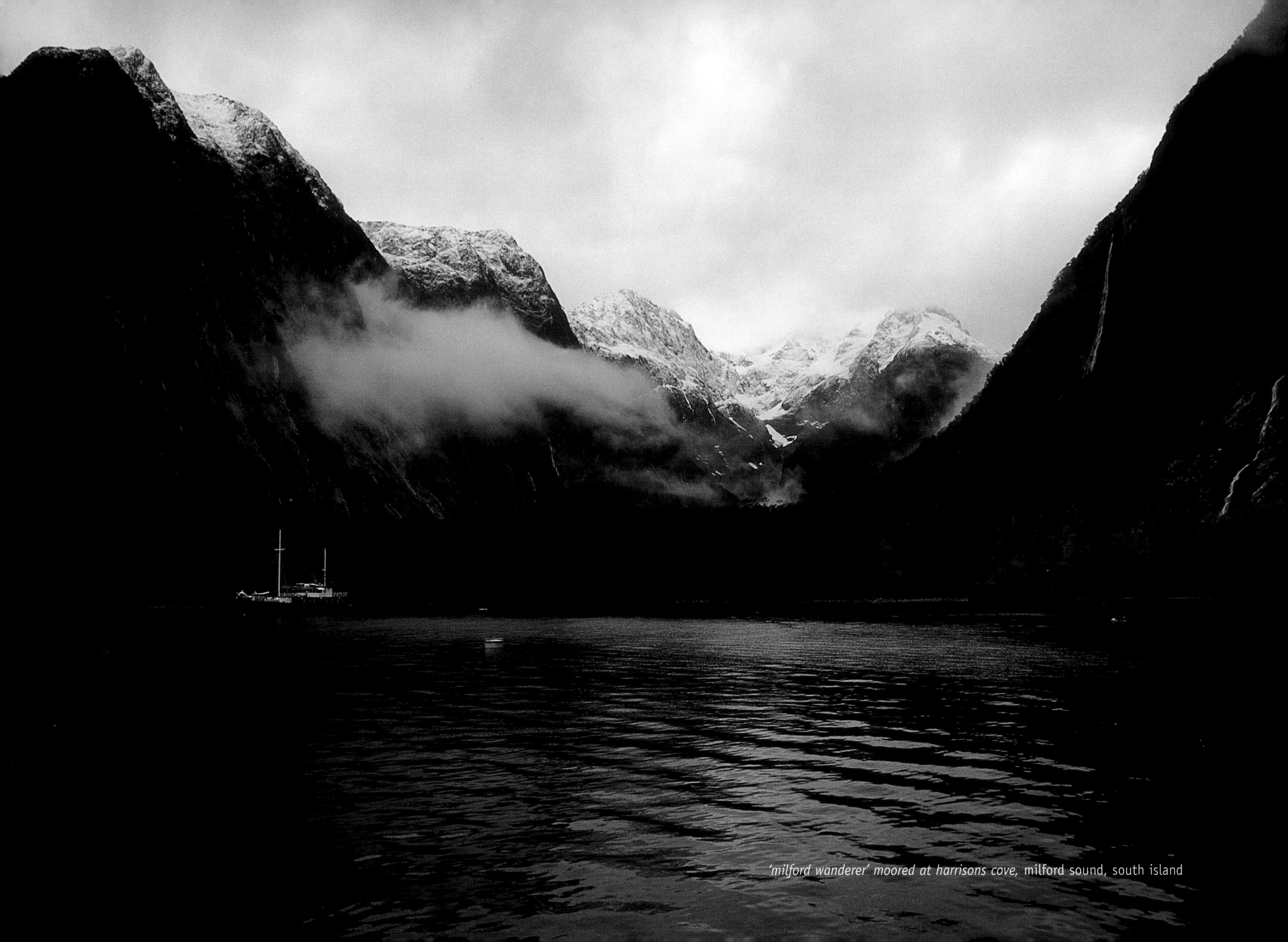

'milford wanderer' moored at harrisons cove, milford sound, south island

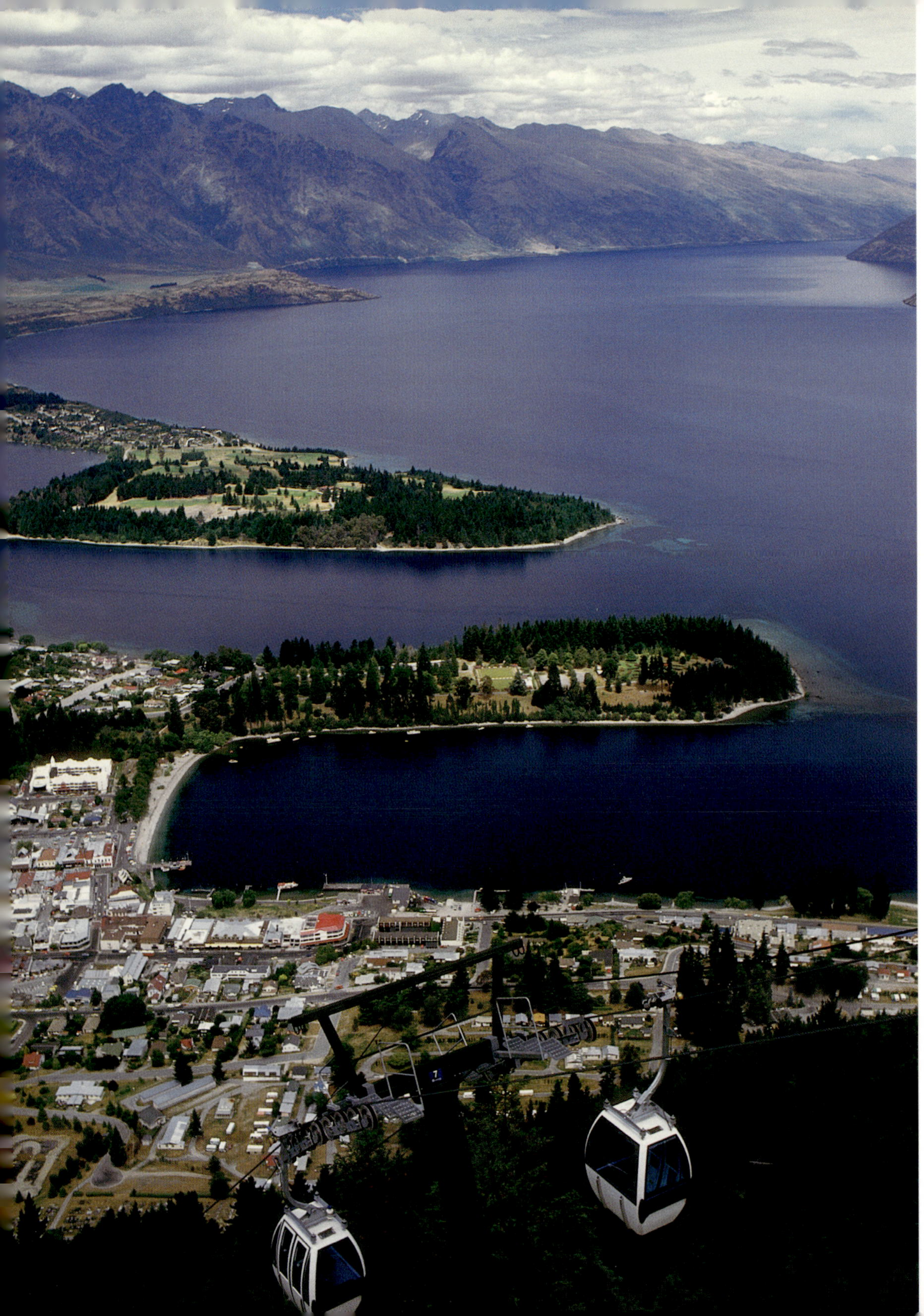

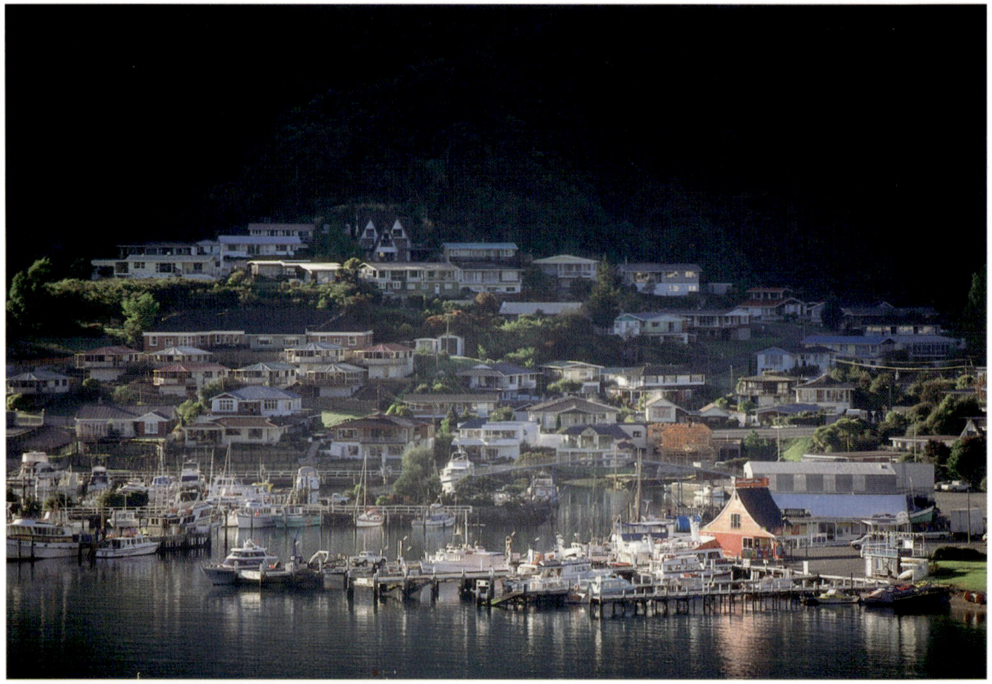

[ABOVE] *picton,*
queen charlotte sound, south island

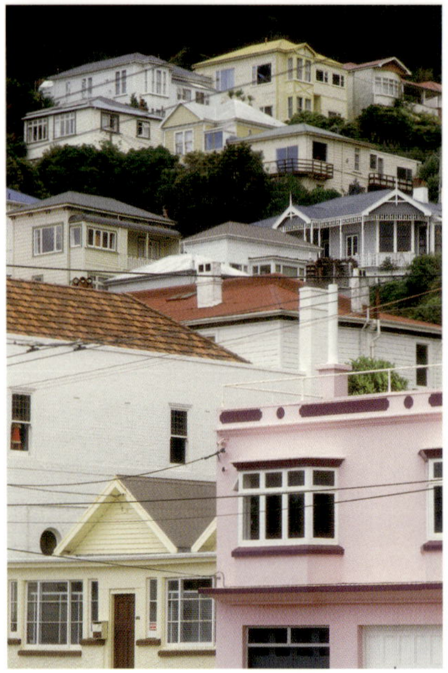

[FAR LEFT] *queenstown, otago,* south island

[LEFT] *wellington,* north island

[RIGHT] *coromandel peninsula,* north island

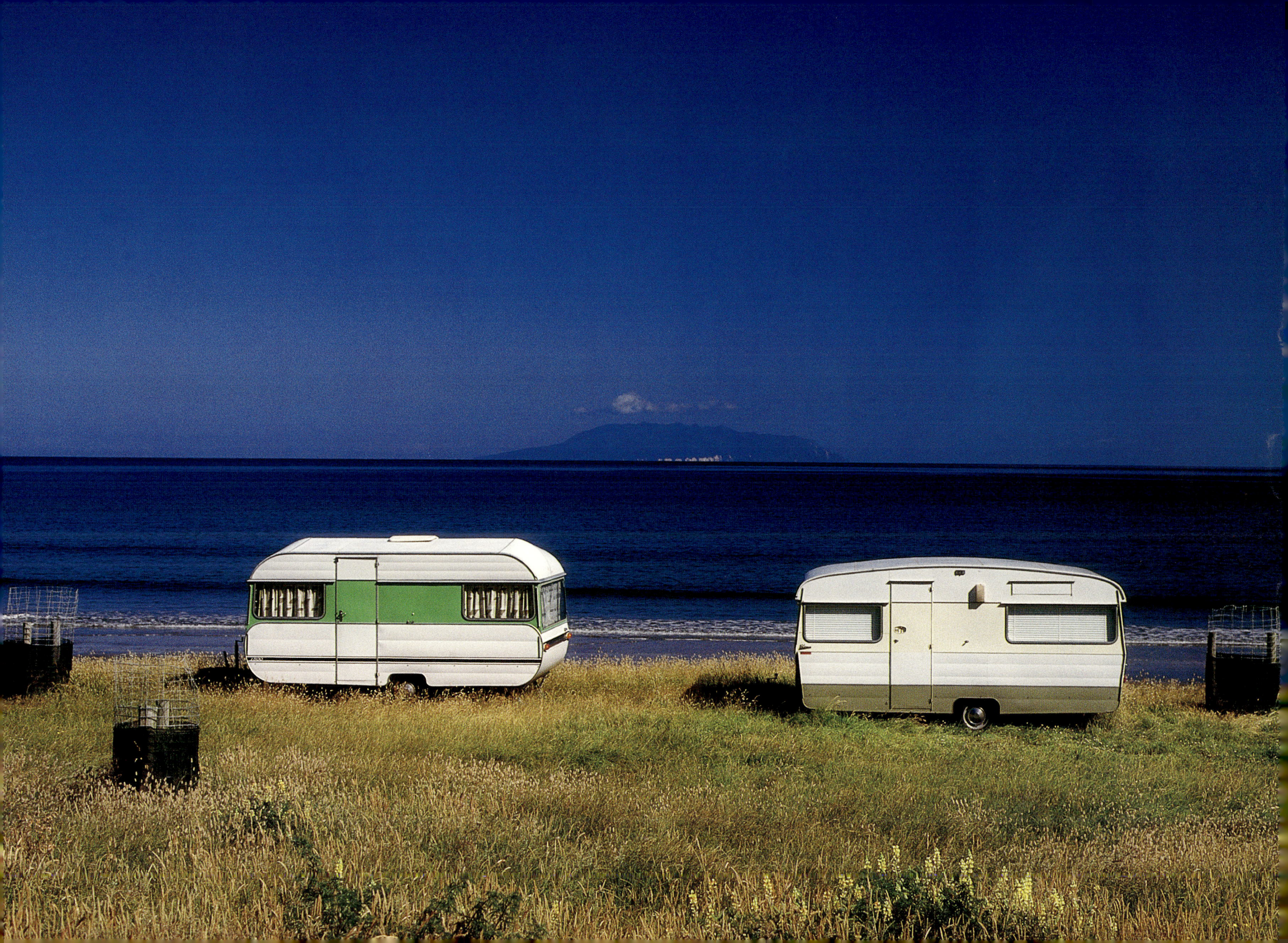

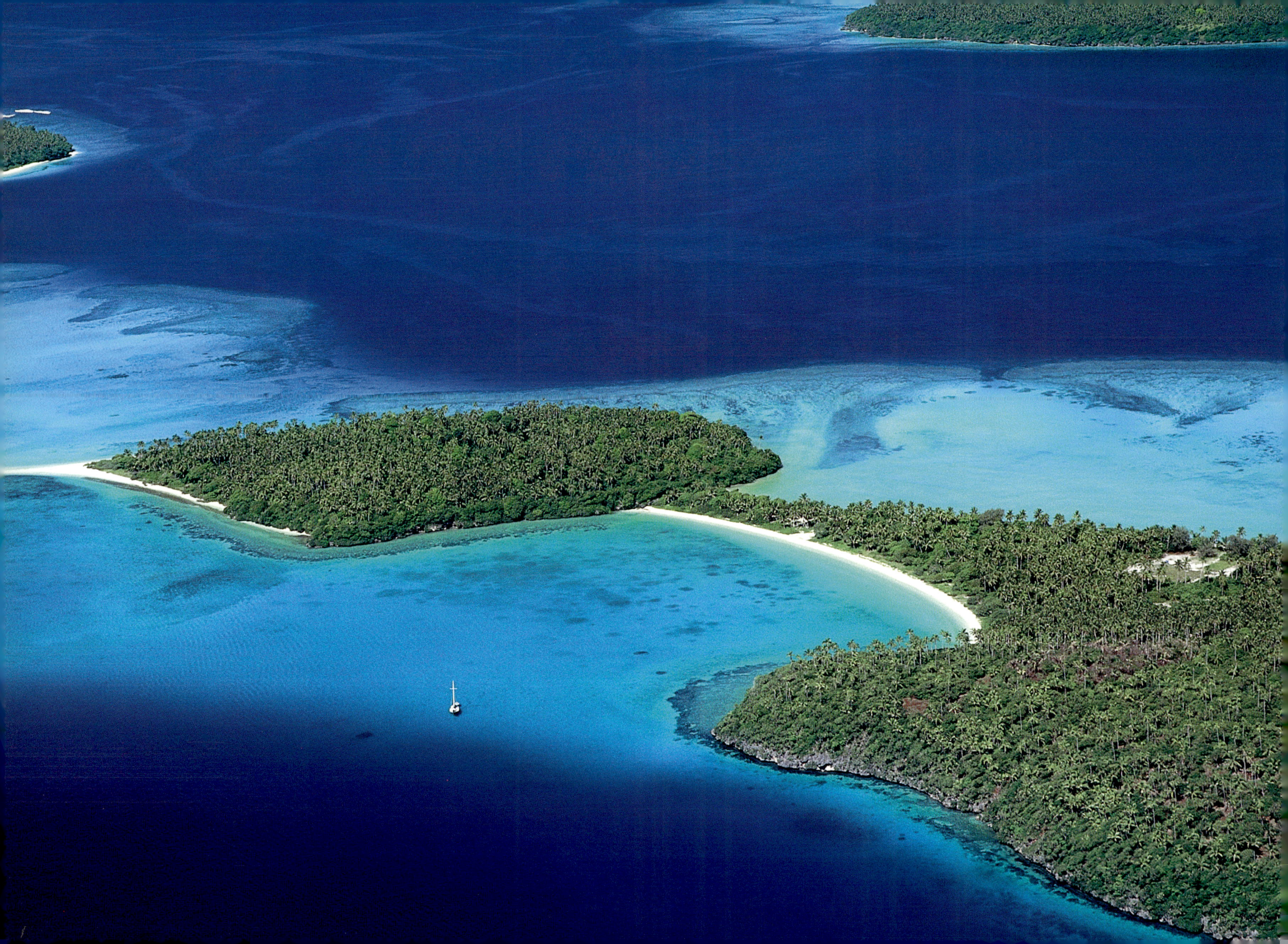

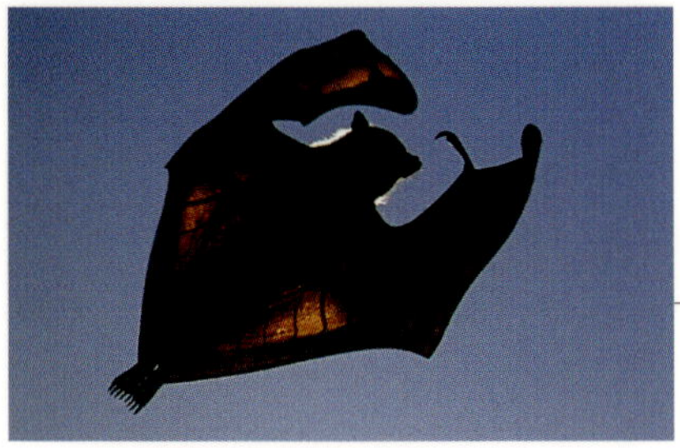

Kingdom of Tonga

TONGA is the Pacific Island's last remaining Polynesian Kingdom, the only island that escaped full colonisation by a European power. The two other Pacific monarchies, Hawai'i and Tahiti, were unable to survive western contact. The Tongan Kingdom, presently headed by a noble of the Tupou dynasty, King Taufa'ahau IV, is highly centralised and tightly governed, which has sometimes occasioned protest from its more democratically minded citizens. With more young Tongans travelling abroad, the pressure for political reform is likely to increase.

The islands which were first settled from Samoa about 500 BC comprise 4 groups of approximately 169 islands. The Southern group of Tongatapu with the capital Nuku'alofa and nearby Eua island, the Ha'apai group 150km to the north and the Vava'u group 100km further north, with the isolated, rarely visited Nivas still further north. Although spread over 700,000sq.km of ocean, Tonga's total land area is only 691sq.km.

During the 10th century there arose a dynasty known as the Tu'i Tonga who were to rule for over 400 years through a hereditary line of 39 kings. In the 13th century, Tongan raiding parties in large double-hulled canoes capable of carrying more than 150 warriors, exerted Tongan influence and domination over a large area of the central Pacific including parts of Samoa, Fiji, Tokelau and Niue.

The main island of Tongatapu is a flat raised atoll of about 259sq.km with many gardens growing vanilla beans, squash, pumpkin and other vegetables for local consumption and export. The capital Nuku'alofa, with the King's timber Victorian style Royal Palace along with the Royal Tombs, is the centre of almost all commercial and business activity in the Kingdom.

The island groups of Vava'u and Ha'apai have many idyllic beaches on their numerous islands. Because there are no rivers in Tonga the water visibility is exceptional. Port of Refuge in Vava'u with its fiord like channels is a favourite destination for cruising yachts and is also the home of one of the Pacific's largest fleet of charter yachts.

The church is extremely important in Tongan life, with over 40% of the population belonging to the Wesleyan church, which is also the state church. Another 15 official churches actively compete for the remainder of the population. No work, trade or sport is allowed on Sundays, with all shops and restaurants not serving the tourist trade, closed.

Originally named the Friendly Islands by James Cook, Tonga today remains very relaxed as if it exists in another time.

[**LEFT**] *vava'u group* [**ABOVE**] *flying fox,* kolovai, tongatapu

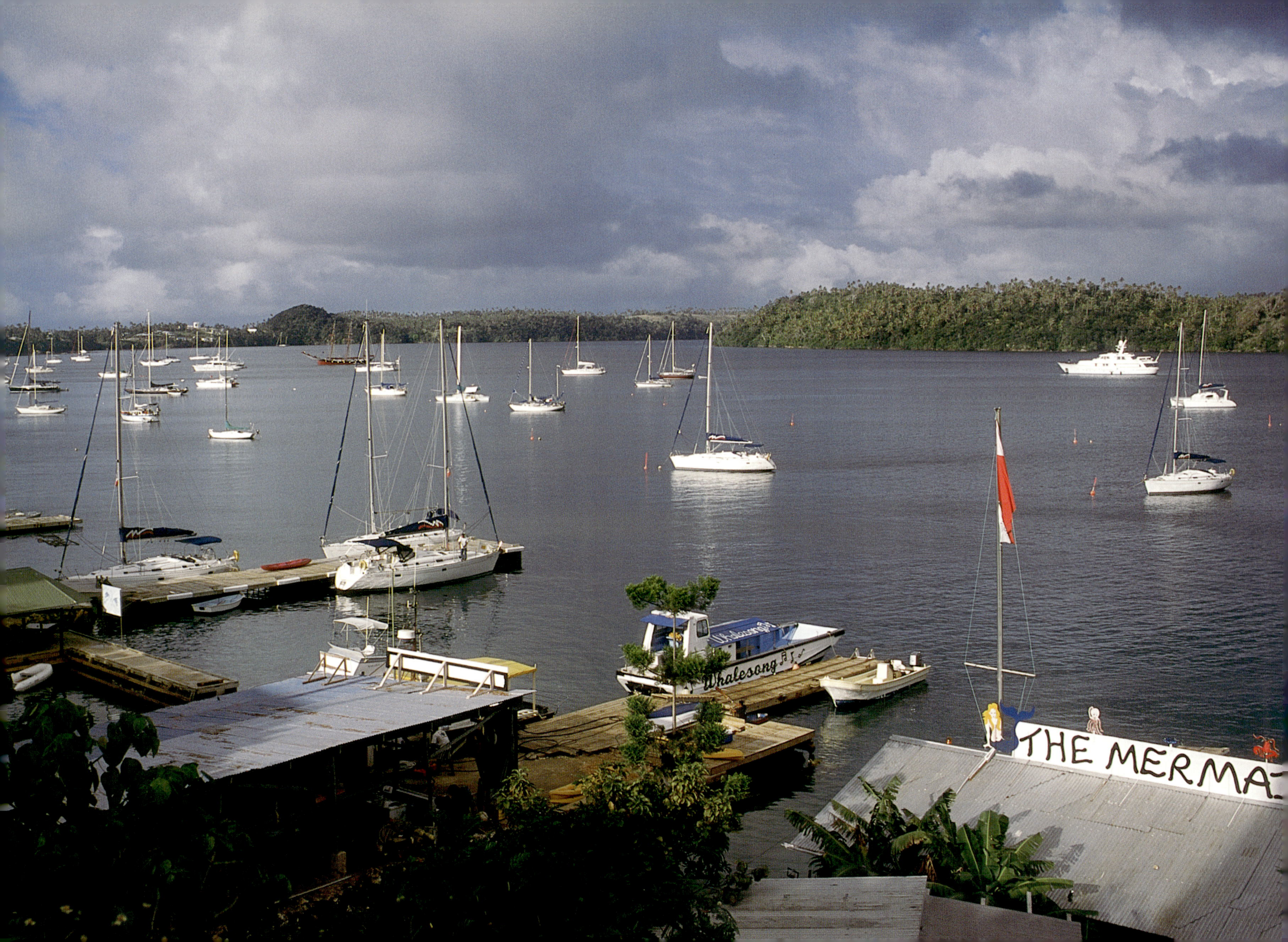
Whalesong
THE MERMA

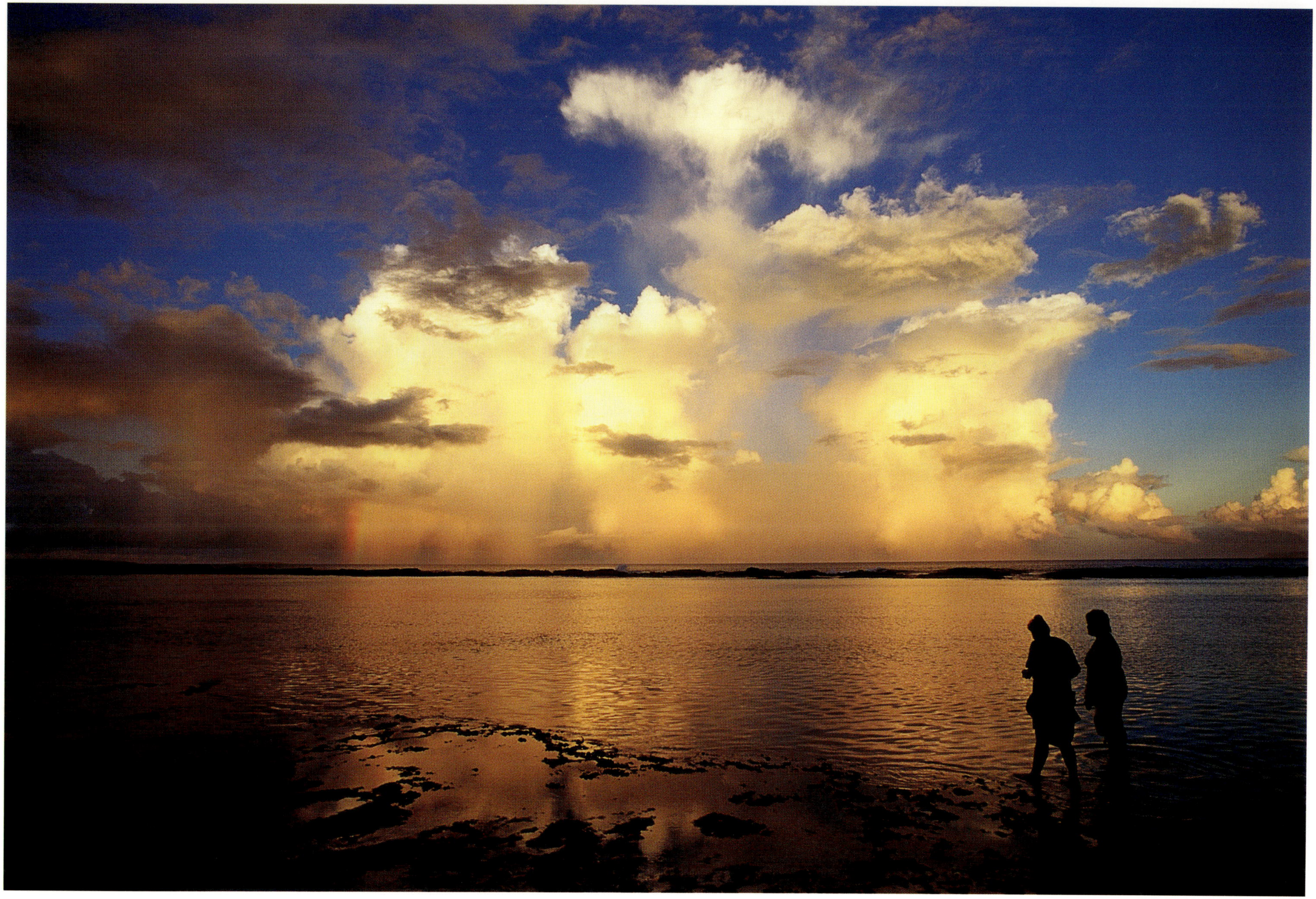

[LEFT] *vaipua inlet and neiafu waterfront,* vava'u

oholei beach, south tongatapu

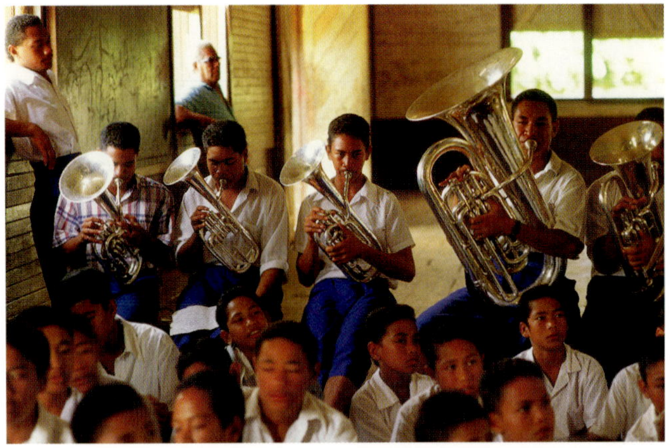

[LEFT] *school band practice,* nuku'alofa [BELOW] *thatched hut,* tongatapu

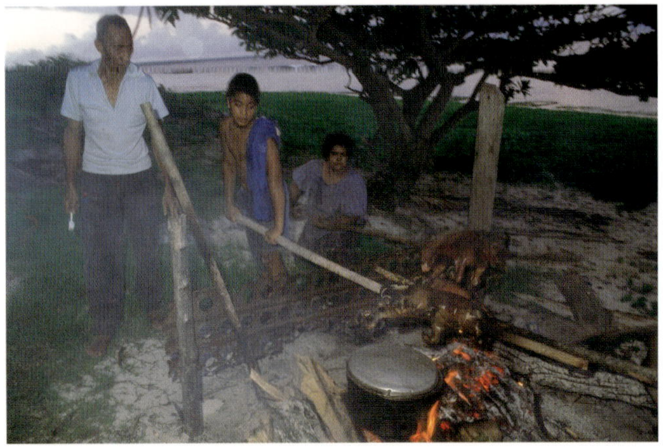

[ABOVE] *roasting suckling pig,* oholei beach, south tongatapu

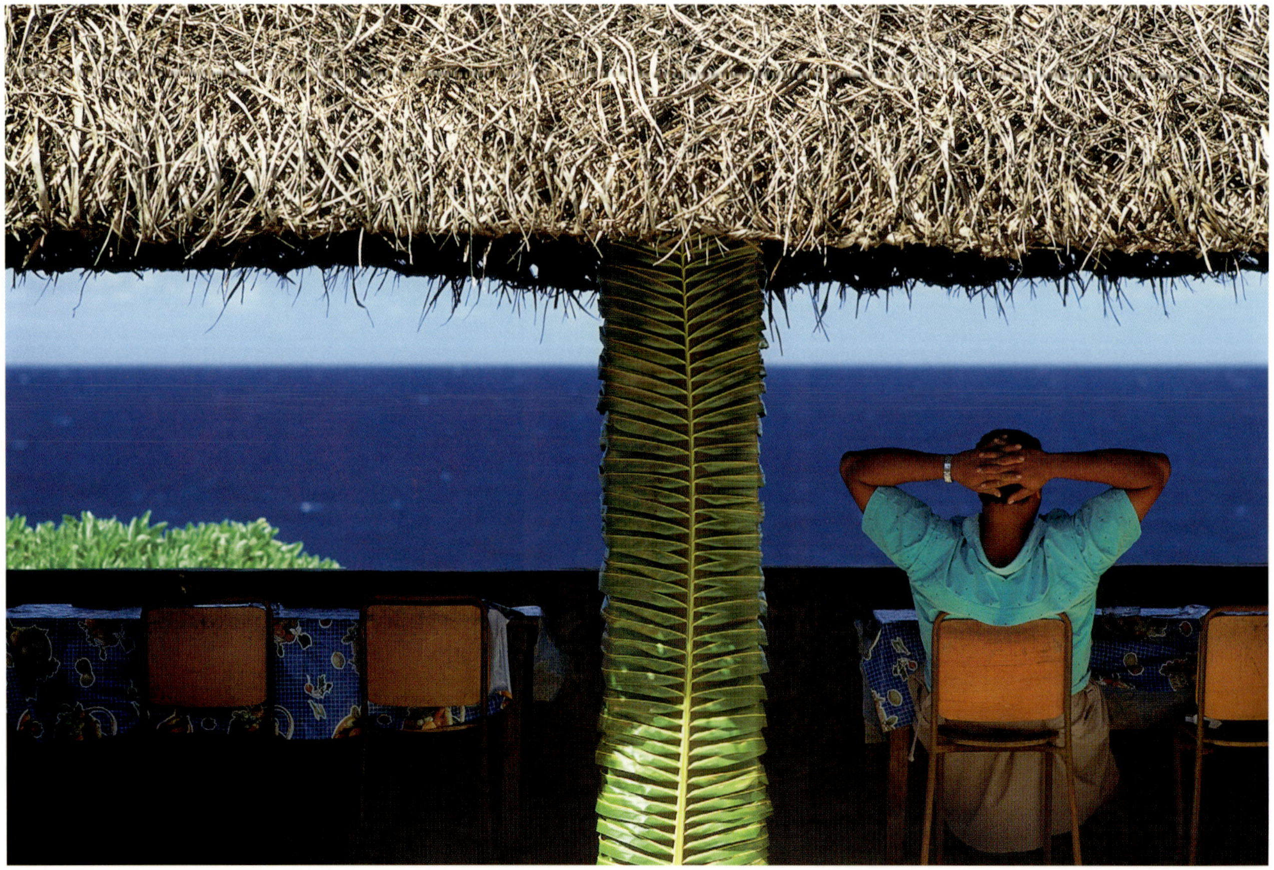

[RIGHT] *nuku'alofa girls school,* tongatapu

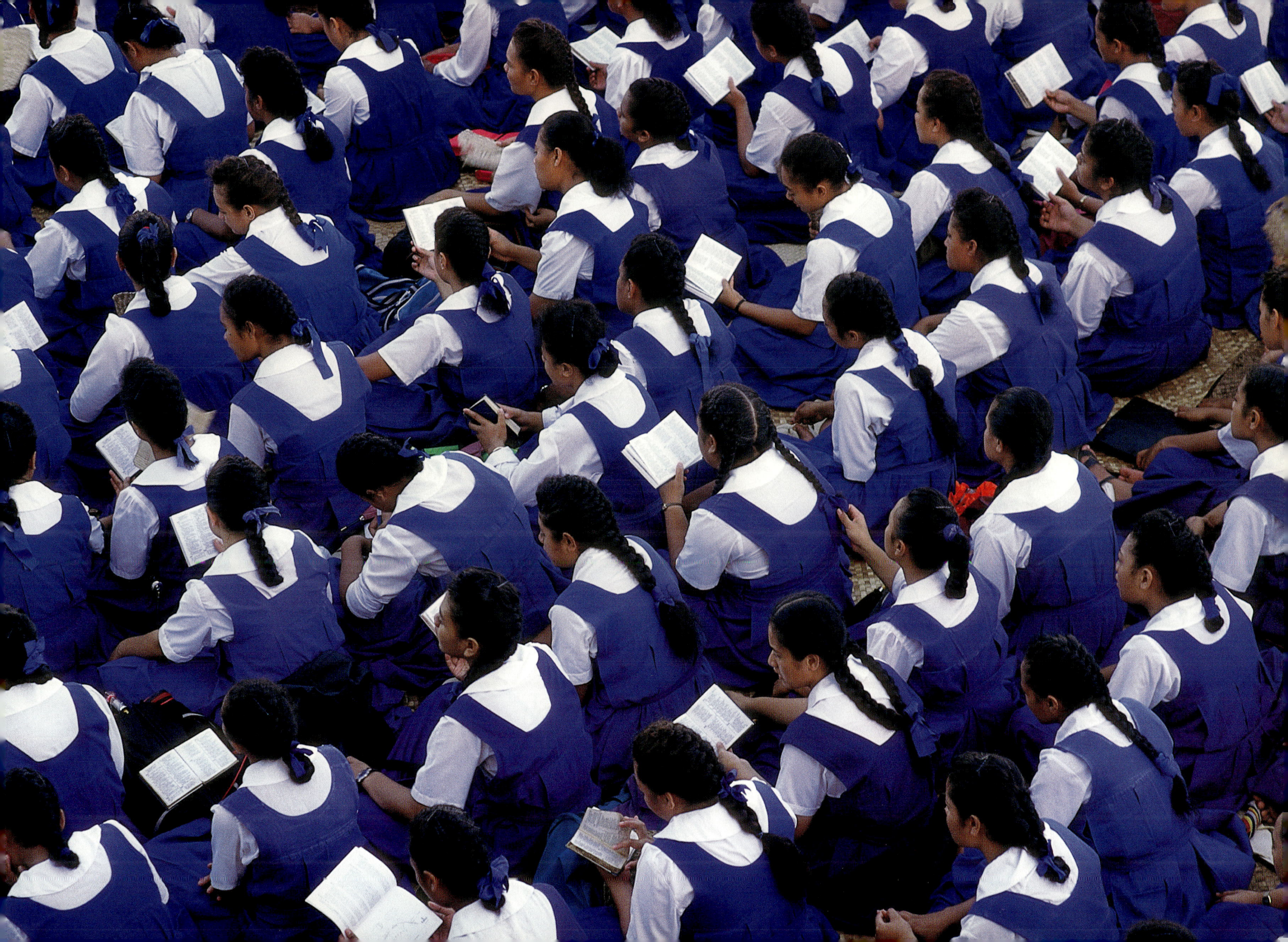

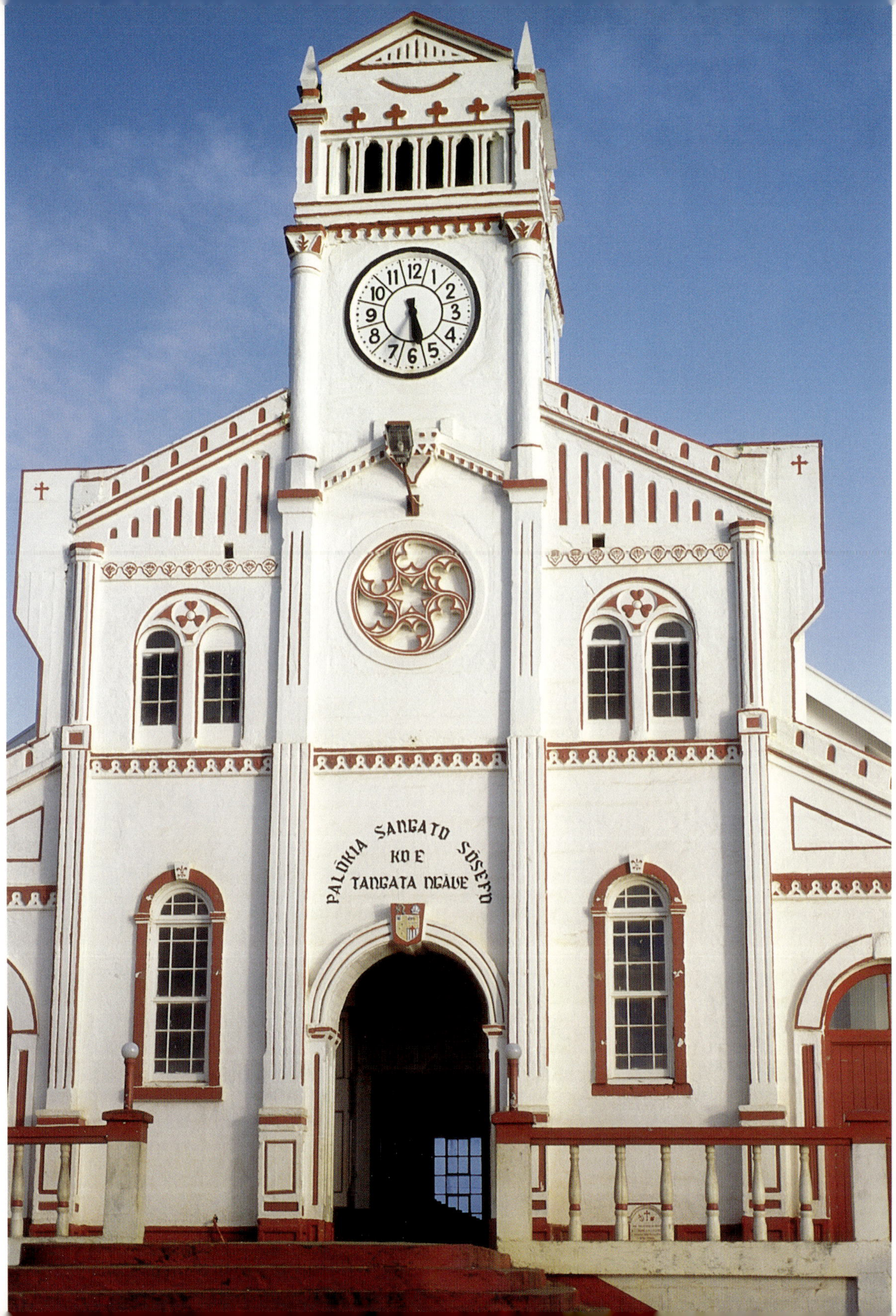

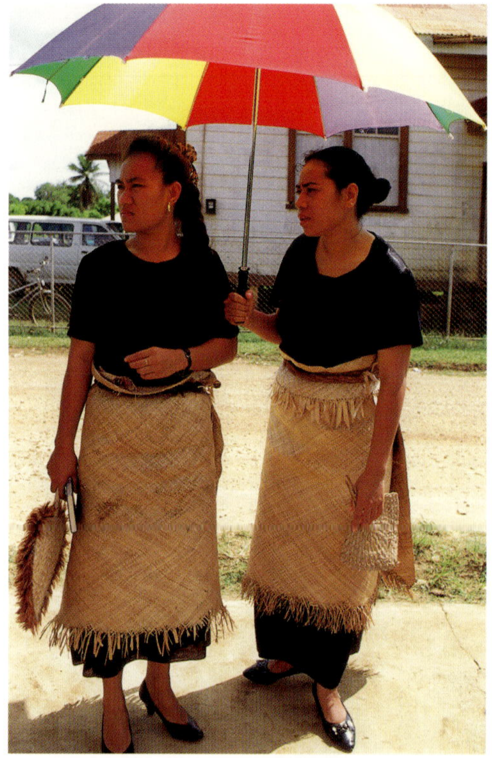

women in traditional tongan dress

[BELOW] *church service,* nuku'alofa, tongatapu

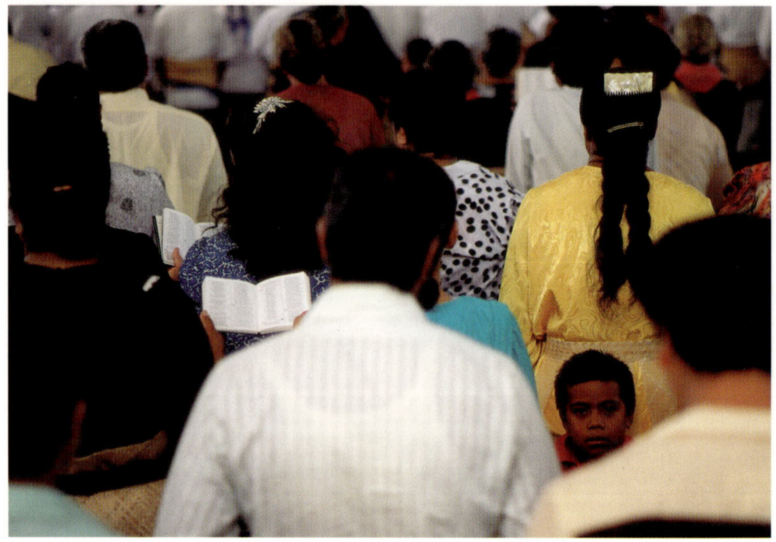

[LEFT] *neiafu catholic church,* vava'u

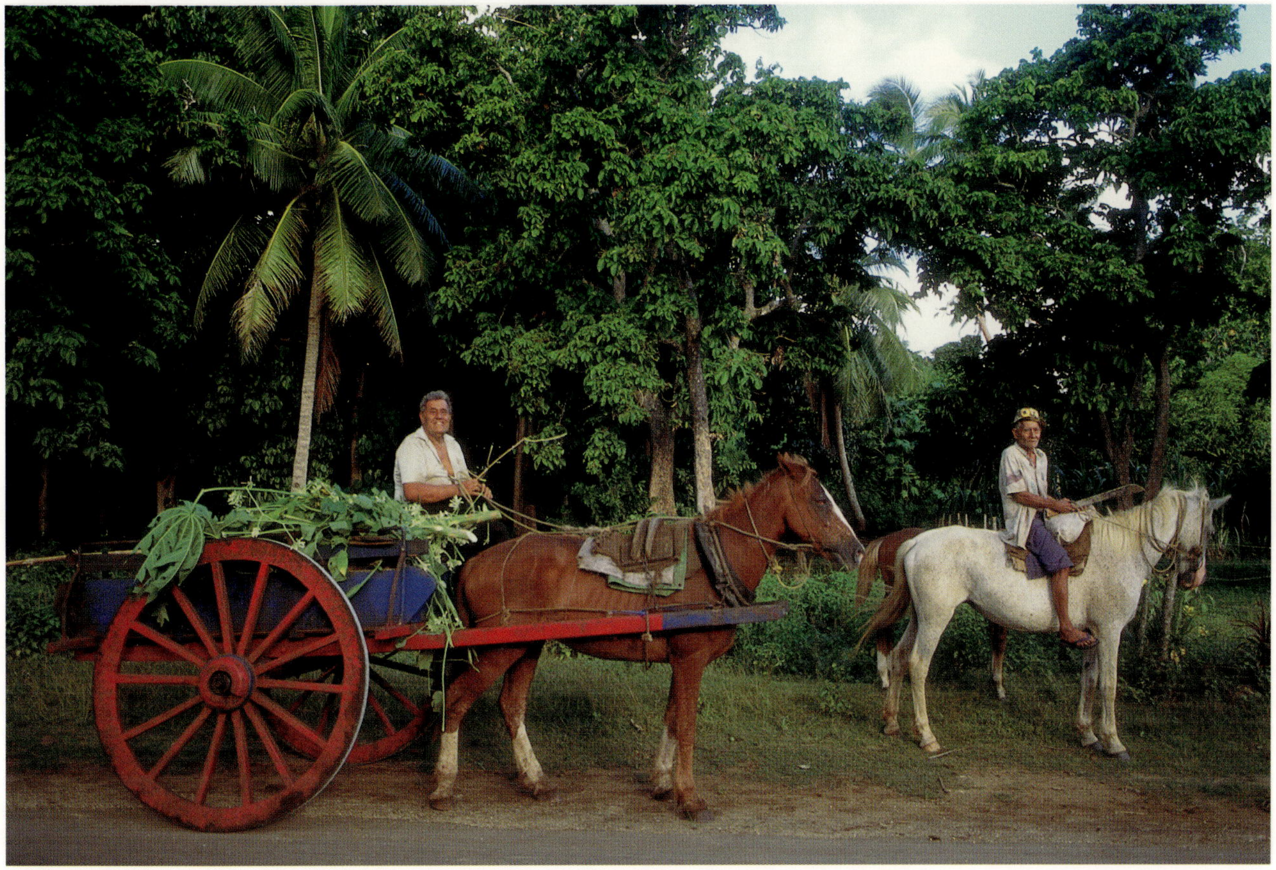

traditional horse drawn cart, tongatapu

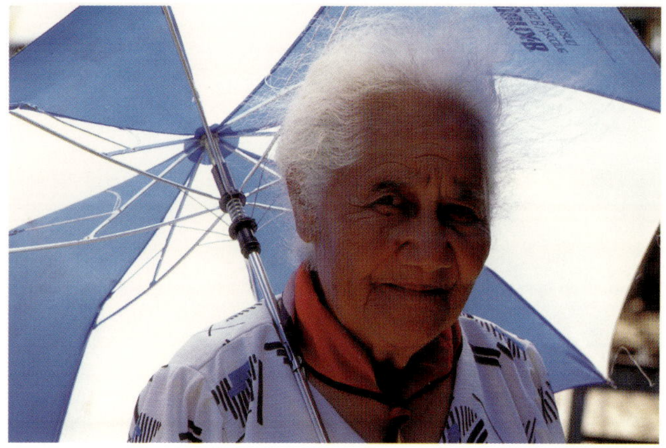

[**RIGHT**] *market day,* nuku'alofa, tongatapu

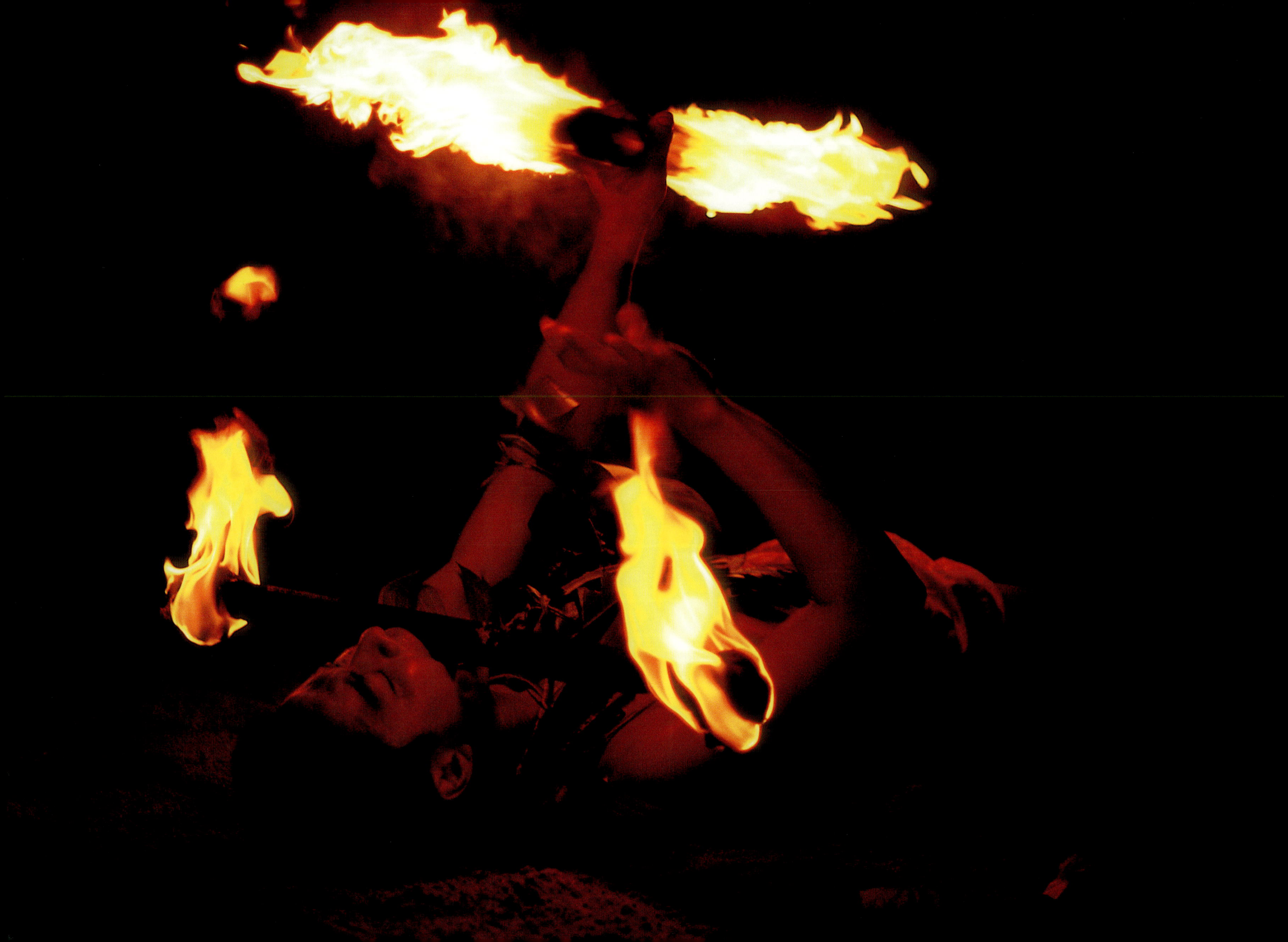

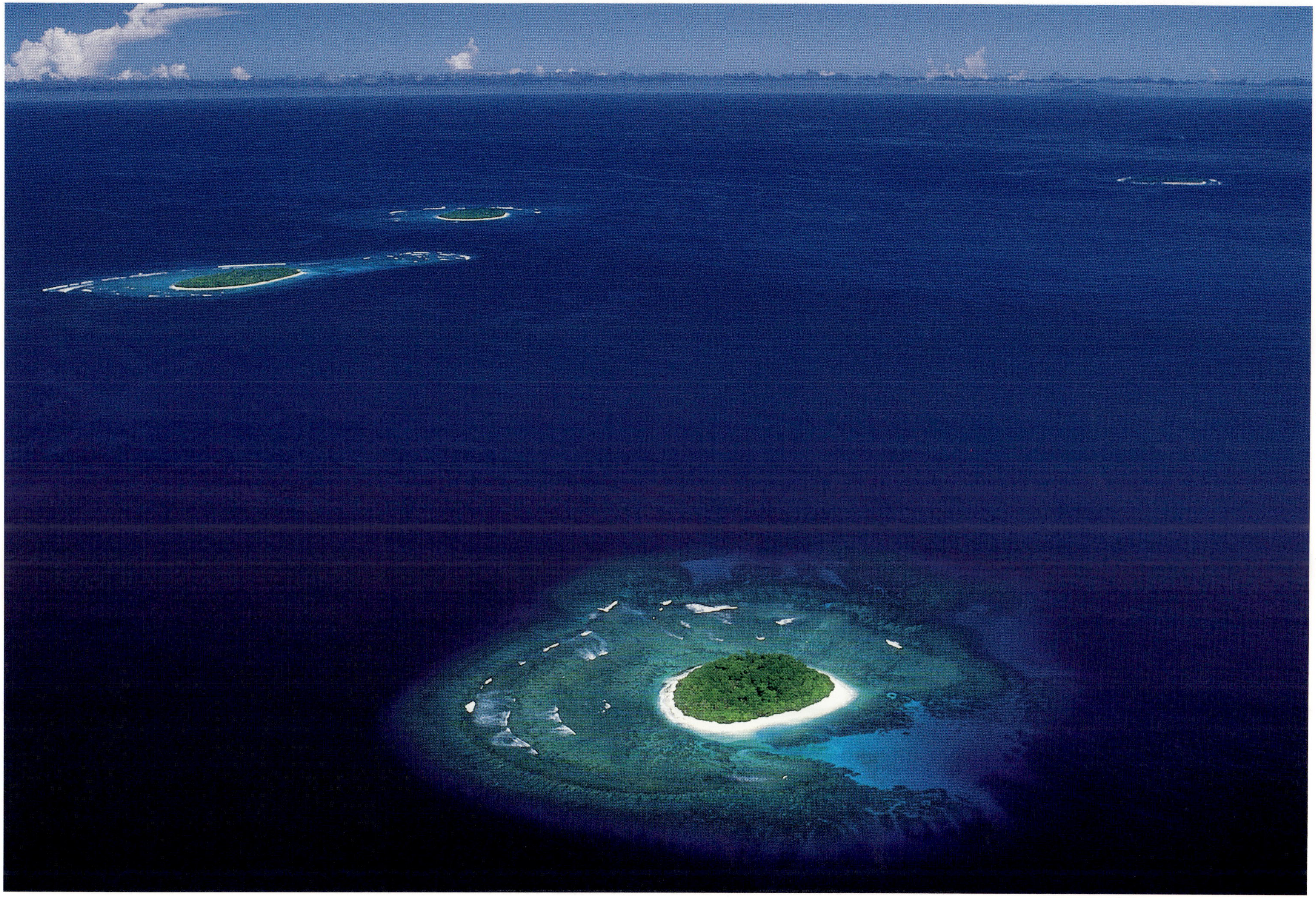

[LEFT] *fire dancer,* tongatapu

motus (small islands), vava'u group

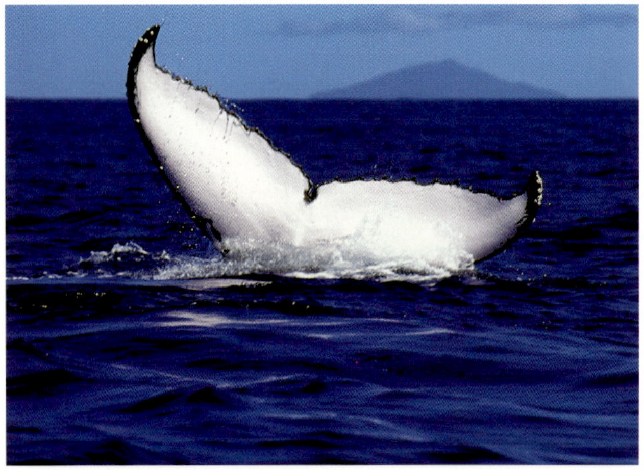

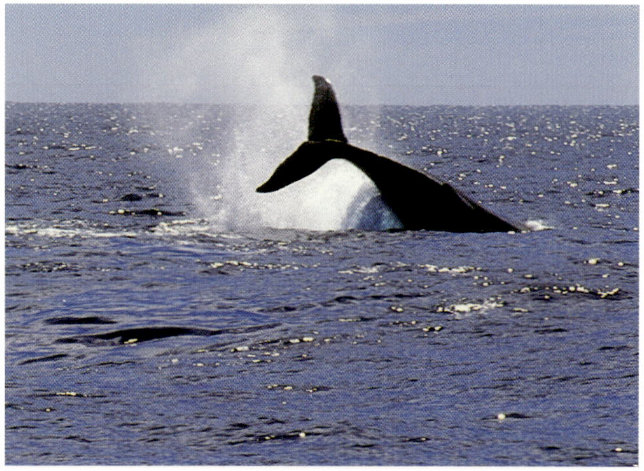

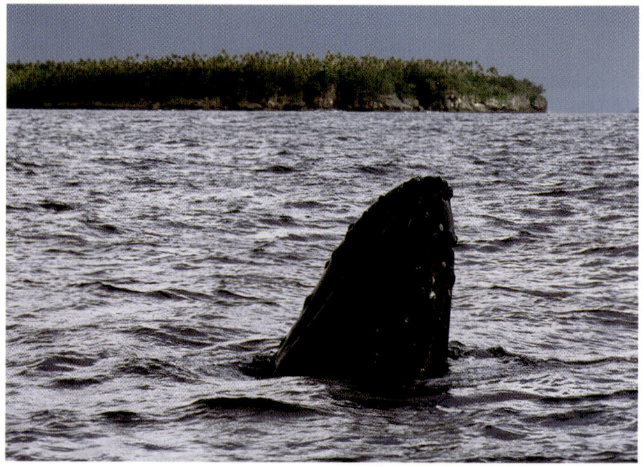

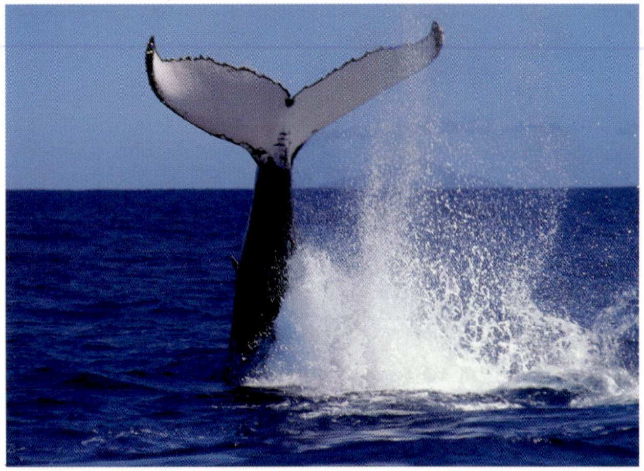

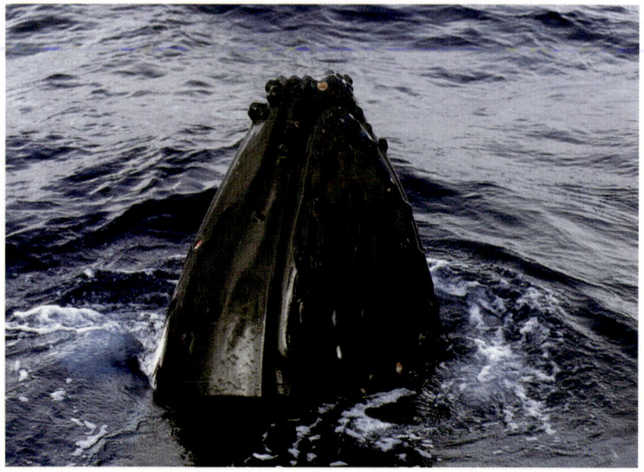

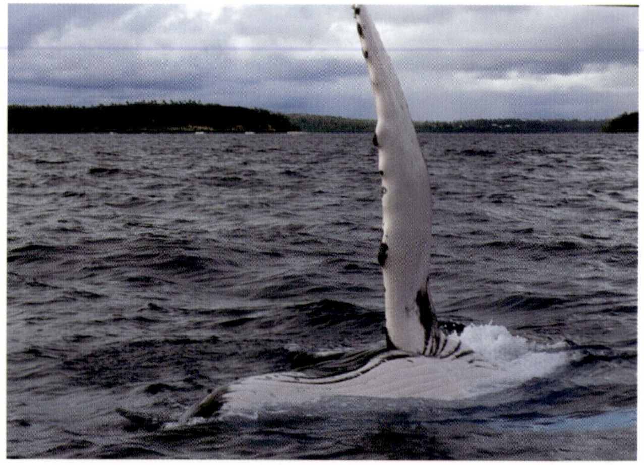

humpback whales migrate from antarctica to vava'u where they mate and calf during the winter

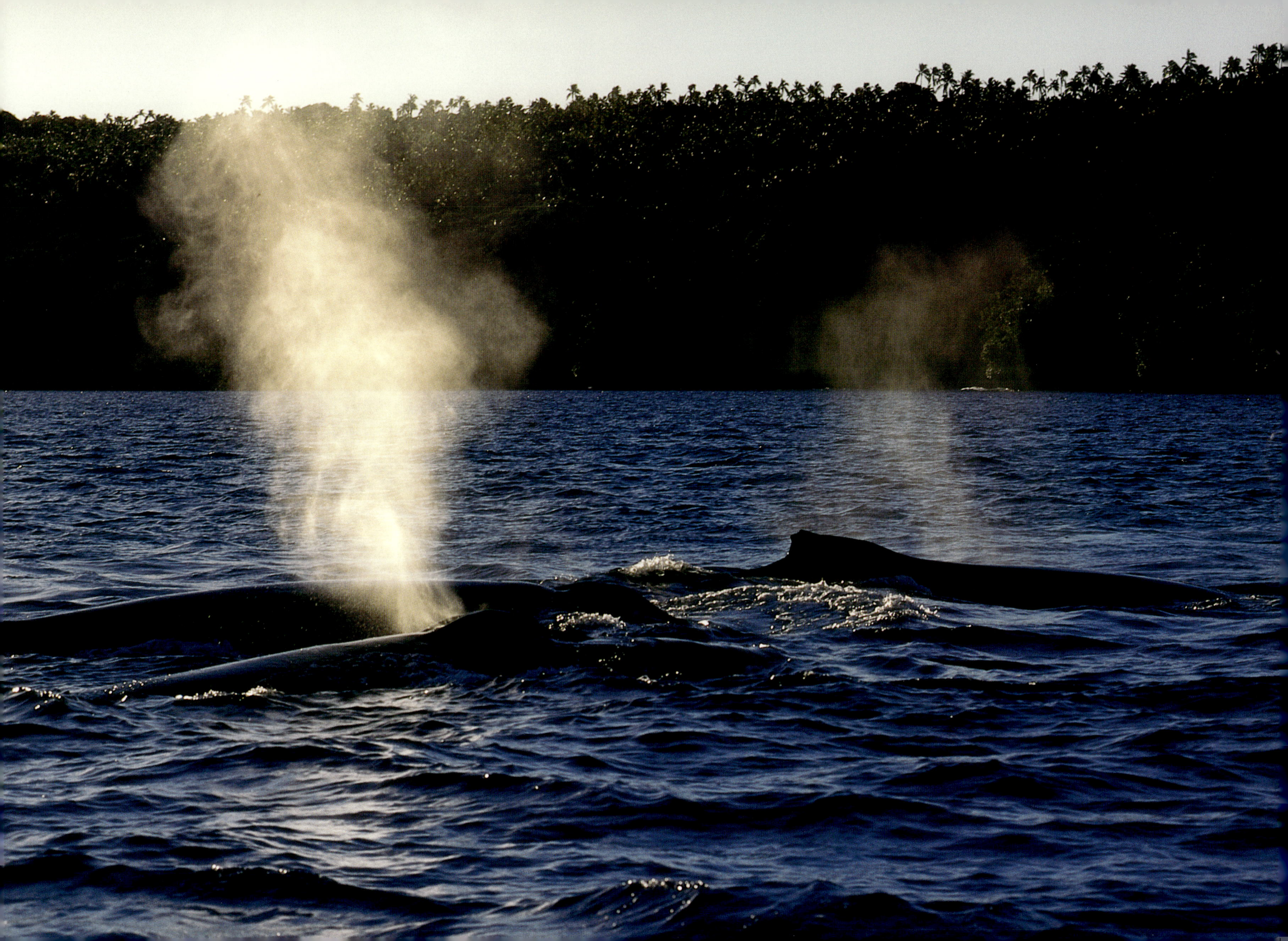

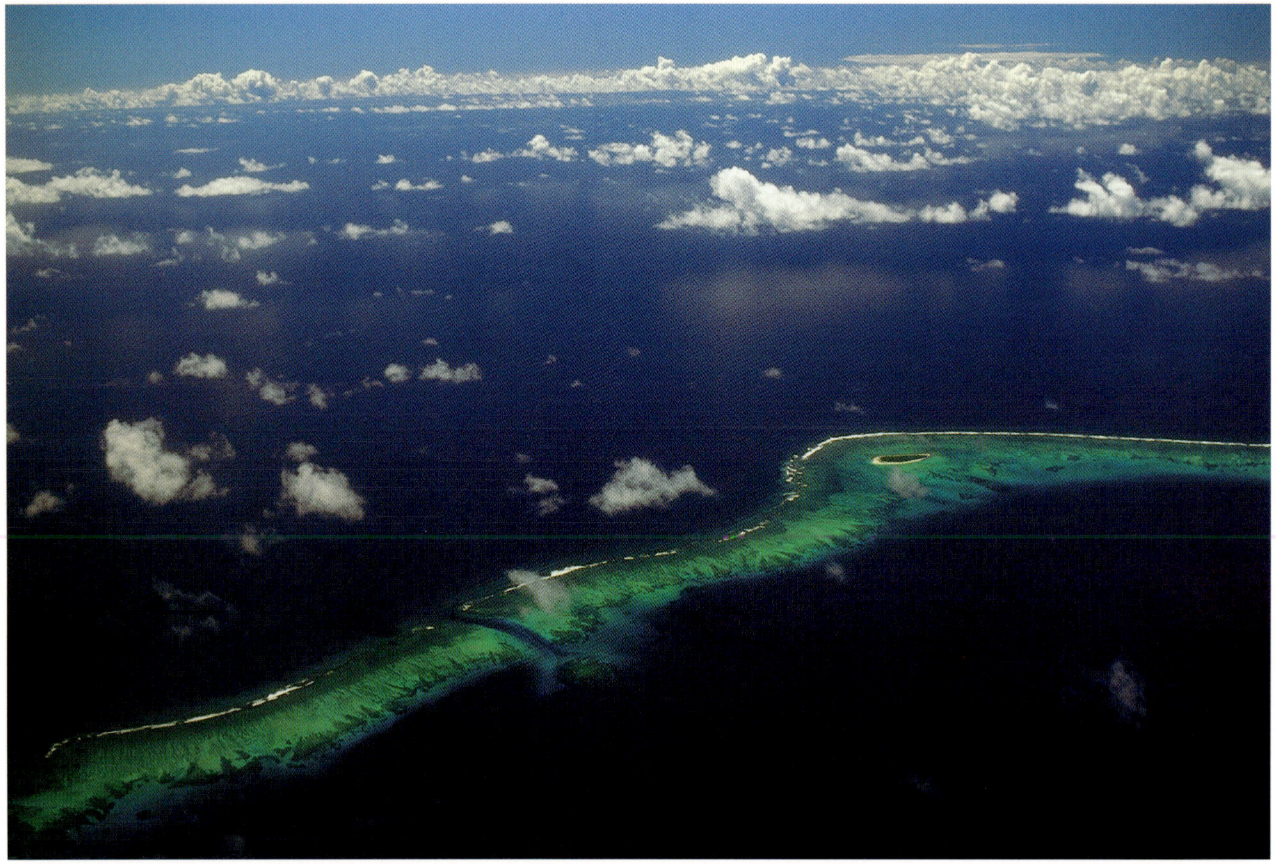

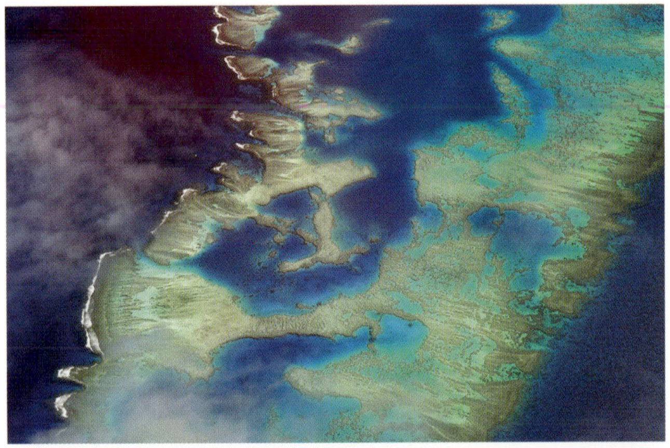

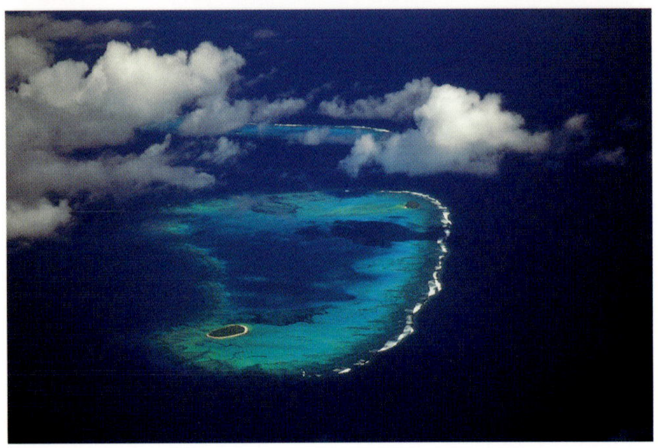

islands and coral reefs in the ha'apai group

[RIGHT] *fafa island across 'the narrows' from nuku'alofa*

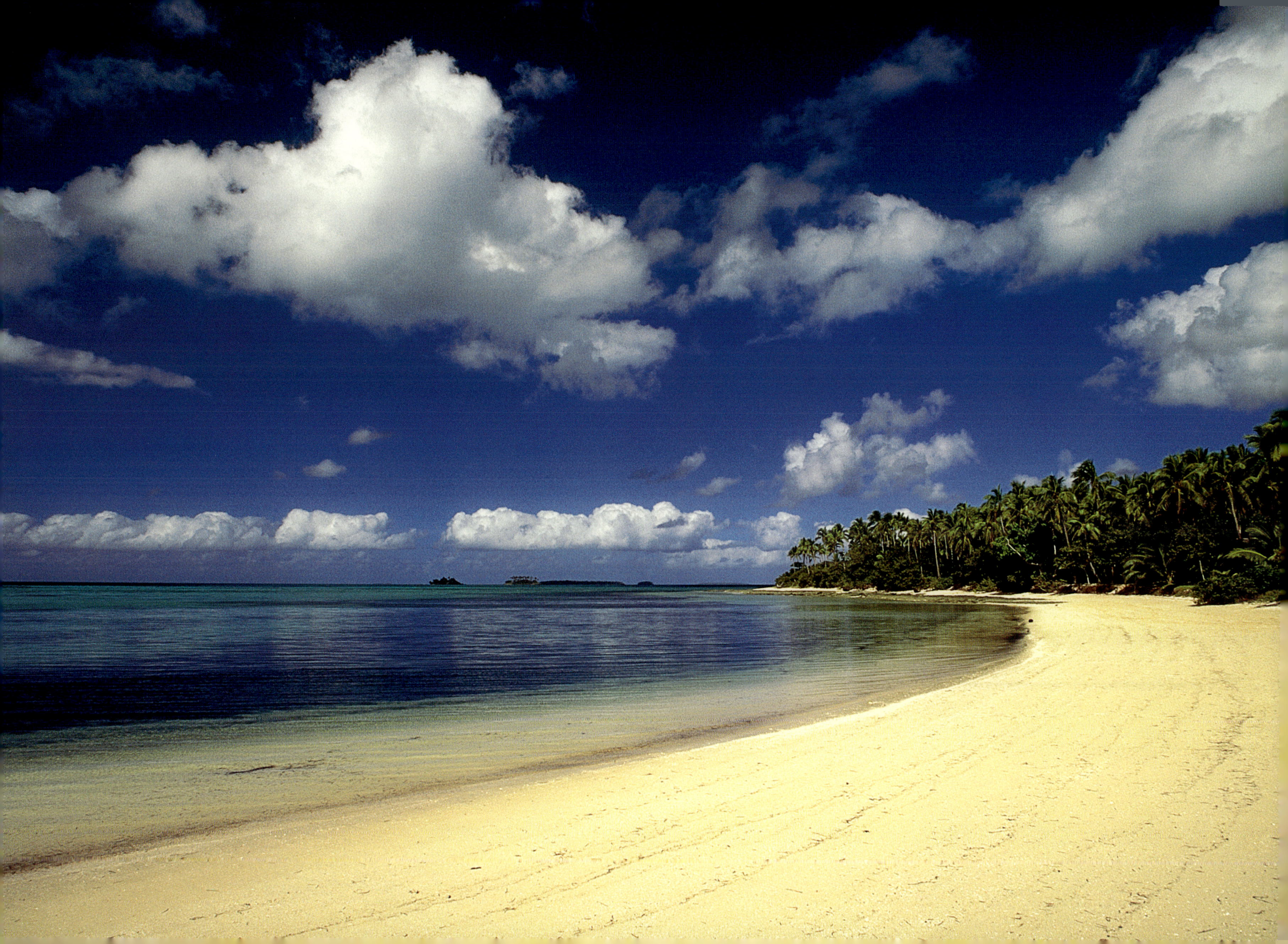

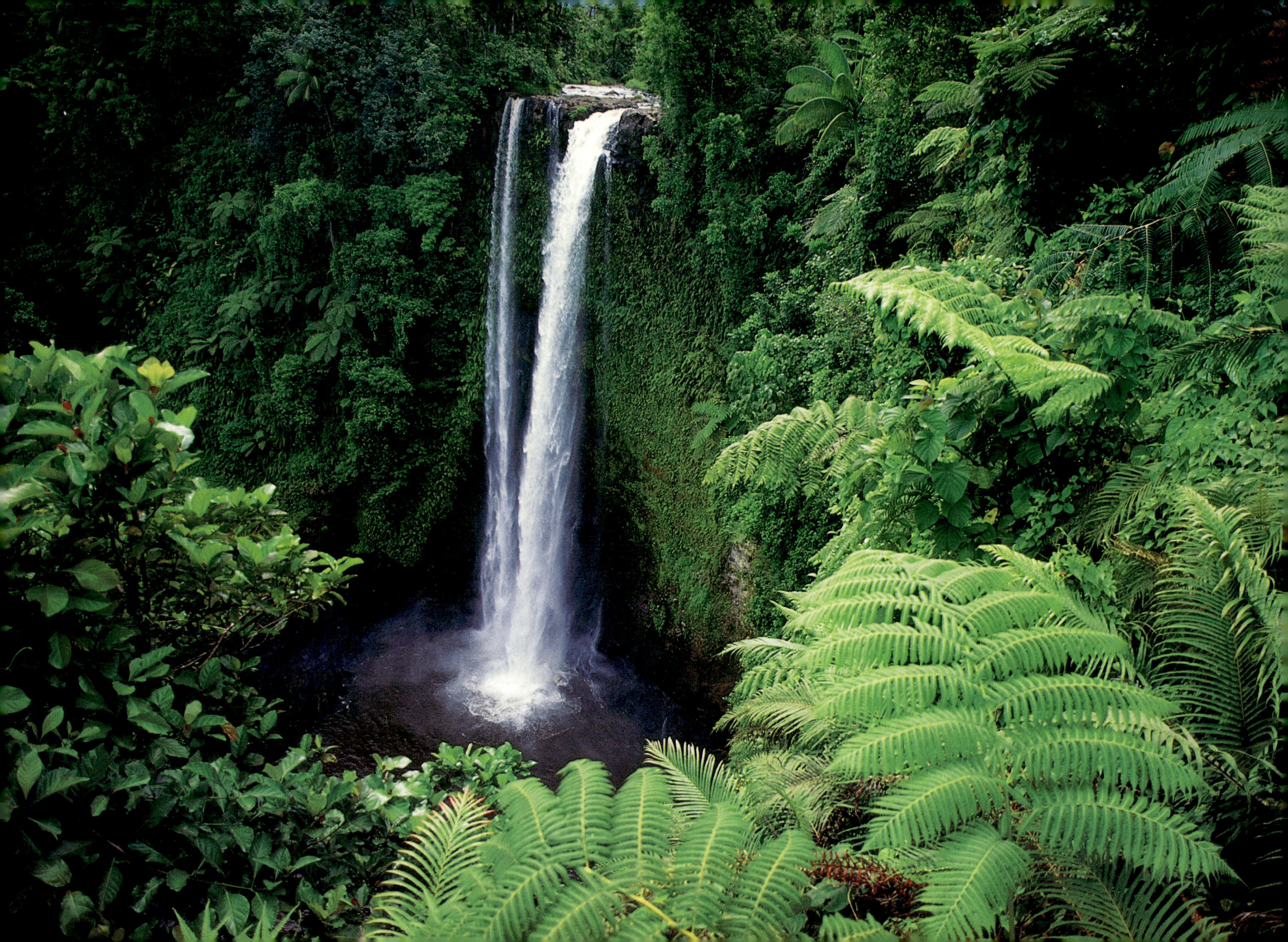

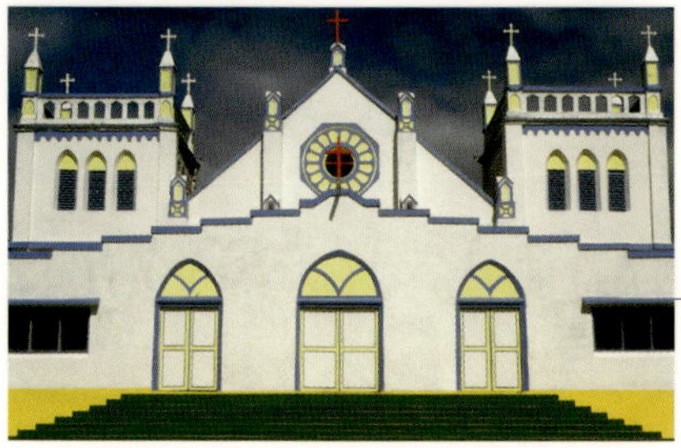

Samoa

KNOWN AS THE 'CRADLE OF POLYNESIA', it was from Samoa, at about the time of Christ, that the Polynesians embarked on their great voyages of exploration and colonisation of the Marquesas, Society Islands and the rest of eastern Polynesia as well as Hawai'i and New Zealand.

Fa'a Samoa - 'the Samoan Way'- remains very much alive and well. The Matai (Chiefs) and the Aiga (extended families) still continue to play crucial roles in society. This reinforces a feeling that this is the spiritual and cultural heart of Polynesia.

Samoa consists of 2 groups of islands, Samoa (formerly known as Western Samoa) and American Samoa, an unincorporated territory of the USA. Although politically separate, the two groups have the same culture and traditions and also speak the same language. Most of the Samoan group consists of high volcanic islands, mountainous with lush vegetation and rocky shorelines and many bays and beautiful beaches. The two largest islands of Upolu and Savai'i comprise the bulk of the land area. Their coastlines are dotted with neat picturesque villages with traditional Samoan houses (fales) their sides open to the cooling breezes. The roadsides are lined with freshly painted white boulders and there is at least one church in a prominent position in each village.

Apia, the capital of Samoa, is one of the classic old South Sea towns with colonial style timber buildings lining the waterfront. Robert Louis Stevenson spent the last years of his life here. His presence can still be felt all over town from the first building he occupied when he arrived in 1889 which is now a popular restaurant on the main Beach Street, to his home 'Vailima' which is a museum and also the name of the local beer. One of the main hotels is named 'The Tusitala', Samoan for 'teller of tales'.

Stevenson was held in deep affection by the Samoans and when he died they hacked a 'Road of the Loving Hearts' through the jungle up the side of Mount Vaeo, where they buried him near the summit overlooking the Samoa he so loved.

The first European to sight Samoa was the Dutchman Jacob Roggeveen in 1722. He was followed by whalers and John Williams from the London Missionary Society. German copra plantations were established in the 1850's.

A growing rivalry between the colonial powers Britain, Germany and the USA led to inter-tribal warfare when they backed different Samoan factions. Eventually Germany gained Samoa as a colony until New Zealand took over after World War One. Independent Samoa was the first Pacific Island to gain independence in 1962.

[LEFT] *fuipisia falls,* upolu [ABOVE] *vaiusu catholic church,* apia

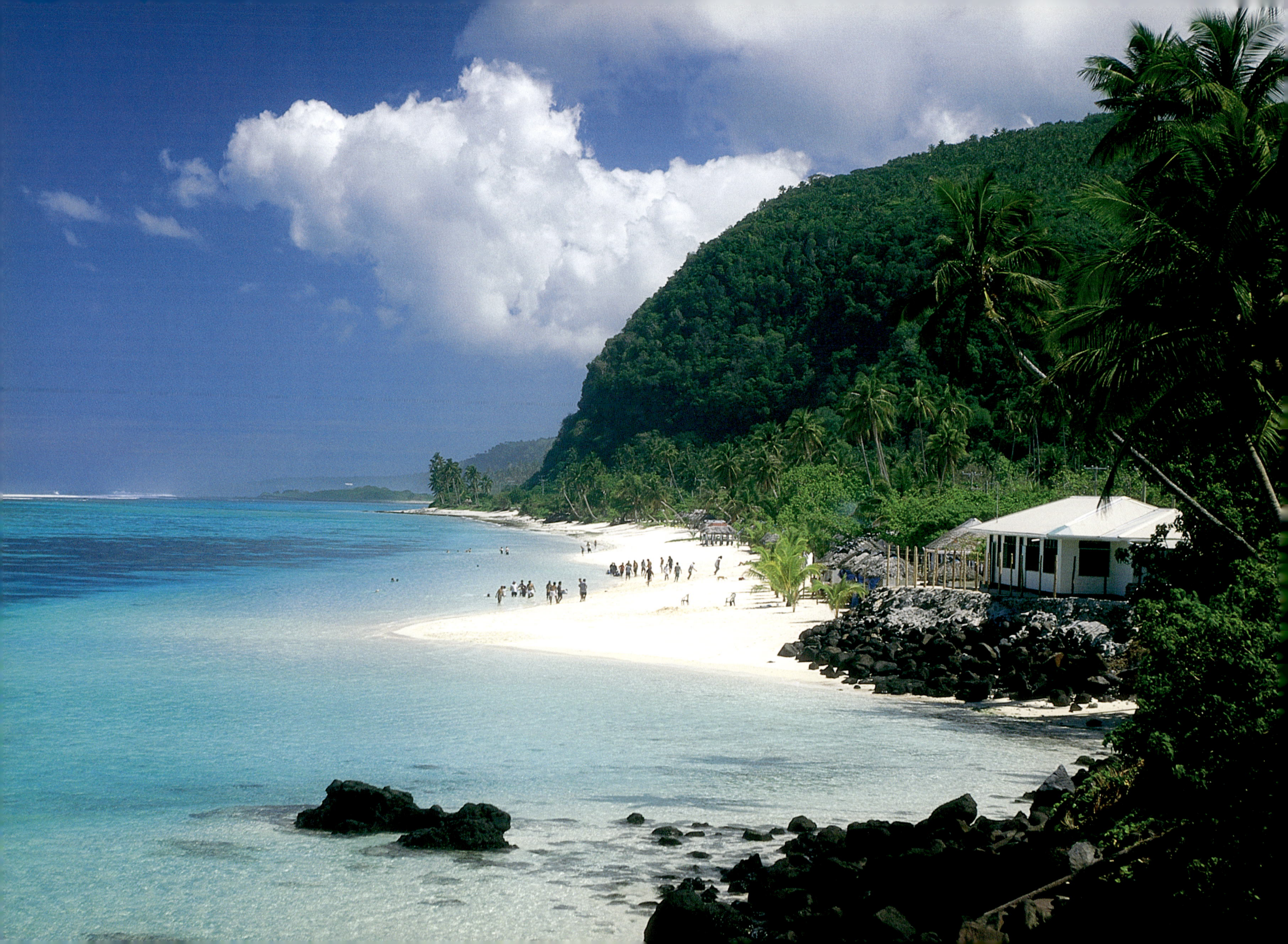

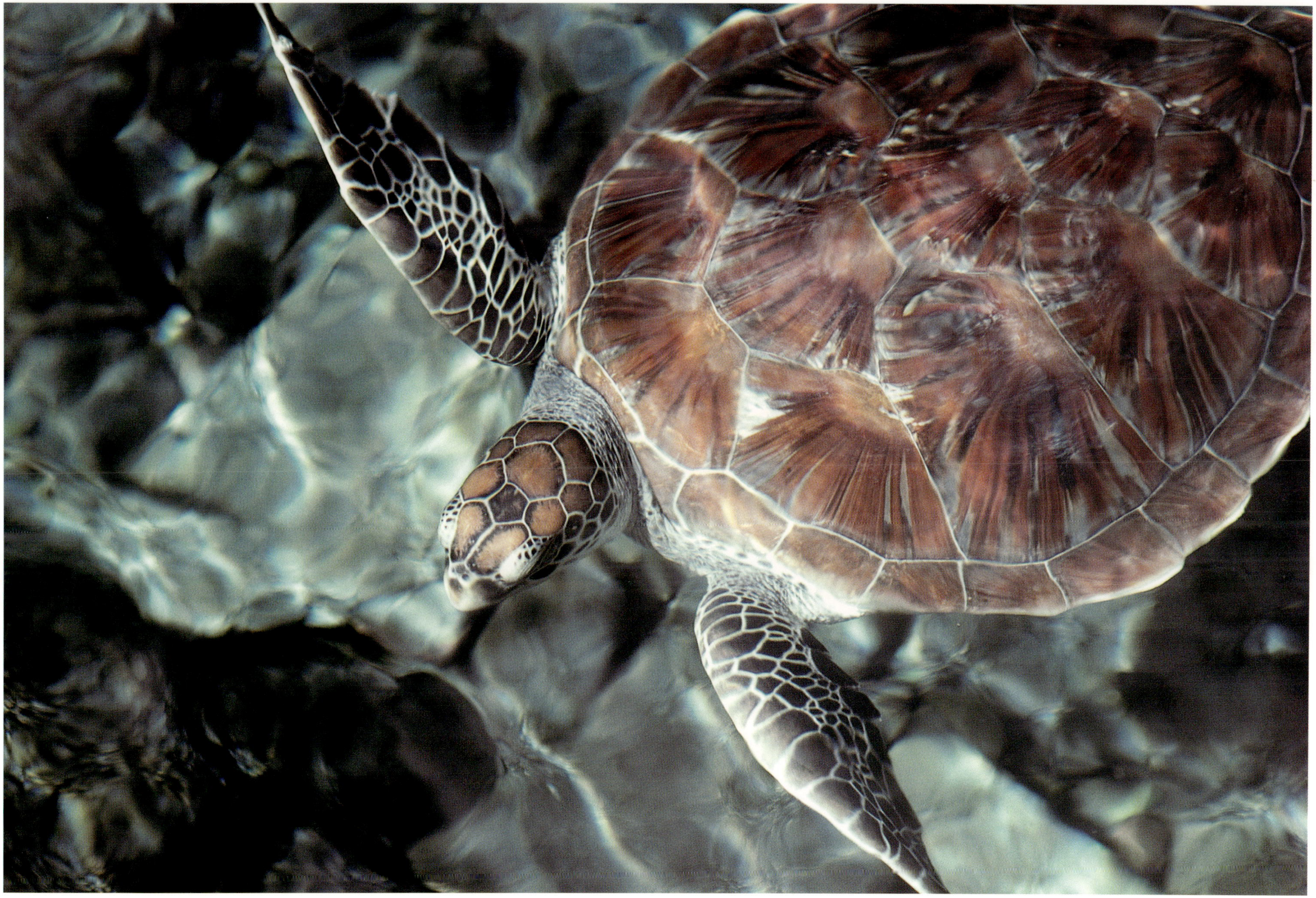

[LEFT] *lalomanu beach*, upolu

green turtle, tidal pool, upolu

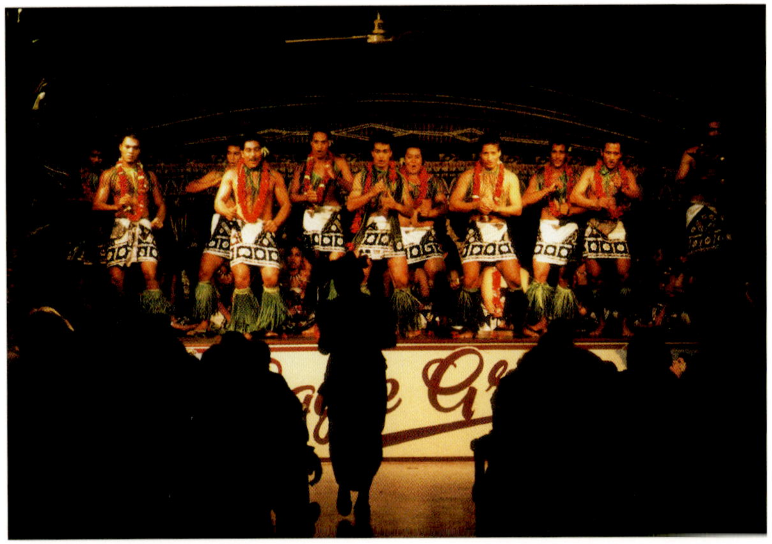

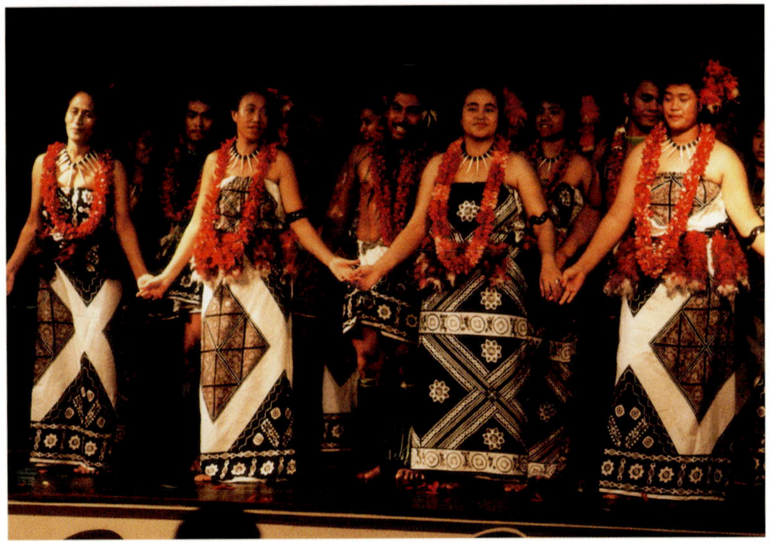

fia fia show at aggie grey's hotel, apia, upolu

[RIGHT] *ofu,* manua islands, american samoa

[FAR RIGHT] *apia market,* upolu

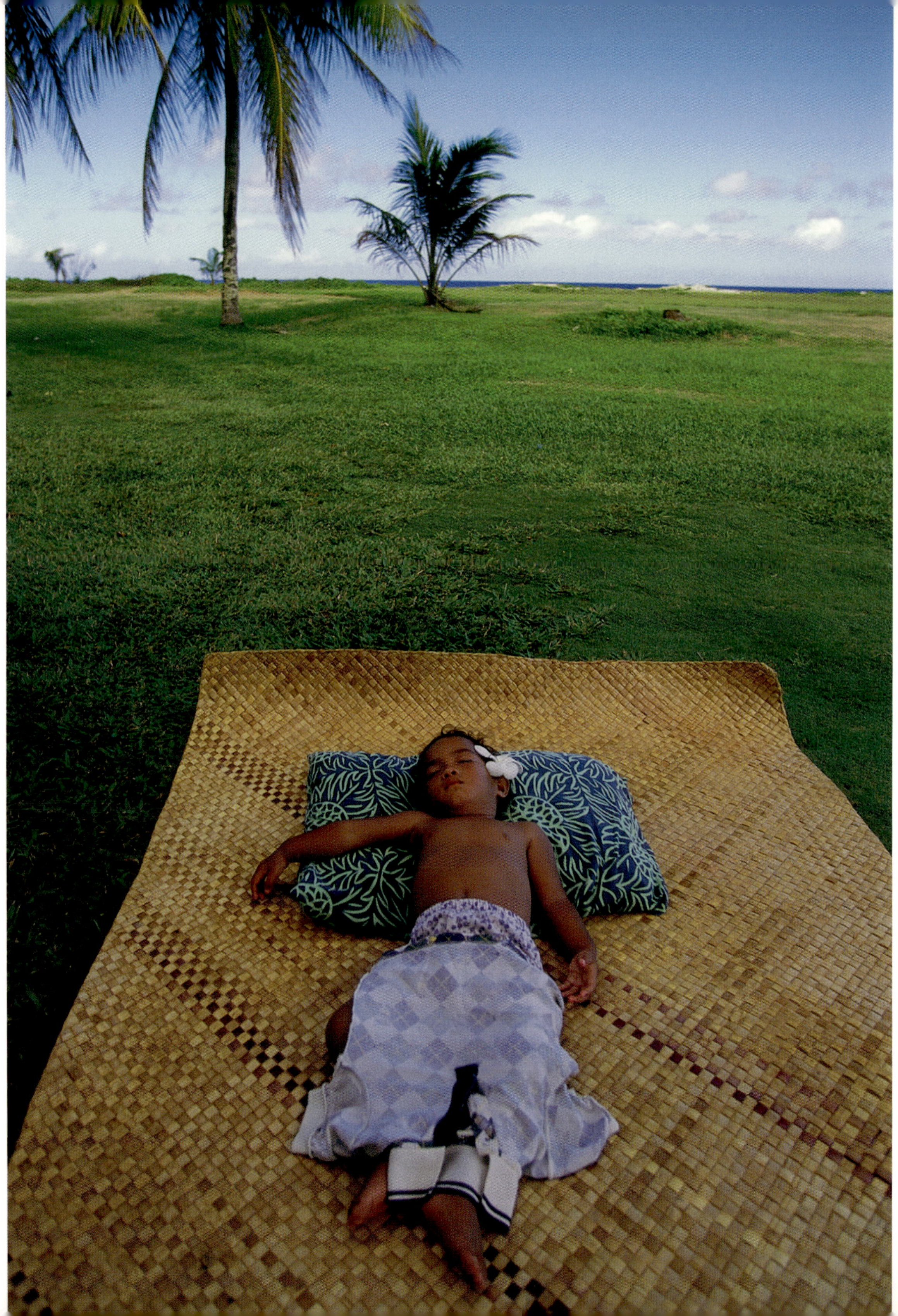

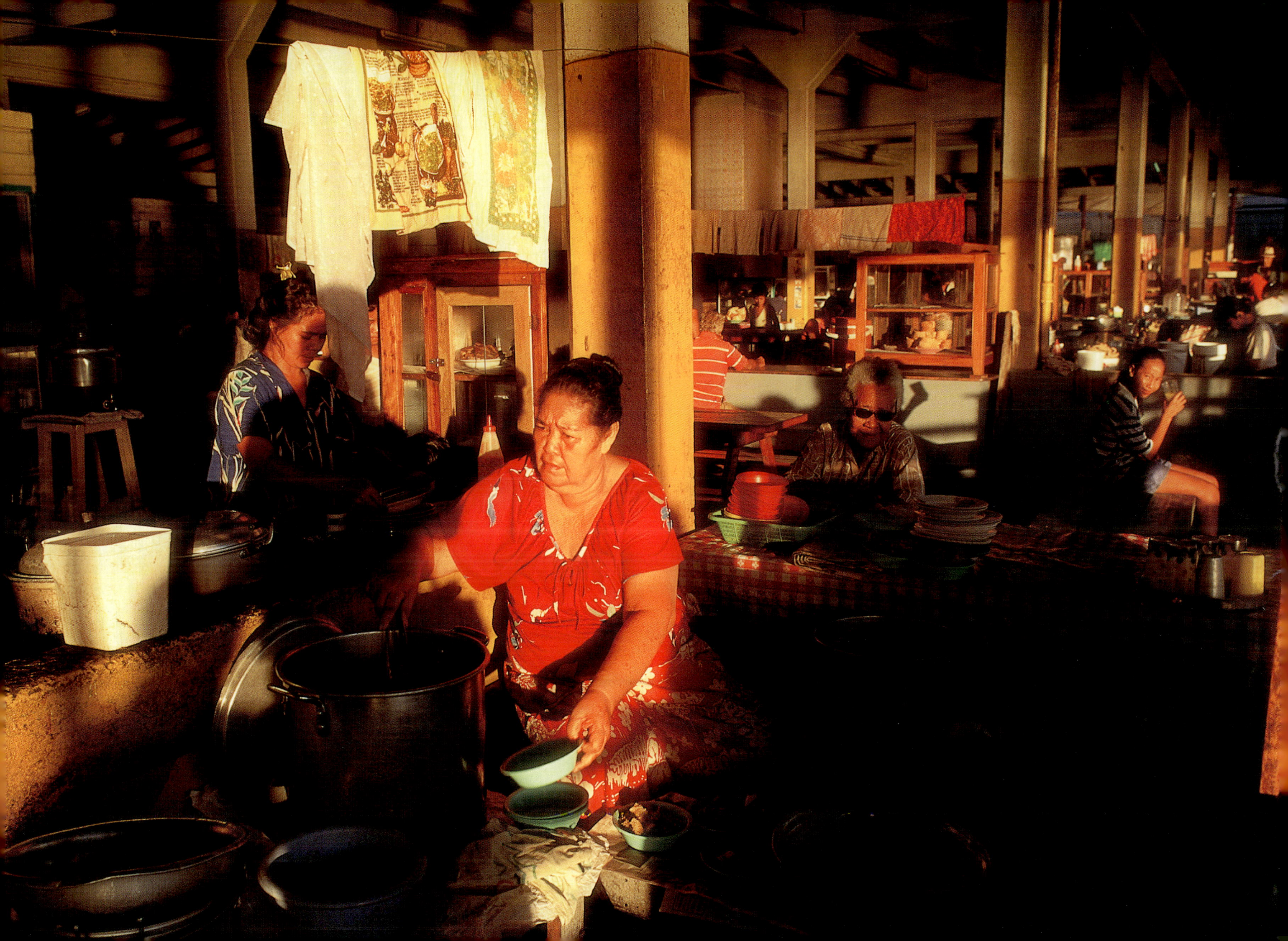

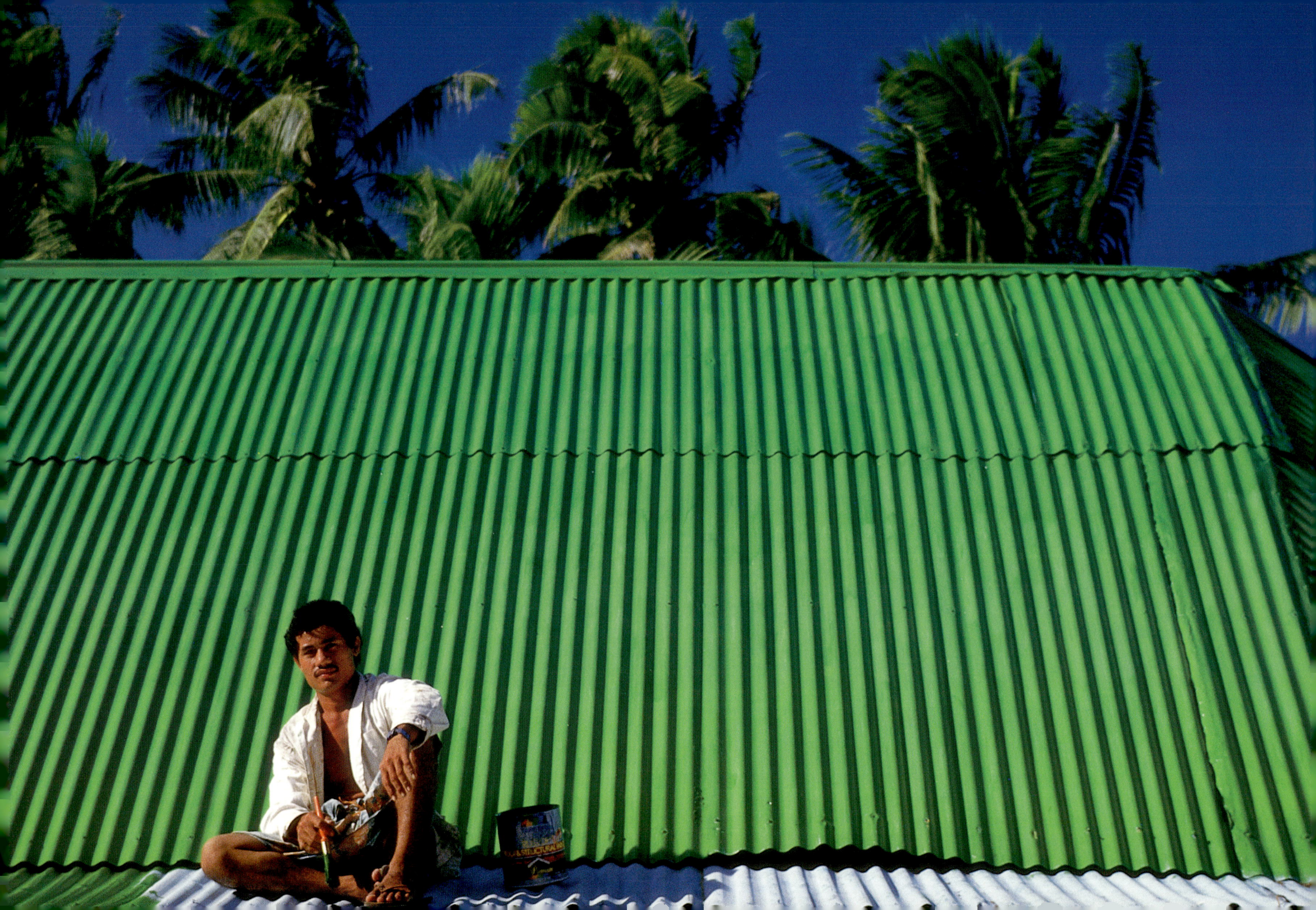

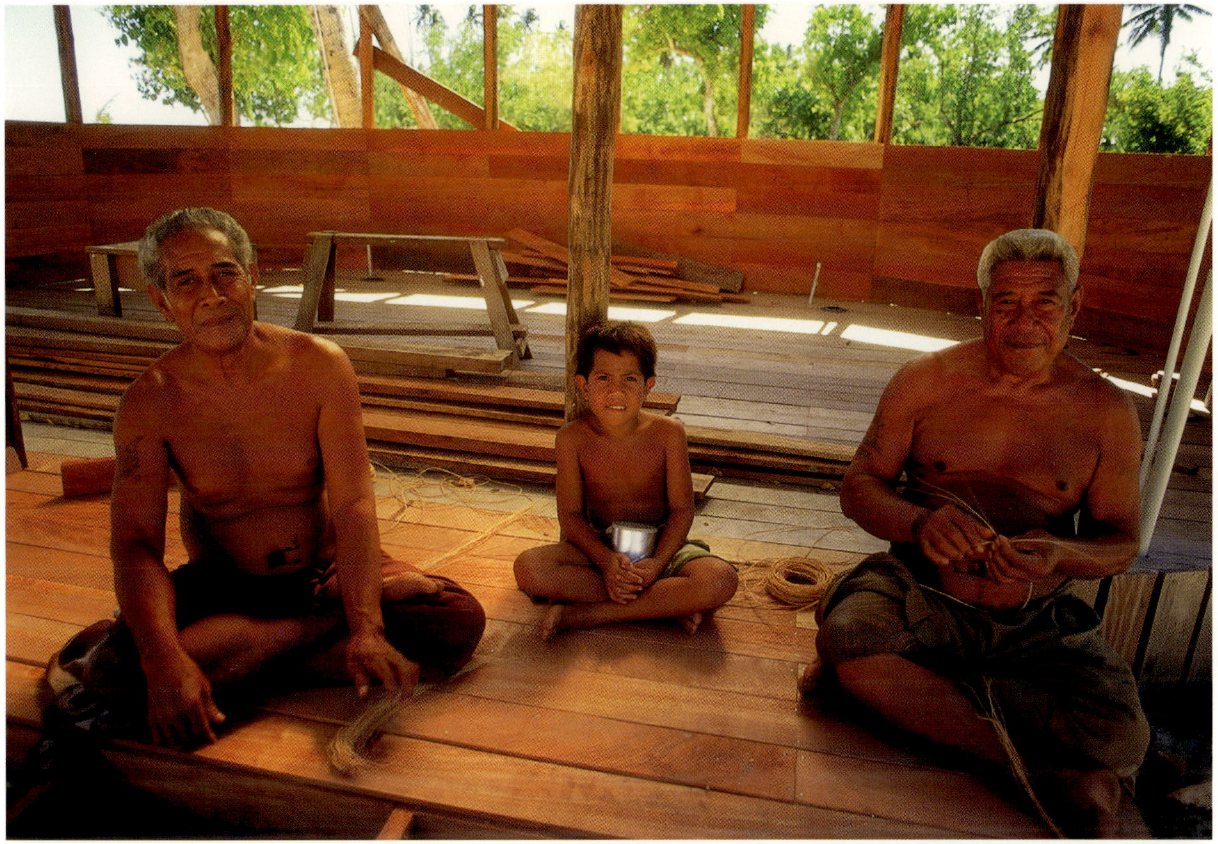

working on site at the coconuts beach club, maninoa, south upolu

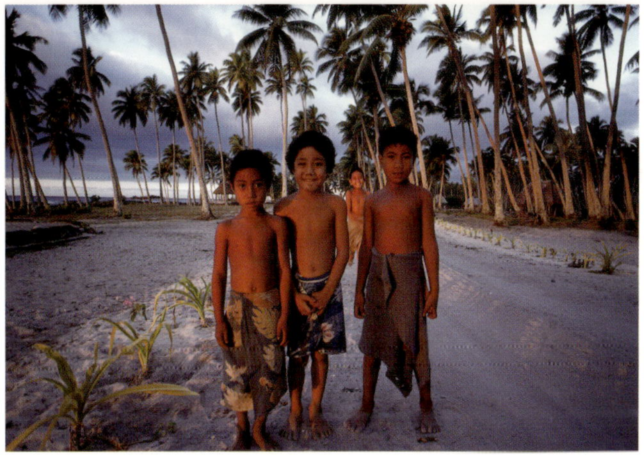

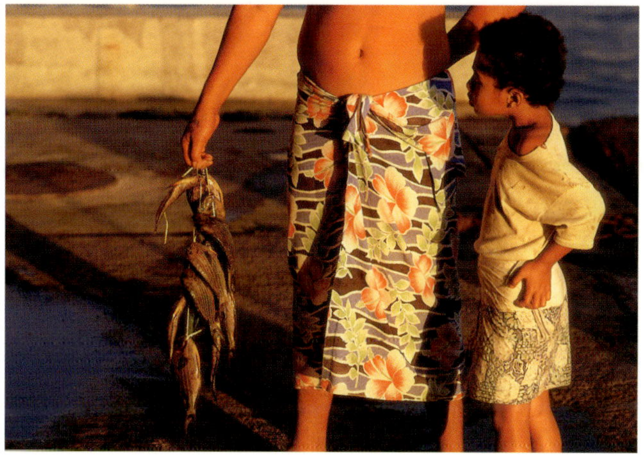

[**LEFT**] *house painter, south coast,* upolu

[**ABOVE RIGHT**] *west coast village,* savai'i [**ABOVE FAR RIGHT**] *apia fish market,* upolu

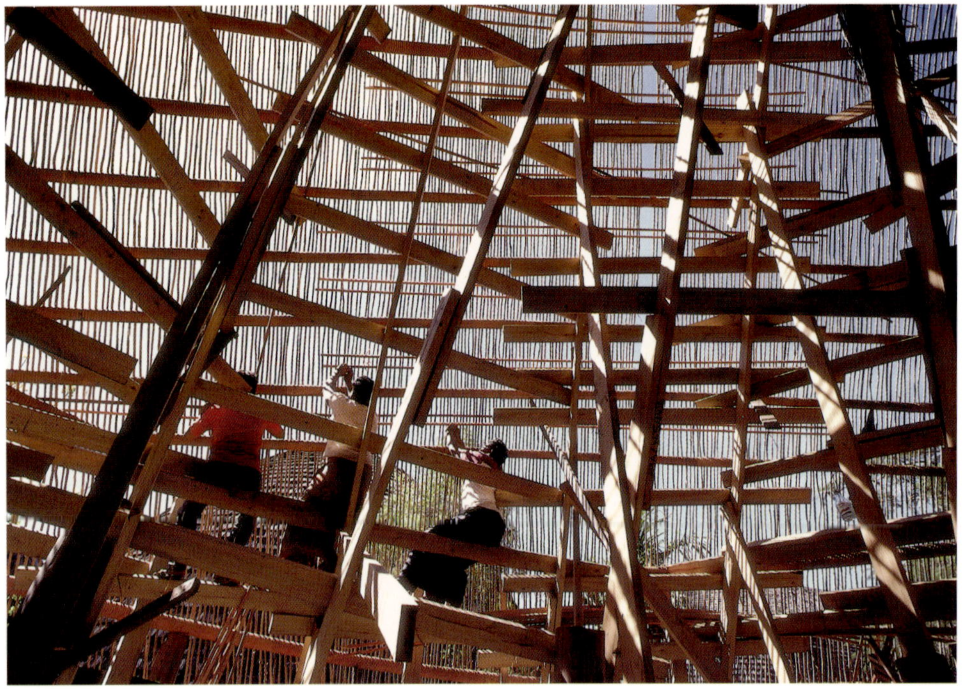

construction of a samoan fale at the tusitala hotel, apia, upolu

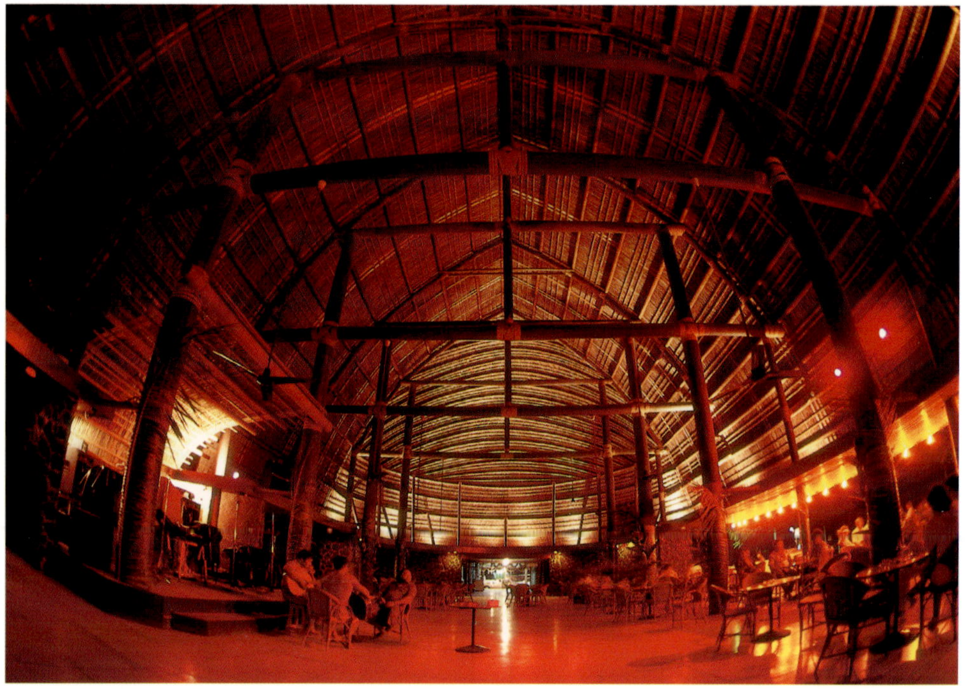

the tusitala hotel's traditional samoan fale, apia, upolu

[RIGHT] *south ofu beach,* manua islands, american samoa

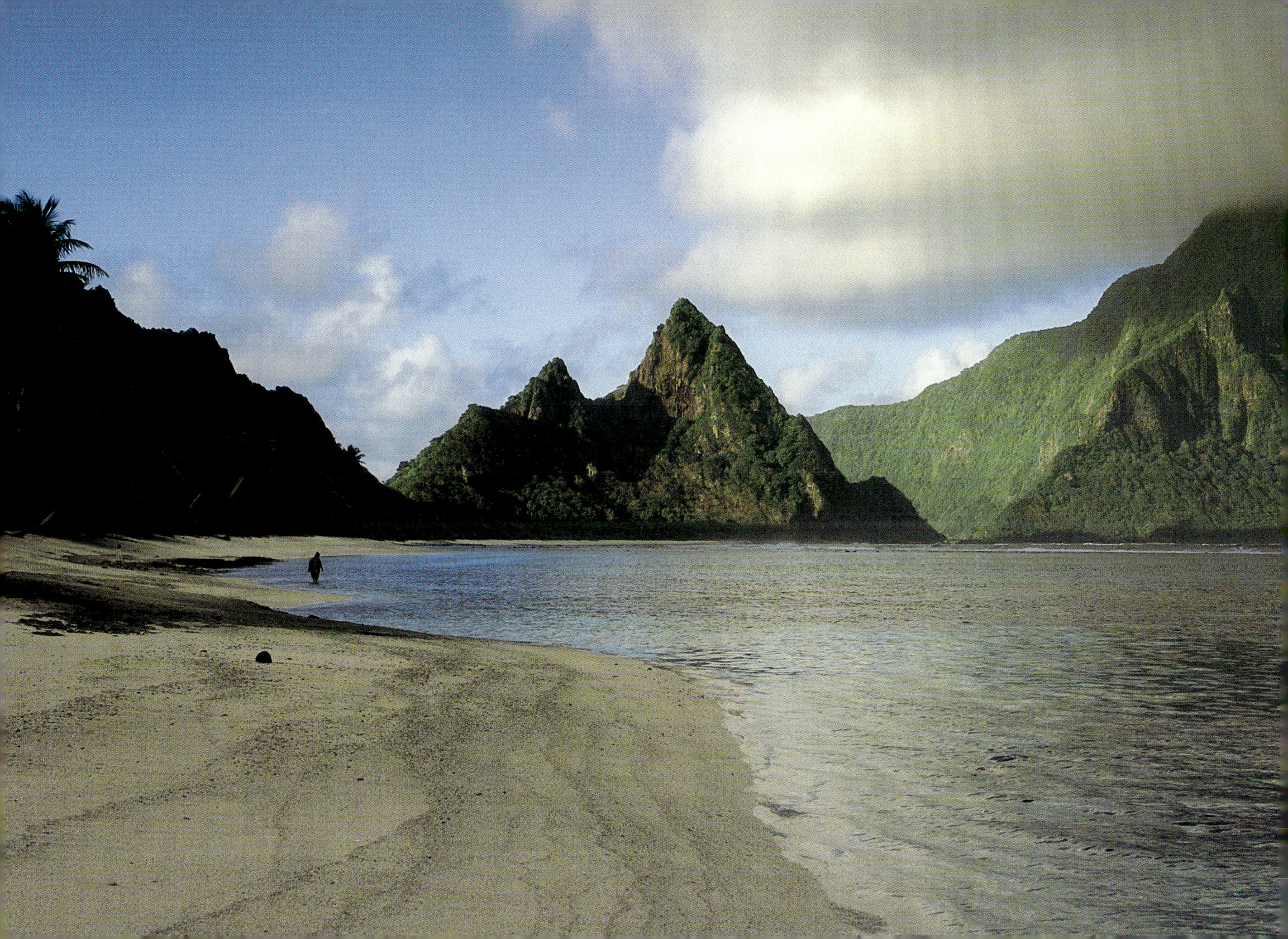

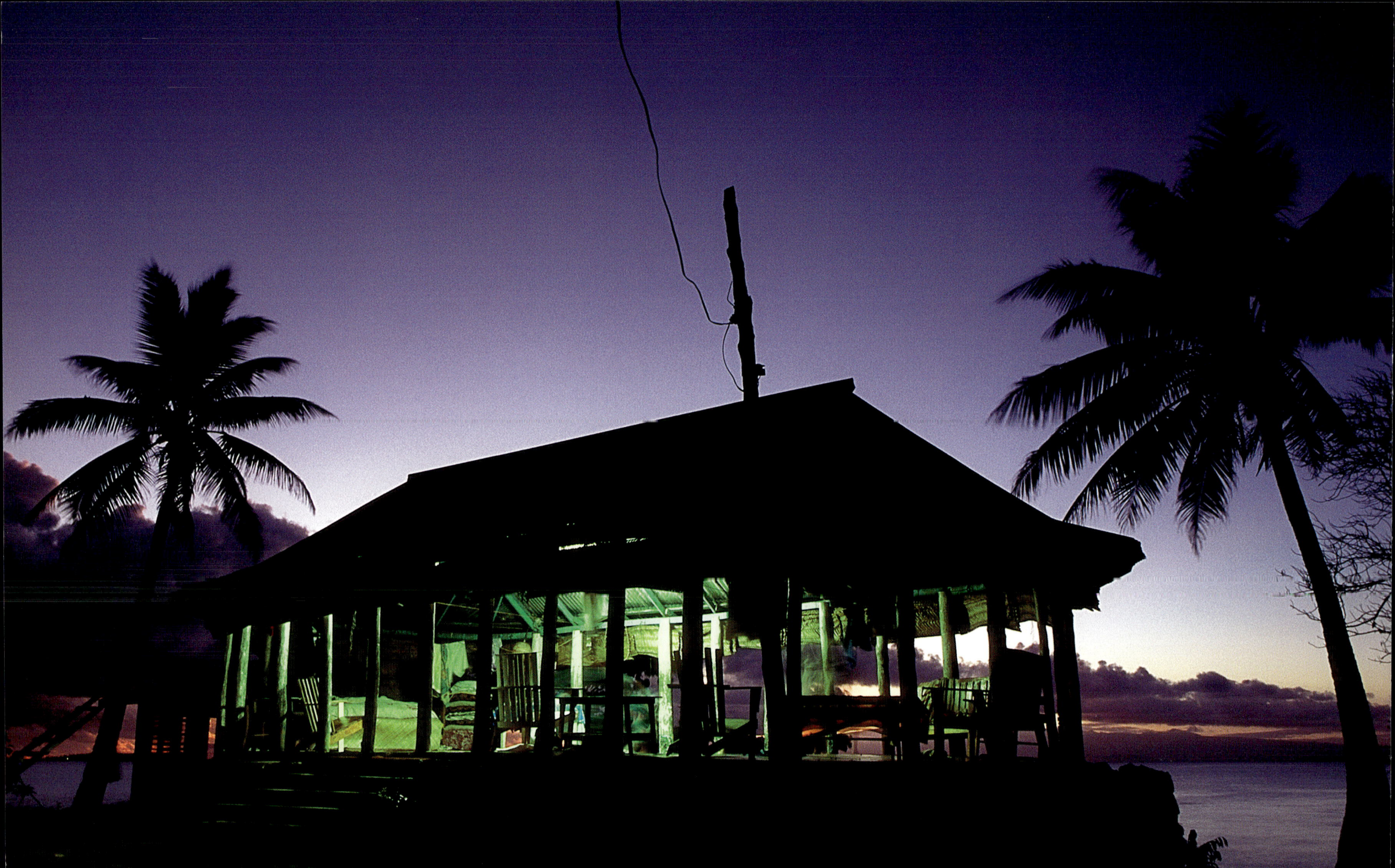

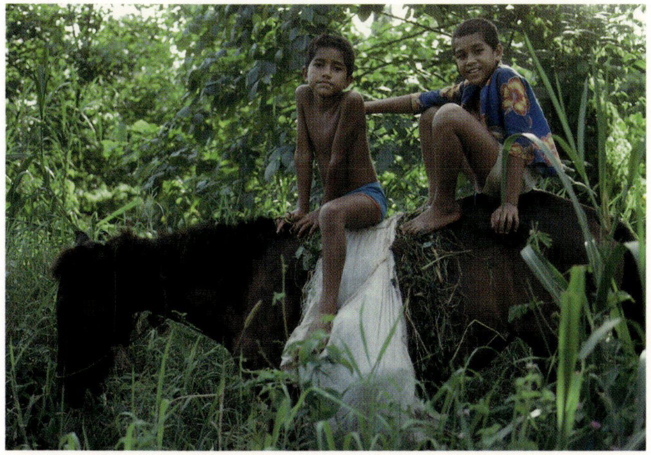

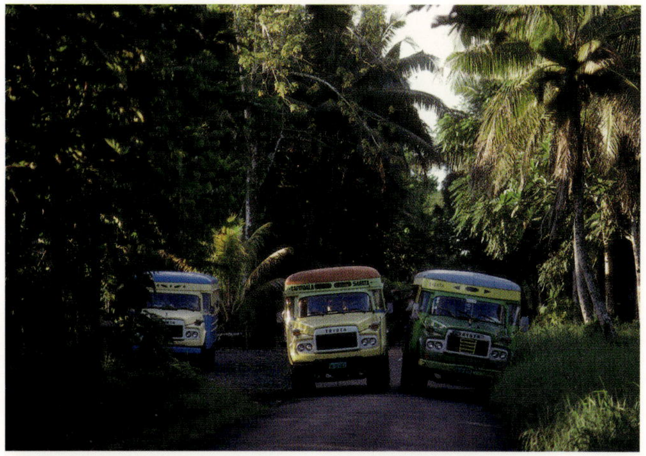

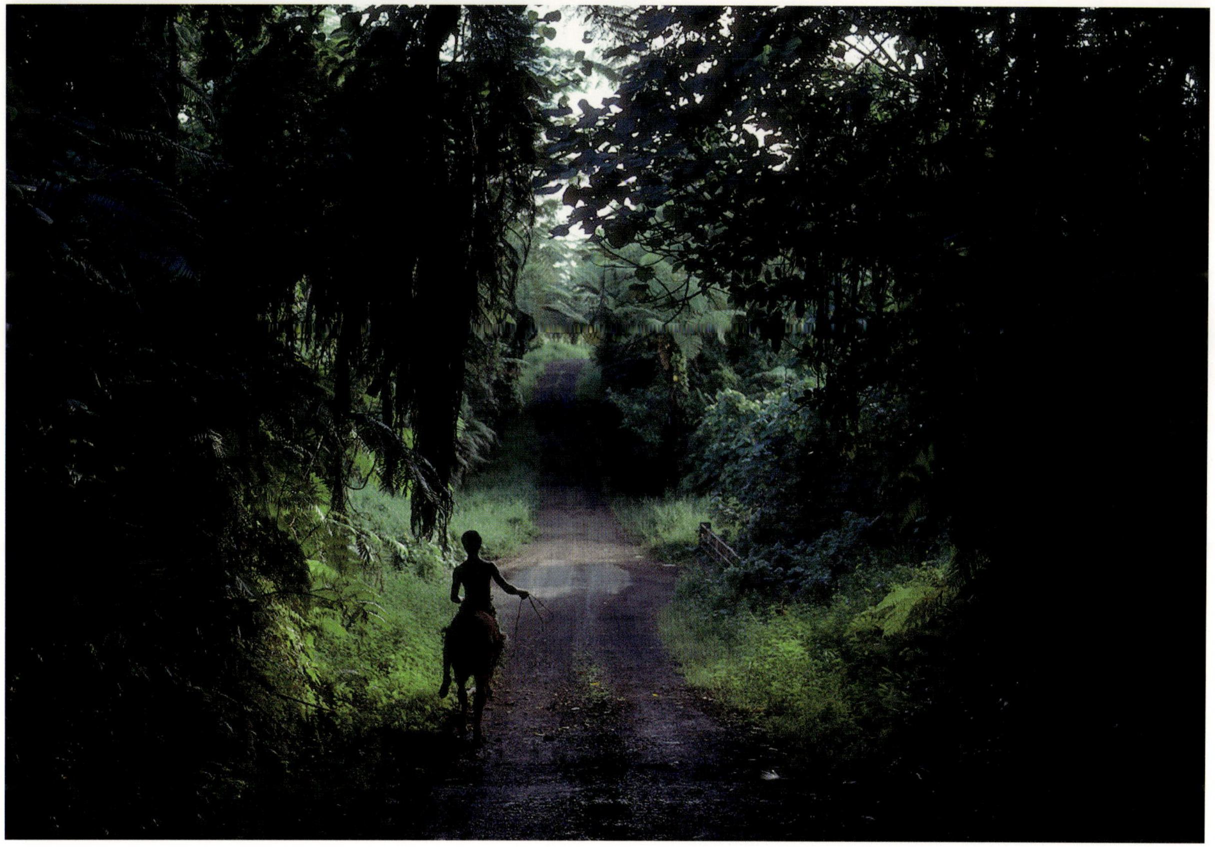

[**ABOVE**] *boys on grazing horse,* upolu

[**ABOVE RIGHT**] *samoan buses on cross island road,* upolu

[**RIGHT**] *bareback horseman on jungle road,* upolu

[**LEFT**] *samoan house on main coast road,* northwest upolu

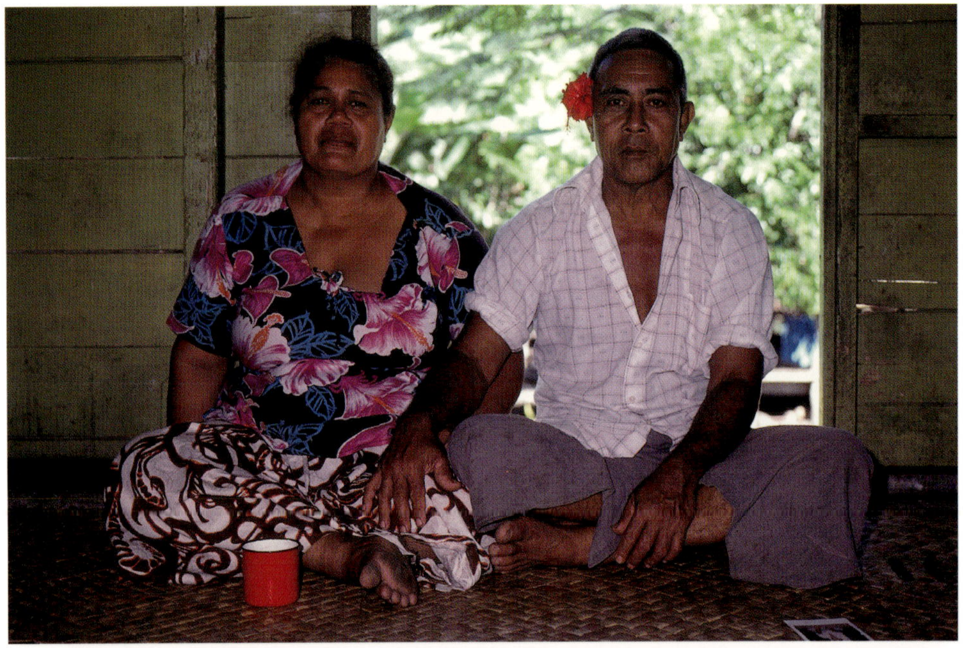

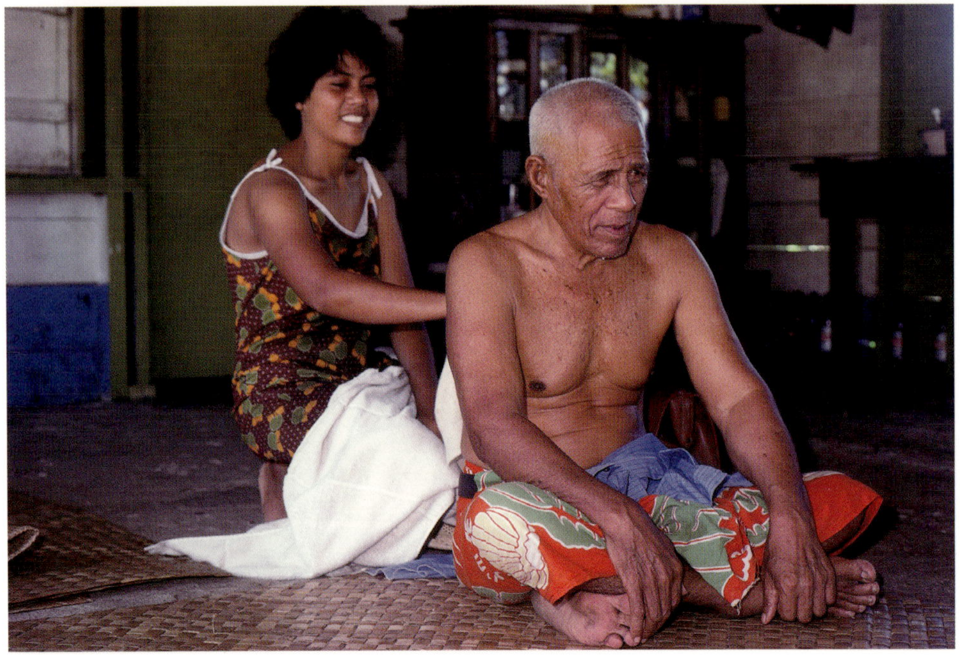

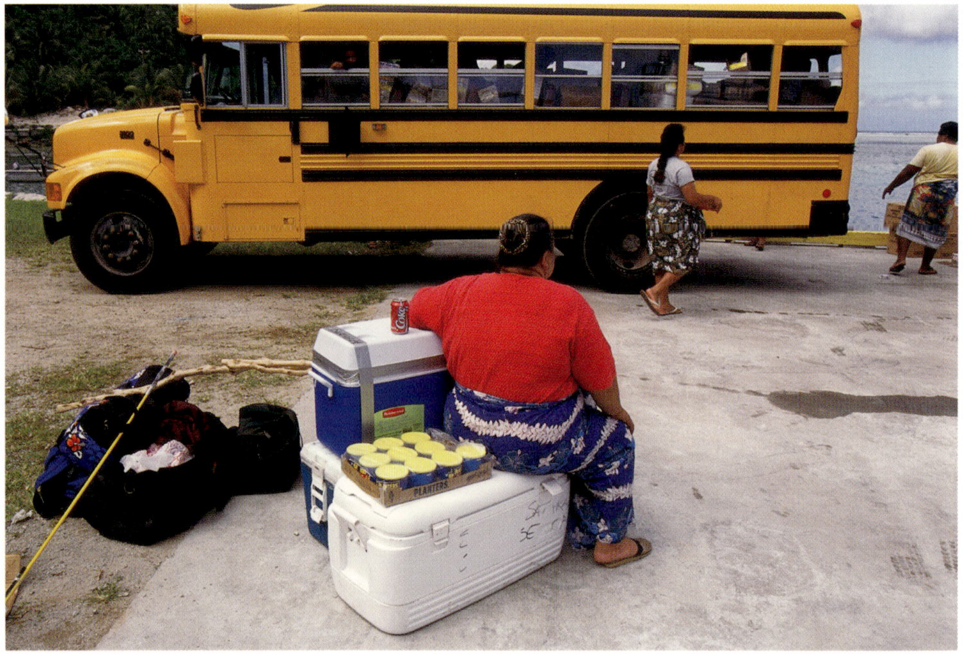

ofu wharf, manua islands

[ABOVE AND BELOW LEFT] *samoan households,* west coast savai'i

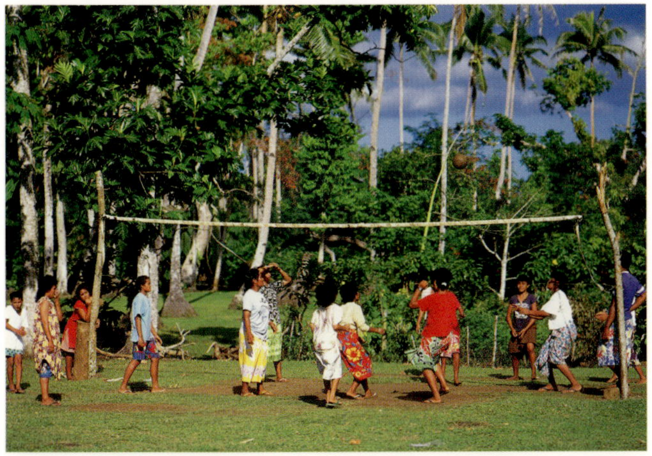

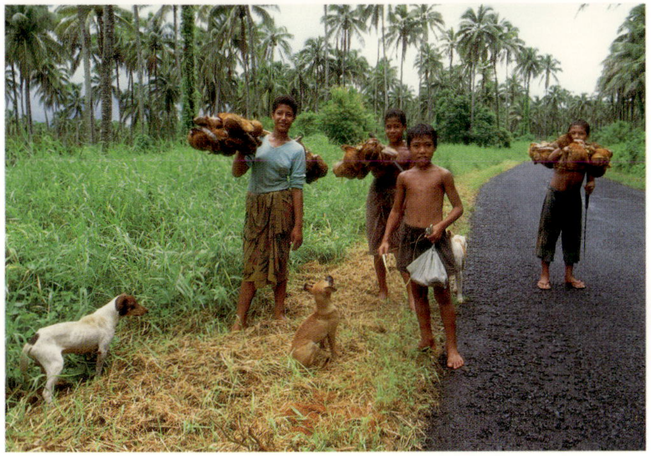

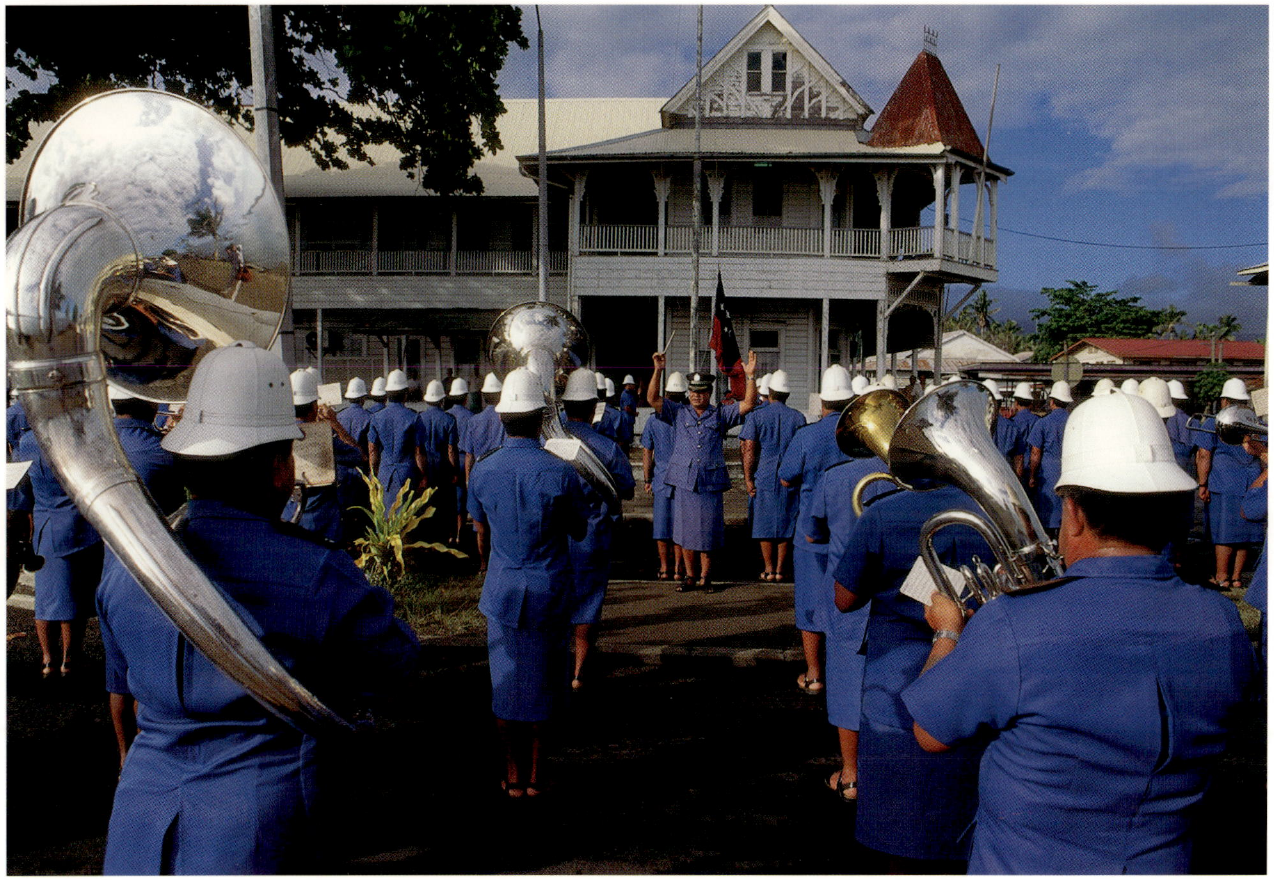

police band on beach road, apia, upolu

[**ABOVE LEFT**] *volleyball on a south coast village,* upolu [**LEFT**] *returning home with coconuts,* cross island road, upolu

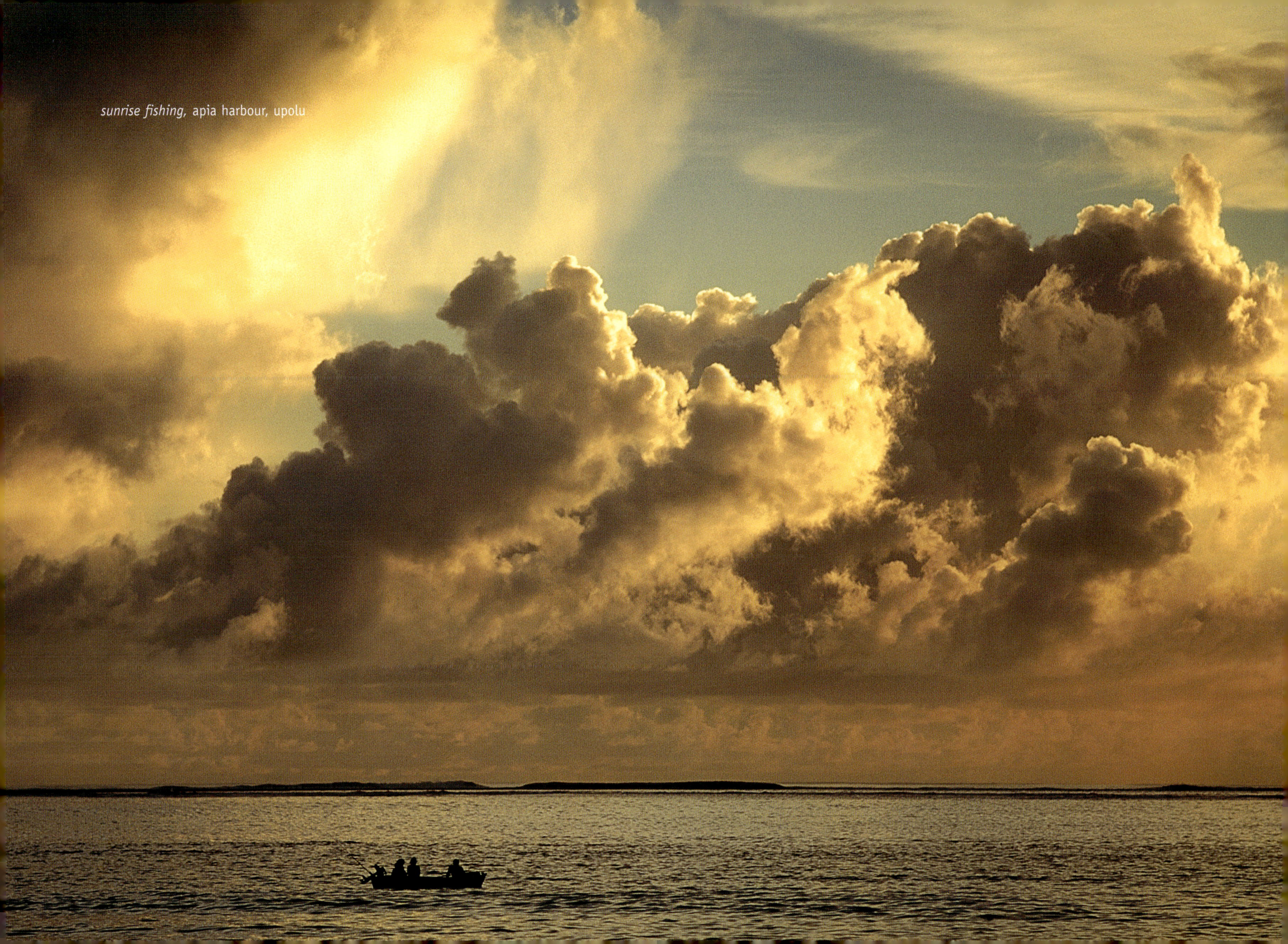
sunrise fishing, apia harbour, upolu

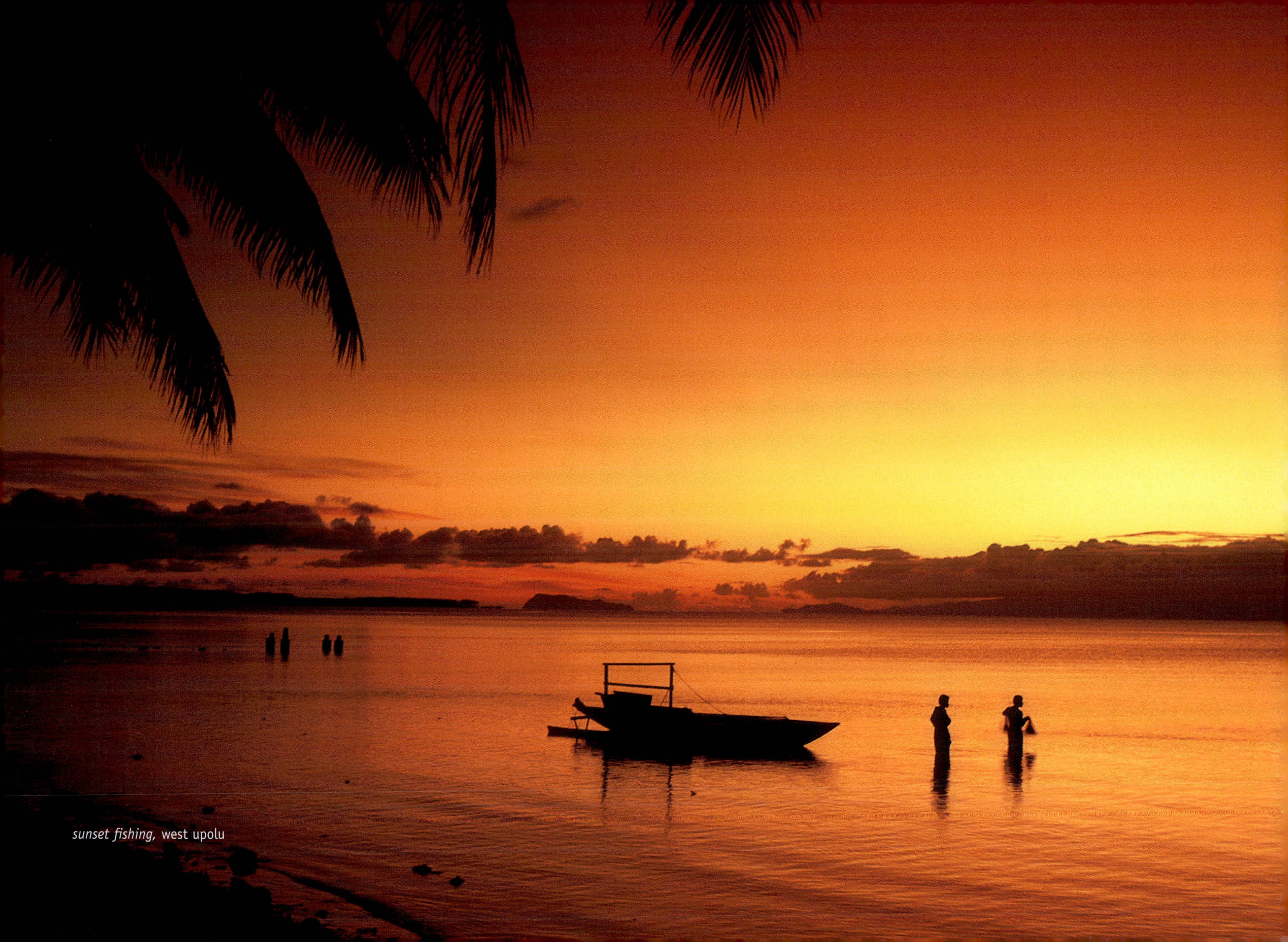

sunset fishing, west upolu

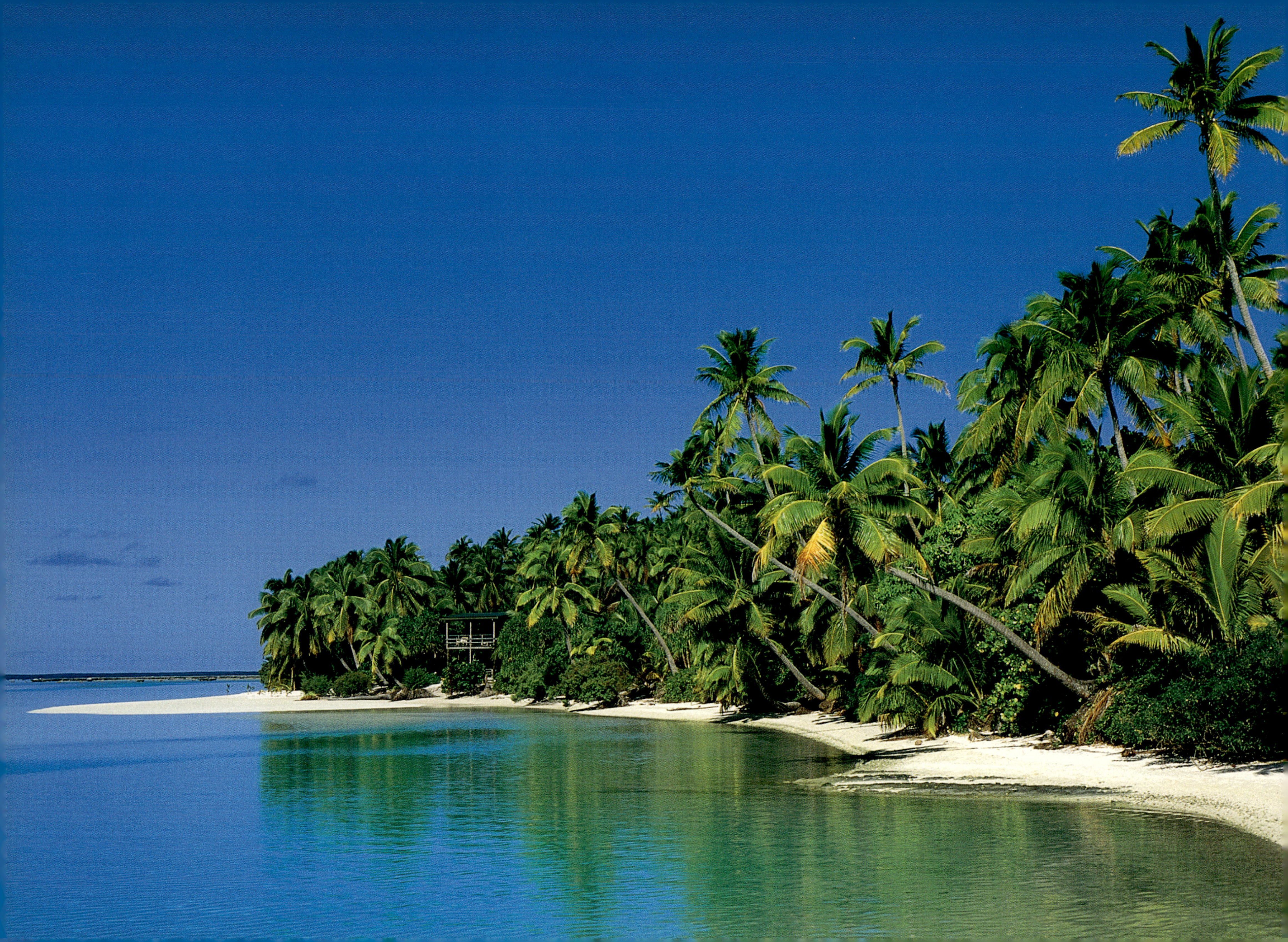

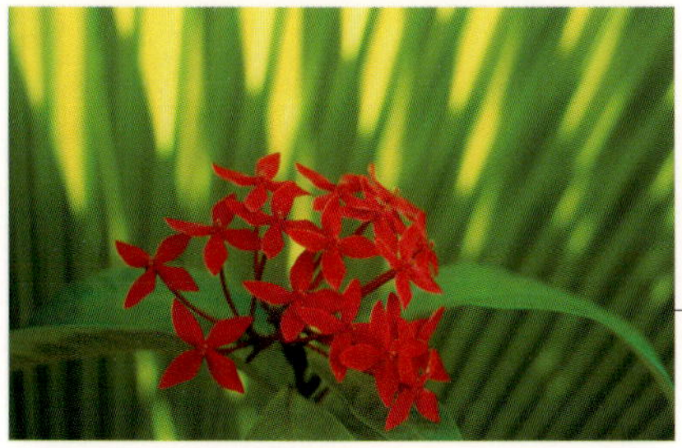

Cook Islands

THE 15 COOK ISLANDS, tiny dots in a vast ocean of over 2 million square kilometres comprise only 241sq.kms of land in two groups. The southern group, with 90% of the land and most of the population, is a mix of raised coral islands, coral atolls and volcanic islands, while the northern group are all coral atolls.

Settled from the Society Islands about 700-900AD, the Cook Islanders still have many cultural and linguistic similarities with their Polynesian cousins. Although no large kingdom evolved, as was the case in Tahiti, the culture still developed sophisticated engineering skills. The Ara Metoa, an ancient paved road that circles the island of Rarotonga a little inland from today's road, with parts that are still in use, is thought to have been constructed 700 years ago.

Rarotonga, the main island, is one of the most beautiful islands in the Pacific; a classic oval shaped volcanic high island with rugged central mountains rising to a height of 650m above sea level, covered in dense tropical vegetation. Its valleys and coastal region with their rich red soils are full of vegetable gardens and orchards of citrus and bananas. The coastal circle road of 32km passes many lovely lagoons and white sandy beaches.

Aitutaki, the second most populated and visited island, is a low volcanic island with a 12km x 15km stunningly beautiful lagoon dotted with 15 small 'Motus' and several sandbars.

The population of the Cooks of about 18,000 is steadily declining with many Cook Islanders leaving to reside in New Zealand (50,000) and Australia (20,000), remitting back considerable amounts of money to the island economy. This along with tourism and New Zealand aid, help to balance an economy heavily dependent on imports. The country is self-governing in free association with New Zealand and has a 24 member Parliament operating on the Westminster System. Local matters are handled by island and village councils.

Black pearls are farmed on the islands of Manihiki and Penrhyn. Finely woven white hats of pandanus leaves and colourful applique quilts and cushion covers are renowned Cook Island handicrafts. The attractive relaxed little capital of Avarua has the charm of old Tahiti without the bustle and expense of modern Papette.

[LEFT] *one foot island,* aitutaki [ABOVE] *red bouvardia,* atiu

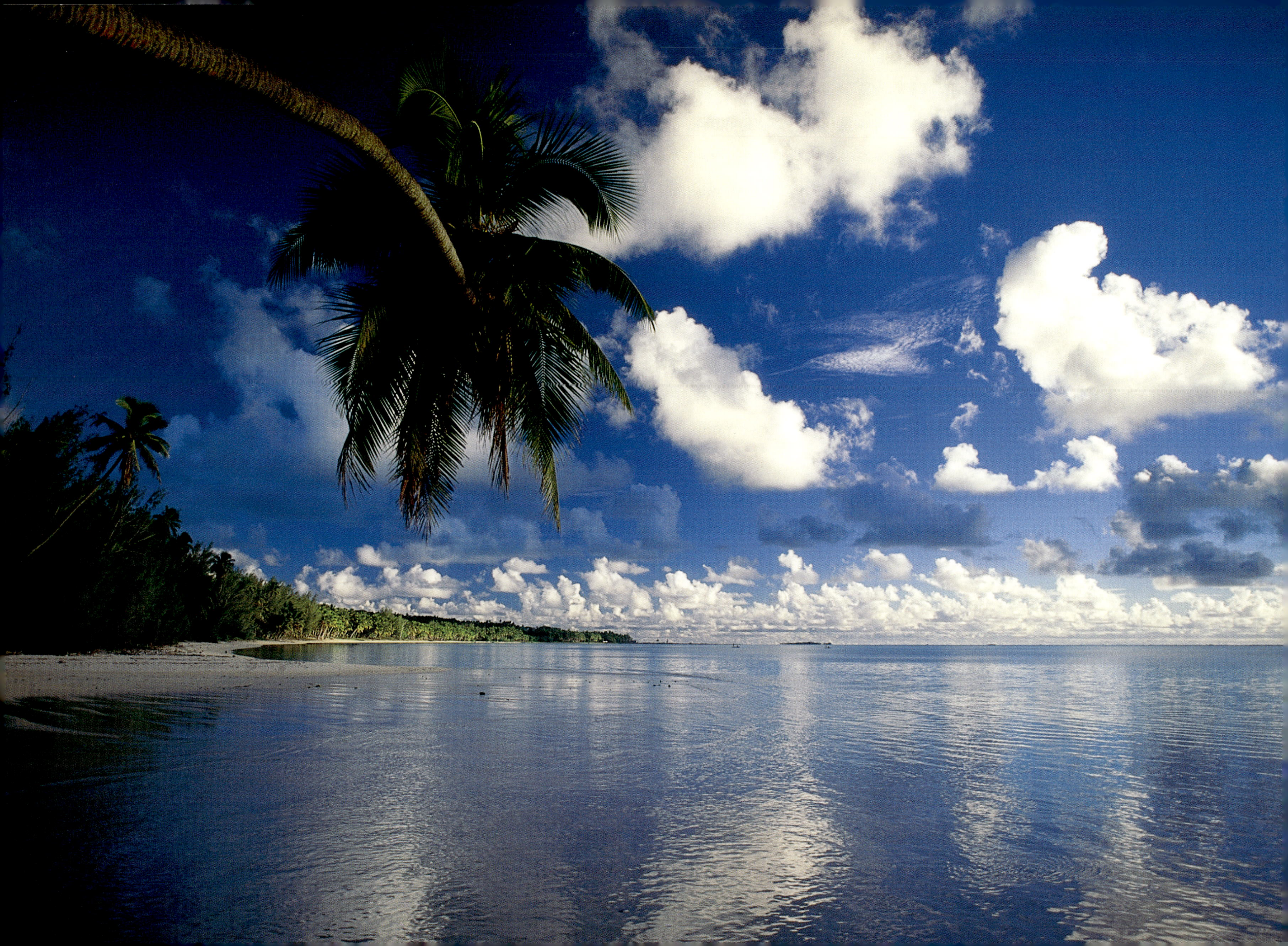

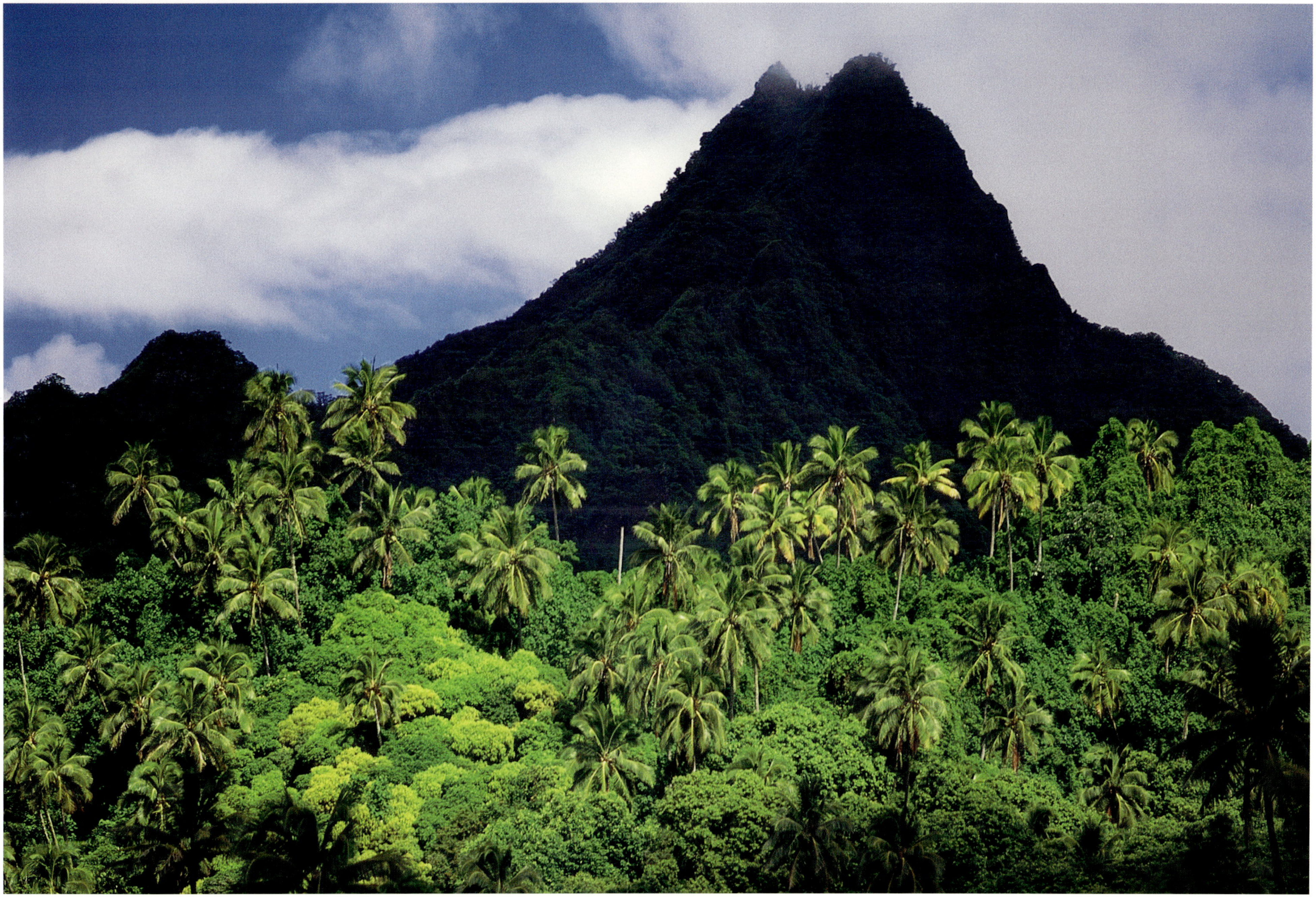

[LEFT] *aitutaki lagoon*

volcanic peak and jungle, rarotonga

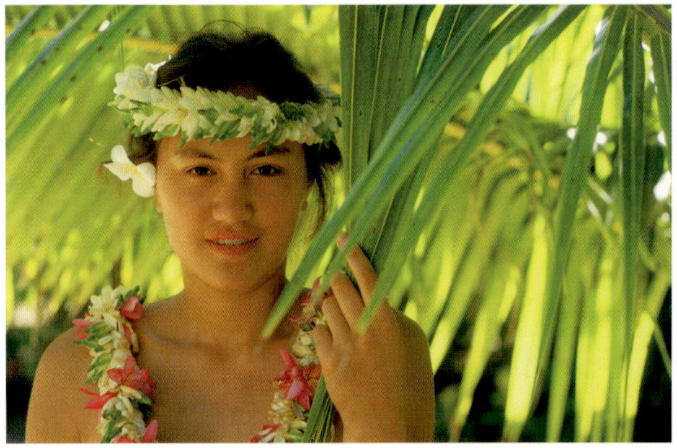

young woman, aitutaki

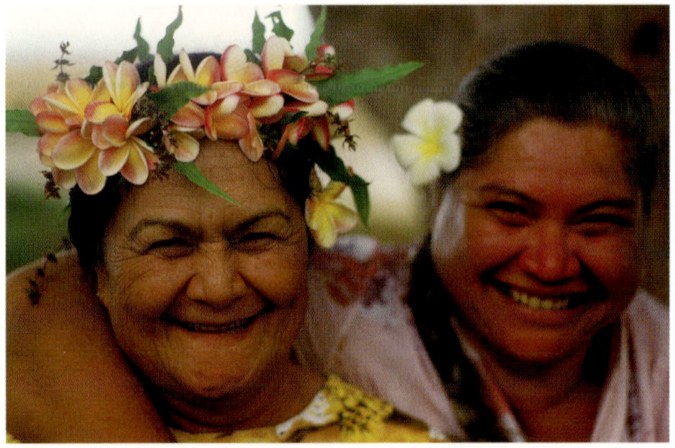

friends, rarotonga

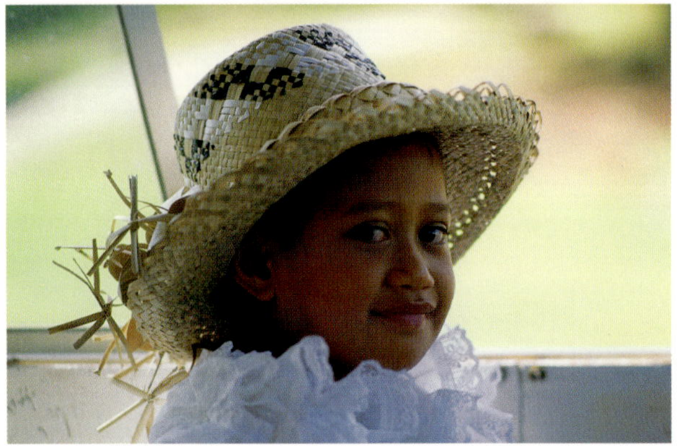

dressed for church, aitutaki

[RIGHT] *church service at avarua,* rarotonga

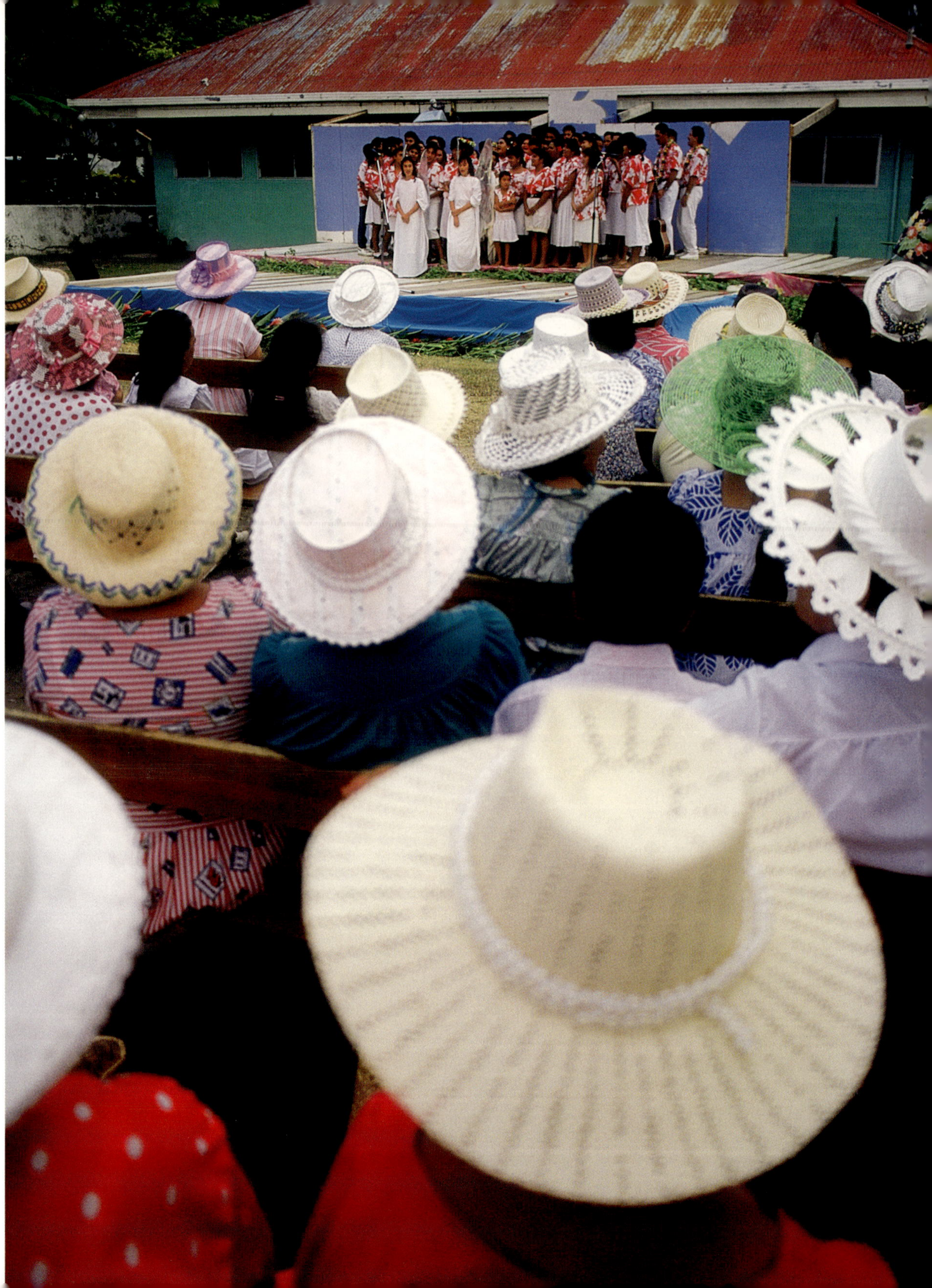

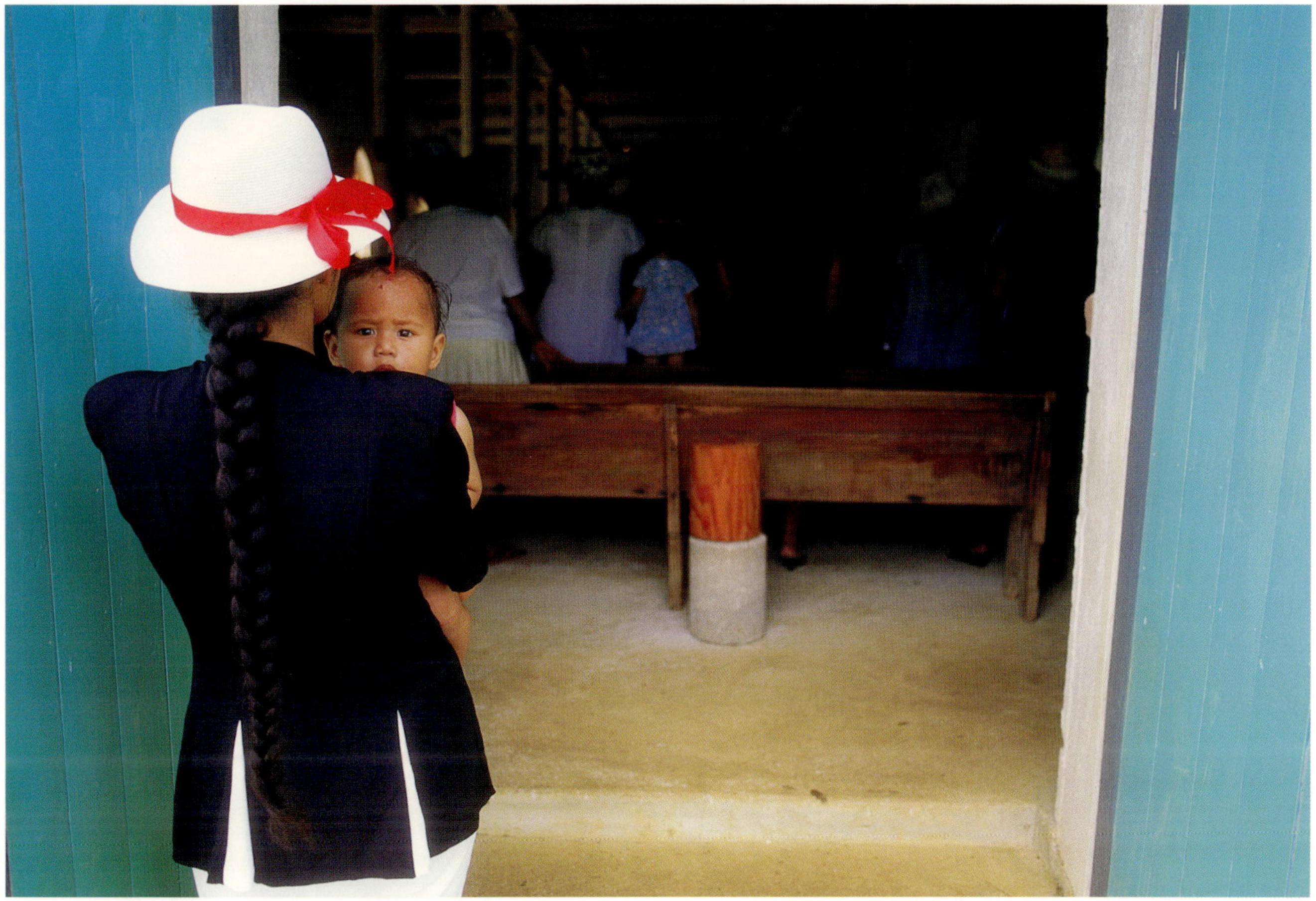

church service, atiu

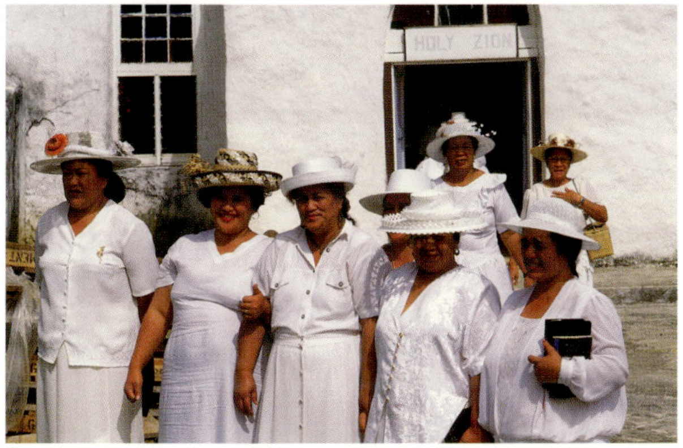

[LEFT] *after church service,* arutanga, aitutaki

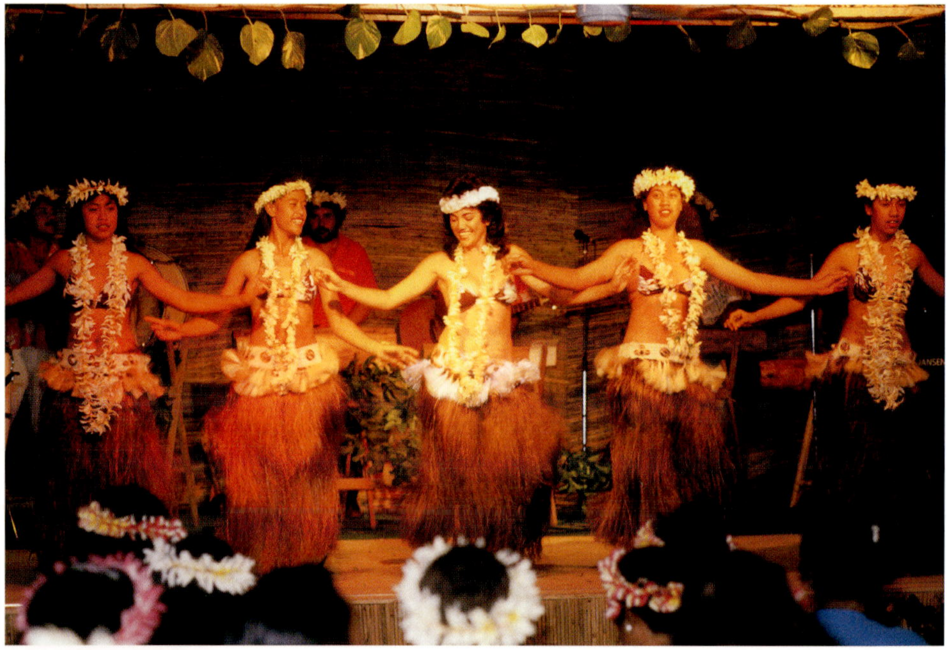

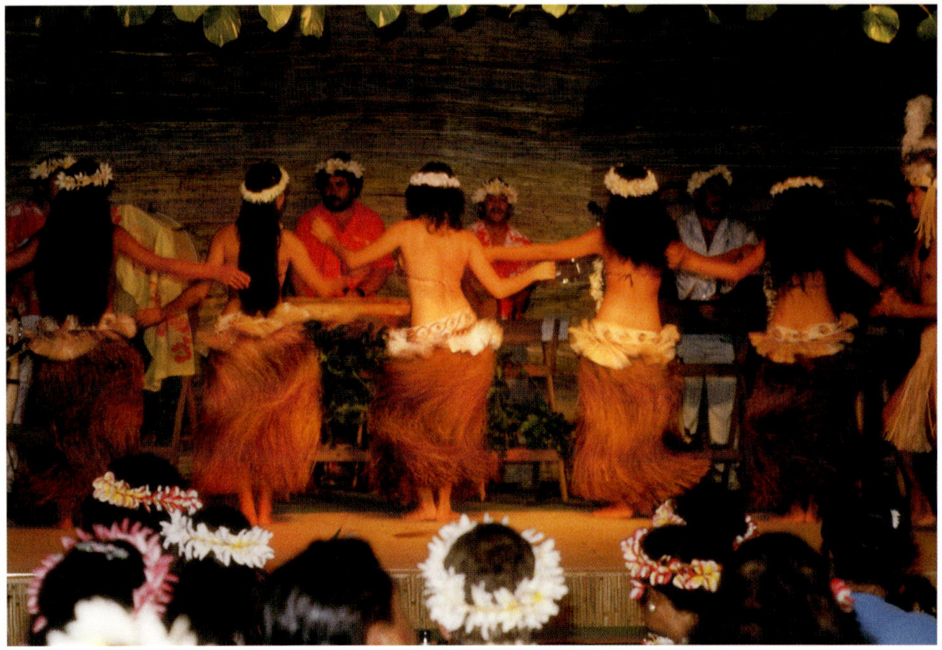

cook island dancers at a rarotongan hotel

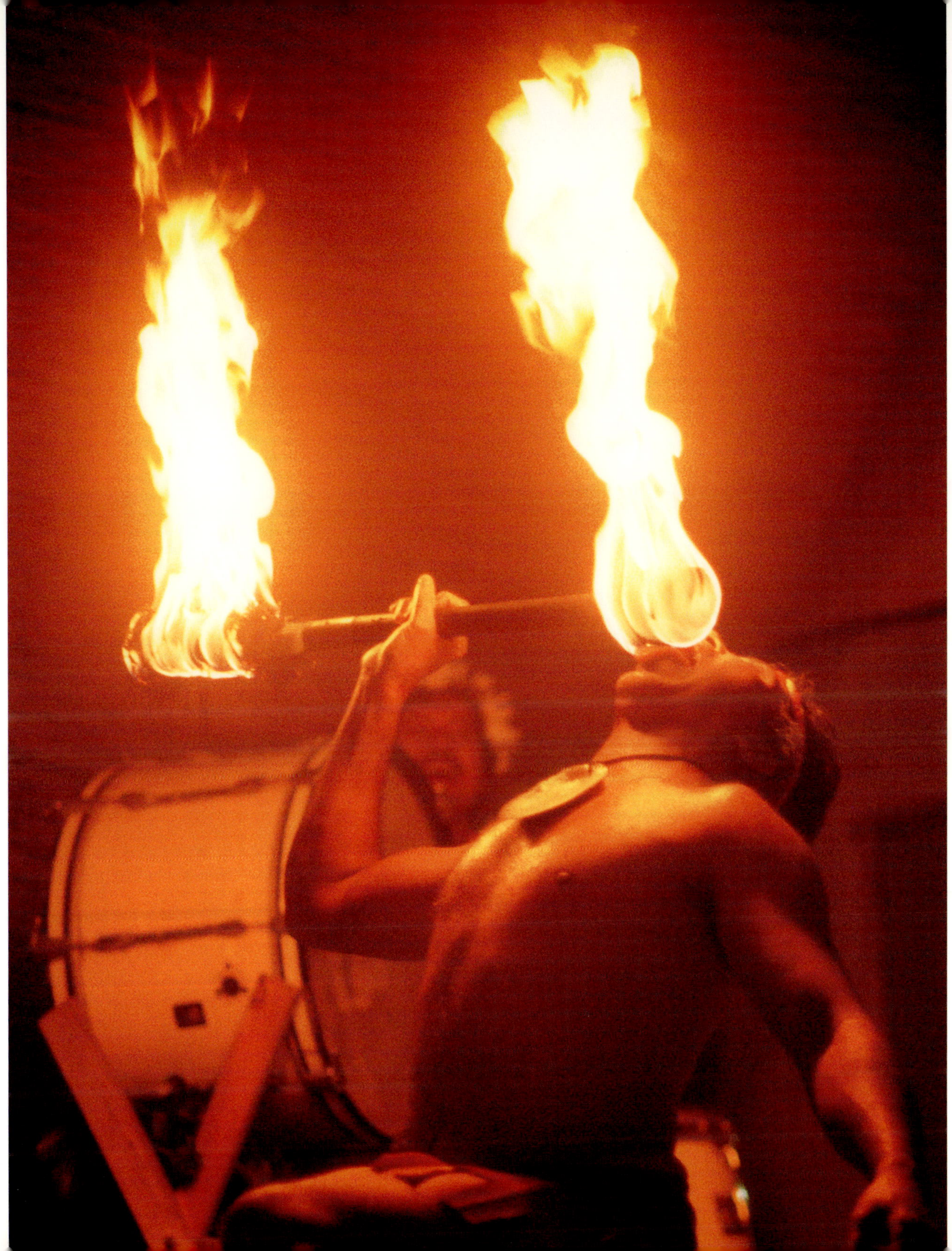

fire dancer, rarotonga

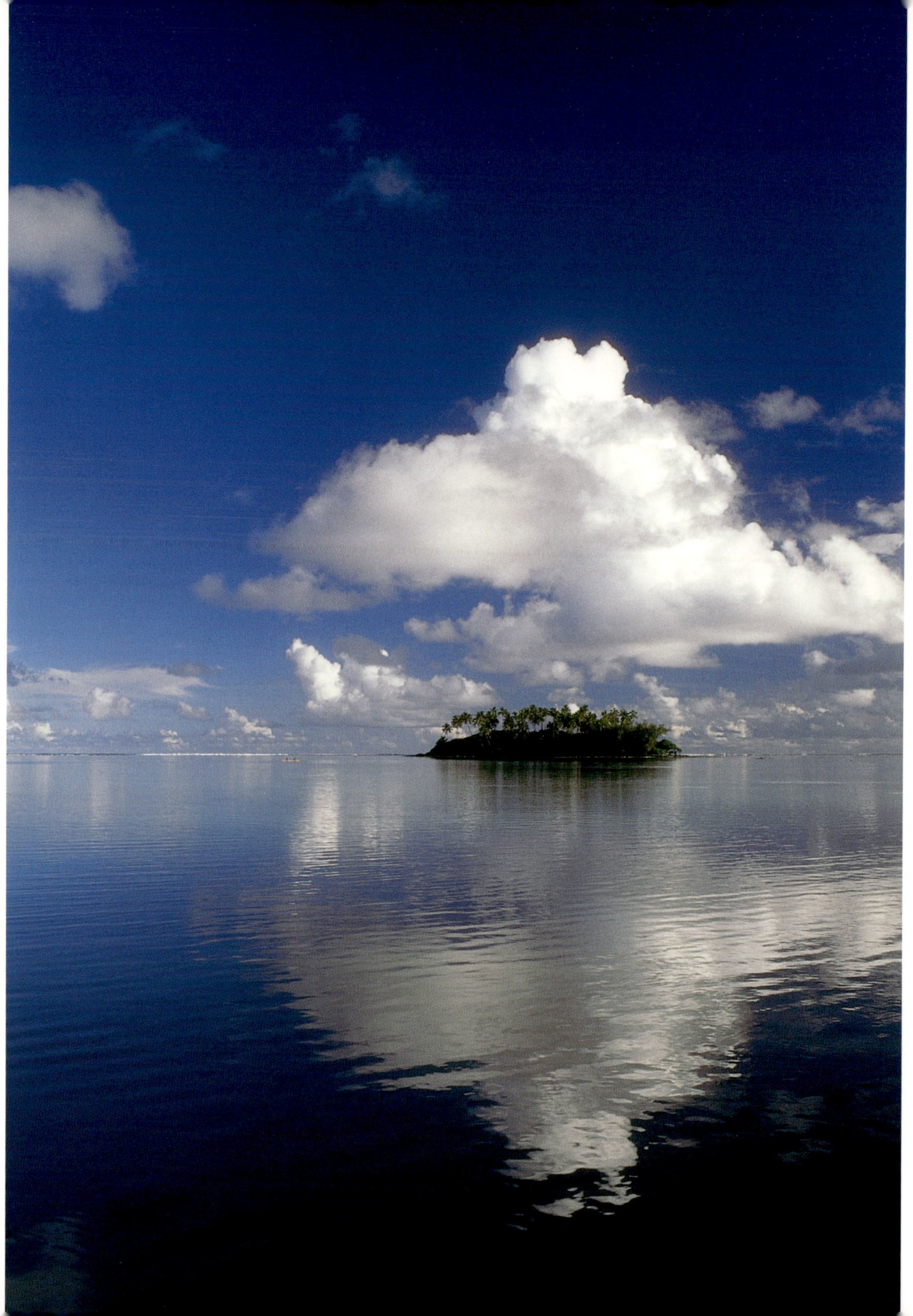

muri lagoon, rarotonga

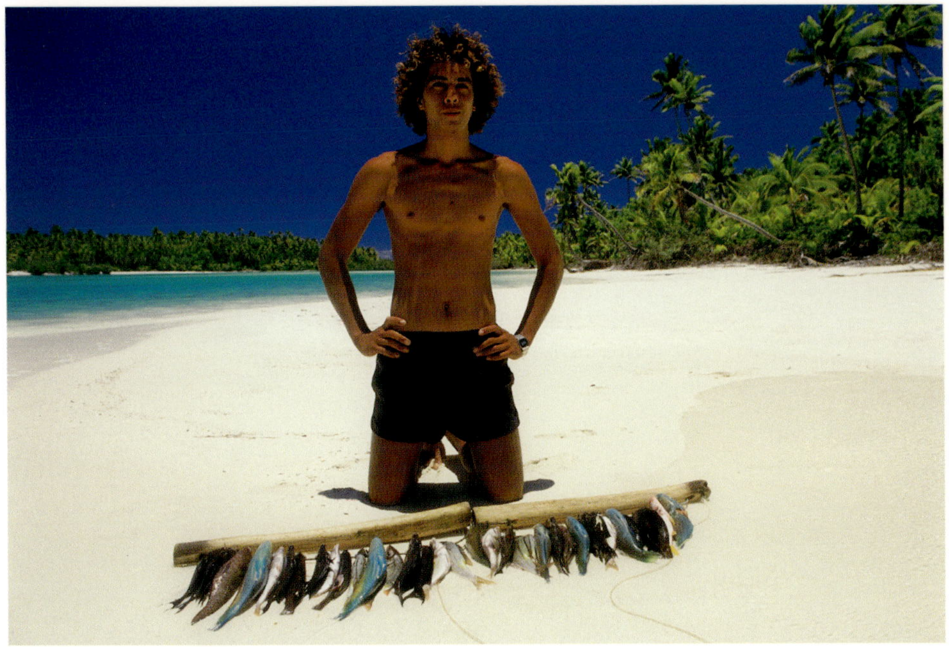

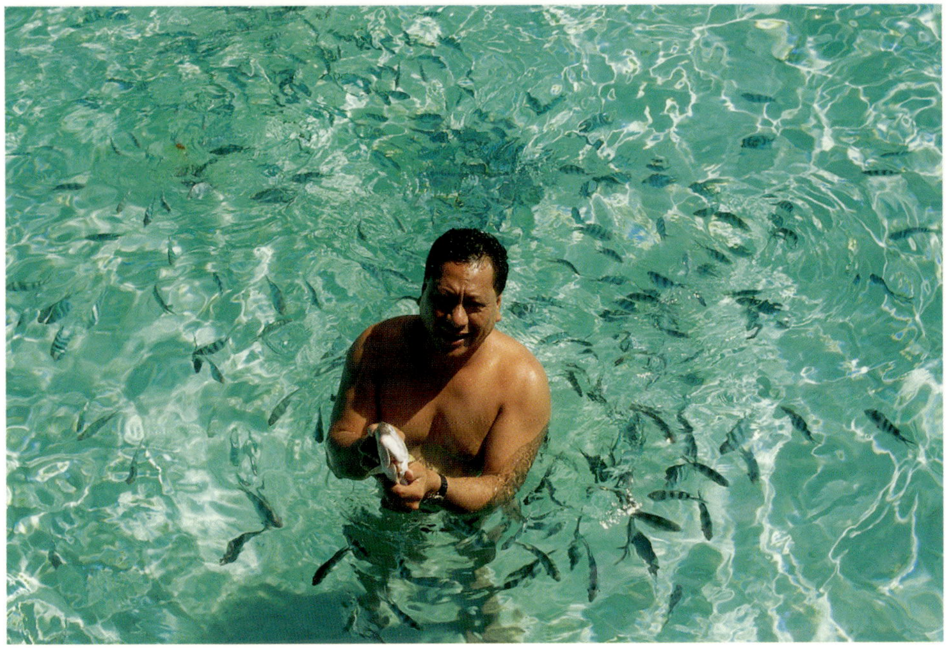

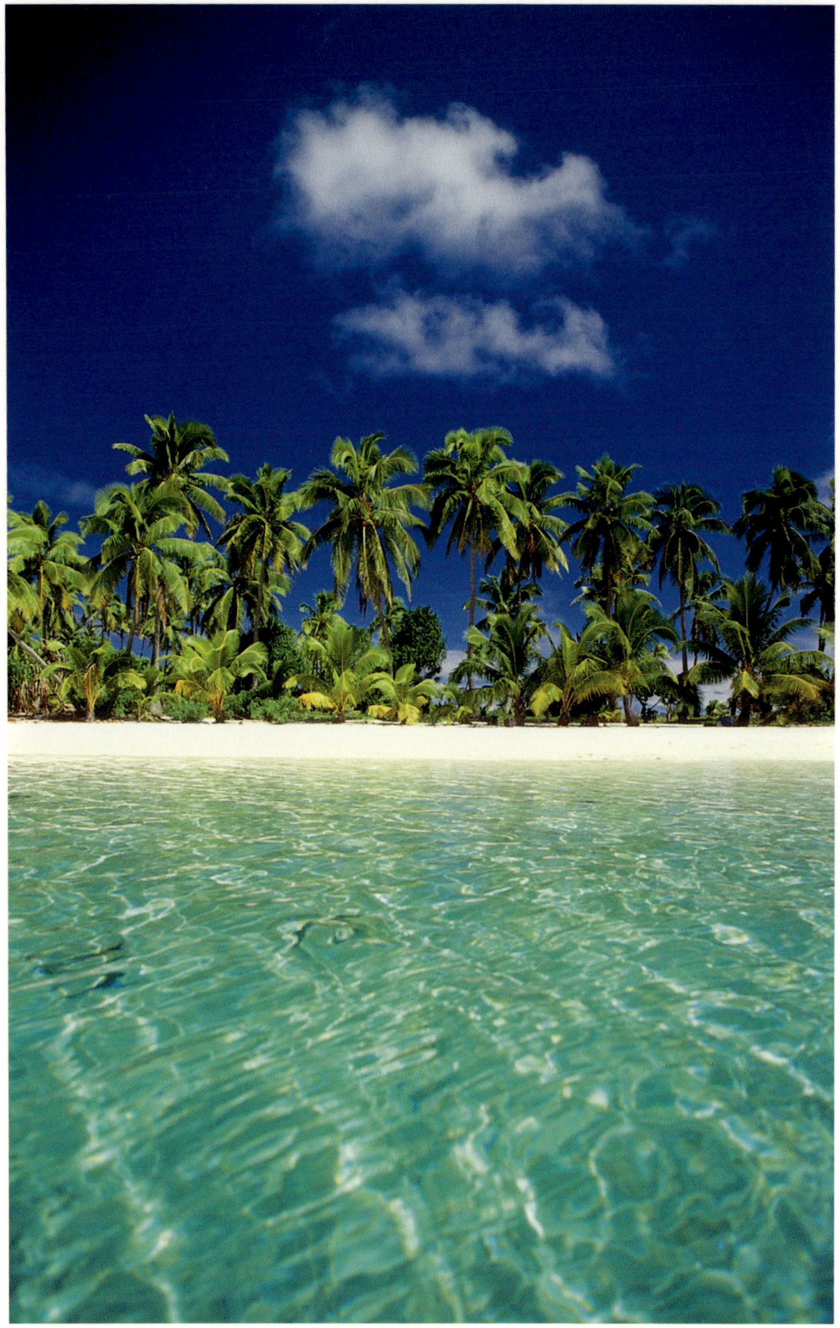

aitutaki lagoon

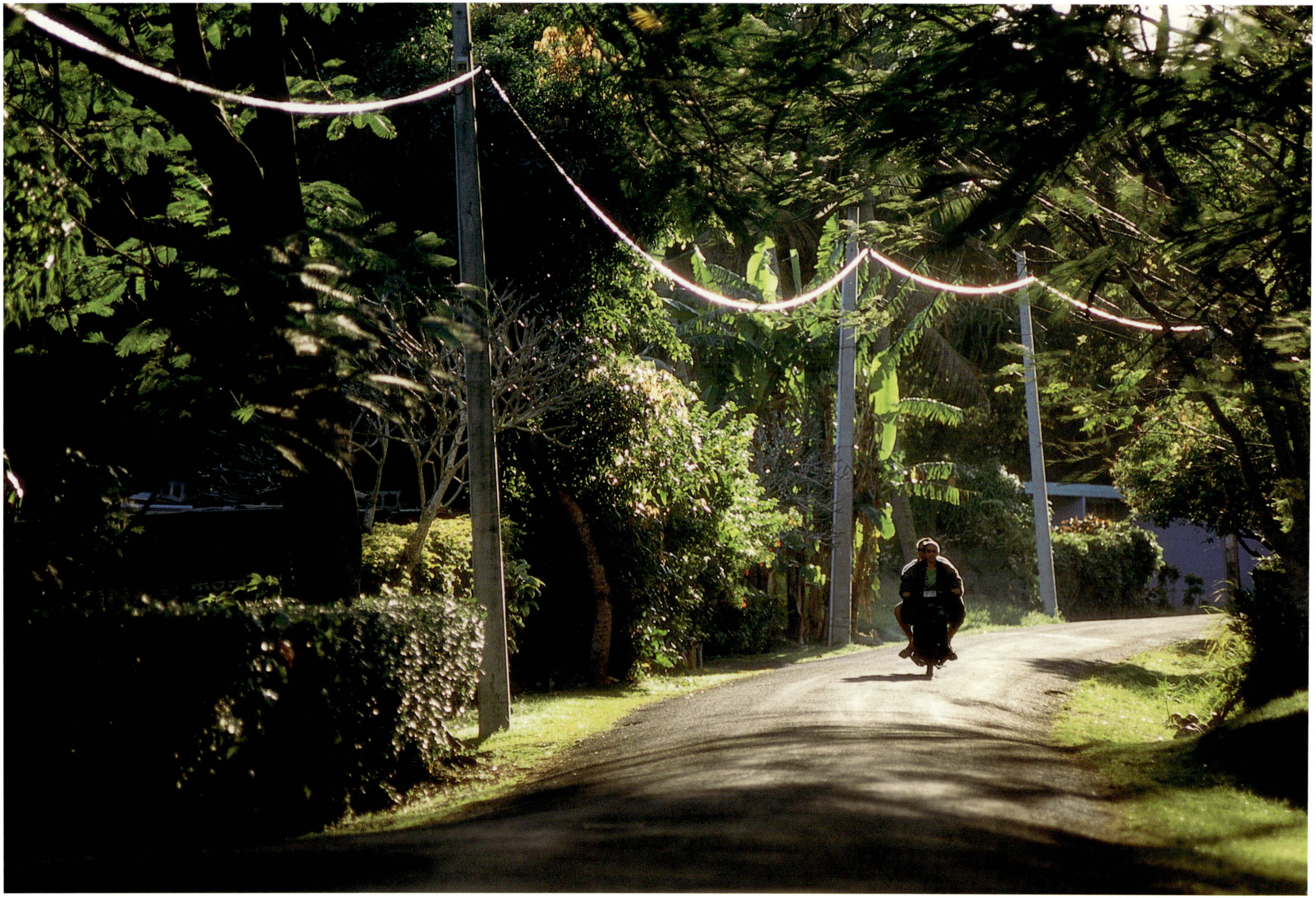

ara metua, the ancient polynesian interior road of rarotonga

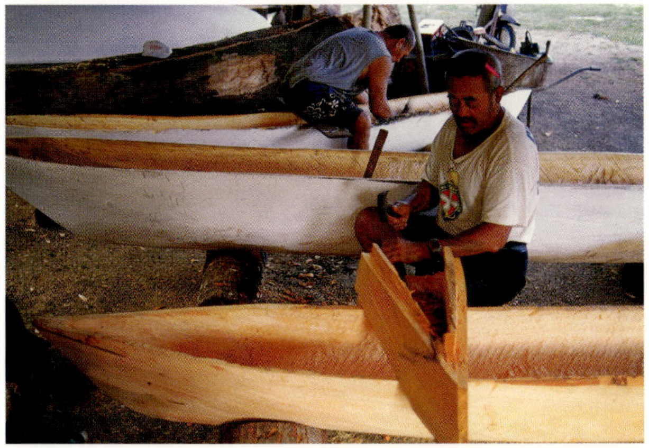

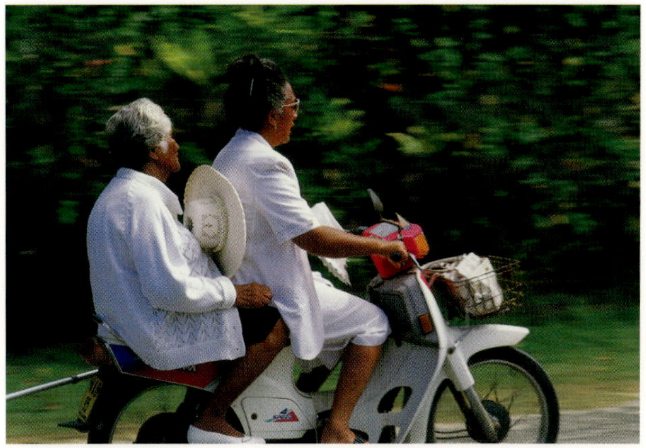

[LEFT] *canoe builder,* aitutaki

returning home from church, aitutaki

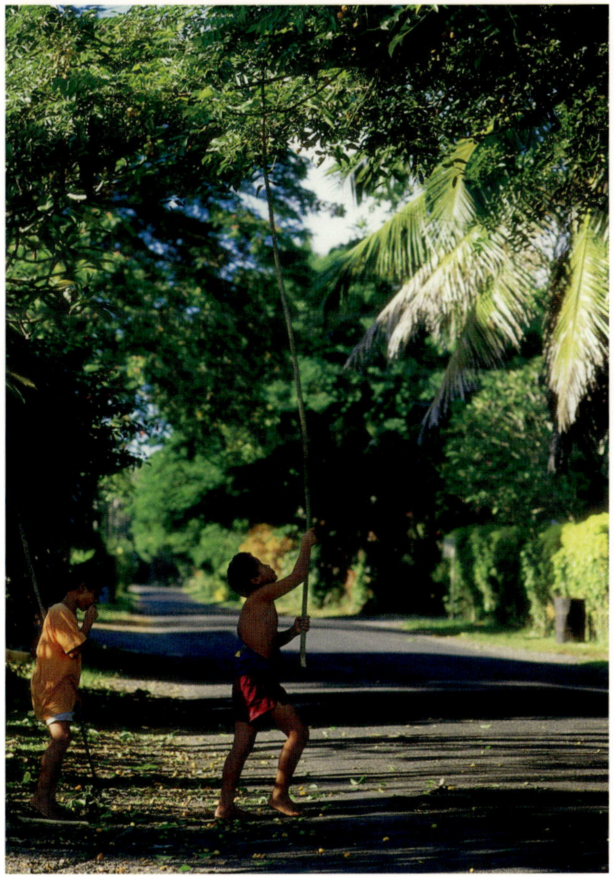

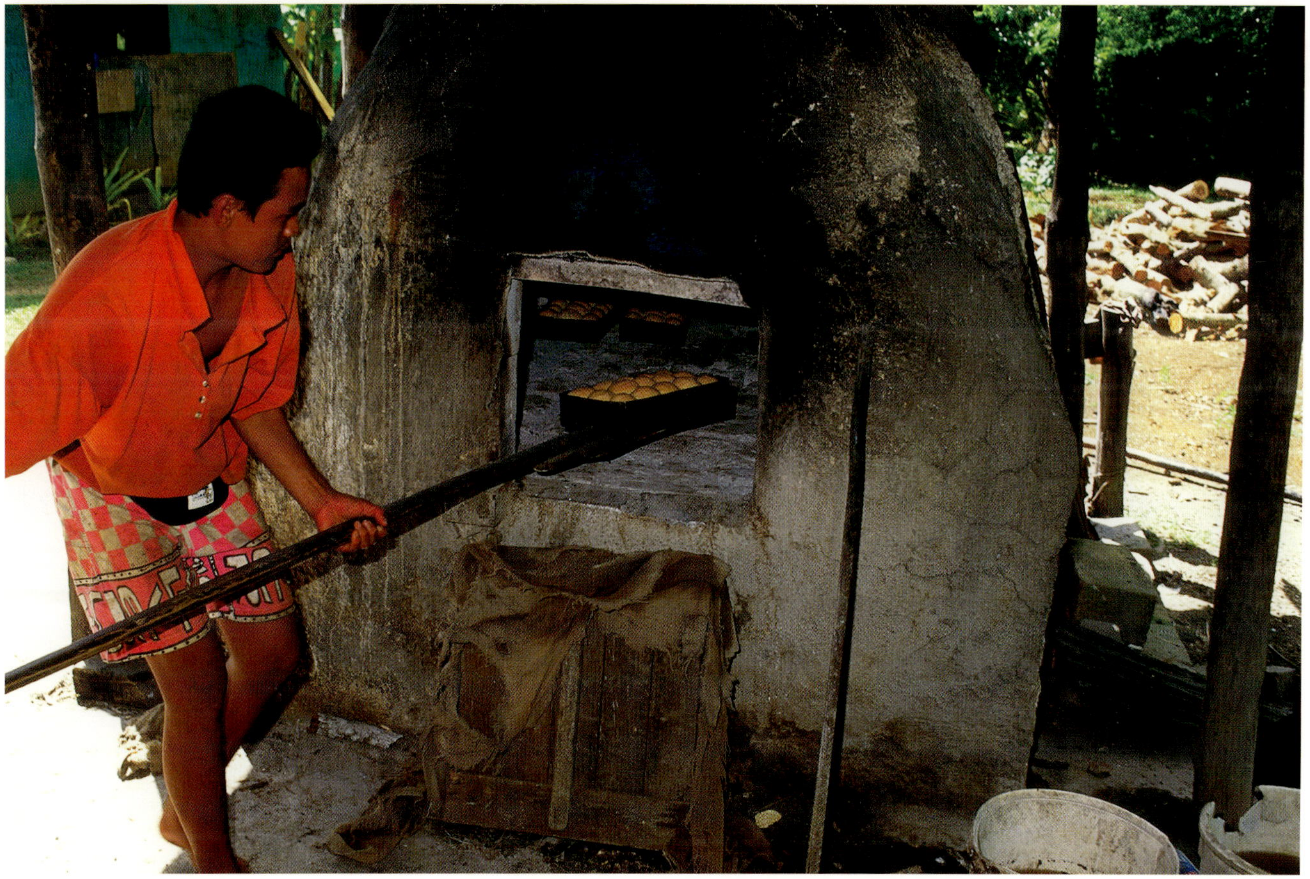

[ABOVE] *children collecting nuts,* rarotonga [RIGHT] *the atiu bakery*

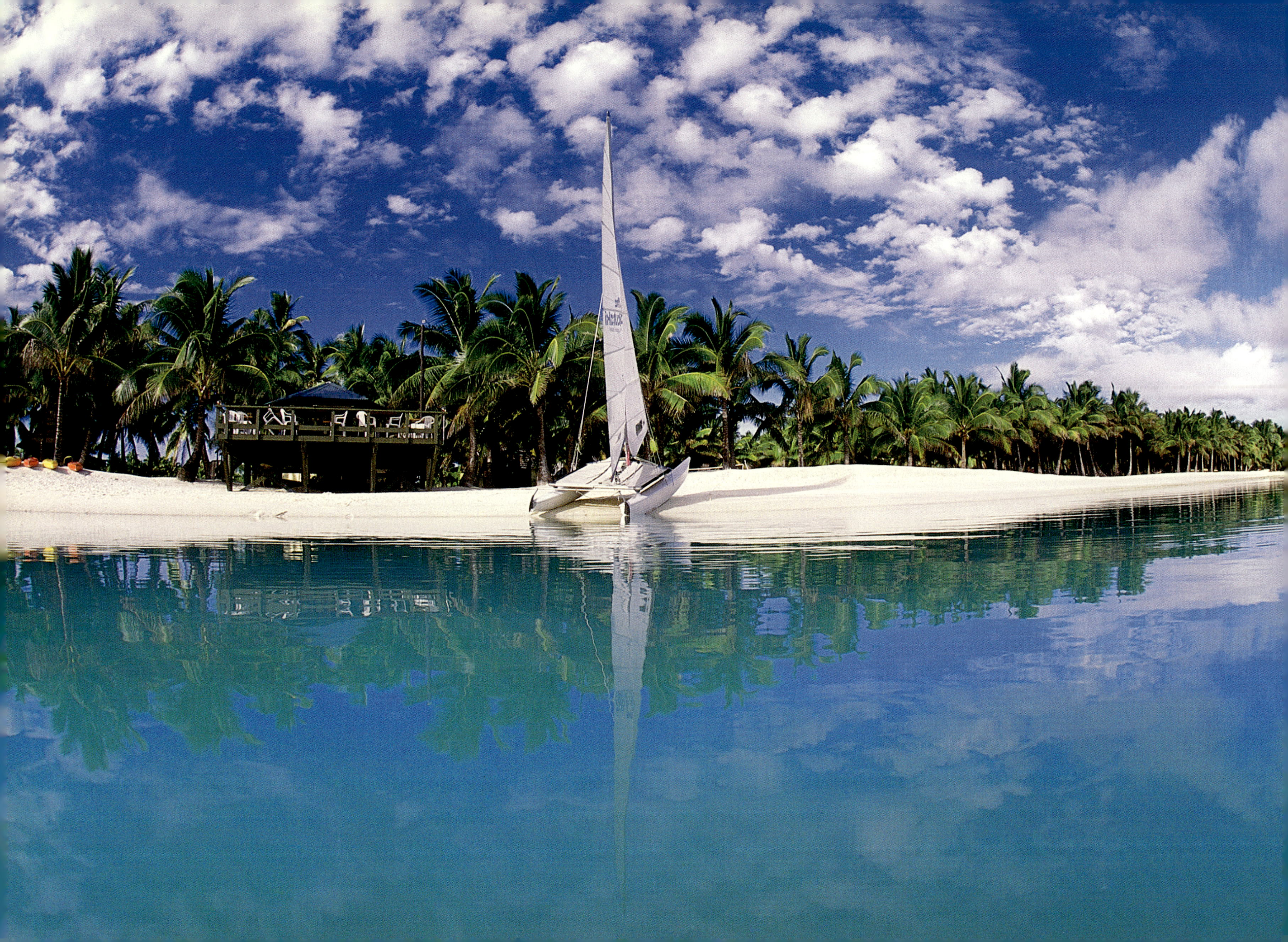

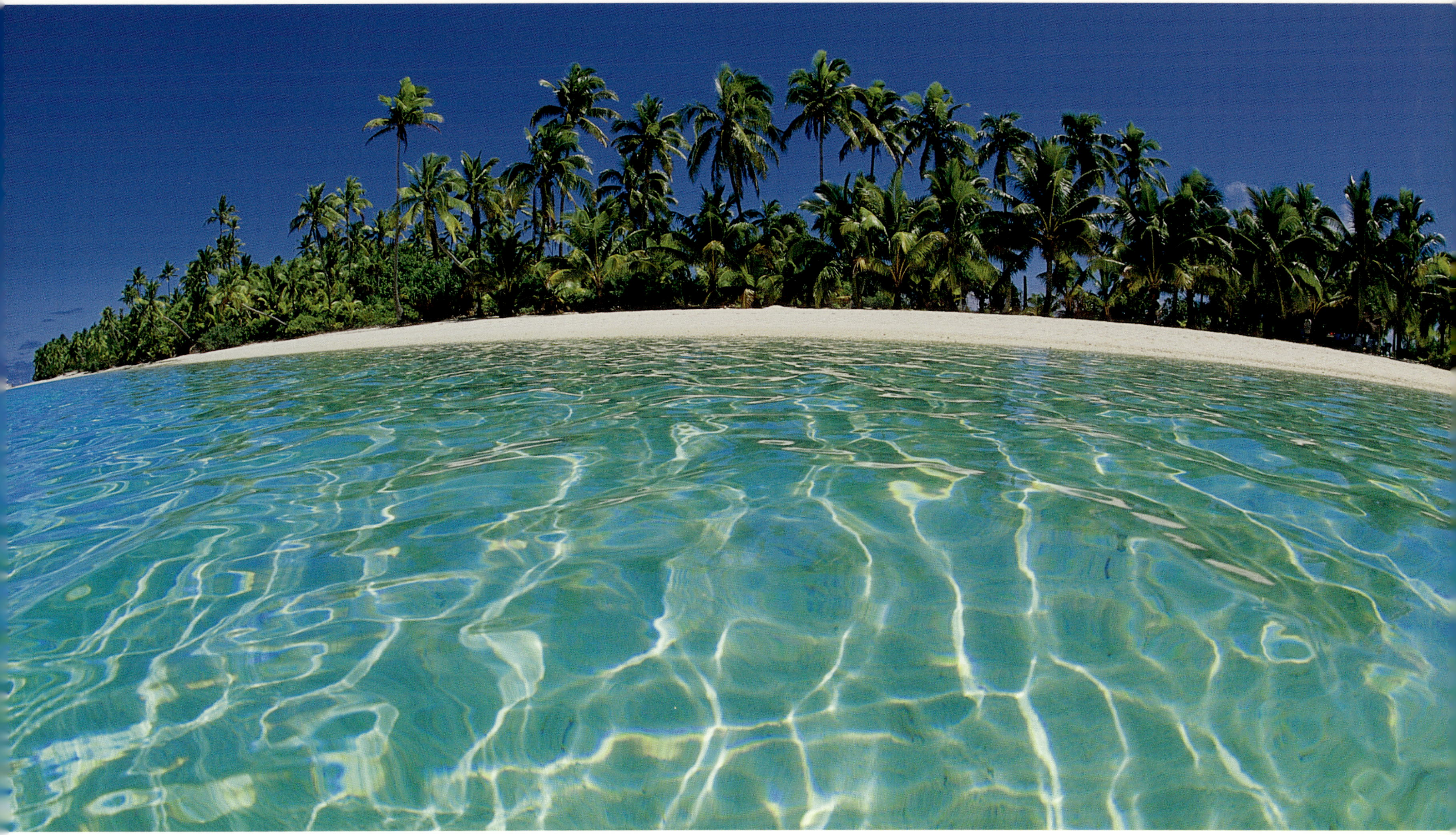

[LEFT] *pearl beach hotel,* aitutaki

one foot island, aitutaki

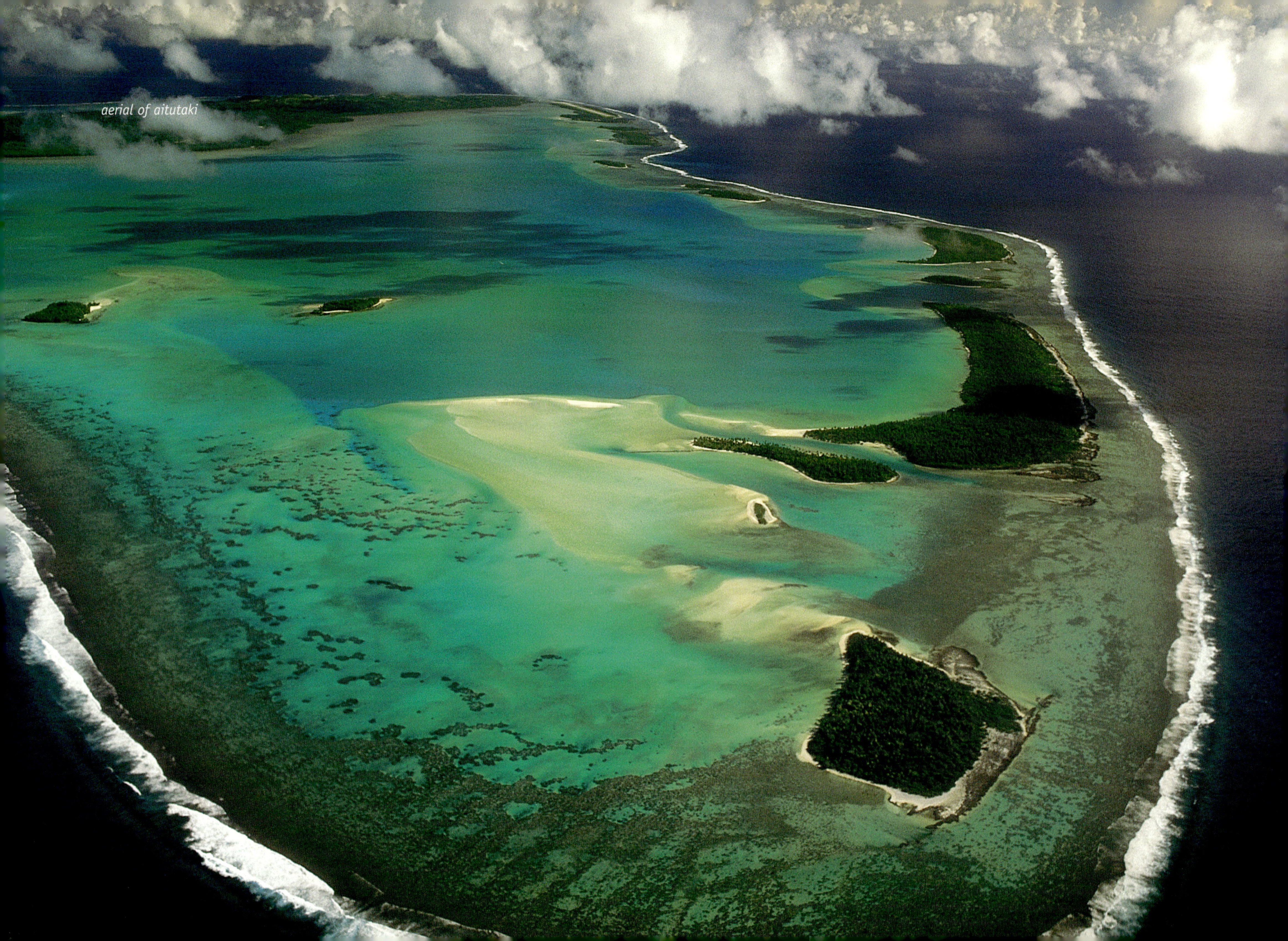
aerial of aitutaki

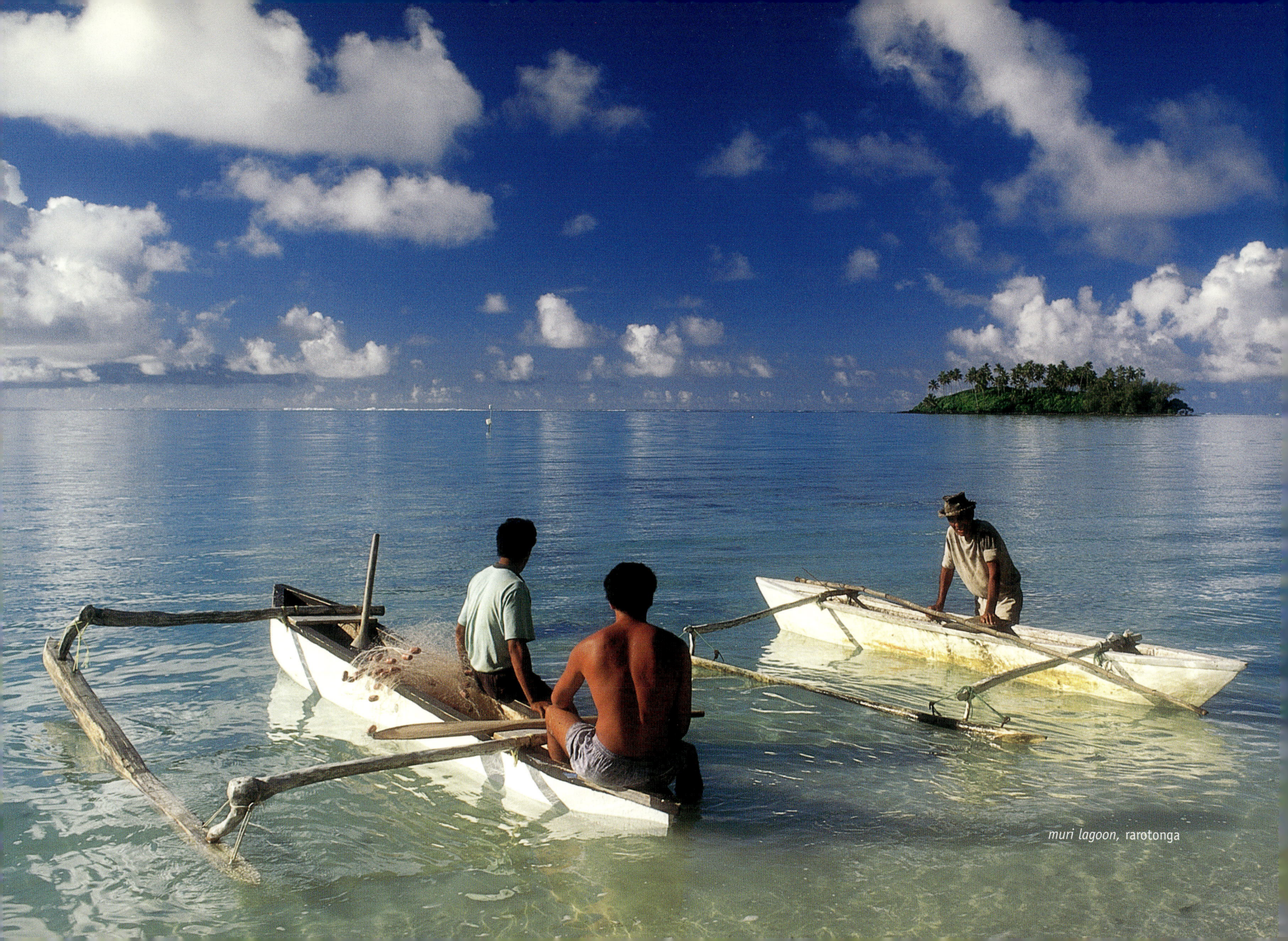

muri lagoon, rarotonga

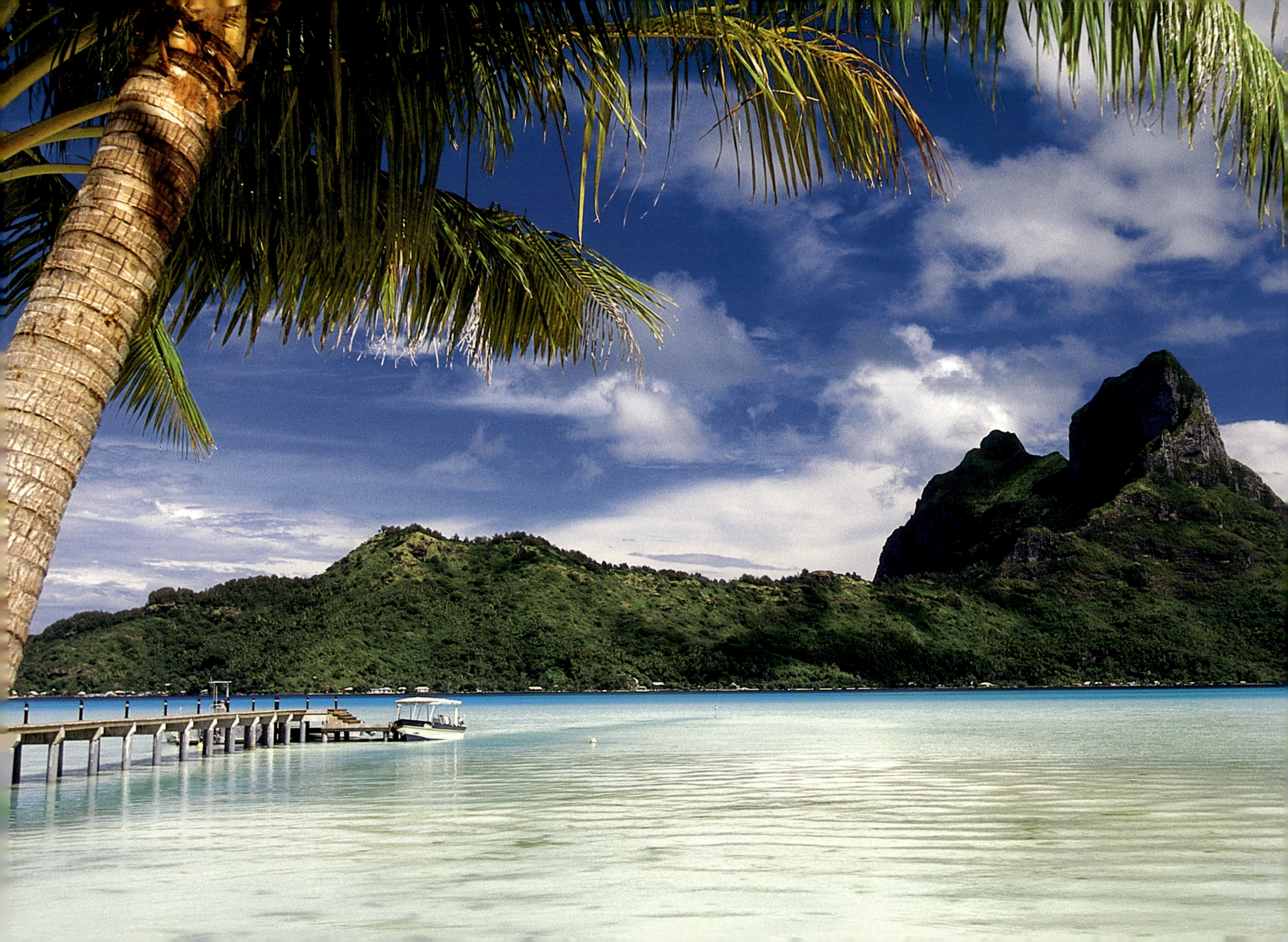

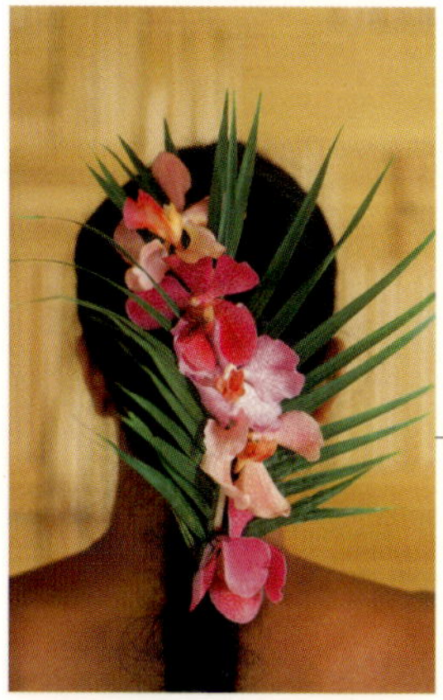

Tahiti and the Society Islands

THE SOCIETY ISLANDS are divided into the Windward (Tahiti and Moorea) and the Leeward (Huahini, Raiatea, Tahua, Bora Bora and Maupiti). These high islands of basaltic volcanic origin are renowned for their beauty, with towering peaks and jagged ridges, lush tropical valleys scented with frangipani and bougainvillea and the idyllic palm tree lined beaches and turquoise lagoons.

Settled originally from the Marquesas around 500AD, the Tahitians developed a complex society of hereditary tribal chiefs. They utilised marine resources, grew crops such as taro, yam, sweet potato, breadfruit, bananas and coconuts and kept chickens, dogs and pigs. The Tahitians had highly developed arts of dance, poetry and oratory and played sports such as surfing, archery, wrestling and canoe racing.

From the earliest years of European settlement, Tahiti exercised a huge fascination on the Western imagination as a place of pleasure and abundance unconstrained by civilised restraints, the abode of the 'Noble Savage'. Much of this fascination flowed from the reports of such navigators as Samuel Wallis, who was the first European to visit Tahiti in 1767, Anton Bougainville, who named it 'La Nouvelle Cythère (after the Greek island where the cult of Aphrodite was centred) and Captain James Cook, who reached Tahiti in 1769 in the 'Endeavour' on a scientific mission to observe the transit of Venus. Cook returned to Tahiti on his second voyage in 1773 and again in 1774 when he returned to England with a Tahitian noble Omai, who soon became a major sensation as a living embodiment of the 'Noble Savage'.

At the time of European contact, rival-ruling families controlled the islands. One of these families, the Pomares, with the help of European mercenaries and weapons, were able to establish themselves as rulers with varying degrees of success from about 1800 to 1881, although for the last 39 years as a figurehead only.

Christian missionaries from the London Missionary Society arrived in the 1790's and together with the French Catholics soon got themselves embroiled in the Island's politics which led to French colonisation in 1842, with Tahiti becoming the first Pacific island to come under the control of a foreign power. During this period the population crashed from an estimated 150-200,000 at the beginning of European contact, to a low of 7169 in 1865 as the effect of introduced diseases, firearms and alcohol decimated the population.

[LEFT] *mount otemanu across bora bora lagoon* [ABOVE] *orchid hair ornament,* huahine

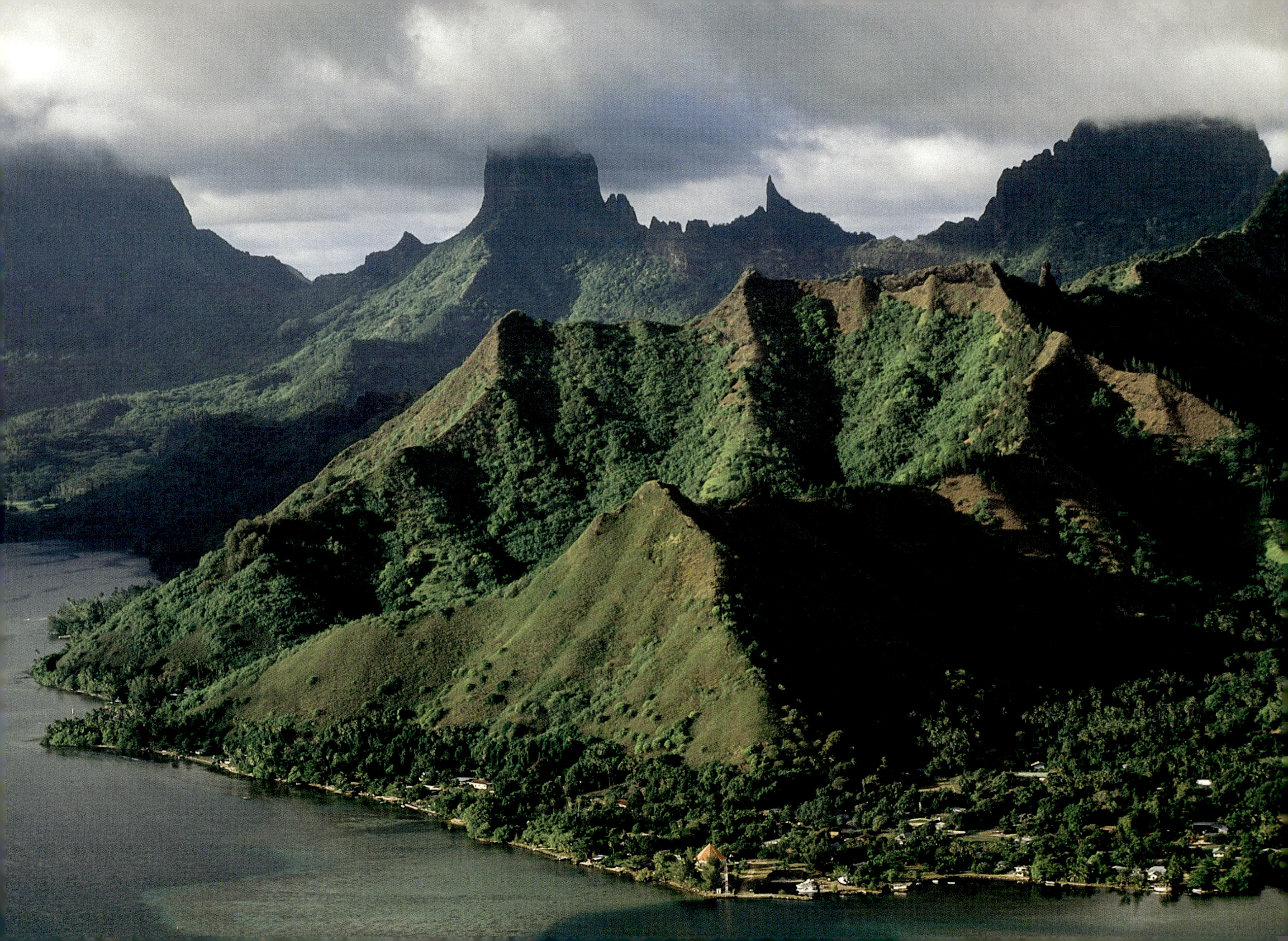

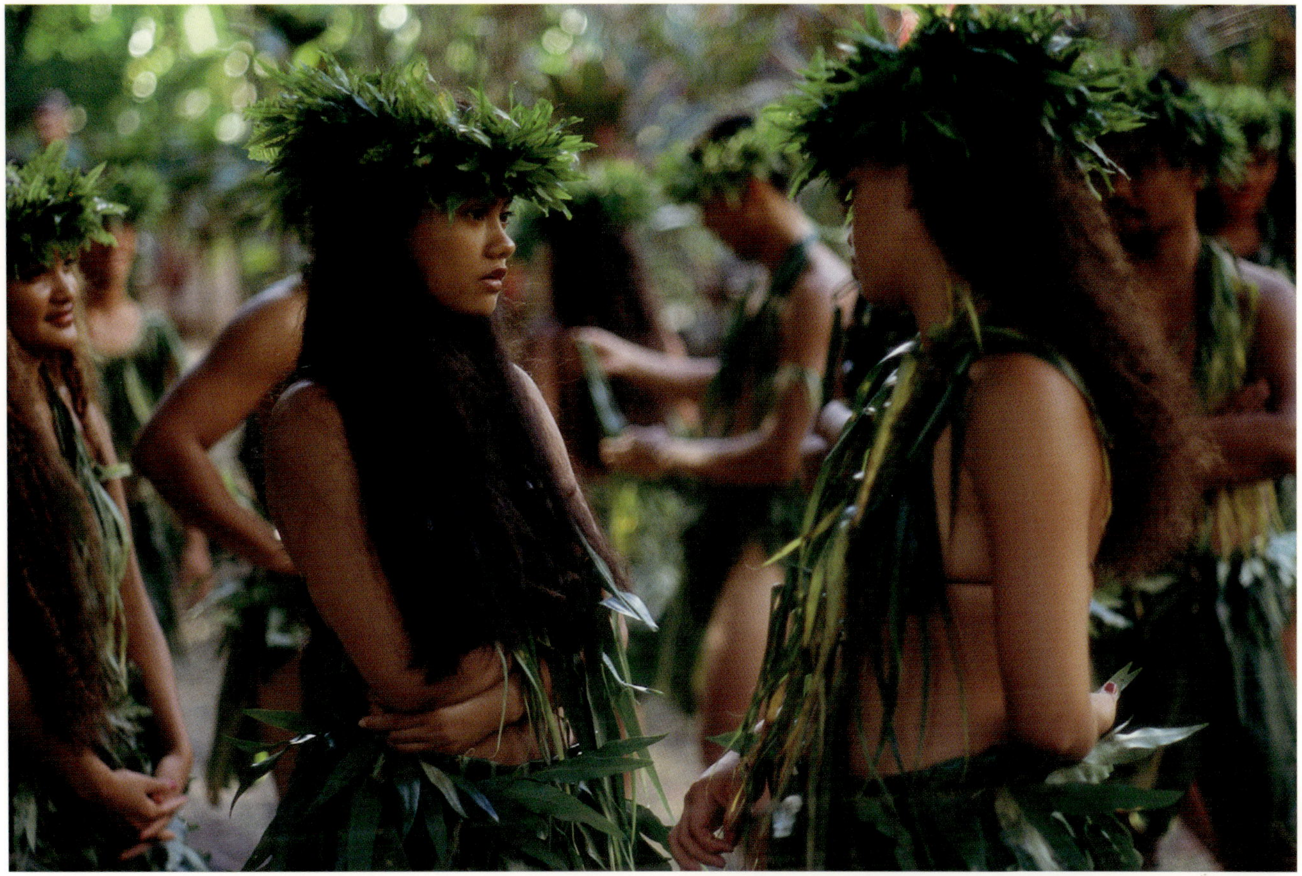

heiva i festival at marae arahurahu, tahiti

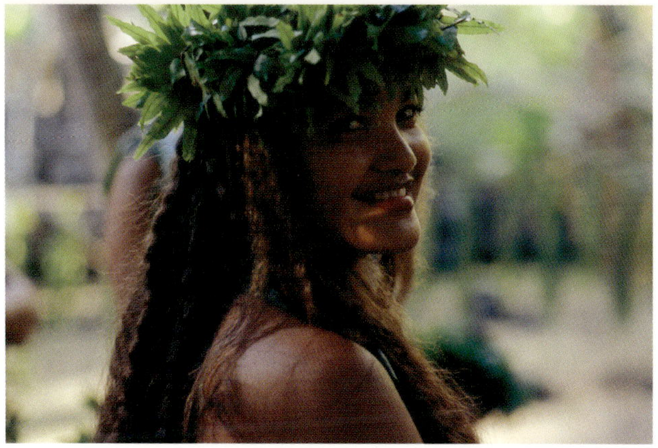

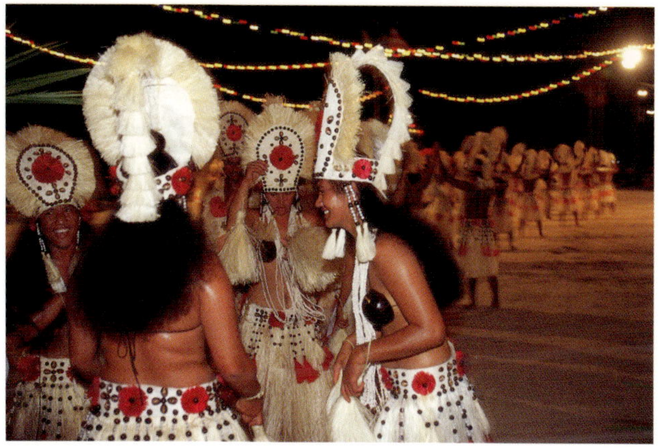

[**LEFT**] *early morning view of moorea island*

[**ABOVE RIGHT**] *heiva i festival at marae arahurahu,* tahiti [**FAR RIGHT**] *heiva i festival,* bora bora

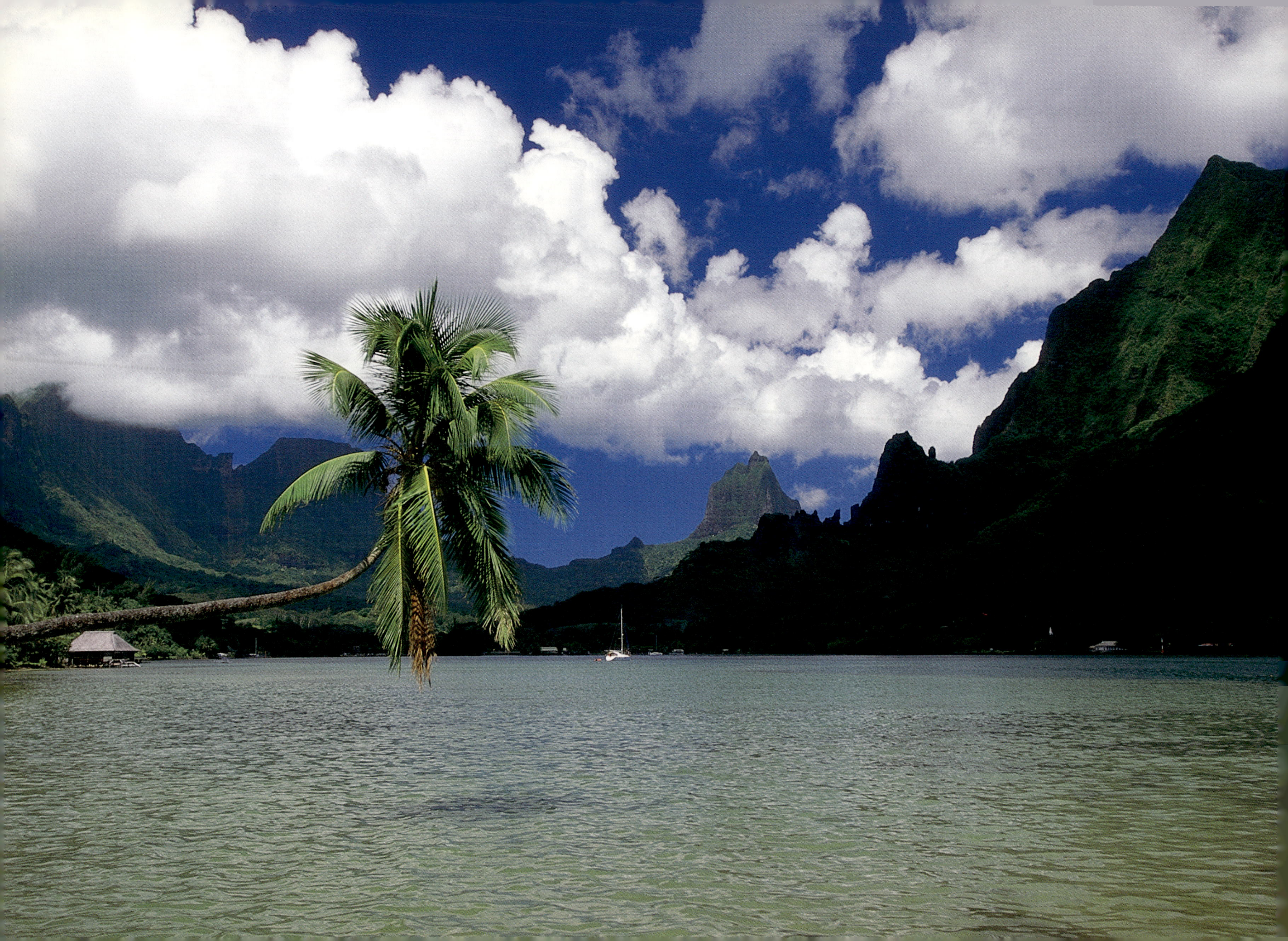

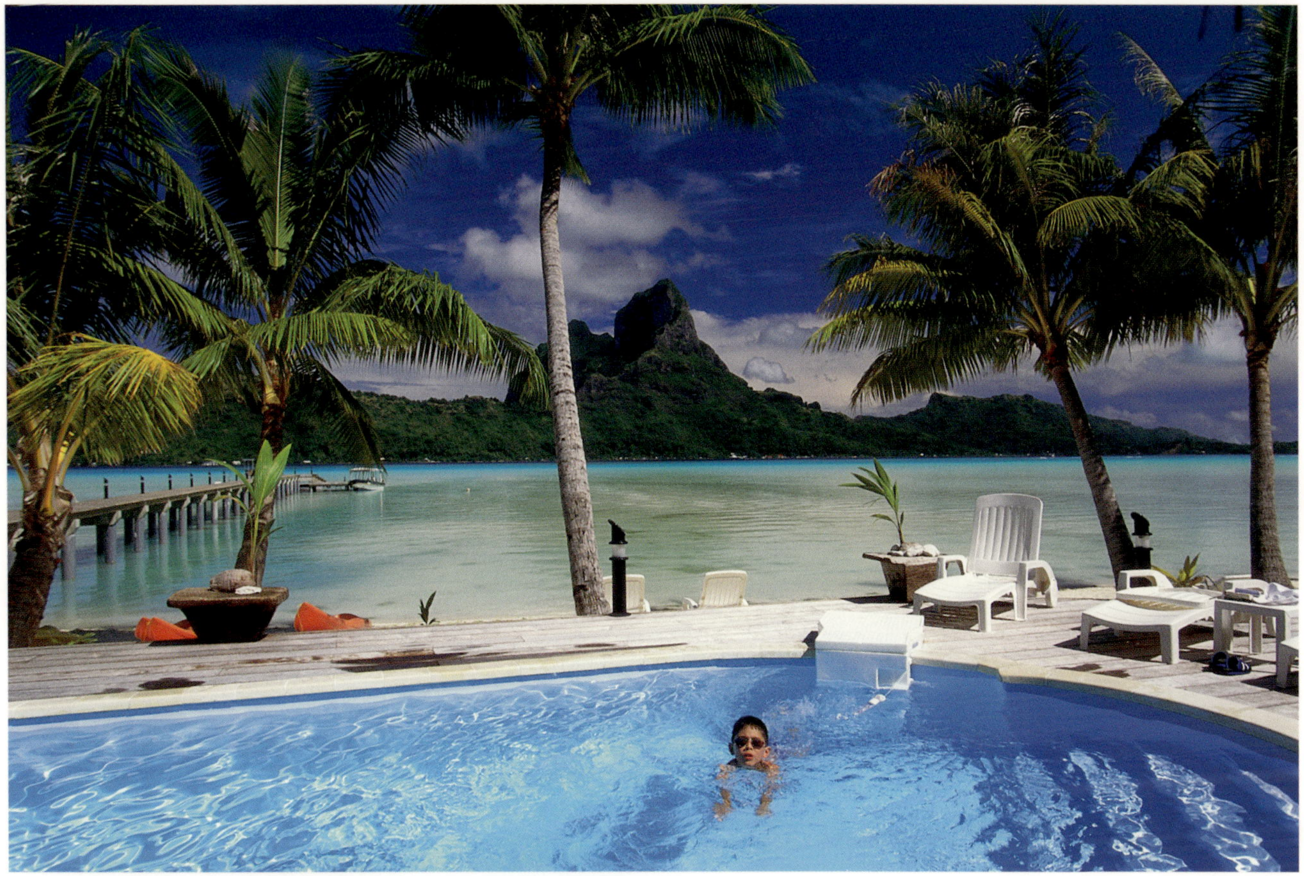

alex hendrie in the eden beach hotel pool, bora bora

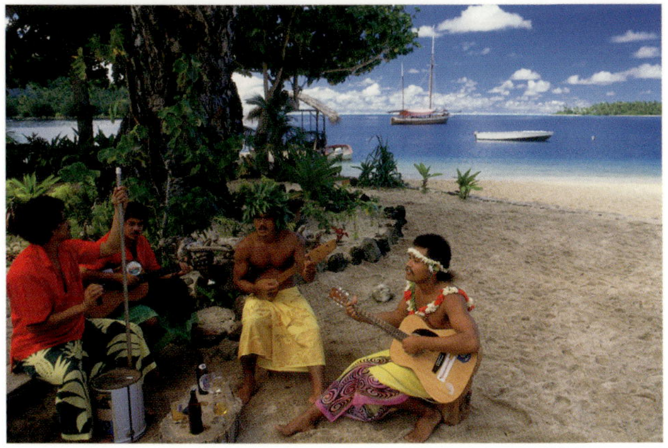

island jam, huahine

[LEFT] *cooks bay,* moorea

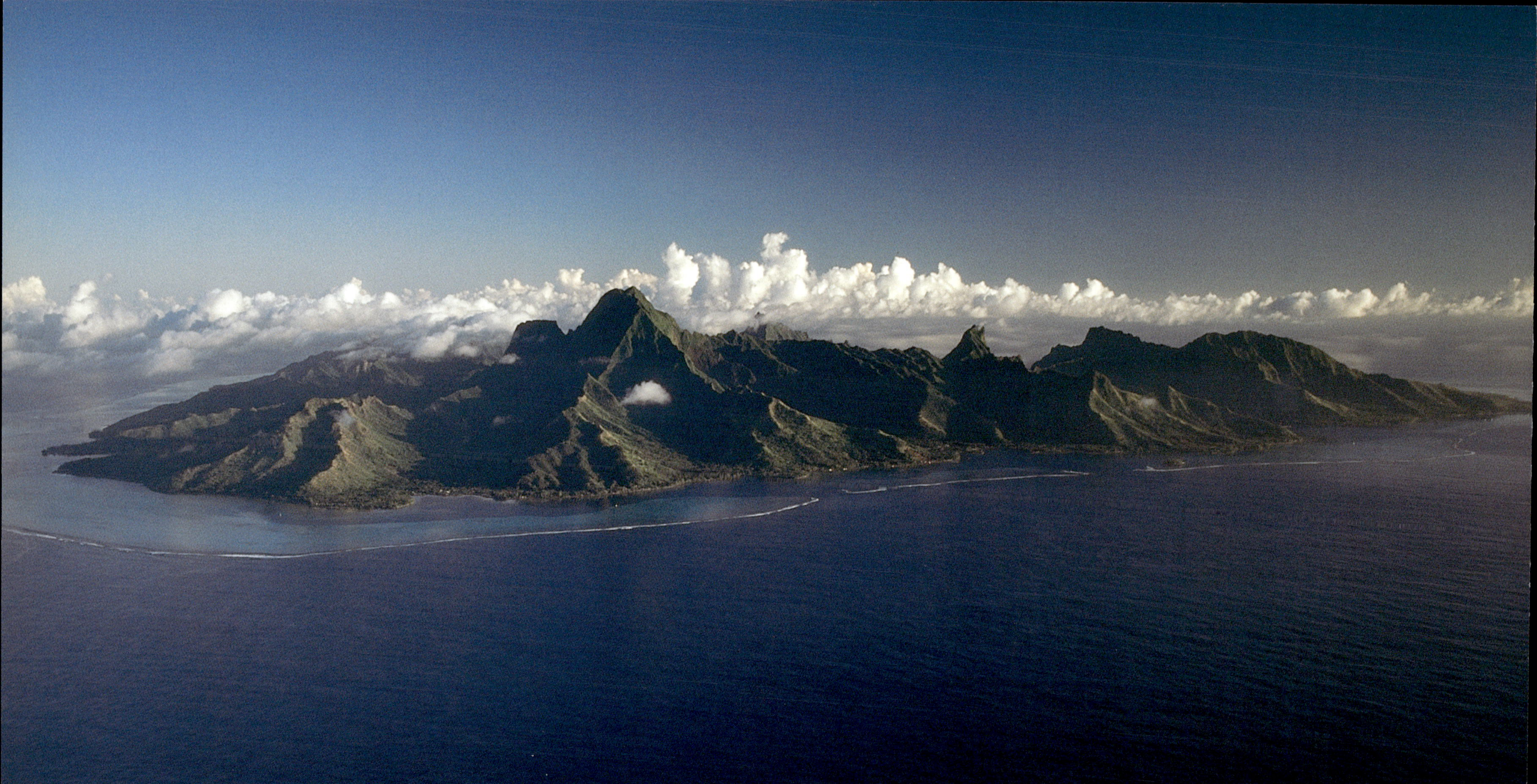

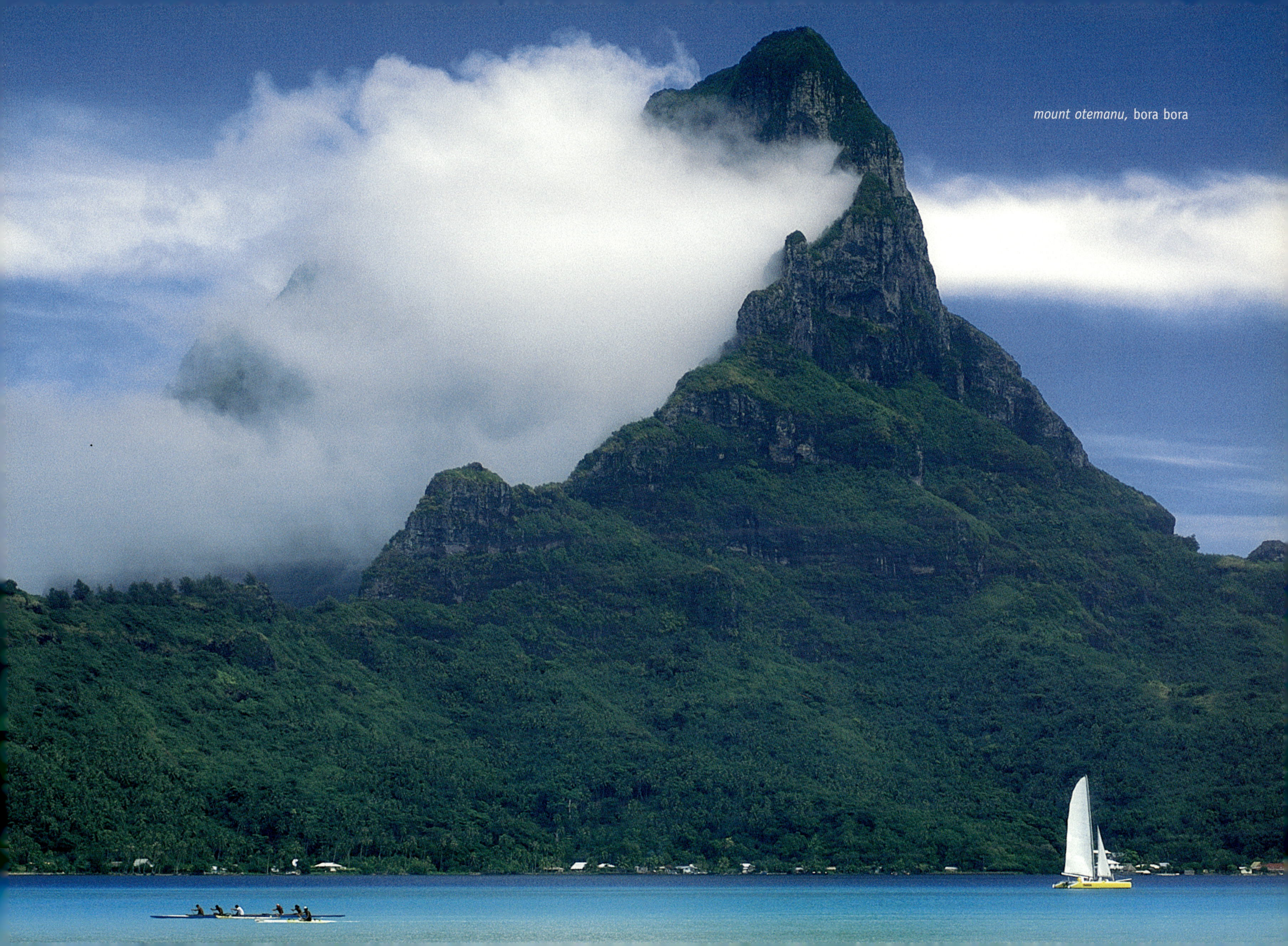

mount otemanu, bora bora

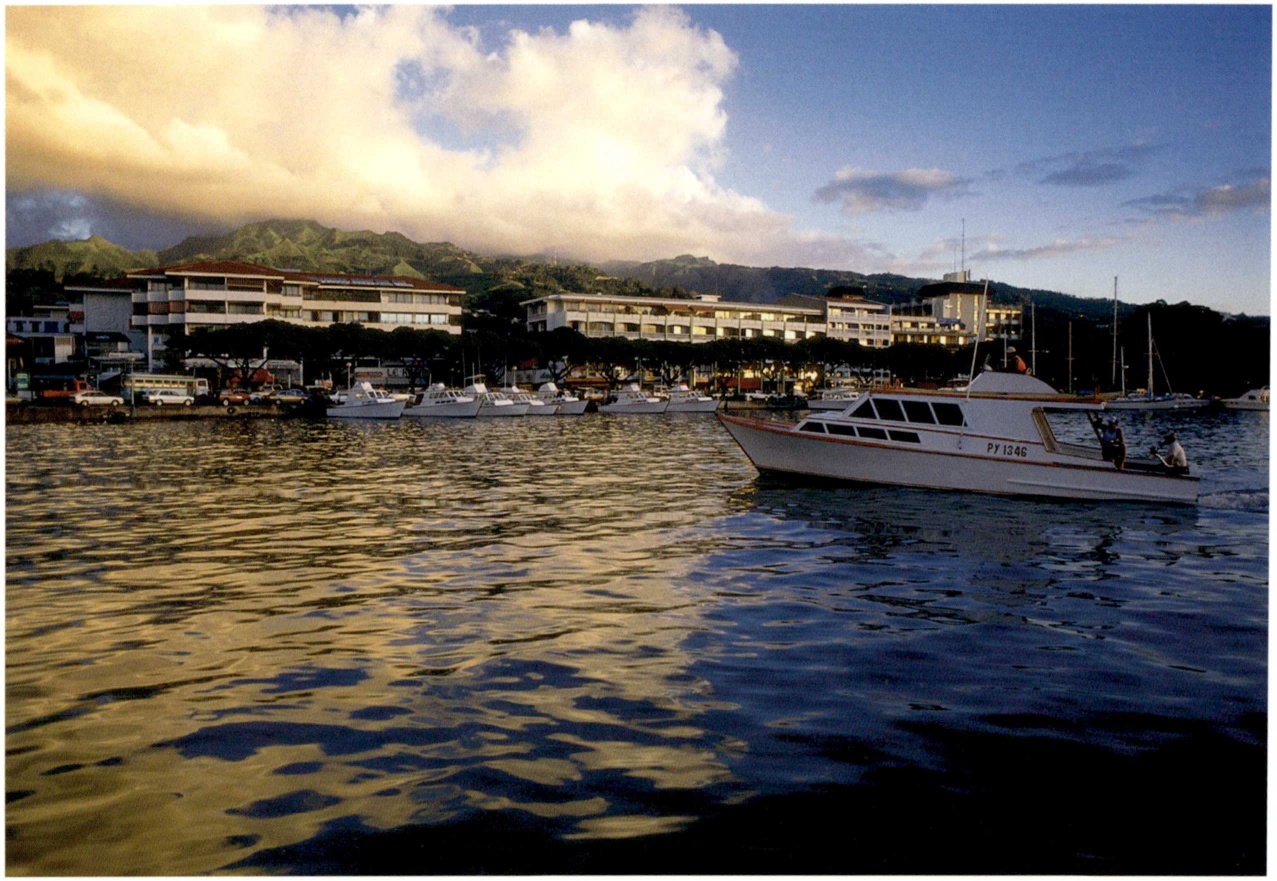

papeete waterfront

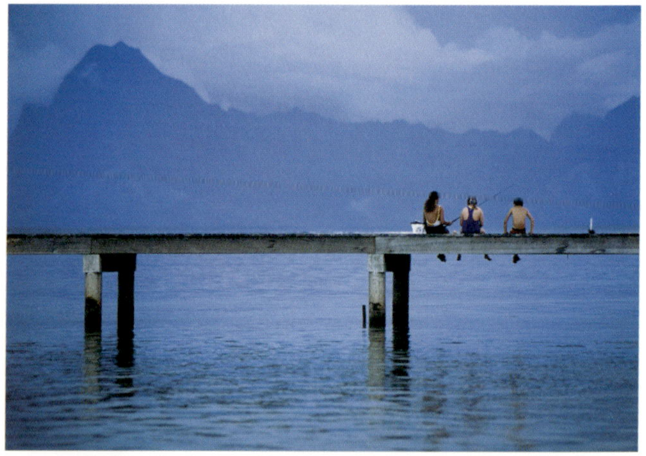

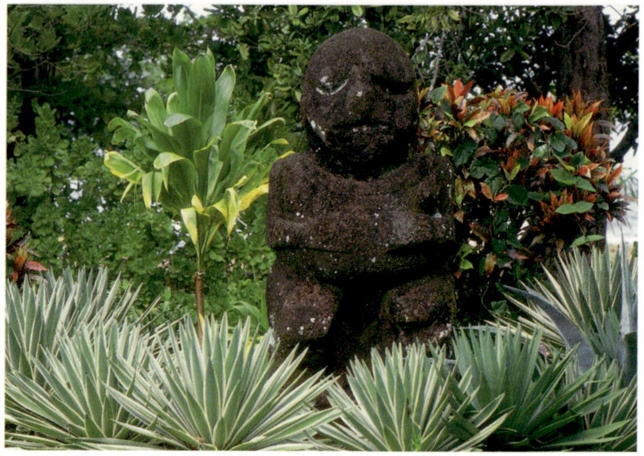

[ABOVE RIGHT] *view of moorea from fishing pier*

[RIGHT] *stone tiki from the astral islands at the gaugin museum,* tahiti

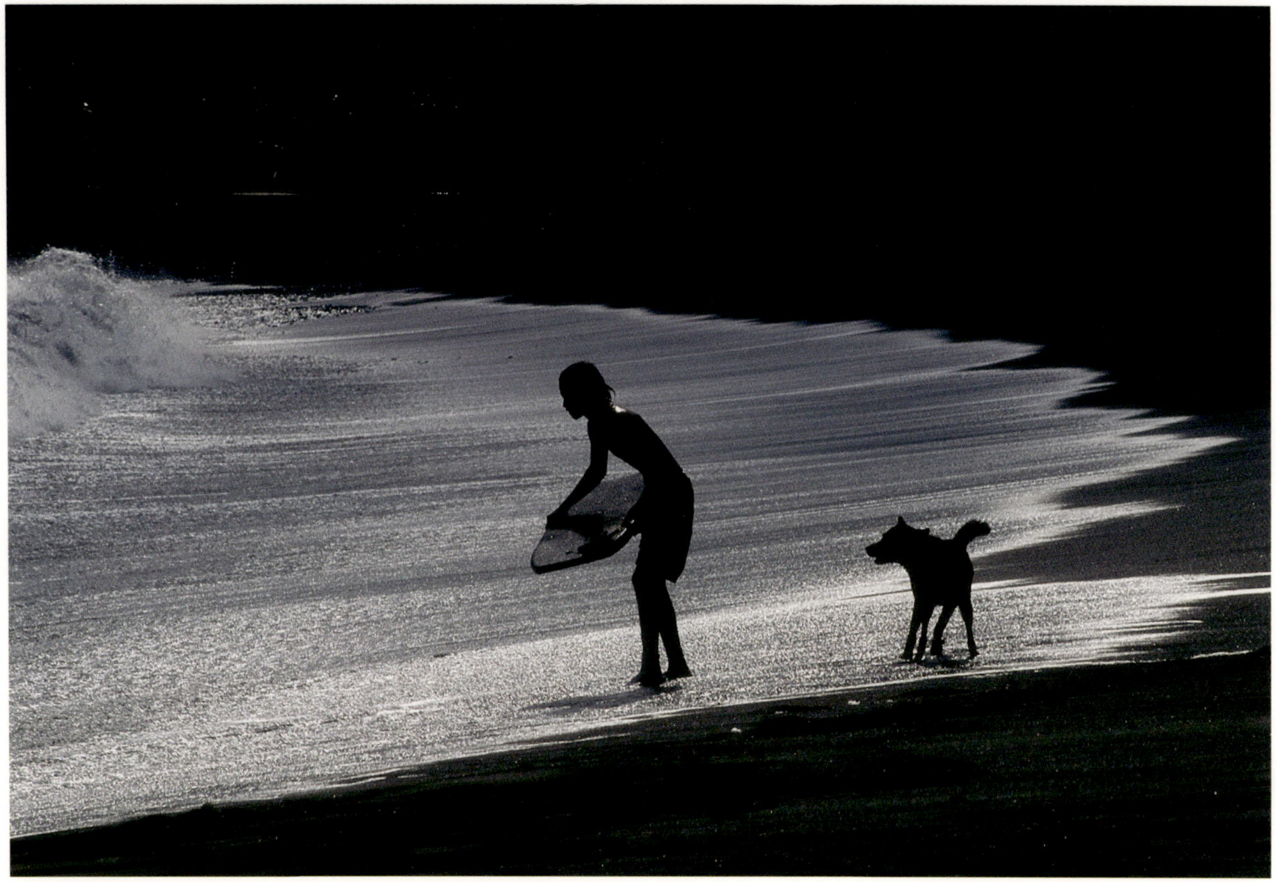

surfing on black sand beach, tahiti

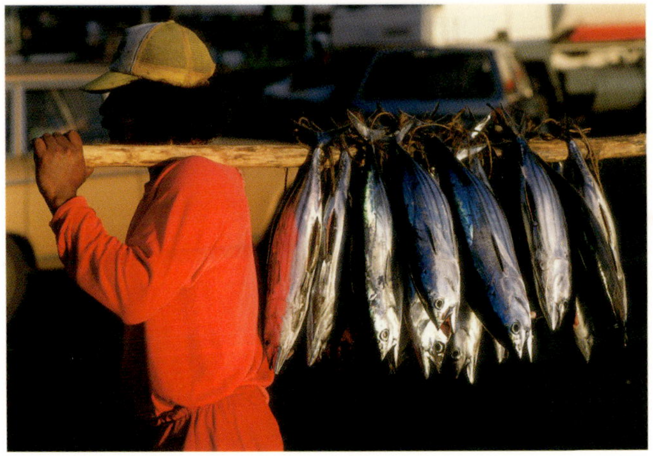

[LEFT] *freshly caught tuna,* papeete waterfront

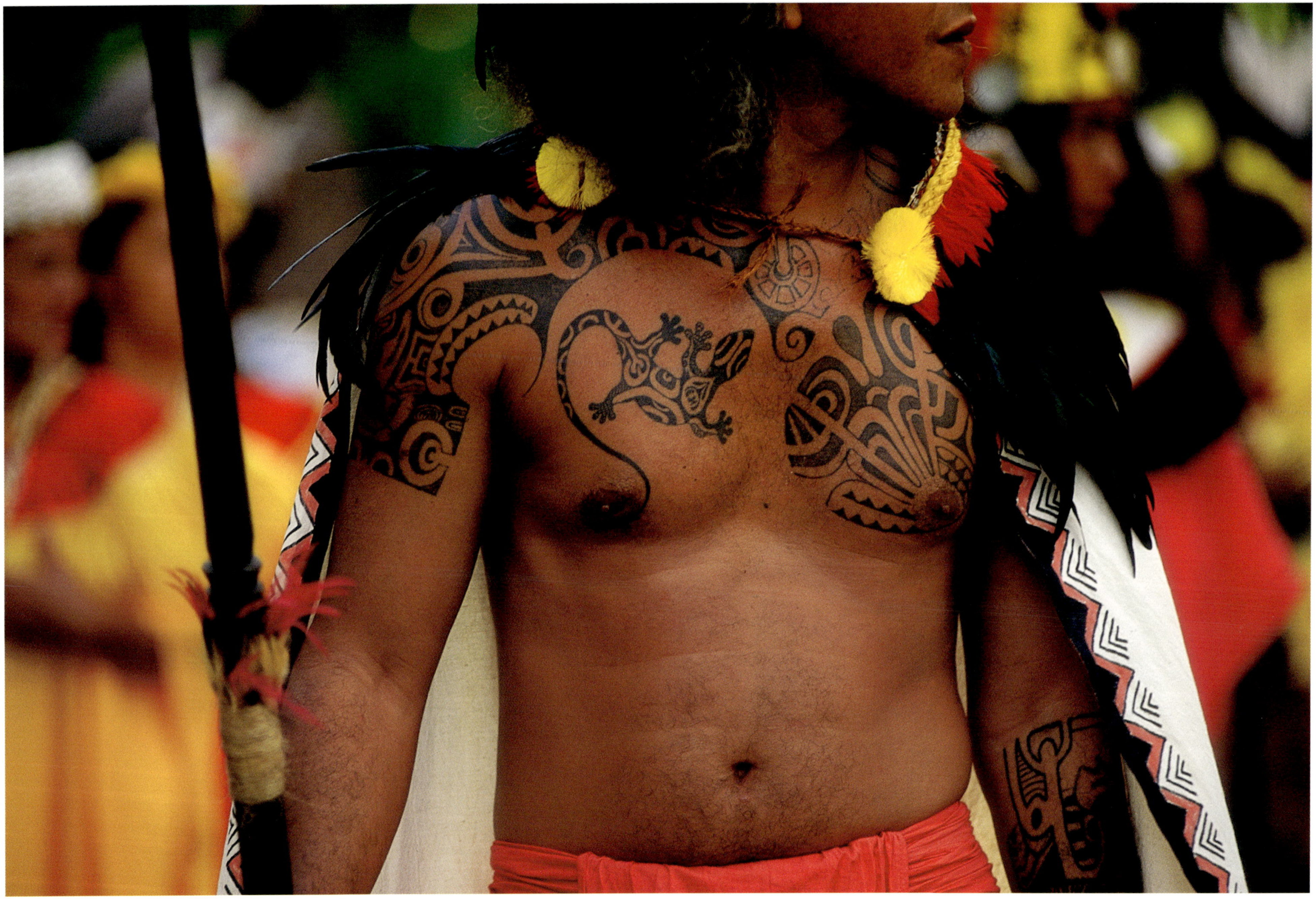

heiva i festival at marae arahurahu, tahiti

[RIGHT] *coral reef and coastline of moorea*

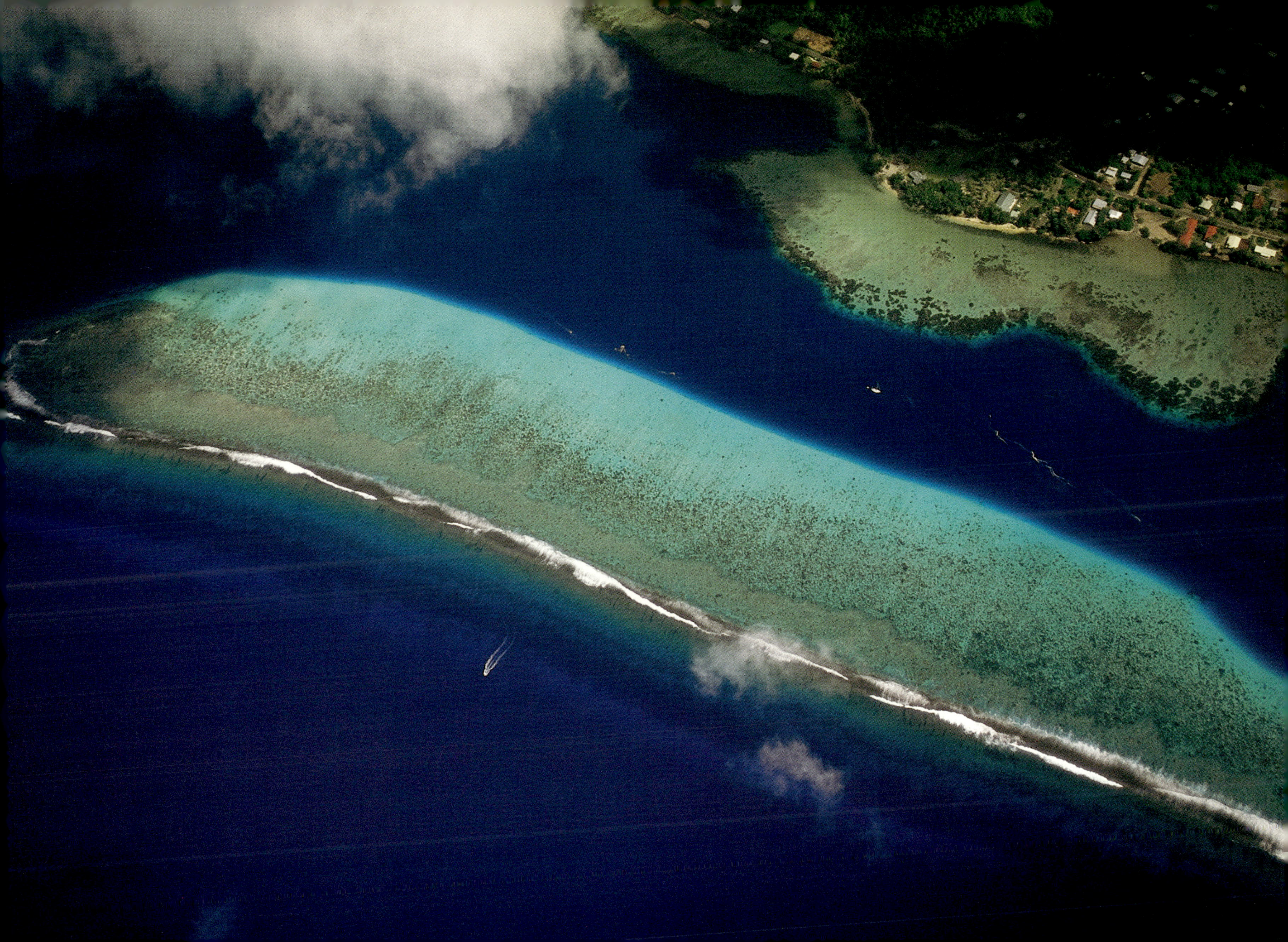

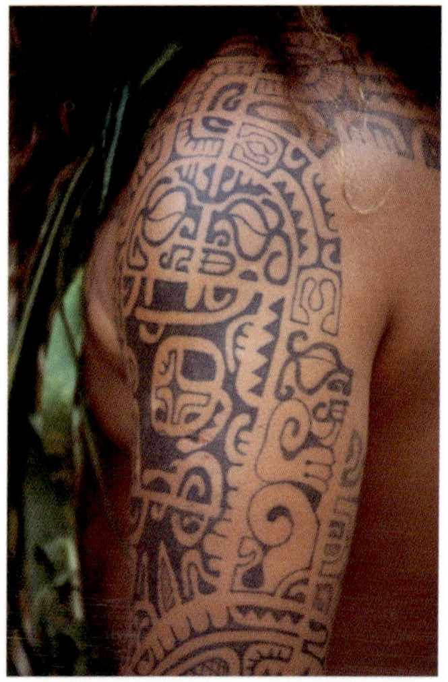

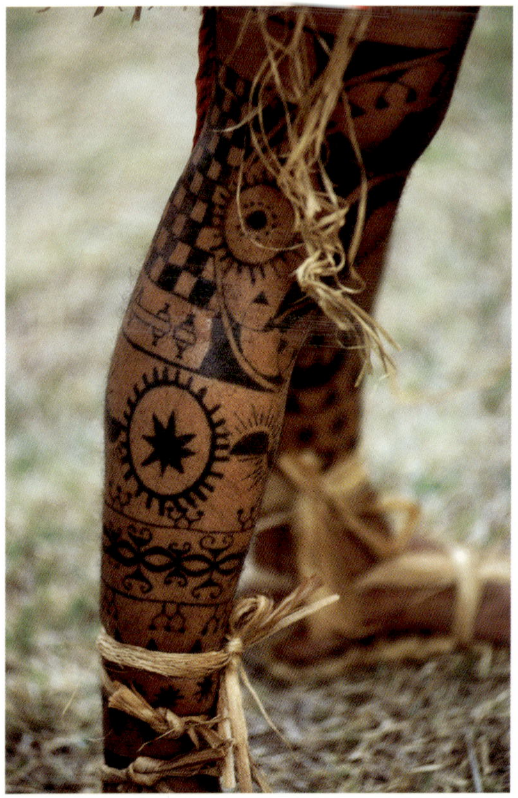

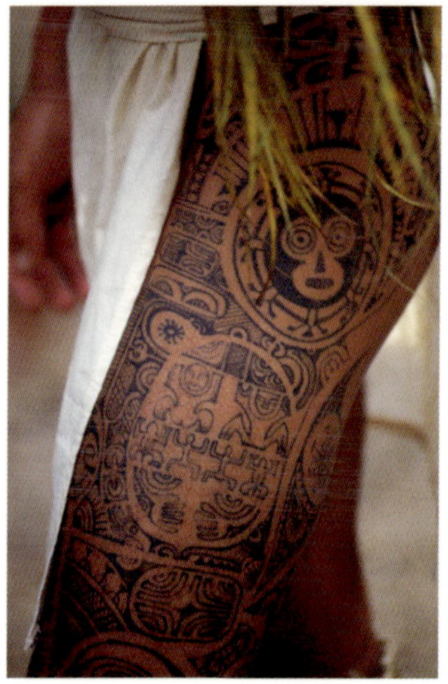

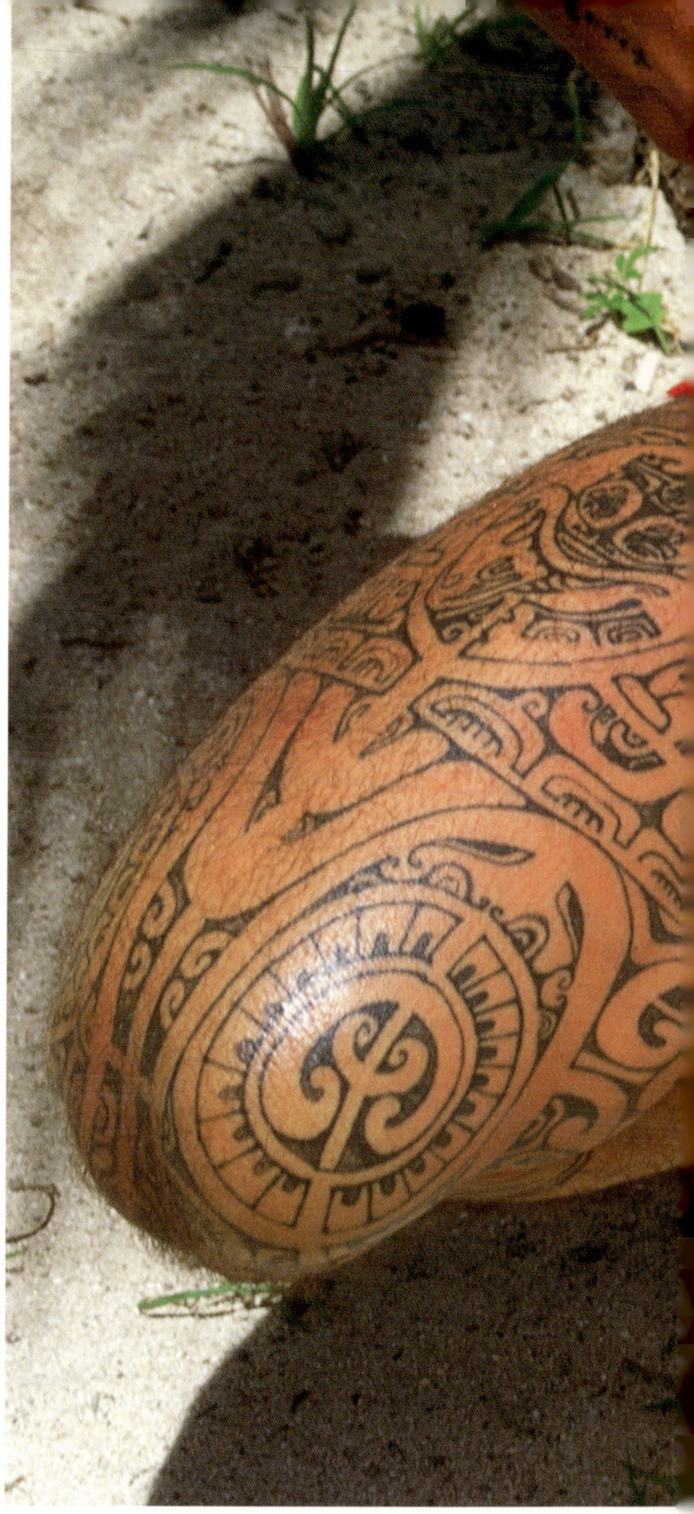

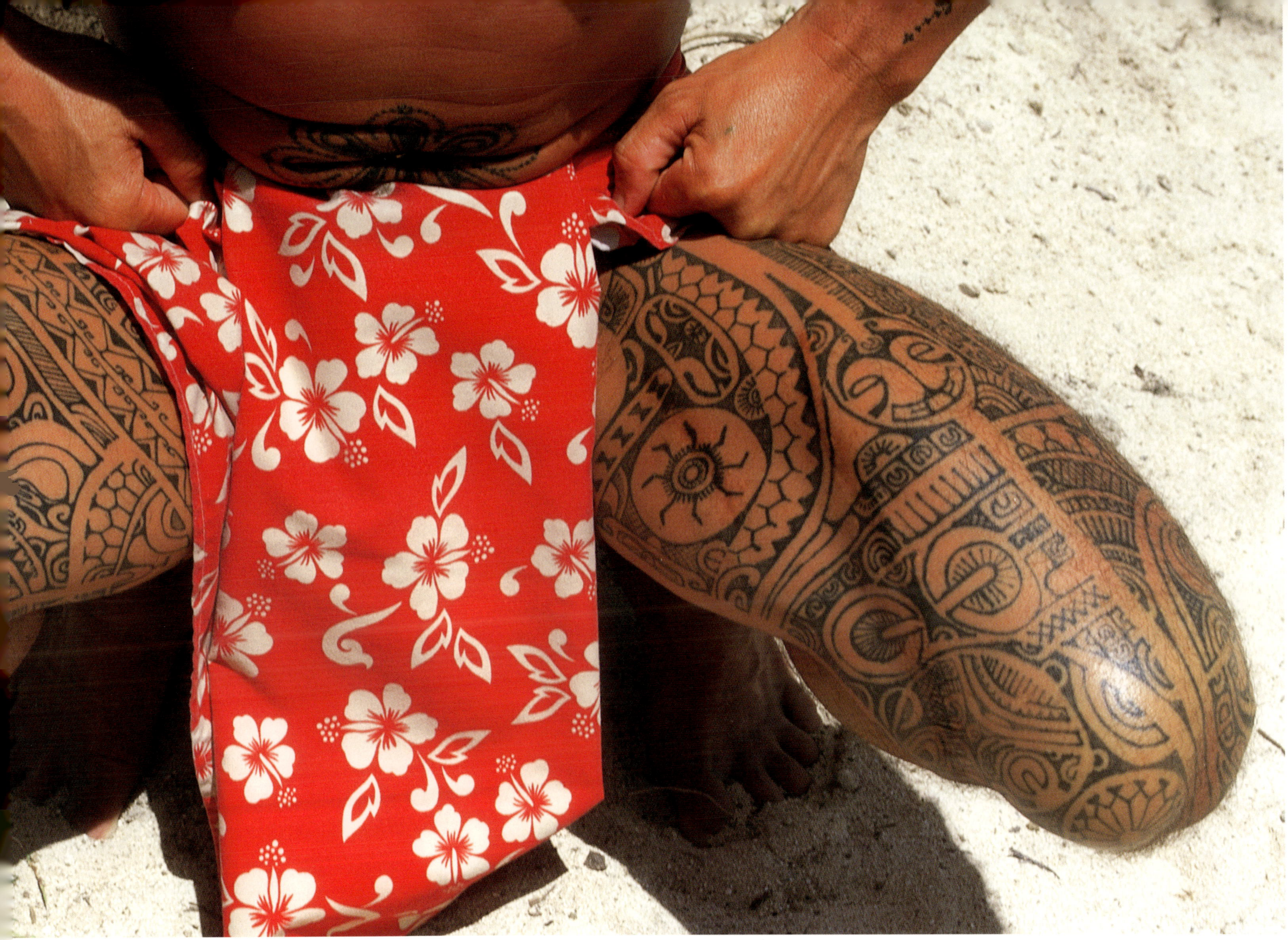

the origins of the tahitian tattoo lay deep in the mythological past and were a reflection of the social status of the wearer

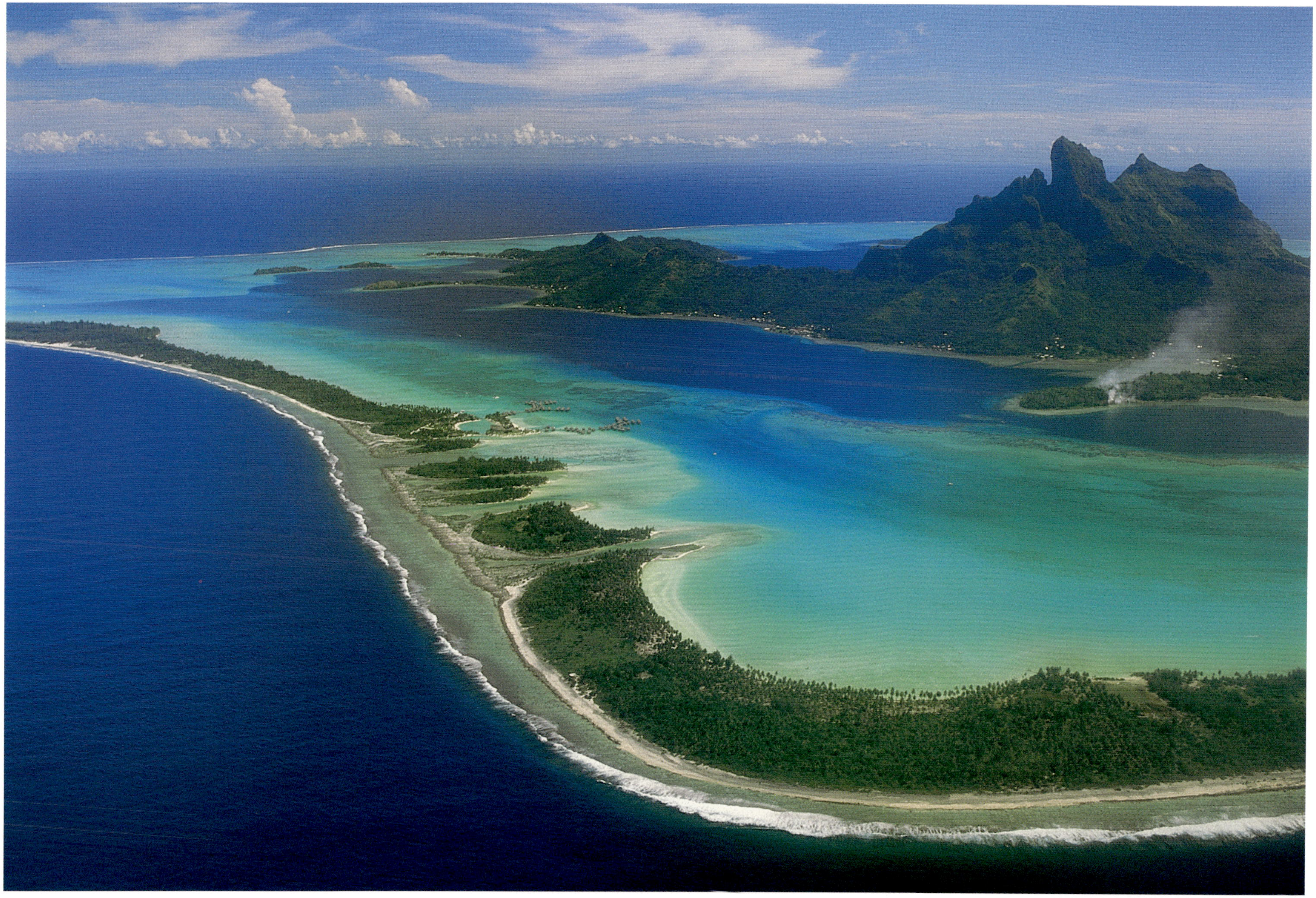

aerial of bora bora lagoon

[RIGHT] *canoeing on the bay of venus between moorea and tahiti*

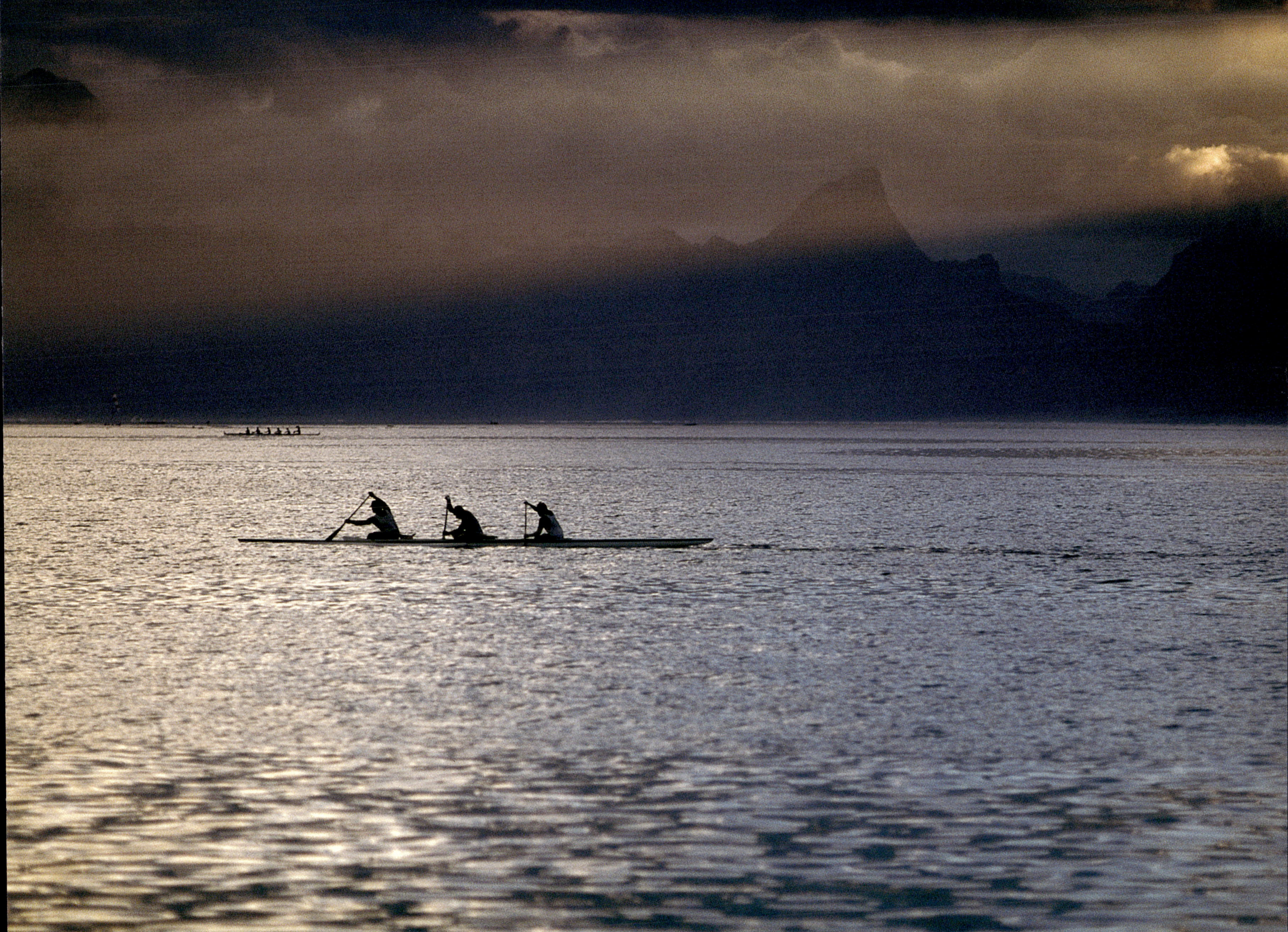

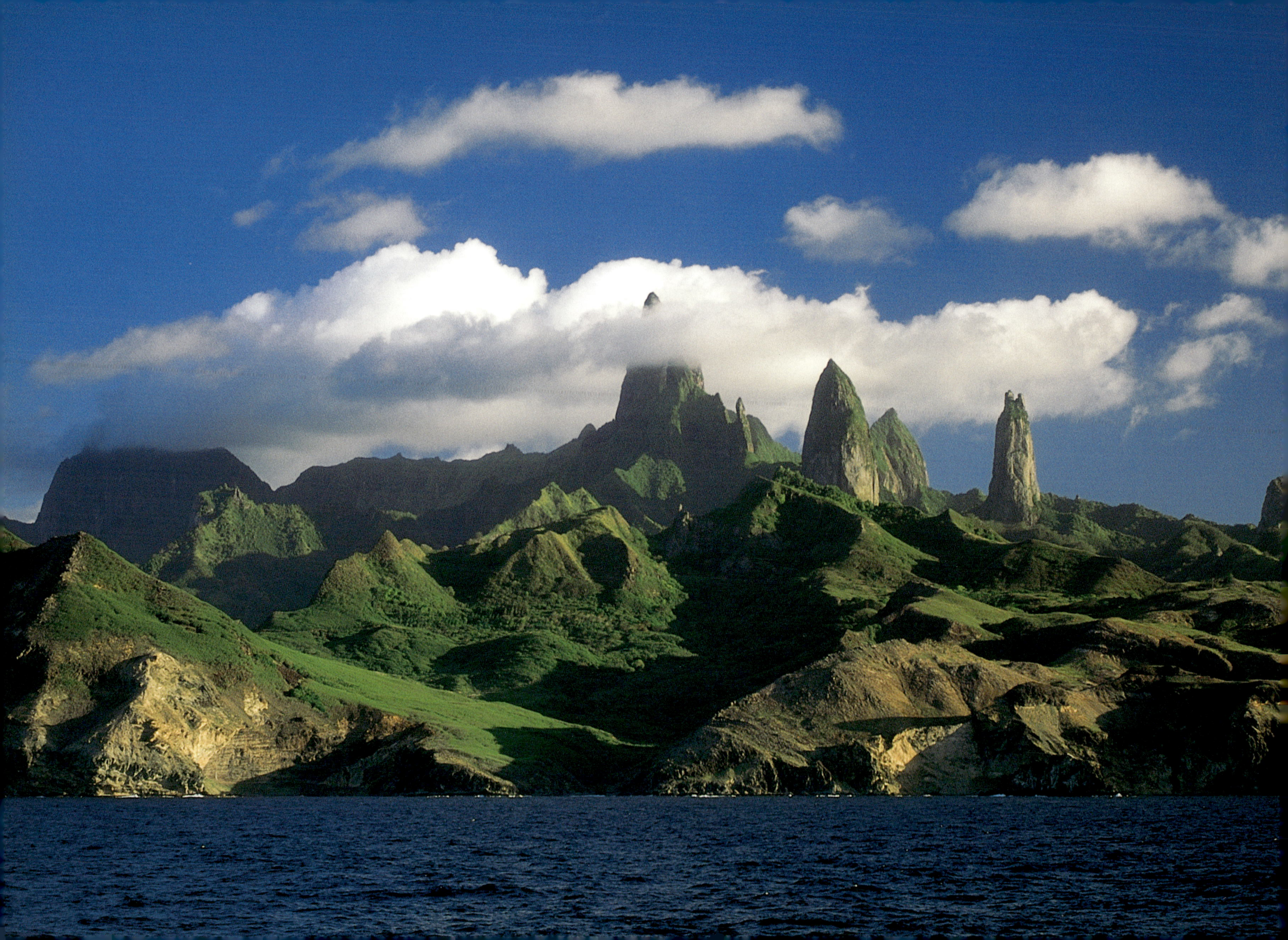

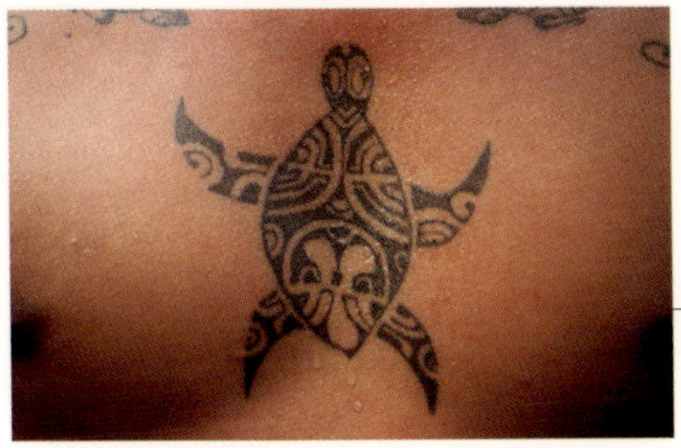

Marquesas Islands

THE MARQUESAS ISLANDS, located between Hawai'i and Tahiti in the eastern Pacific, consist of 10 main islands of which six are presently inhabited. They are part of French Polynesia, a French Overseas Territory.

Settled from Samoa about 300AD, the Marquesas are known as the embarkation point for the exploration and colonisation of most of the eastern Pacific from Hawai'i to Easter Island and New Zealand via Tahiti.

The high volcanic islands are geologically very young with few reefs and none of the lagoons of many of the other island groups. Since there are no flat coastal plains, there are no circle roads. Instead, deep narrow river valleys isolated from each other by serrated razor-backed ridges kept the tribes separated in olden times, as they impede communication even today. Marquesans were unable to develop a stable large scale society of the type found elsewhere in Polynesia because of constant tribal warfare, with the result that no one leader or tribe could consolidate control over the entire group. The Marquesans practised cannibalism on defeated enemies as a way of taking their life force or 'mana'.

The Marquesans were famous for their tattooing which sometimes covered men's entire body. The sexual attraction of tattoos by the Marquesans interested European sailors, creating the tattooed sailor tradition.

The traditional culture was creative and dynamic, as seen from some of its remnants hidden in dark jungles where mysterious over-grown archaeological sites hint at a civilisation long gone. The depopulation that occurred with European contact left the valleys quiet and empty and that remains mostly the case today.

The skilled sculptors and carvers of the Marquesas attracted European artists and writers. Paul Gauguin arrived in 1901 to live and paint on Hiva Oa. There is a reconstruction of his 'House of Pleasure' at Atuona and he is buried near the French singer Jacques Brel in the little cemetery of Calvary on the hill overlooking the town. Also, in 1842 Herman Melville, the American author, who deserted from a whaling ship at Taiohae on Nuku Hiva, spent some time in the Taipi Vai valley as a captive of a cannibal tribe. His book 'Typee' contributed greatly to the popular romantic image of the Pacific.

[LEFT] *volcanic spires,* ua poa [ABOVE] *turtle tattoo*

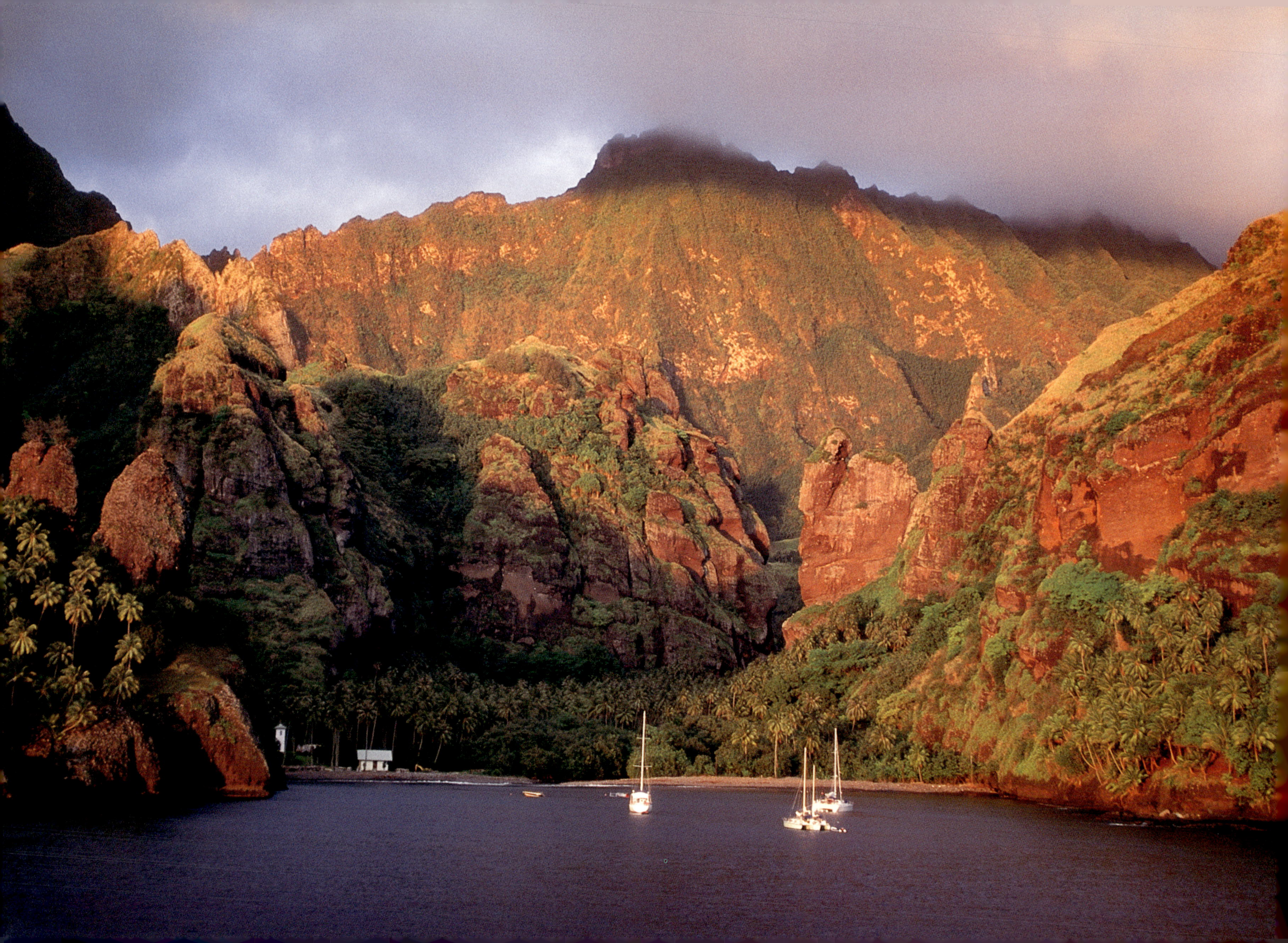

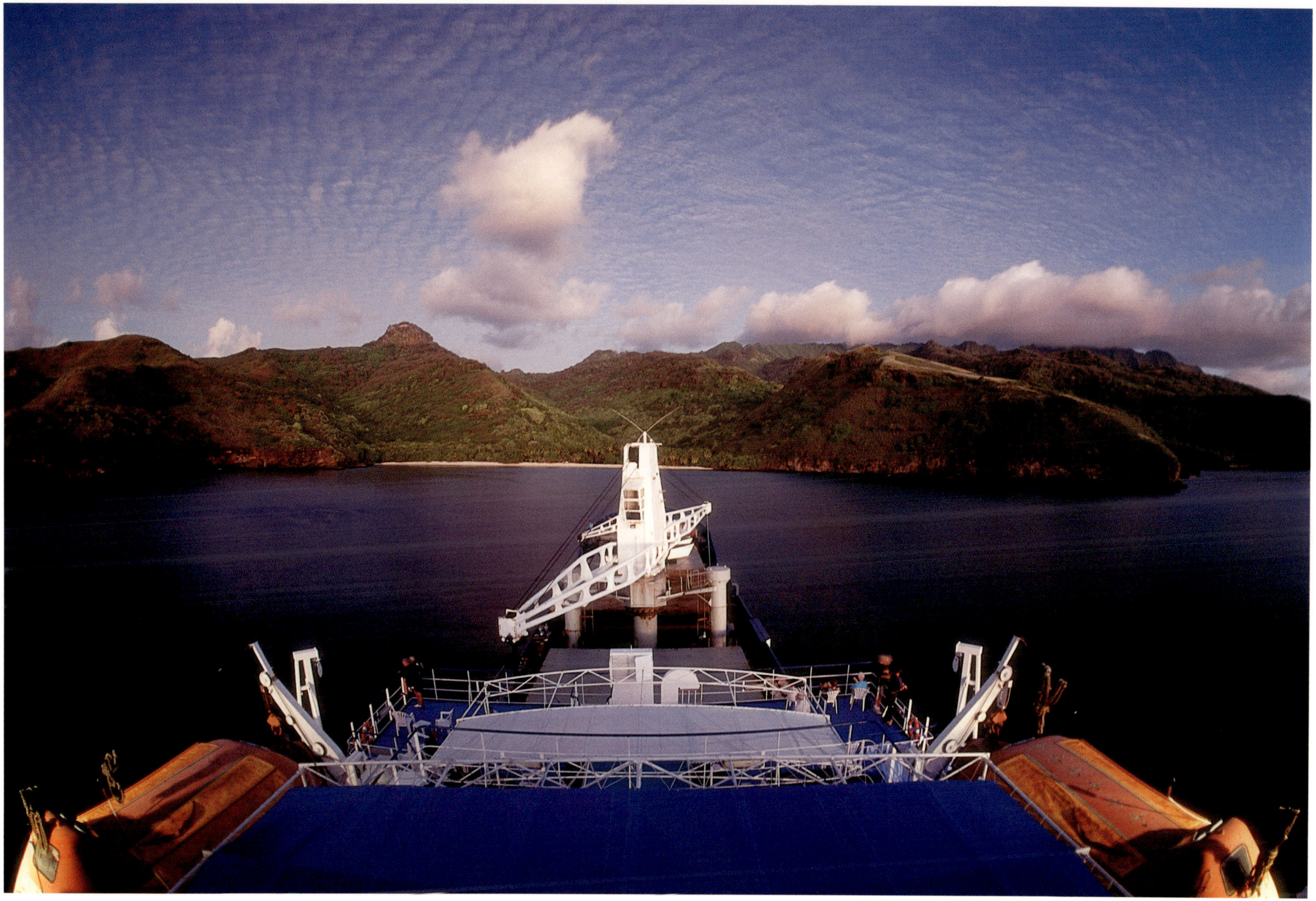

[LEFT] *bay of virgins,* hanavave, fatu hiva

'the aranui' moored at tahuata

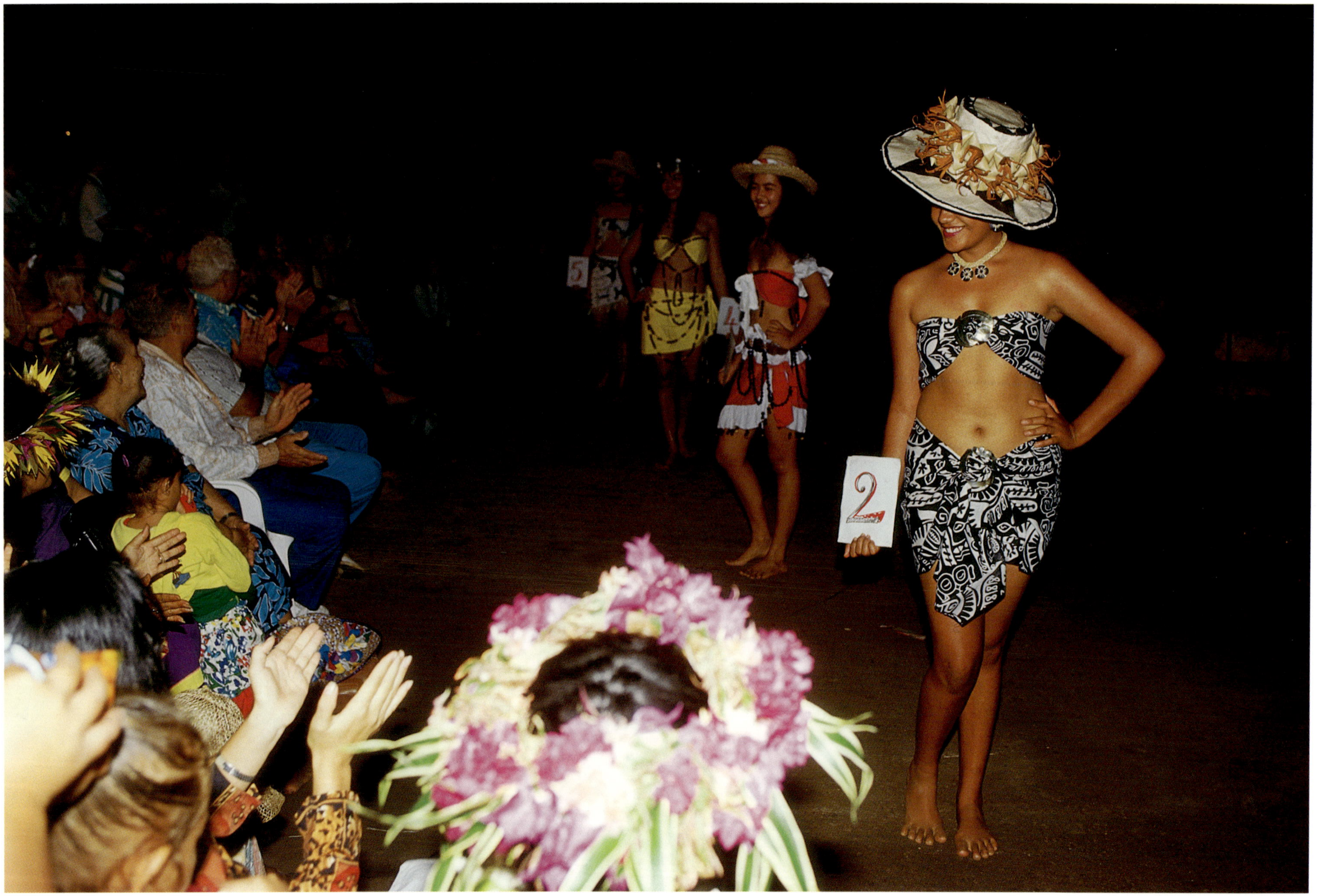

bastille day beauty contest, vaipaee, ua huka

[RIGHT] *dancers at heiva i festival,* vaipaee, ua huka

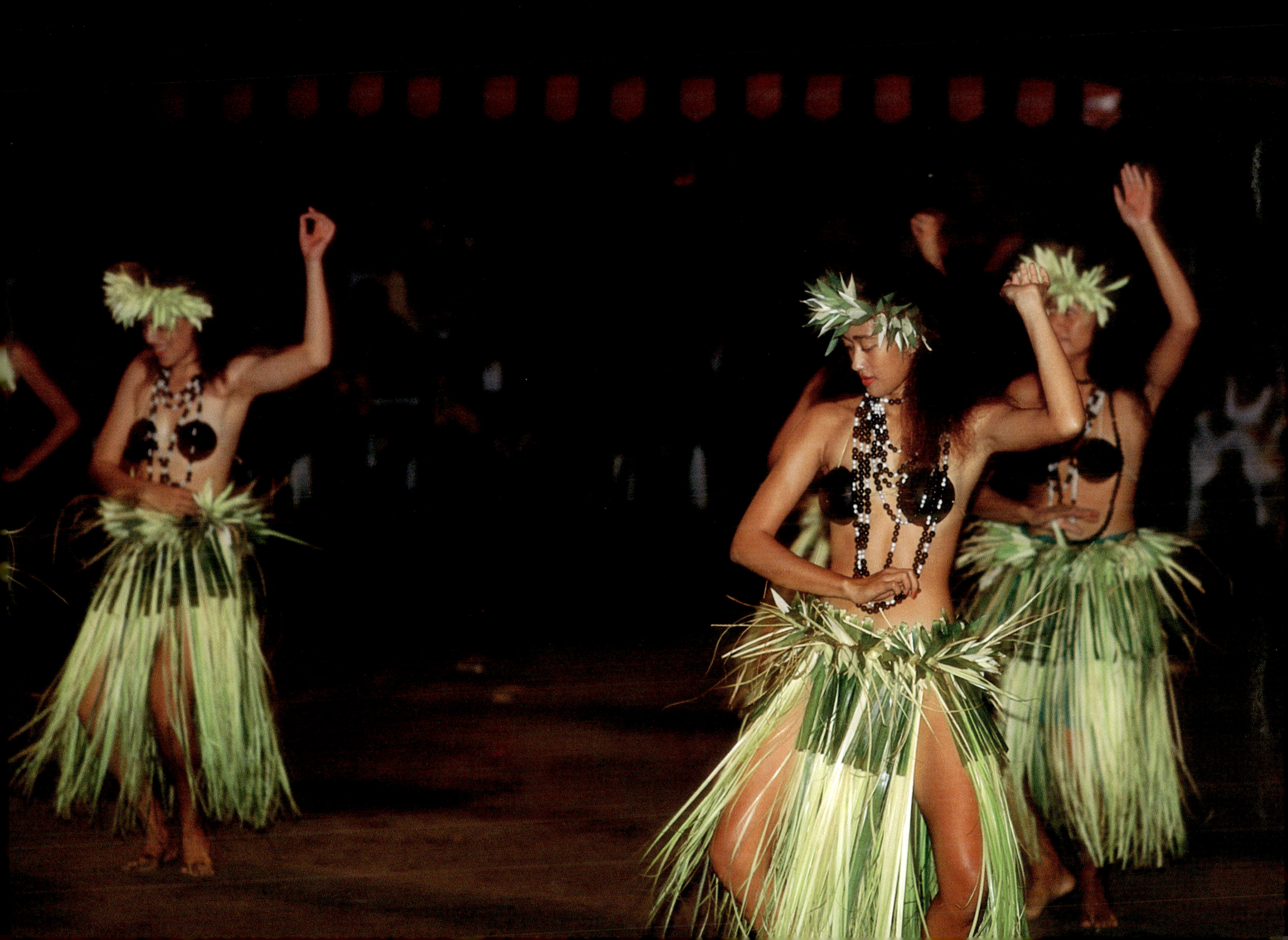

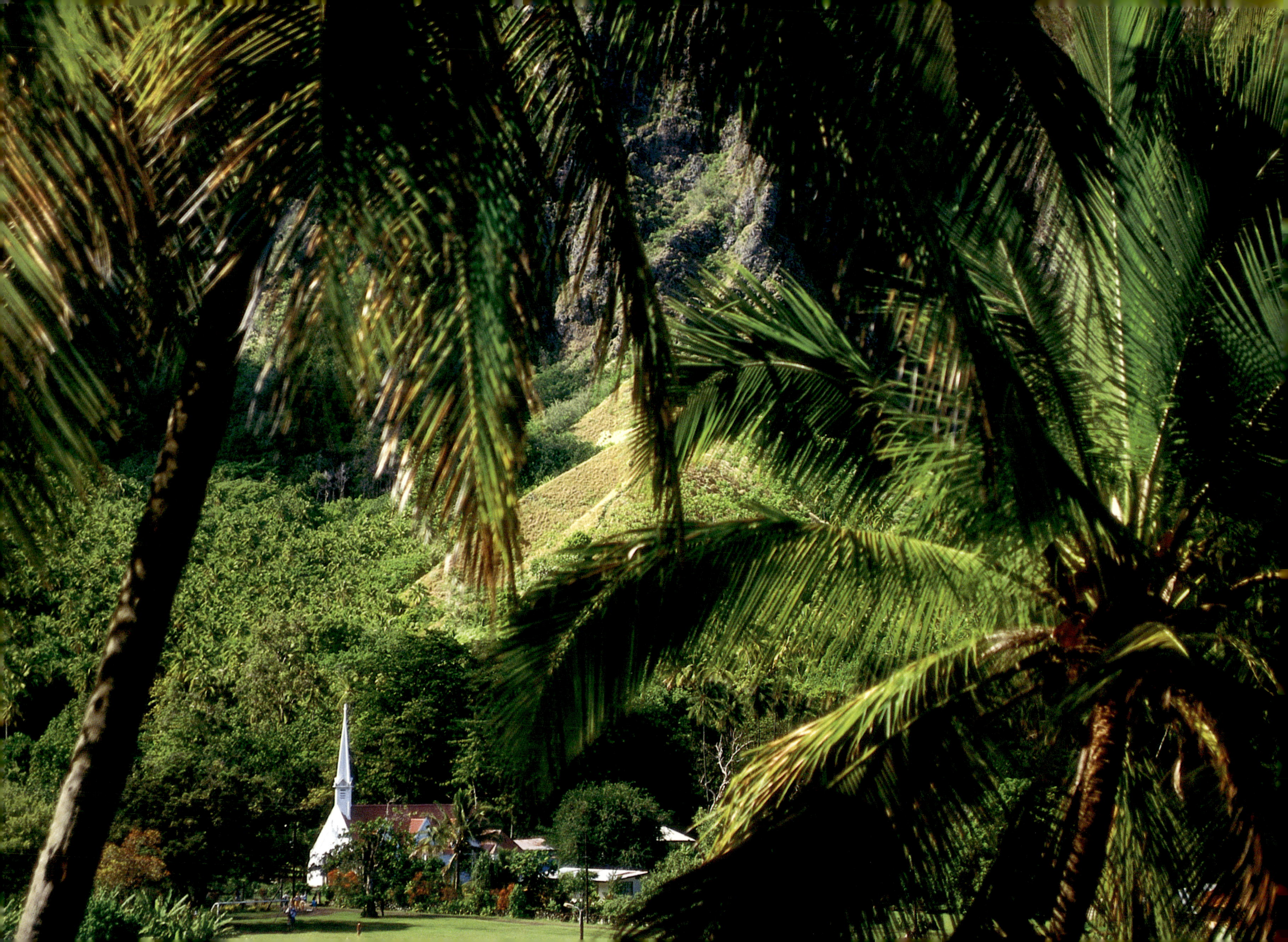

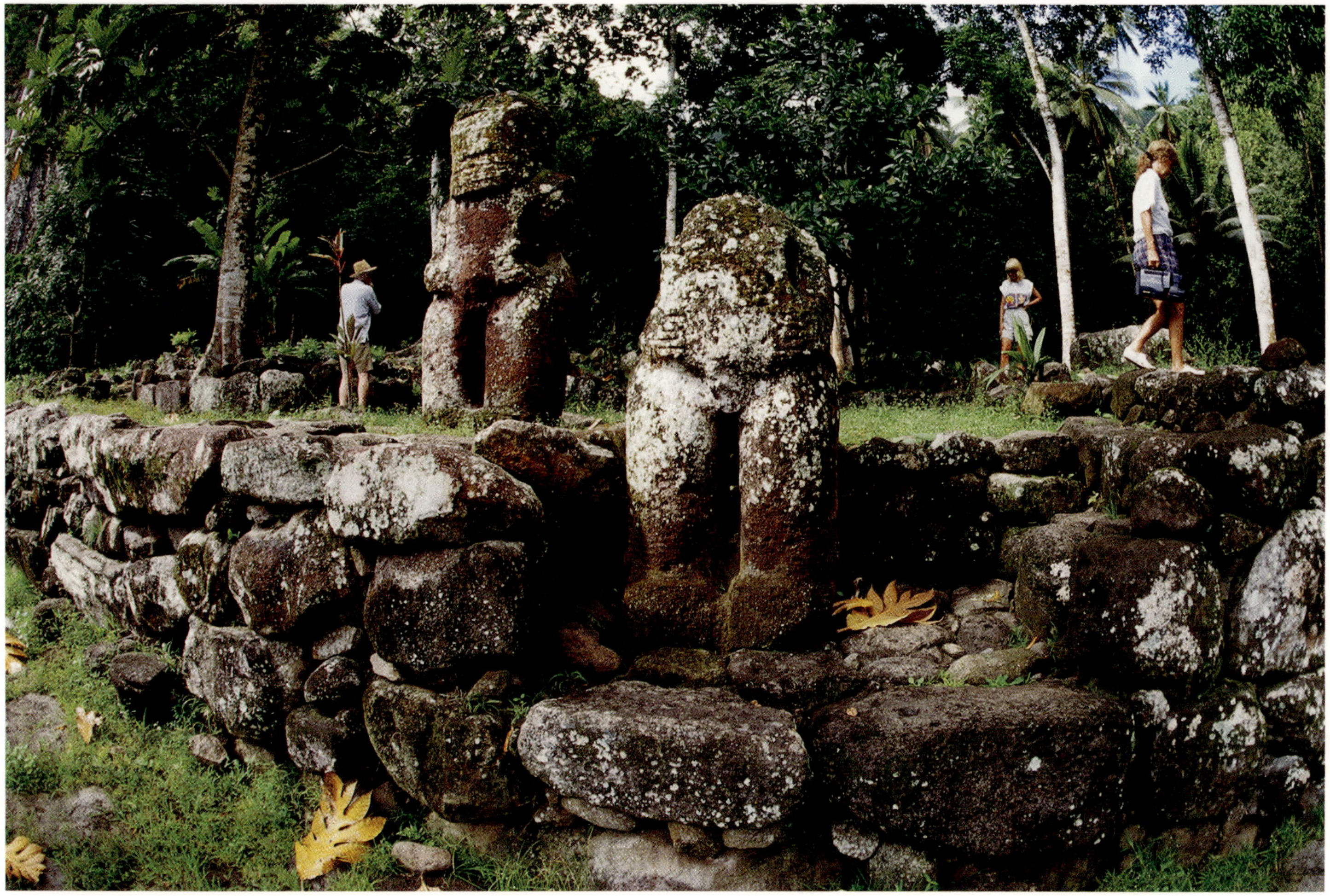

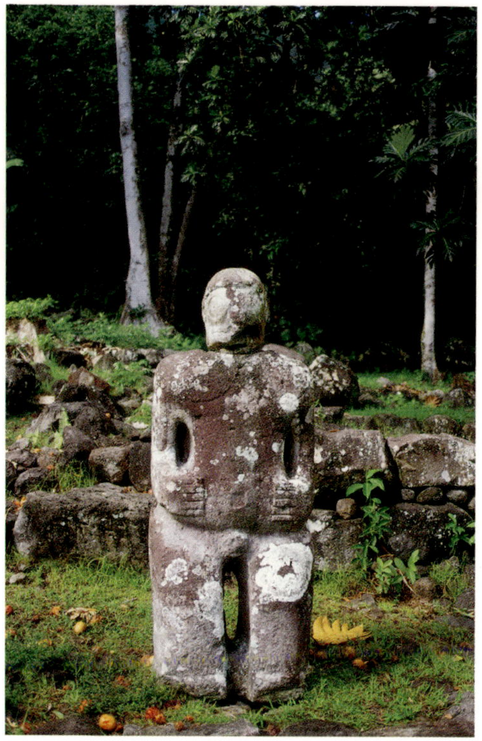

[ABOVE AND RIGHT] *stone tikis on the te l'ipona me'ae,* puamau, hiva oa

[LEFT] *church at omoa,* fatu hiva

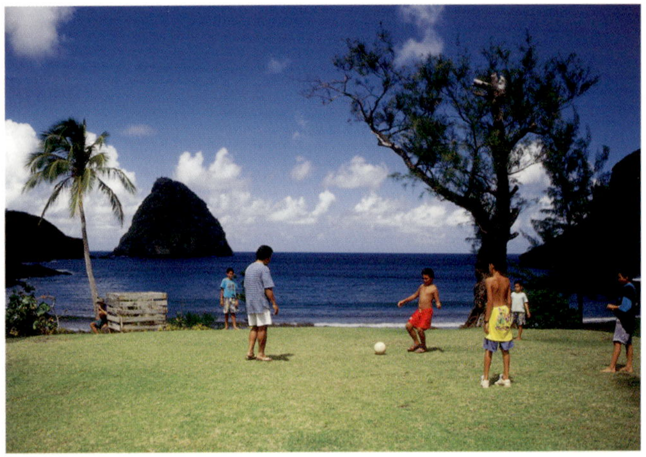

[LEFT AND BELOW] *football game,* hane, ua huka

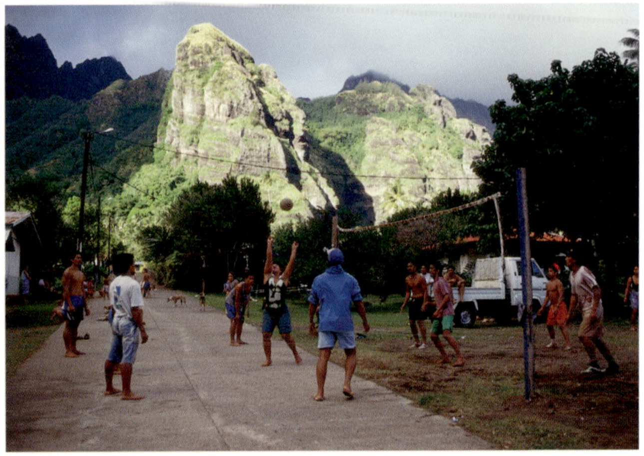

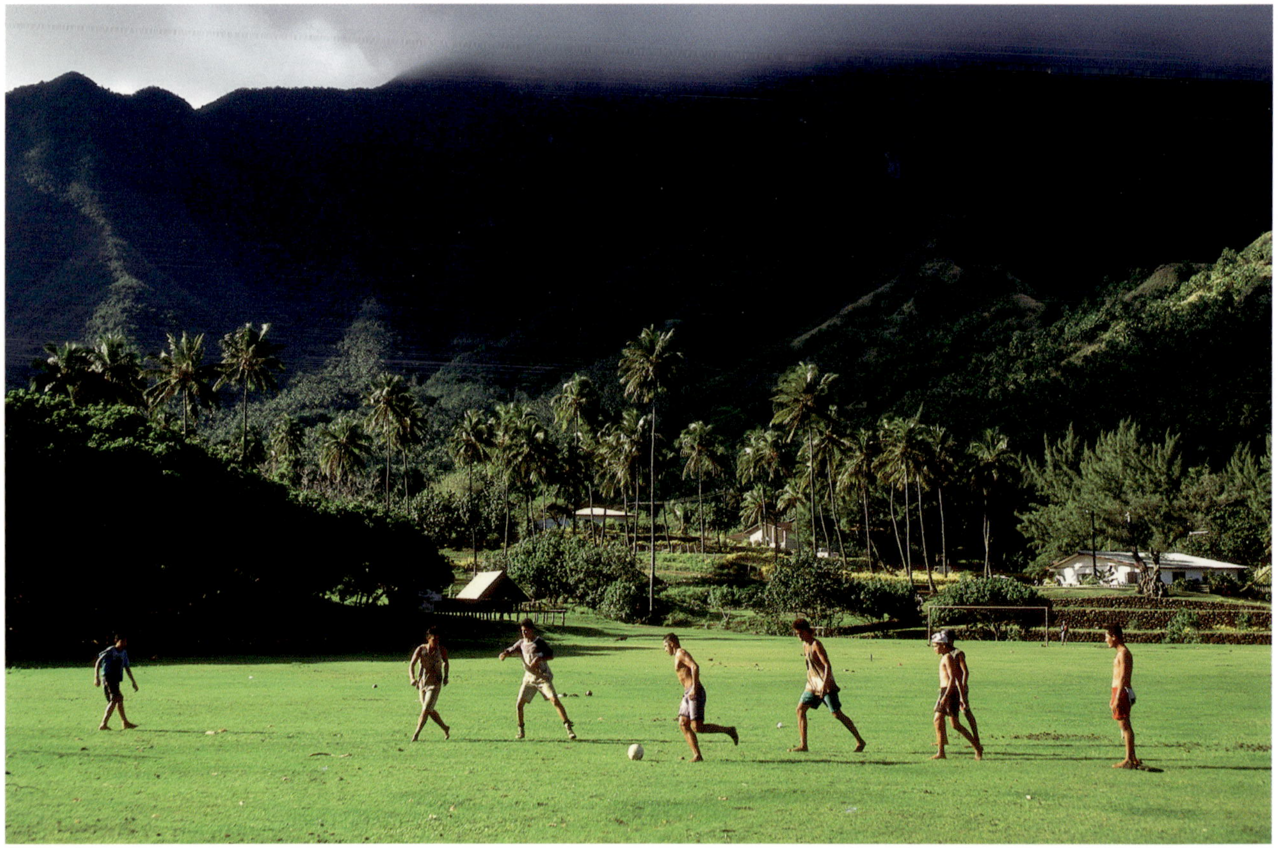

[ABOVE] *volleyball at hanavave,* fatu hiva

[RIGHT] *bareback horserace,* vaipaee, ua huka

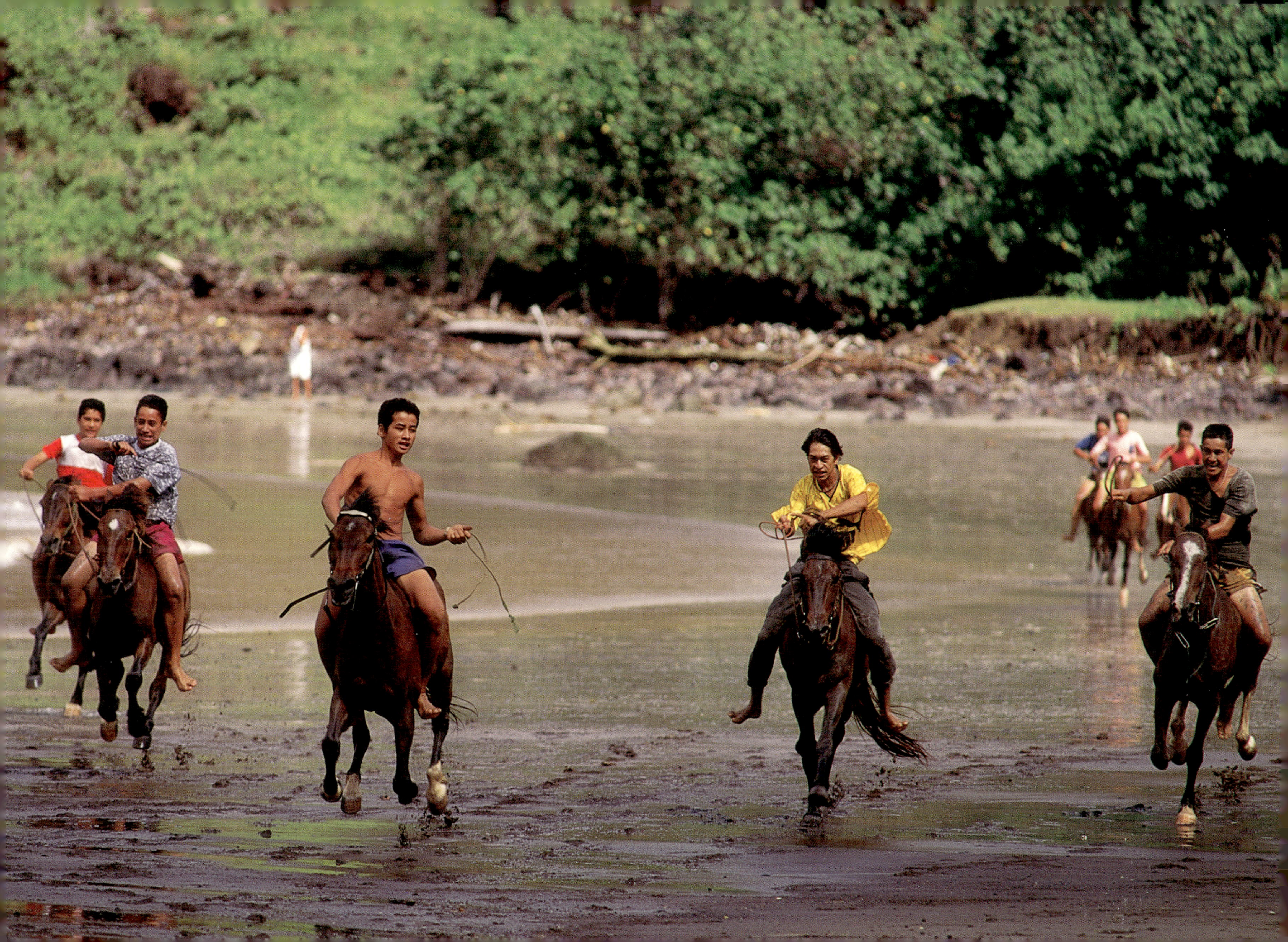

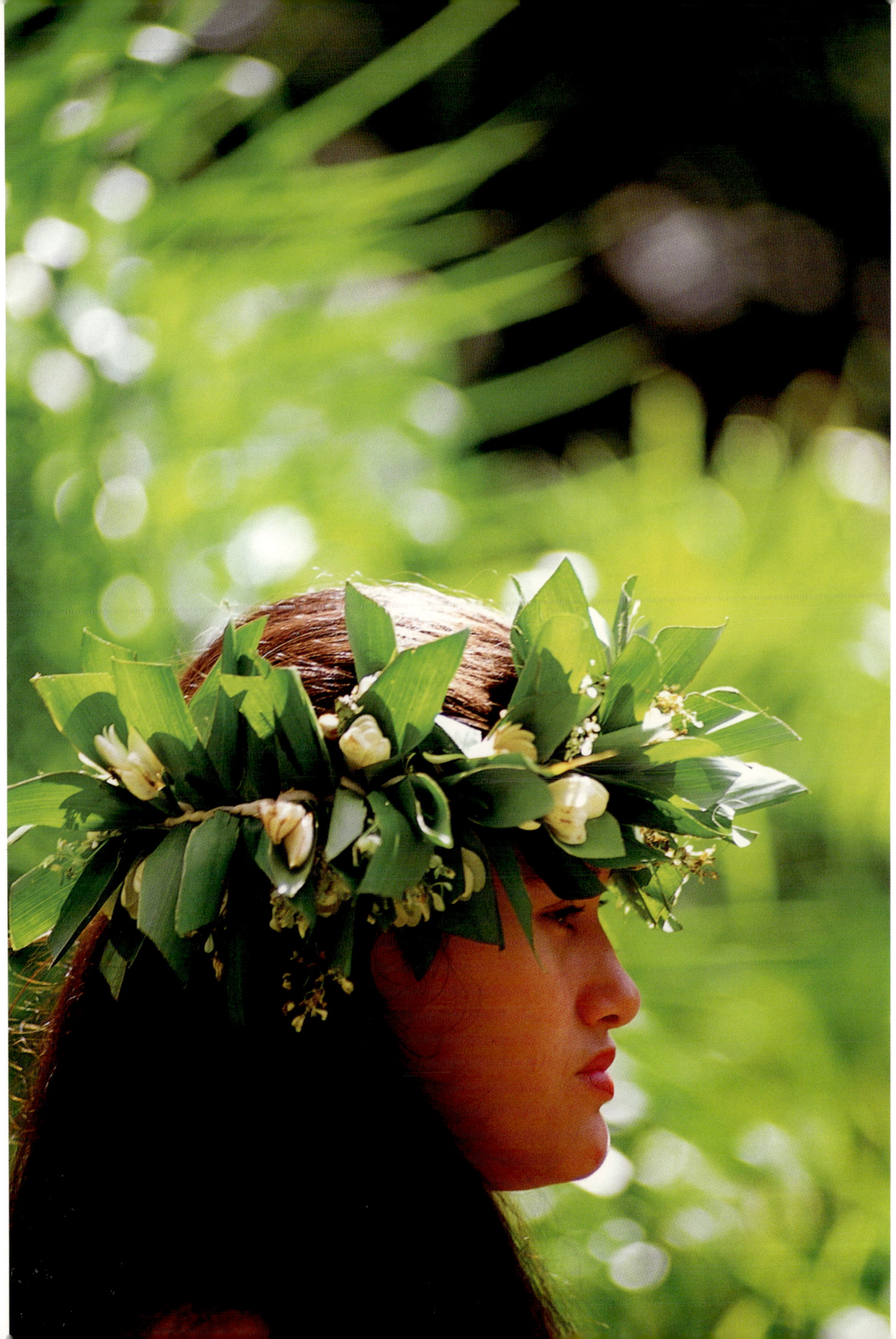

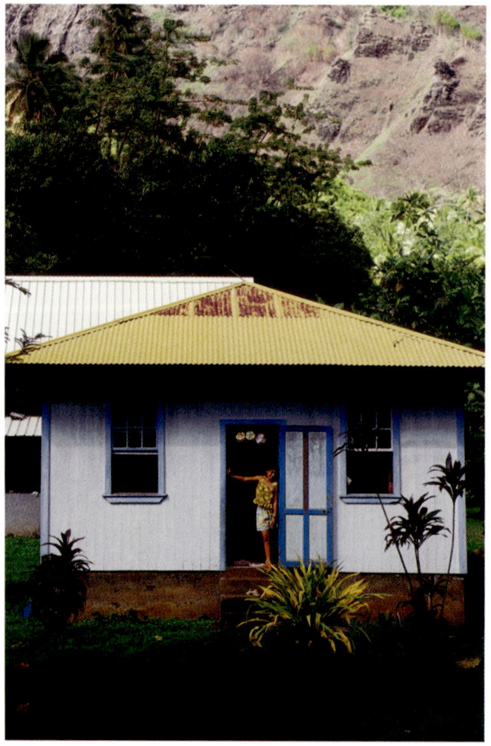

[ABOVE] *hanavave village,* fatu hiva

[LEFT] *marquesan woman at atuona,* hiva oa

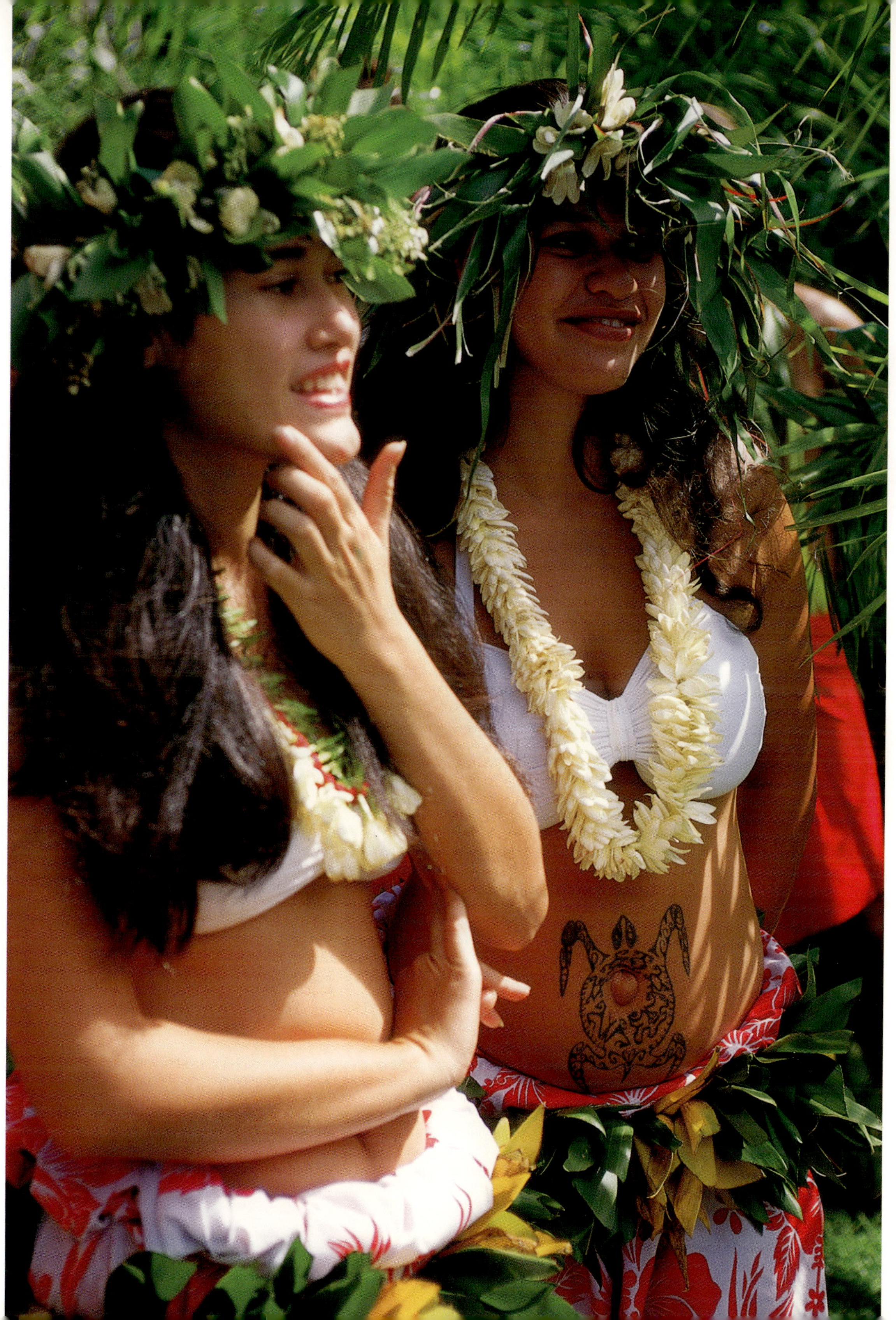

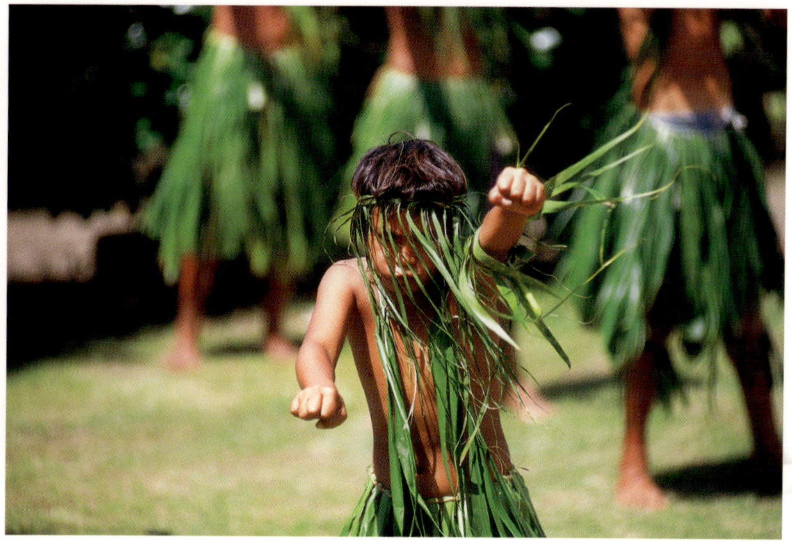

dancing boy, ua pou

[LEFT] *dancers at atuona,* hiva oa

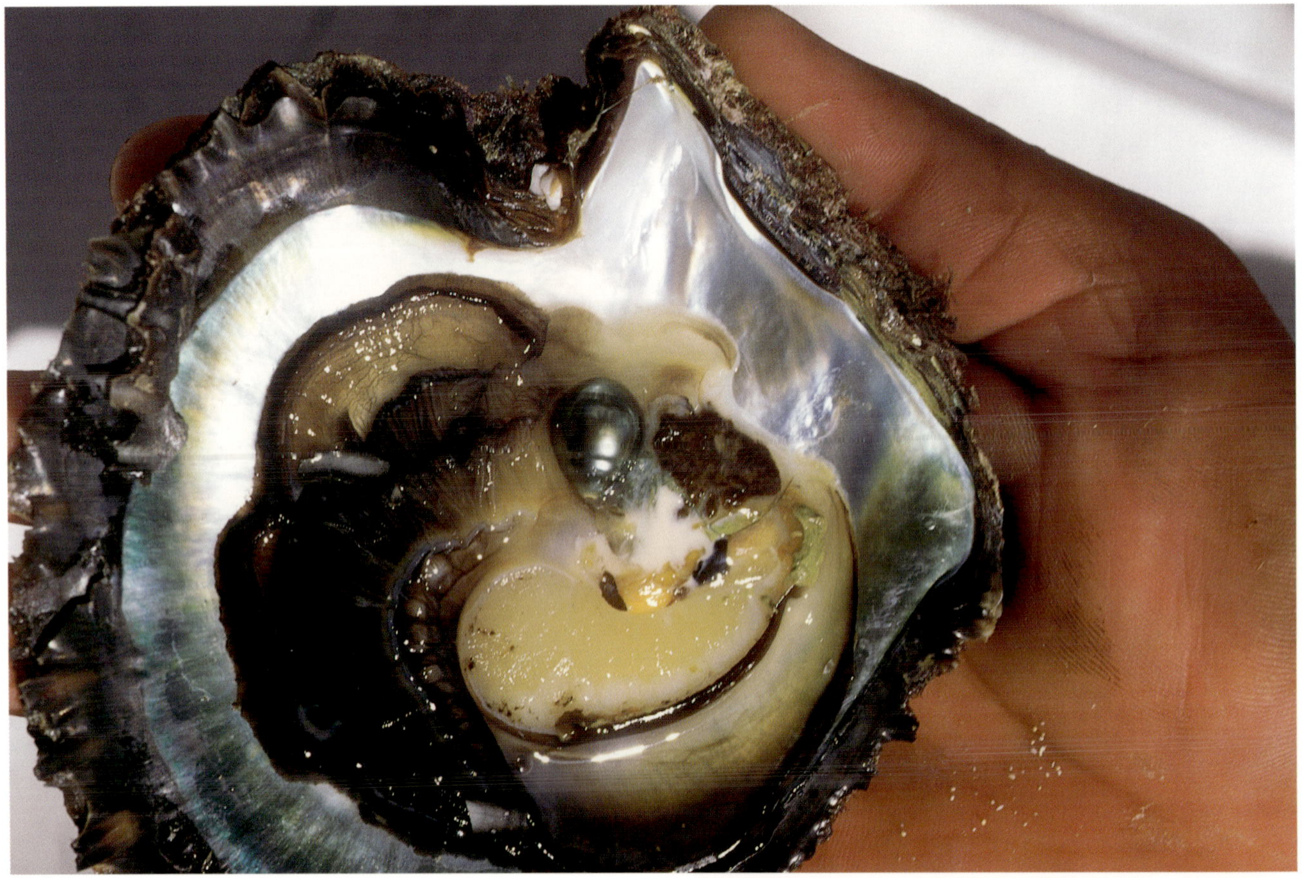

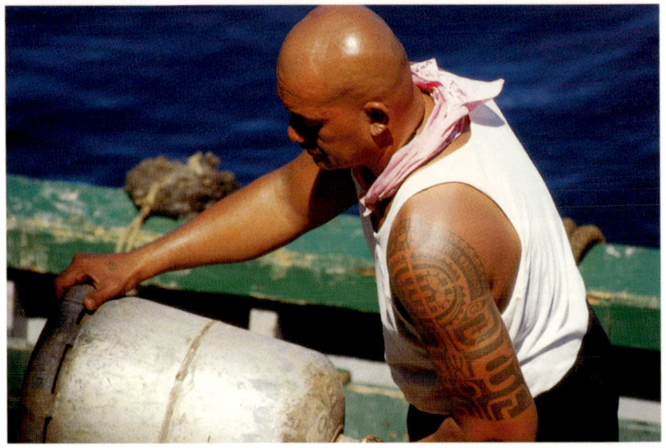

[**ABOVE**] *black pearl from takapoto lagoon,* tuamotu islands [**RIGHT**] *tattooed aranui crewman*

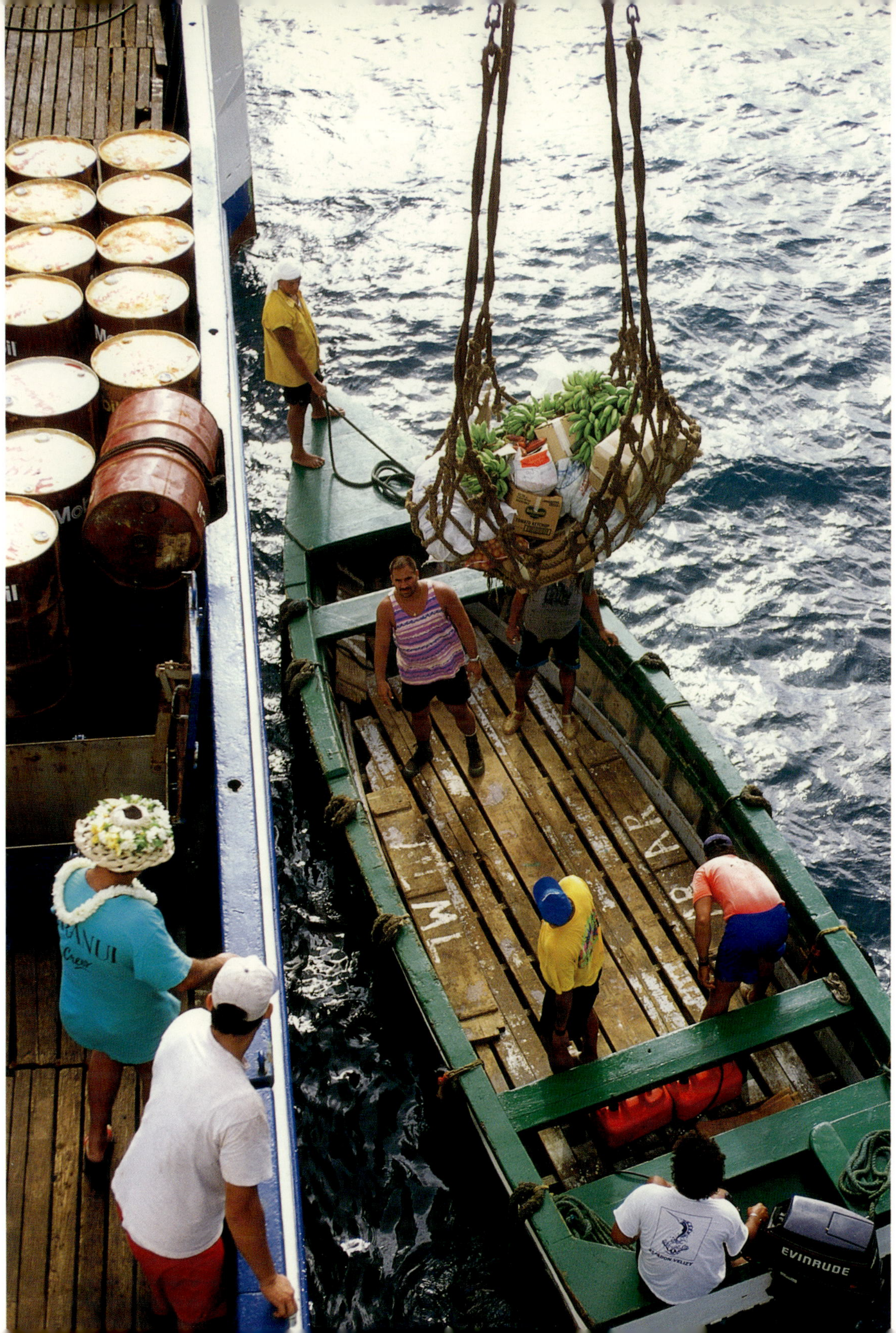

loading cargo, hiva oa

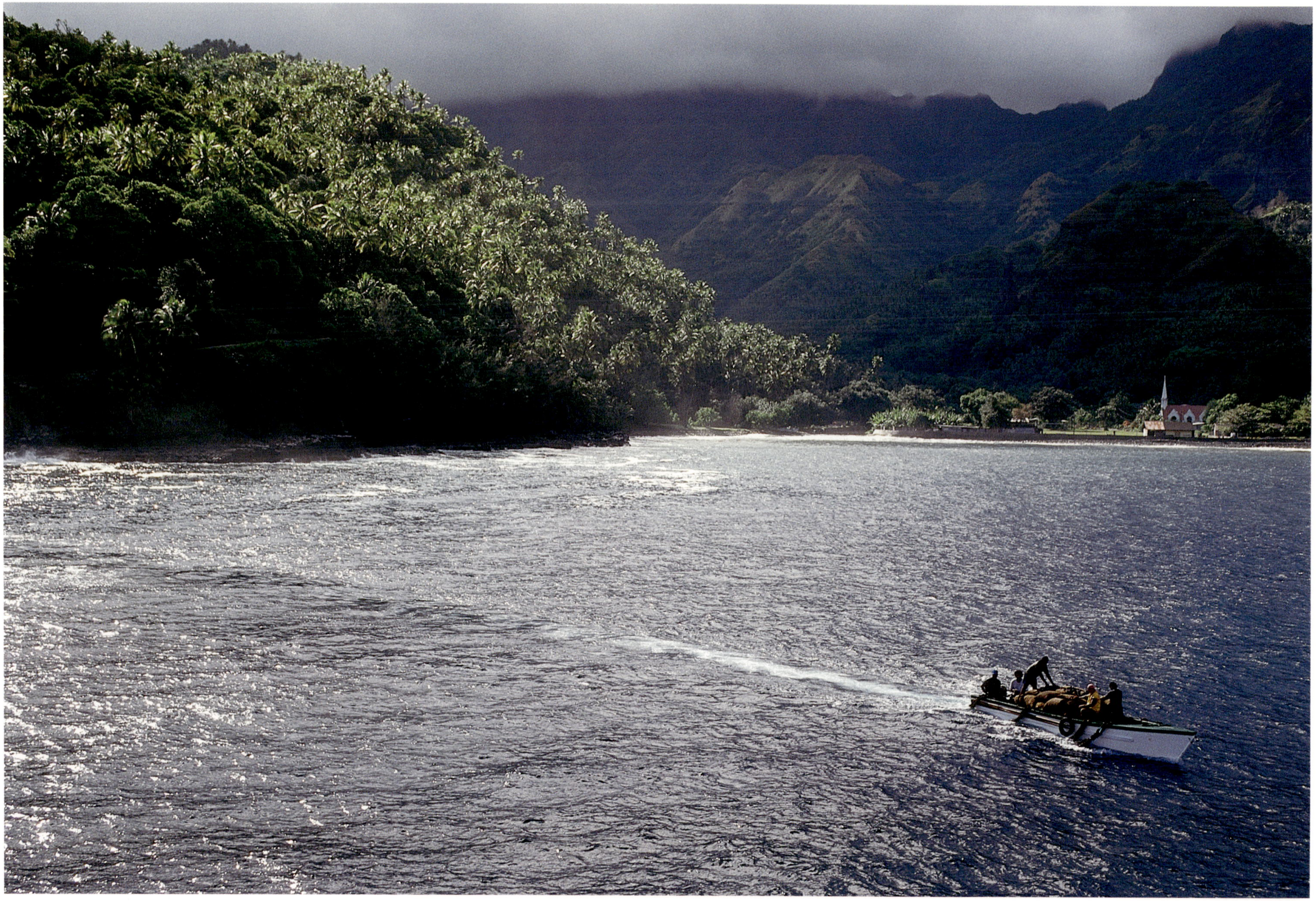

whale boat transporting cargo, omoa, fatu hiva

[RIGHT] *'the aranui' at sunset*

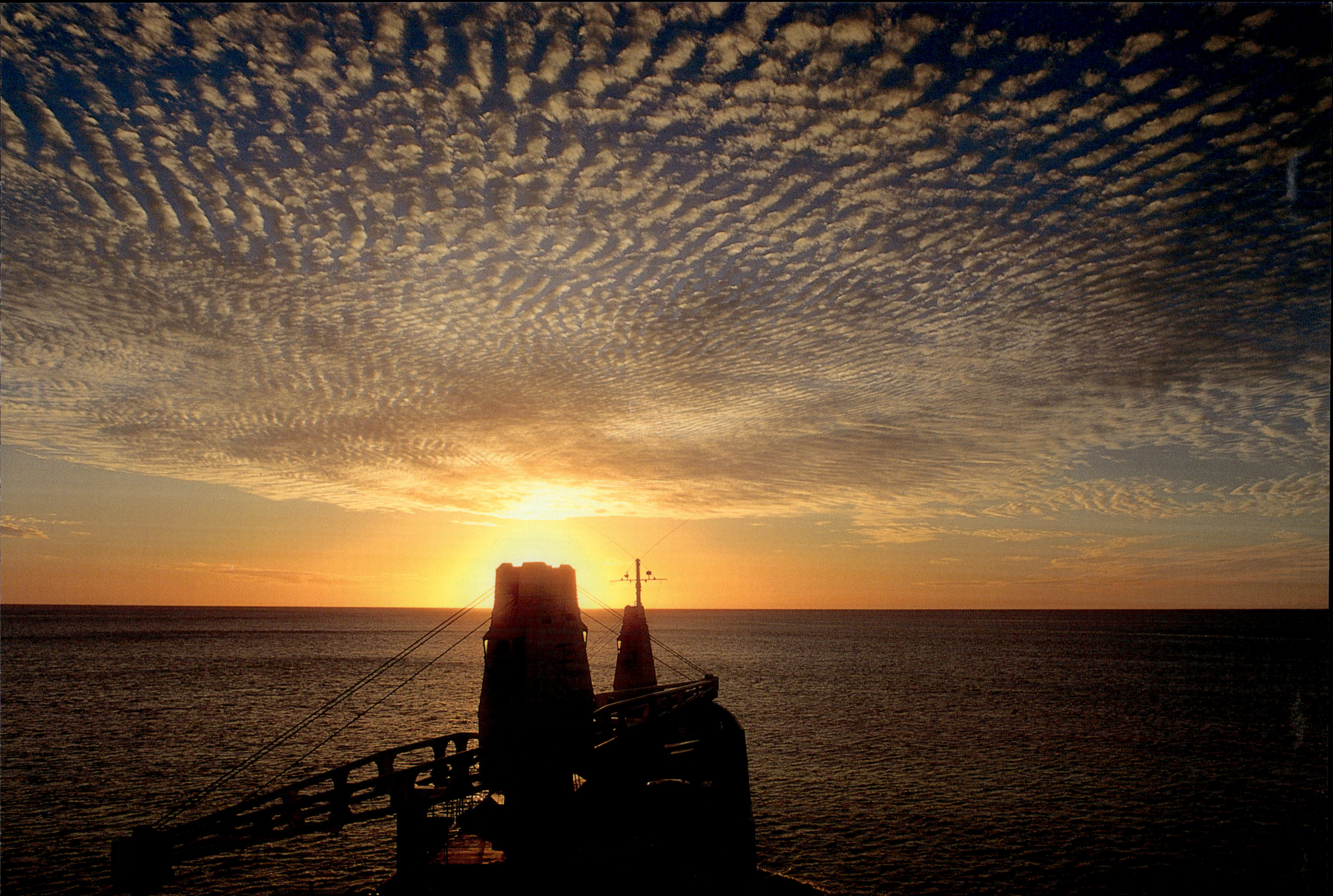

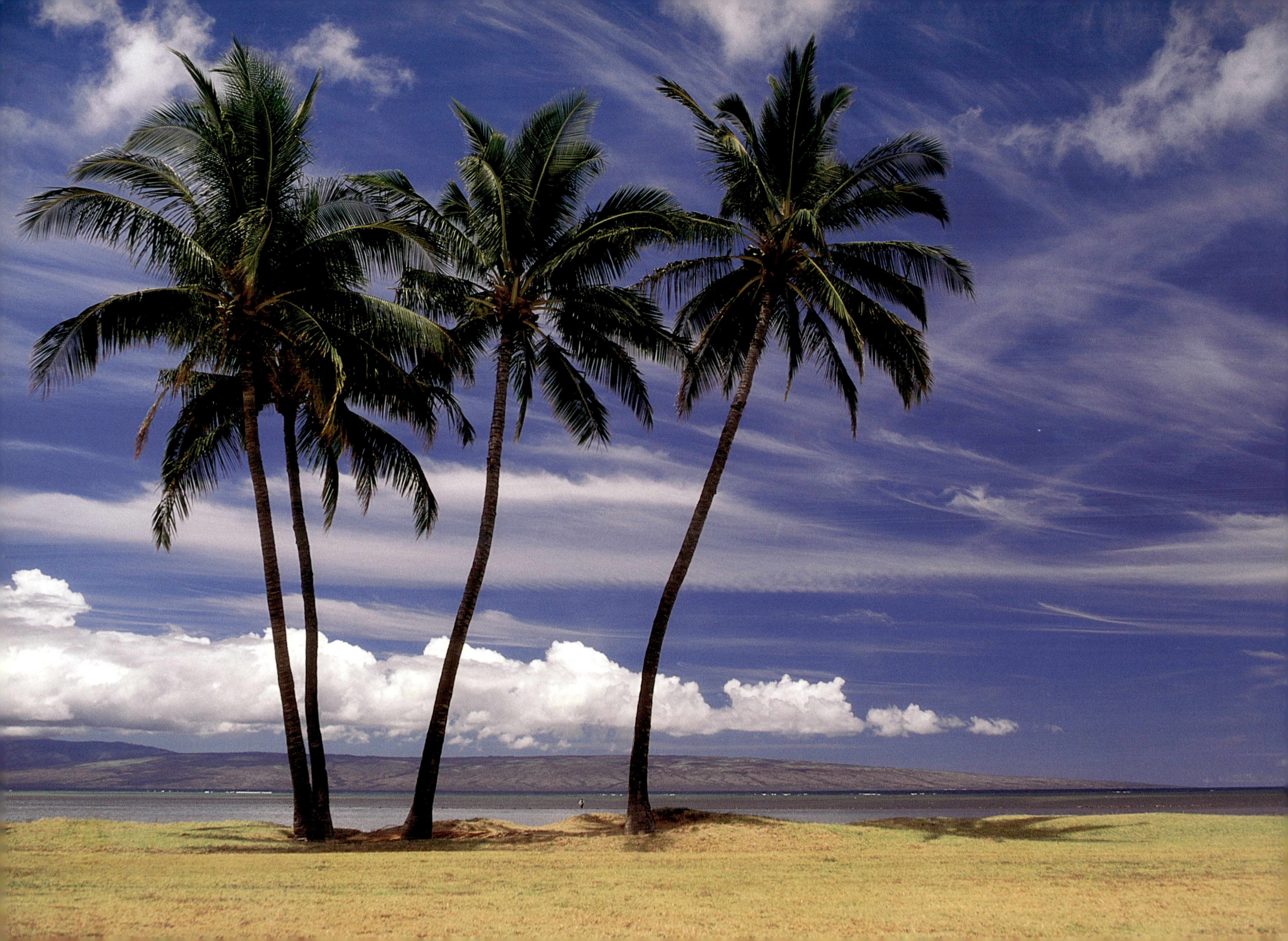

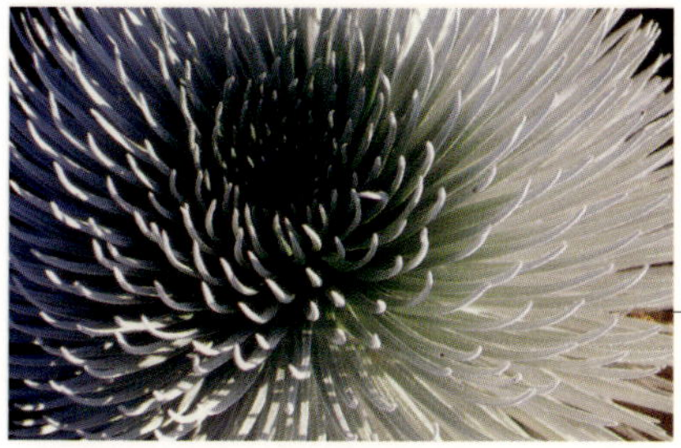

Hawai'i

THE HAWAIIAN ISLANDS are a chain of volcanic islands in the centre of the North Pacific halfway between the USA and Japan. The main islands of Oahu, Maui, Kauai, Molokai, Lanai and Hawai'i have a varied range of scenery, from snow-capped mountains like Maunakea and active volcanoes like Kilauea on Hawai'i, desert-like landscapes in dormant craters on Maui, the mini-Grand Canyon of Waimea to the dramatic coast of Na Pali on Kauai. Waterfalls, white and black sand beaches, valleys covered in tropical rainforest and spectacular cliffs plunging into the ocean, are everywhere. The Hawaiian Islands have some of the most spectacular and accessible scenery in the Pacific.

These islands were settled originally from the Marquesas Islands between 500-800 AD with a second migration from Tahiti after 1000 AD. The Tahitians probably became the dominant class subjugating the earlier arrivals. Hawaiians developed a complex hierarchical culture and political system with a rich oral history. Hawai'i eventually became a united kingdom in the late 18th century under the astute leadership of Kamehameha I, a leading member of a chiefly family from the island of Hawai'i. The Hawaiian Kingdom under different kings and queens of varying abilities and political skills survived until 1893.

The Hawaiian Islands were the last Polynesian islands to be discovered by Europeans. Lying in the northern Pacific they were by-passed by the Spanish and Portuguese explorers sailing from Central and South America to Southeast Asia in the 16th and 17th centuries. Captain James Cook, after exploring and charting many islands in the Pacific, sighted Hawai'i in 1778. He was killed at Kealakekua Bay the following year with the reasons and significance of his death becoming a matter of intense debate among scholars.

The islands developed with the whaling industry, with Honolulu becoming the busiest port in the Pacific in the 19th century. Ships traded in sandalwood to sell in China and the port provisioned the whalers for their journeys to the far reaches of the Pacific. The missionaries of the American Board of Commissioners for Foreign Missions arrived in 1820 and achieved immediate success by converting the female Chief Ka'ahumanu who had succeeded King Kamehameha I. Tapu was broken, Sabbath introduced and an ancient religion cast aside. Idols were smashed and temples destroyed, a new code of conduct and morality enforced and Christian schools started.

Western intrusion was disastrous for the Hawaiians, with the population plunging from at least 300,000 (perhaps many more) at the time of contact, to 40,000 by the 1890's. With the decline of whaling in the 1860's, a sugar industry was developed. Workers from China, Japan, Korea, Puerto Rico and the Philippines were brought in to work the cane fields, greatly contributing to the ethnic diversity that is seen today.

In 1959 Hawai'i became a state of the USA having been annexed by Congress in 1898 as a territory. Today it has by far the most visitors of any island group in the Pacific.

[**LEFT**] *kapuaiwa coconut grove,* molokai [**ABOVE**] *silversword,* haleakala crater, maui

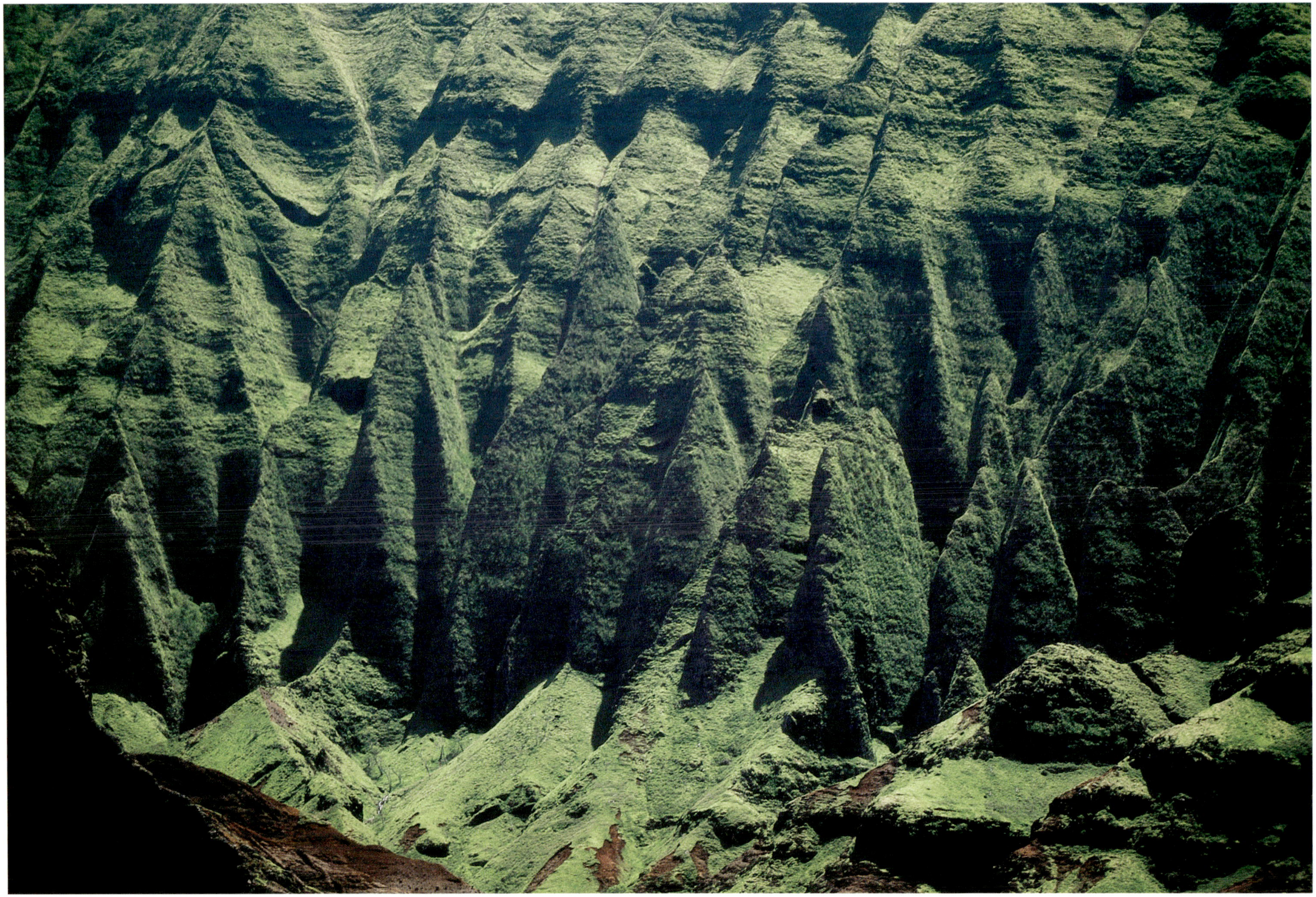

[ABOVE AND RIGHT] *the na pali coast,* kauai

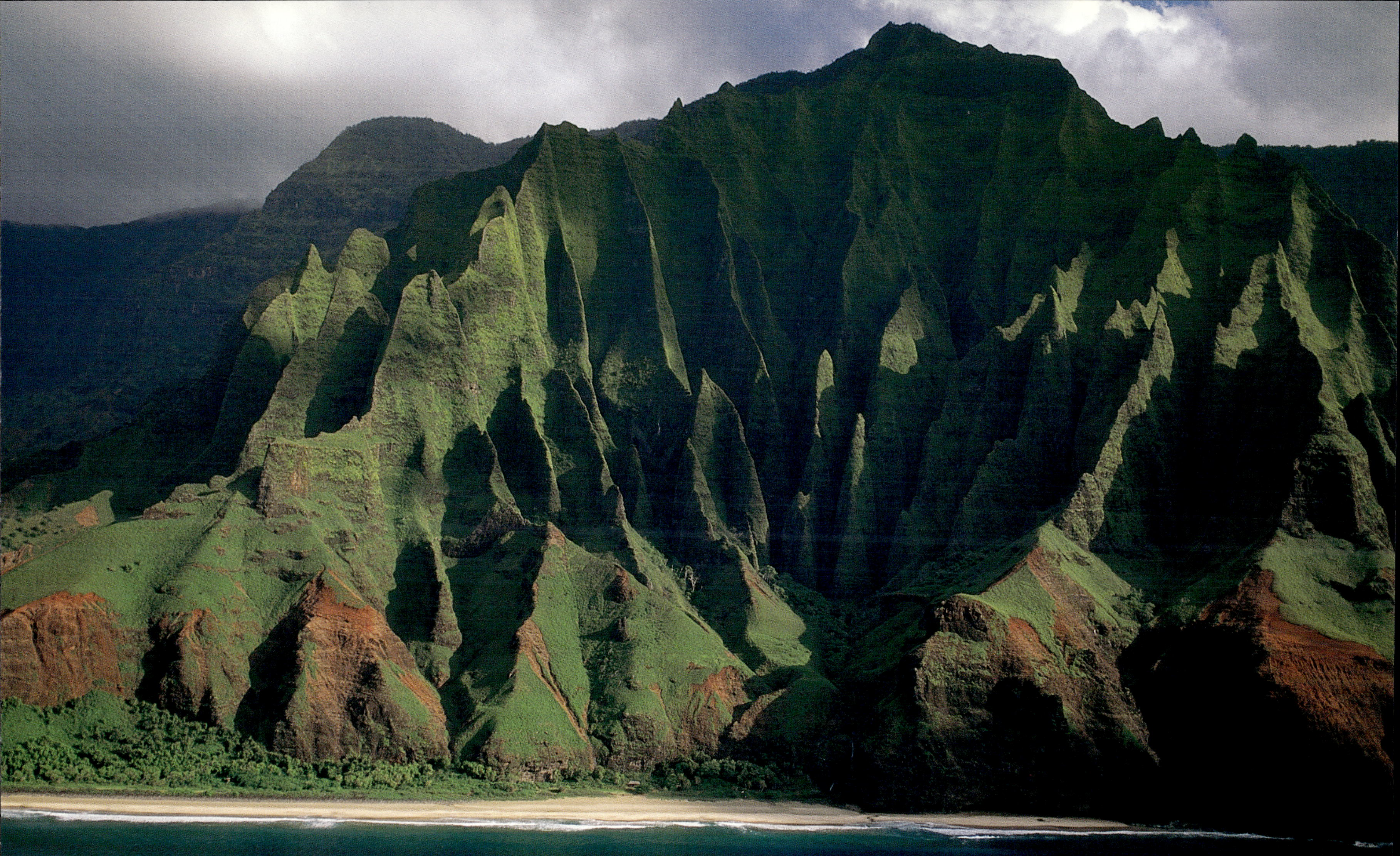

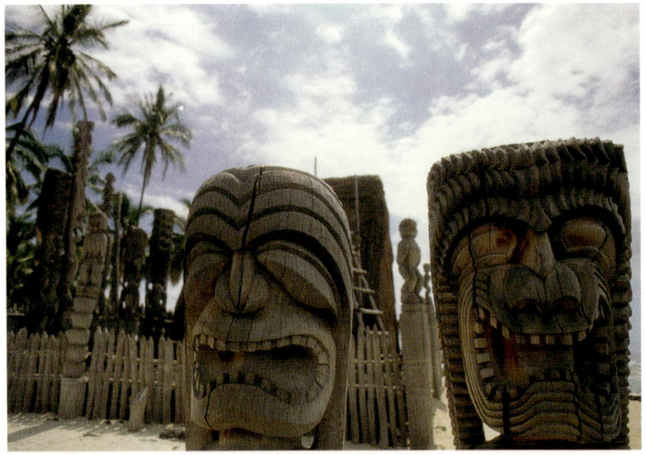

[LEFT] *hale o keawe heiau temple,* hawai'i

[BELOW LEFT] *petroglyphs,* waikoloa, hawai'i

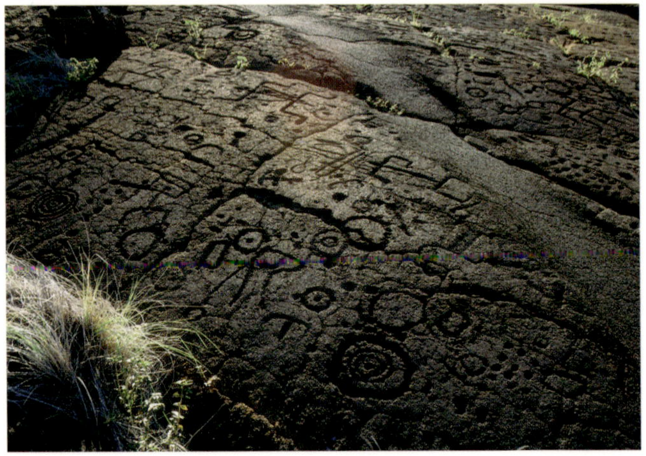

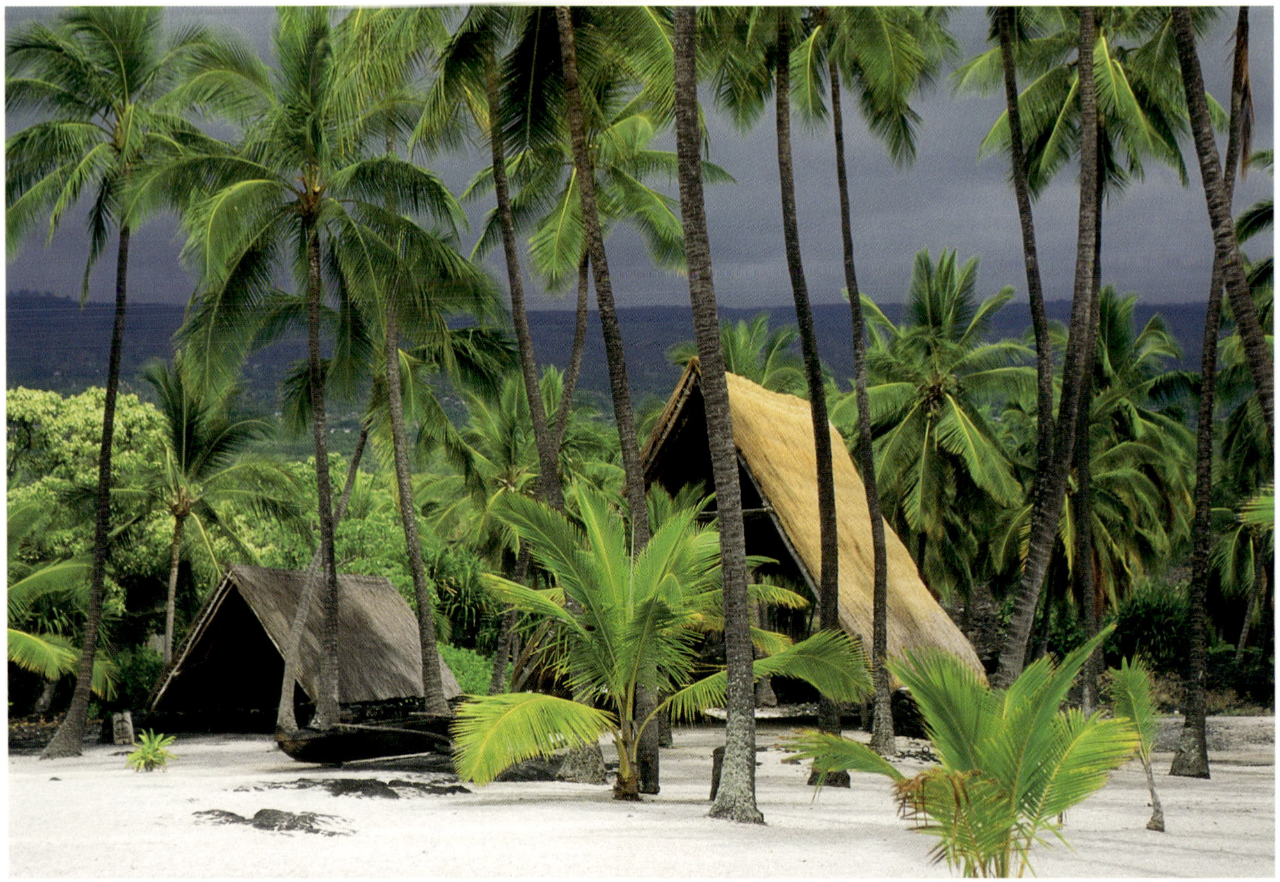

[RIGHT] *hale o keawe heiau temple,* hawai'i

[FAR RIGHT] *sugarcane village,* kauai

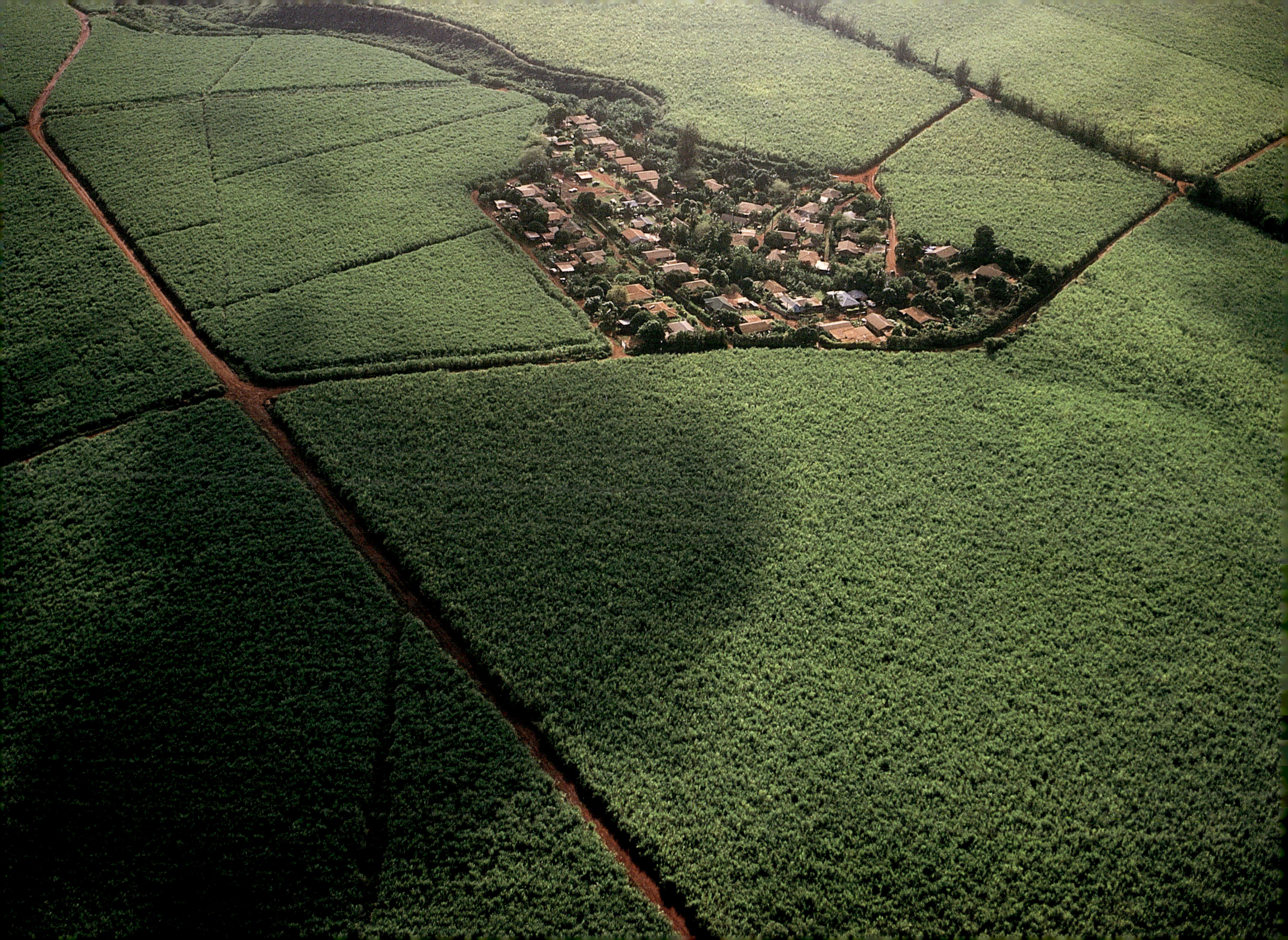

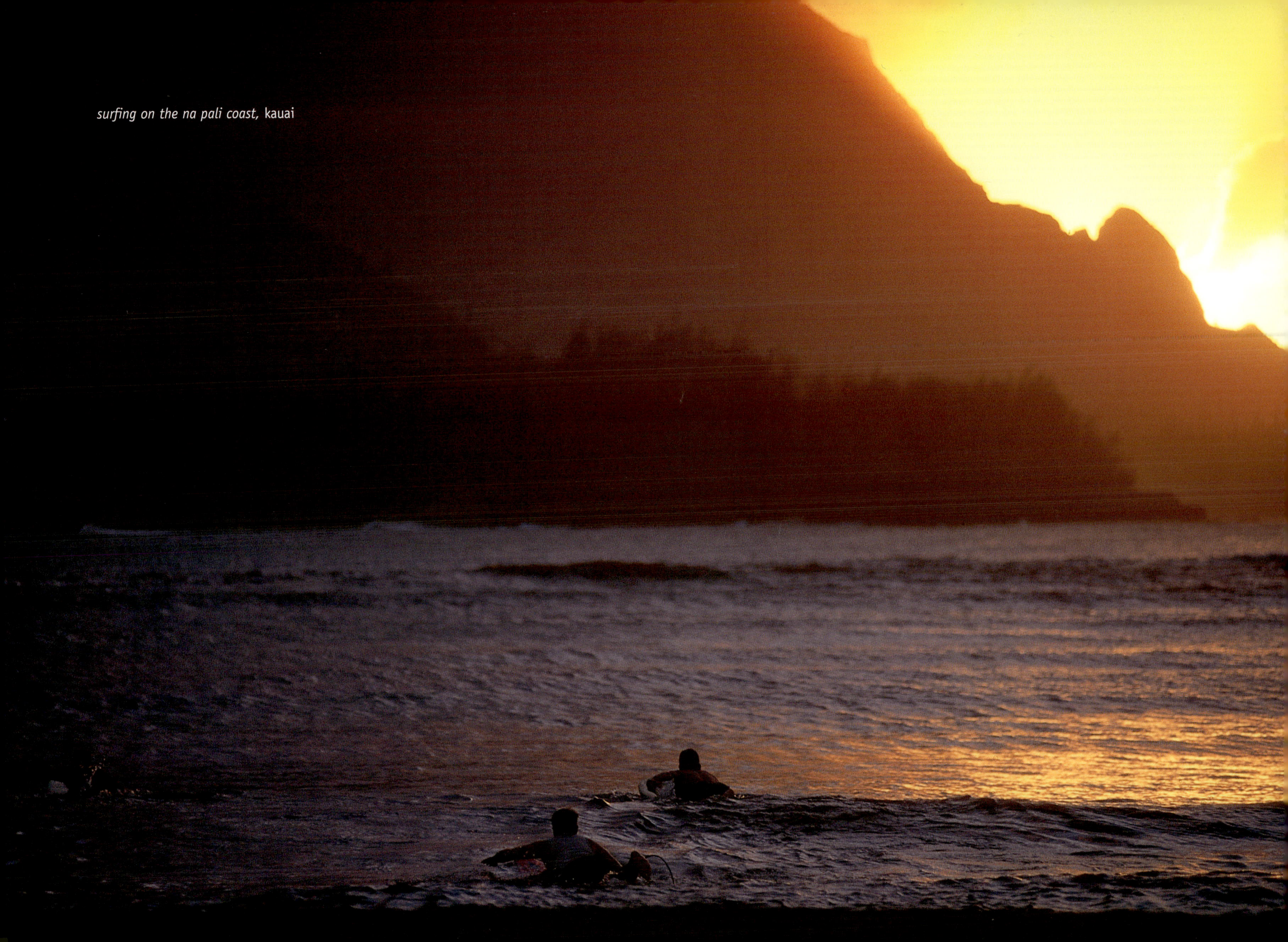

surfing on the na pali coast, kauai

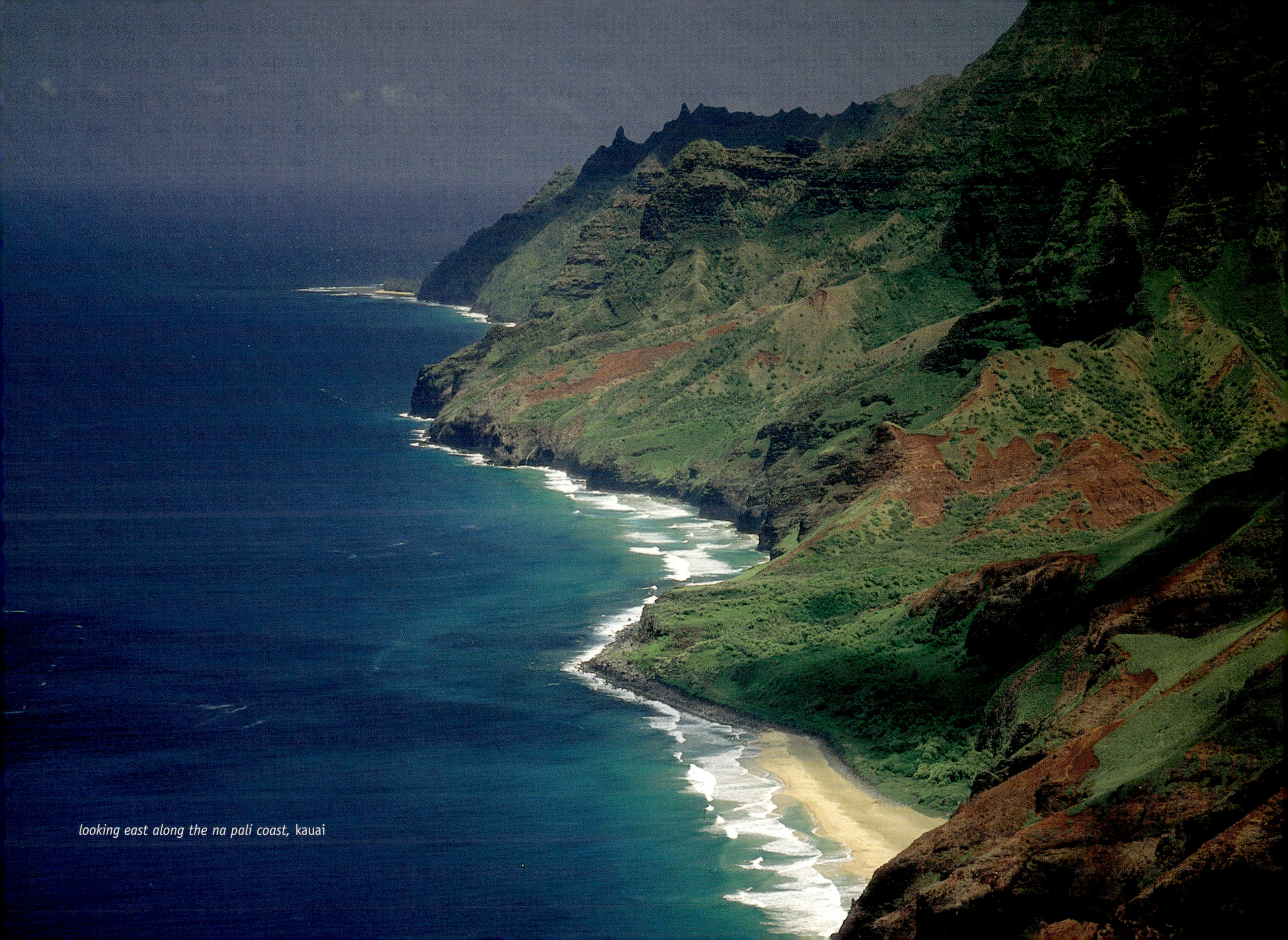

looking east along the na pali coast, kauai

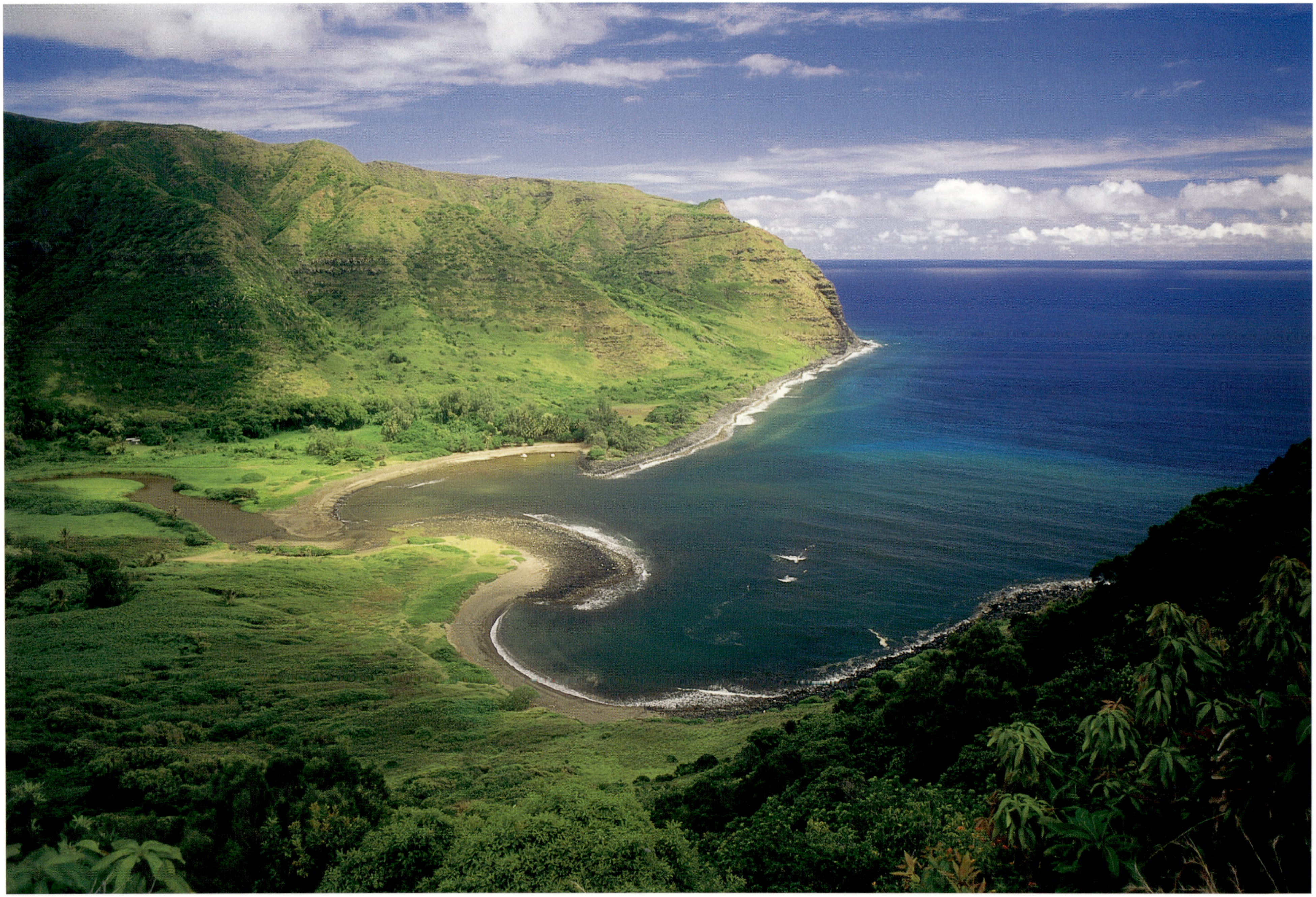

halawa bay, molokai

[RIGHT] *waimea canyon,* kauai

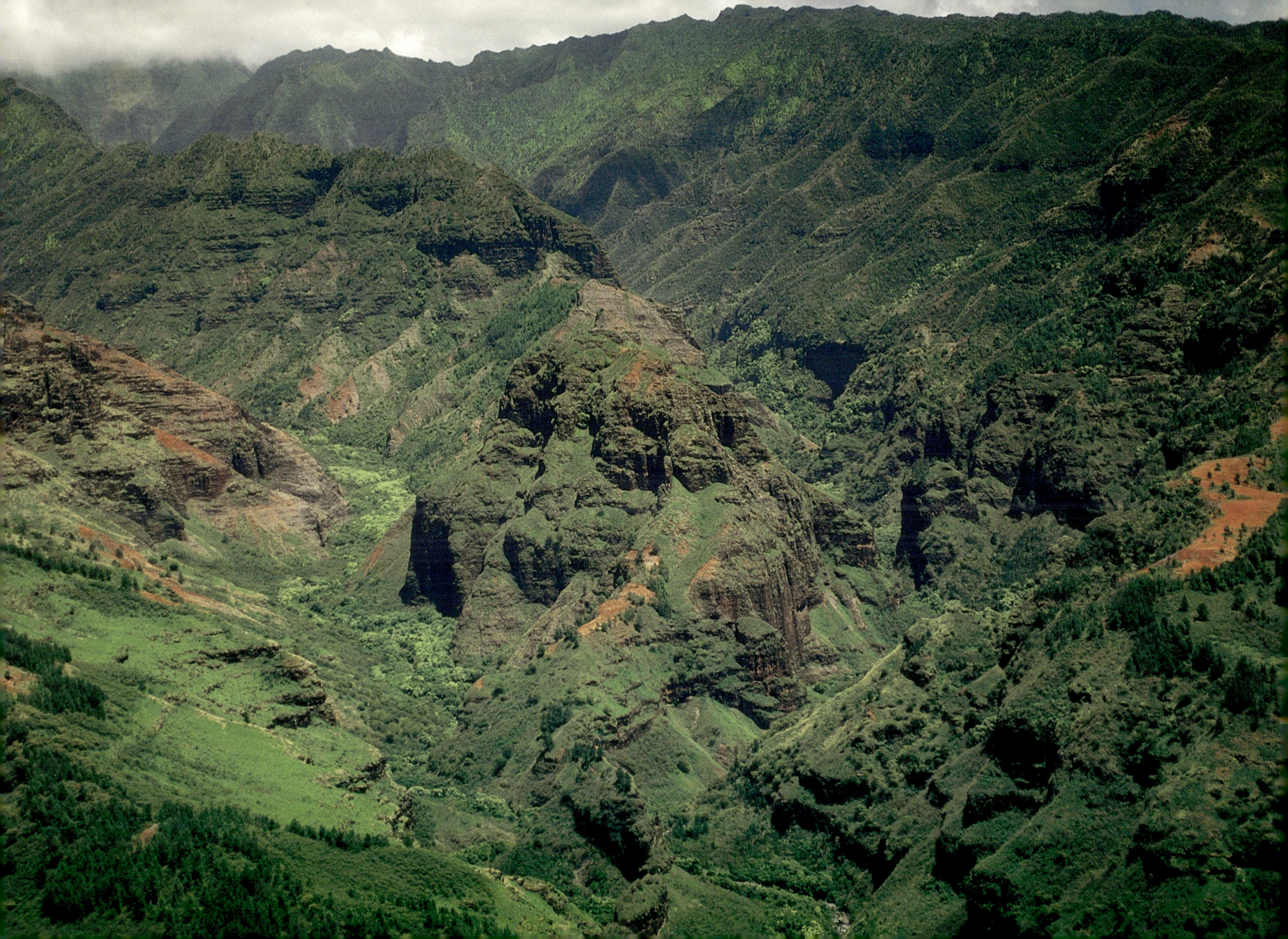

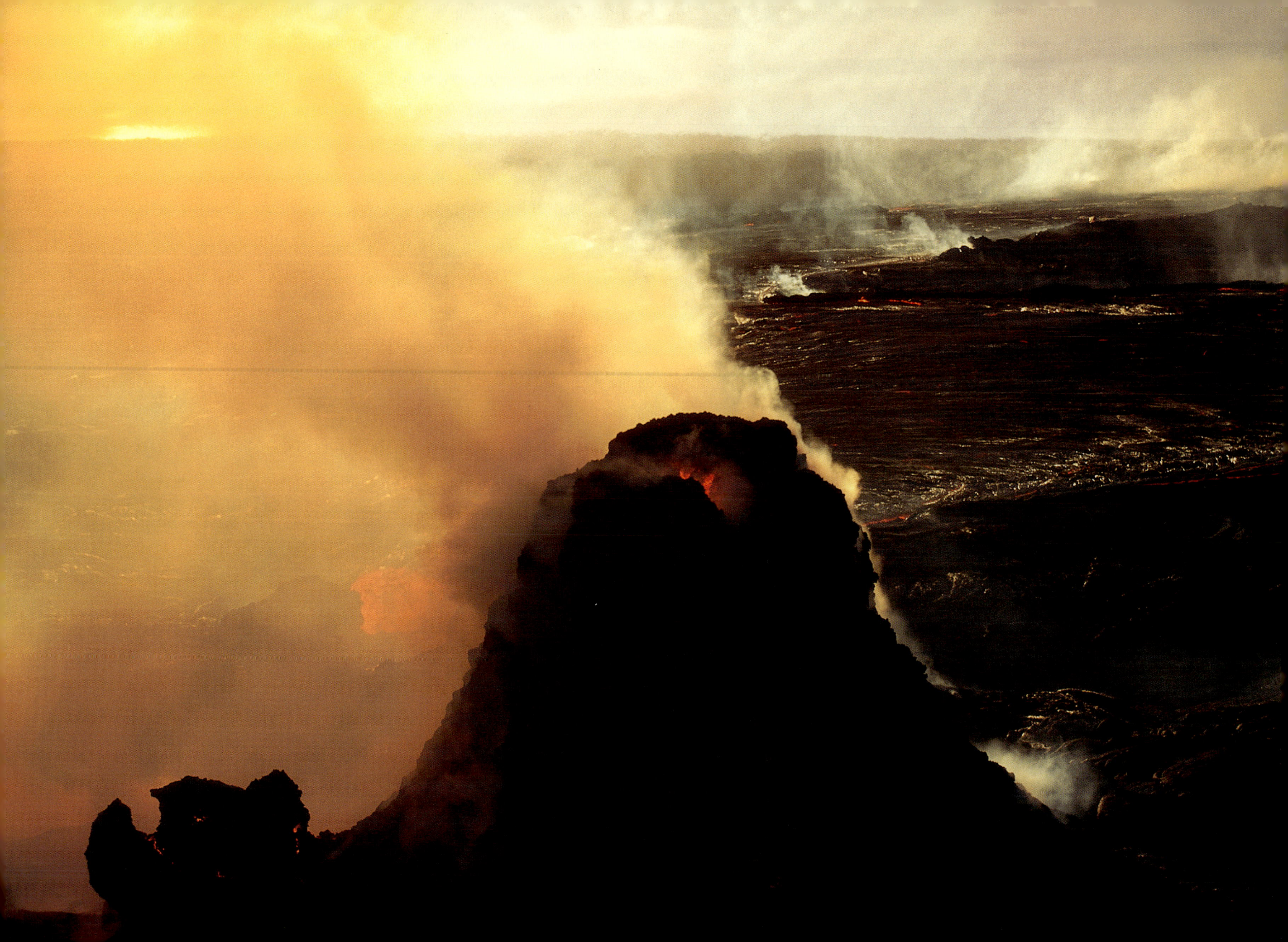

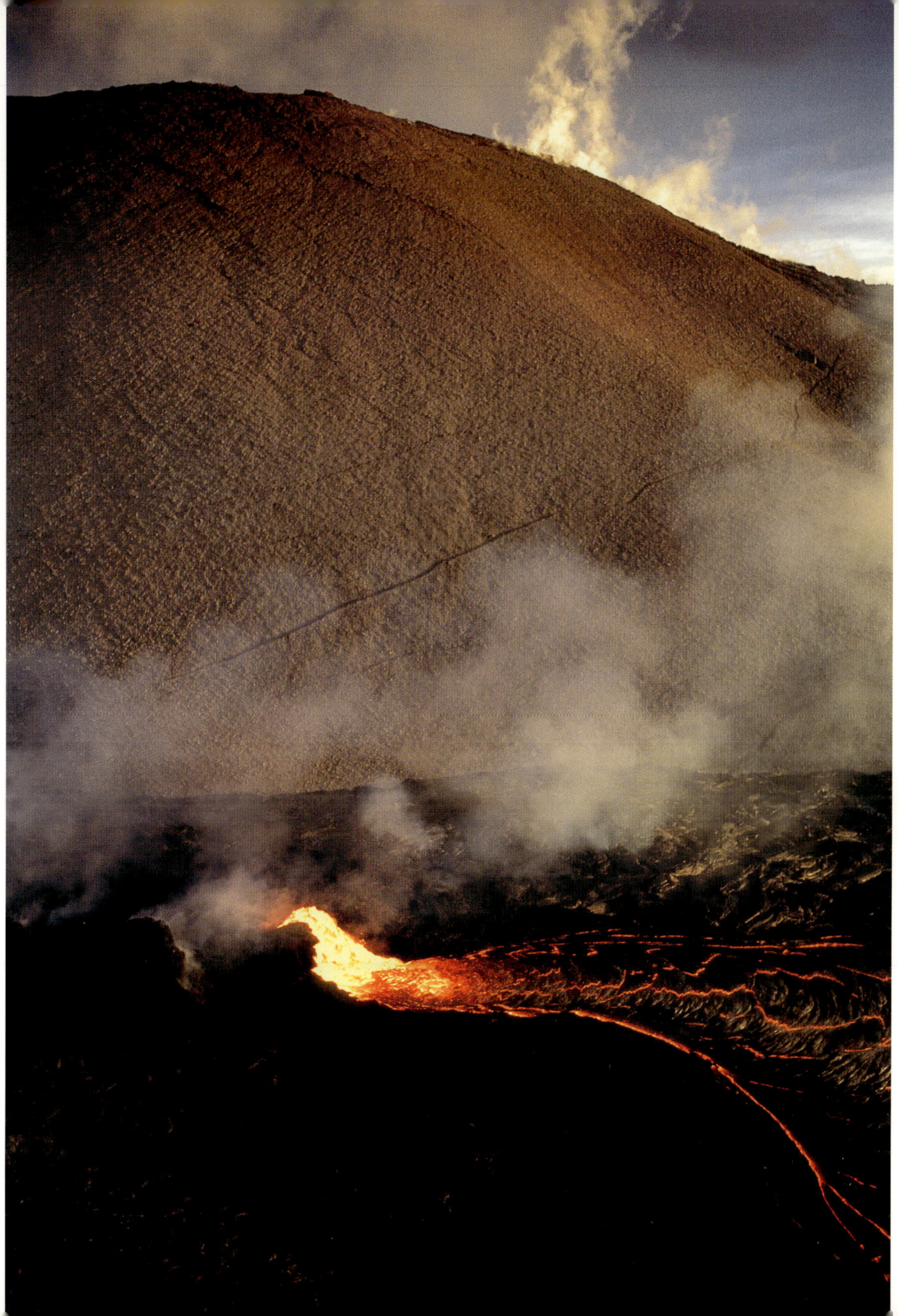

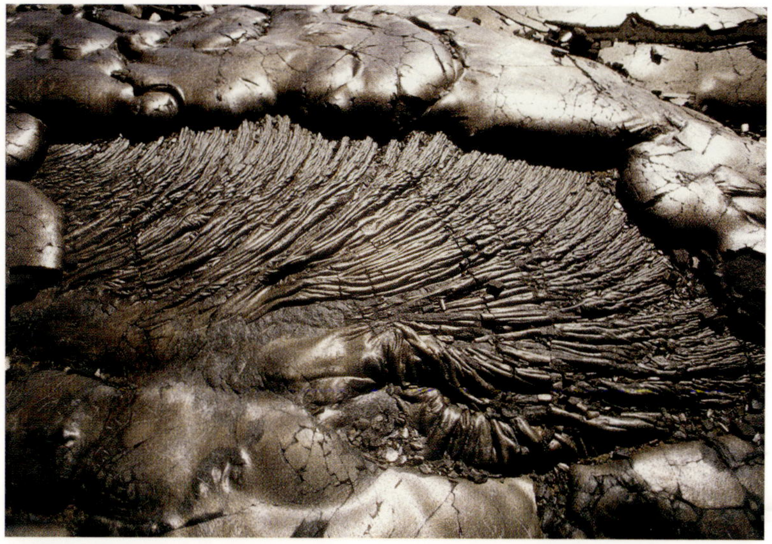

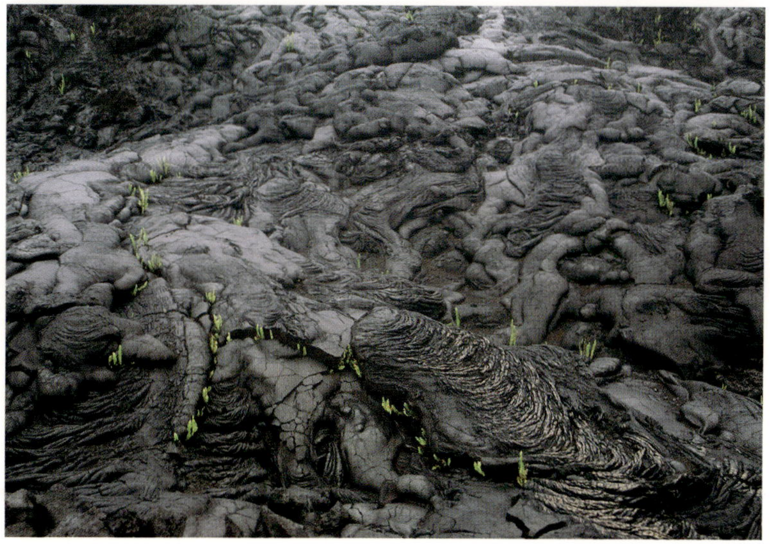

[ABOVE] *cooled pahoehoe lava flow,* kilauea volcano, hawai'i

plants reclaiming lava flow area

[LEFT AND FAR LEFT] *kilauea volcano,* hawai'i

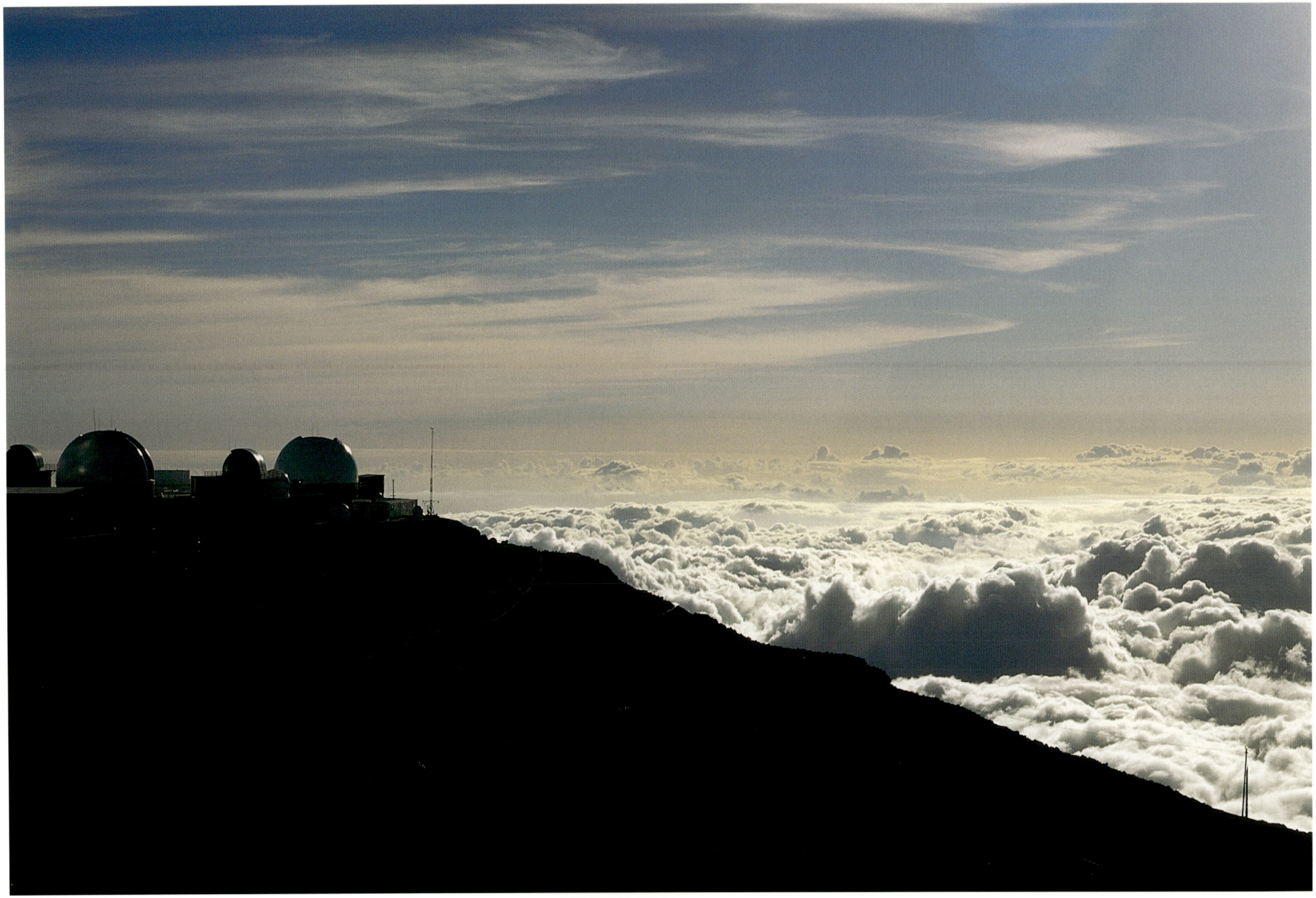

science city, haleakala, maui

[RIGHT] *moonscape,* haleakala crater, maui

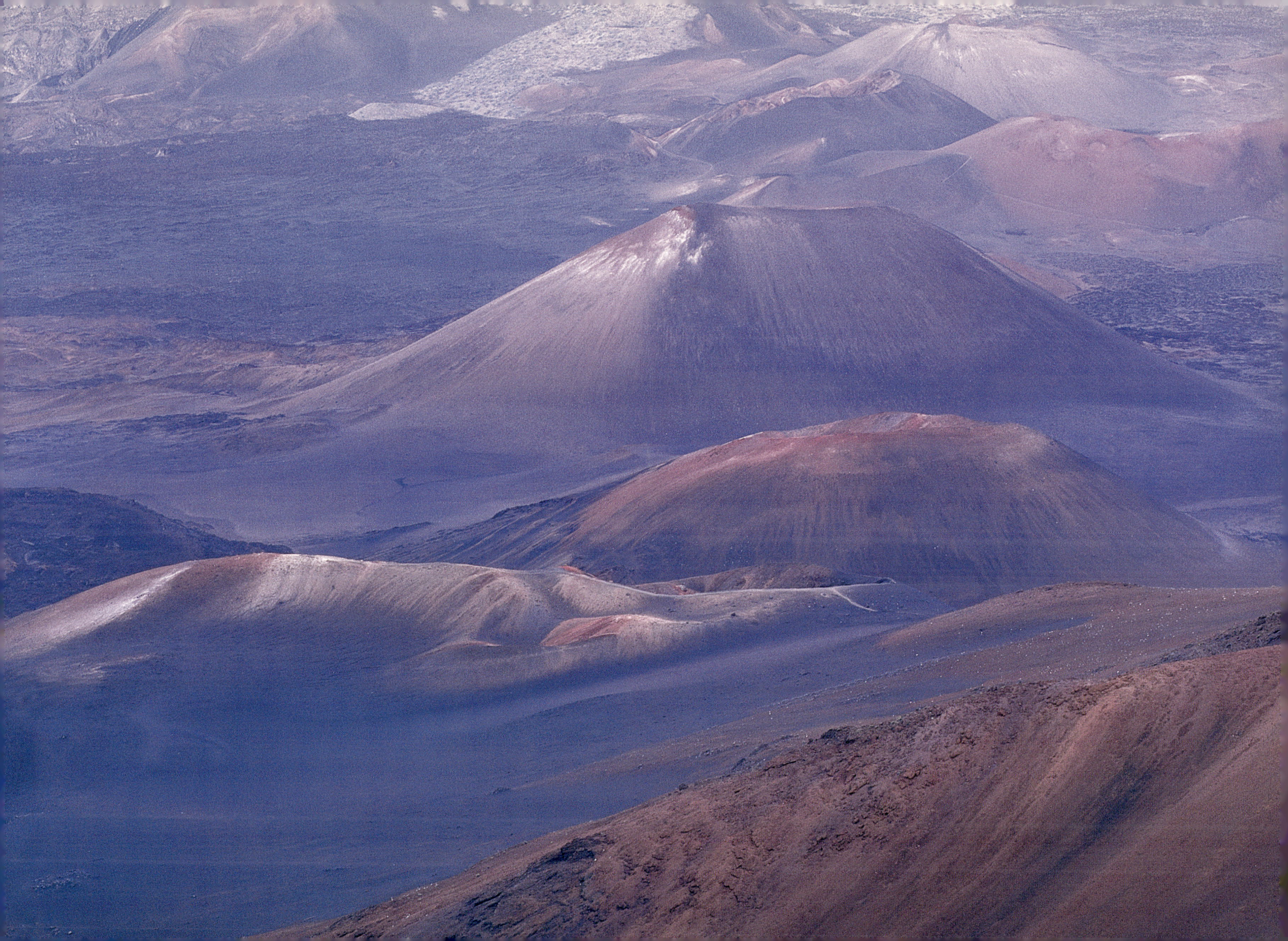

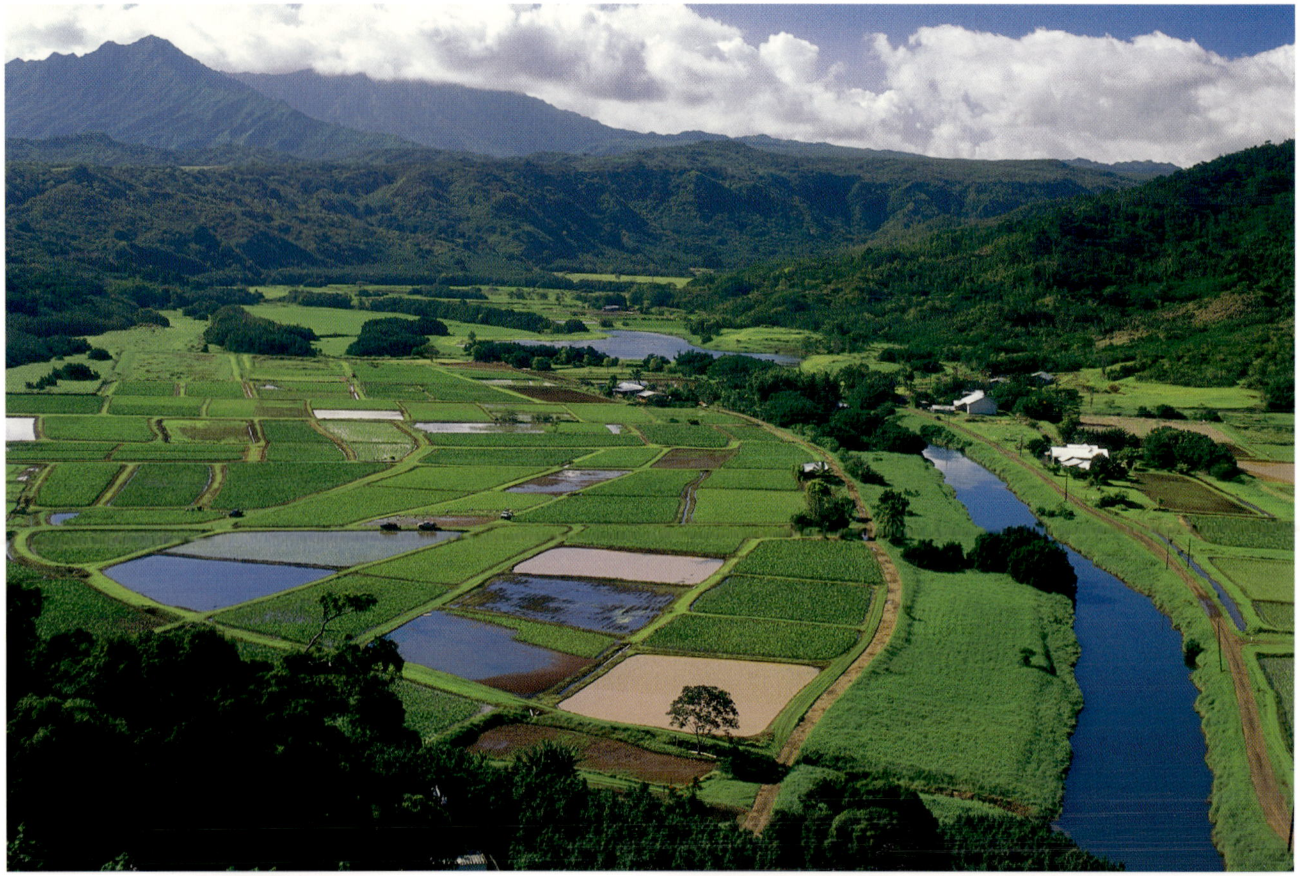

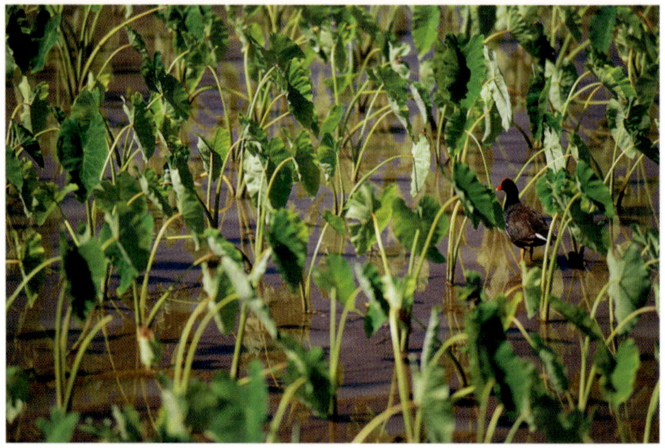

[ABOVE] *hanalei valley,* kauai [RIGHT] *taro field,* hanalei valley, kauai [FAR RIGHT] *moaula falls,* halawa valley, molokai

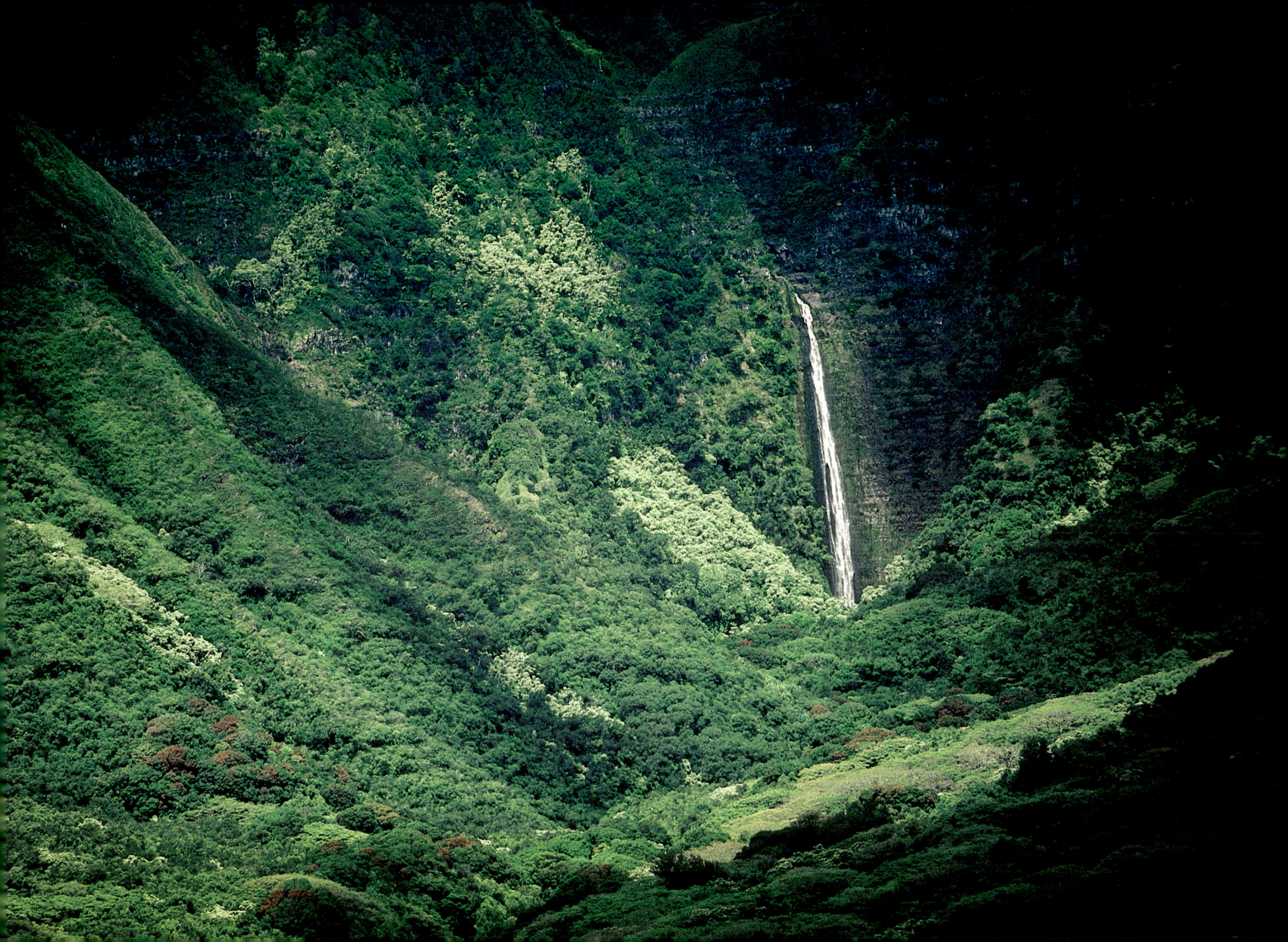

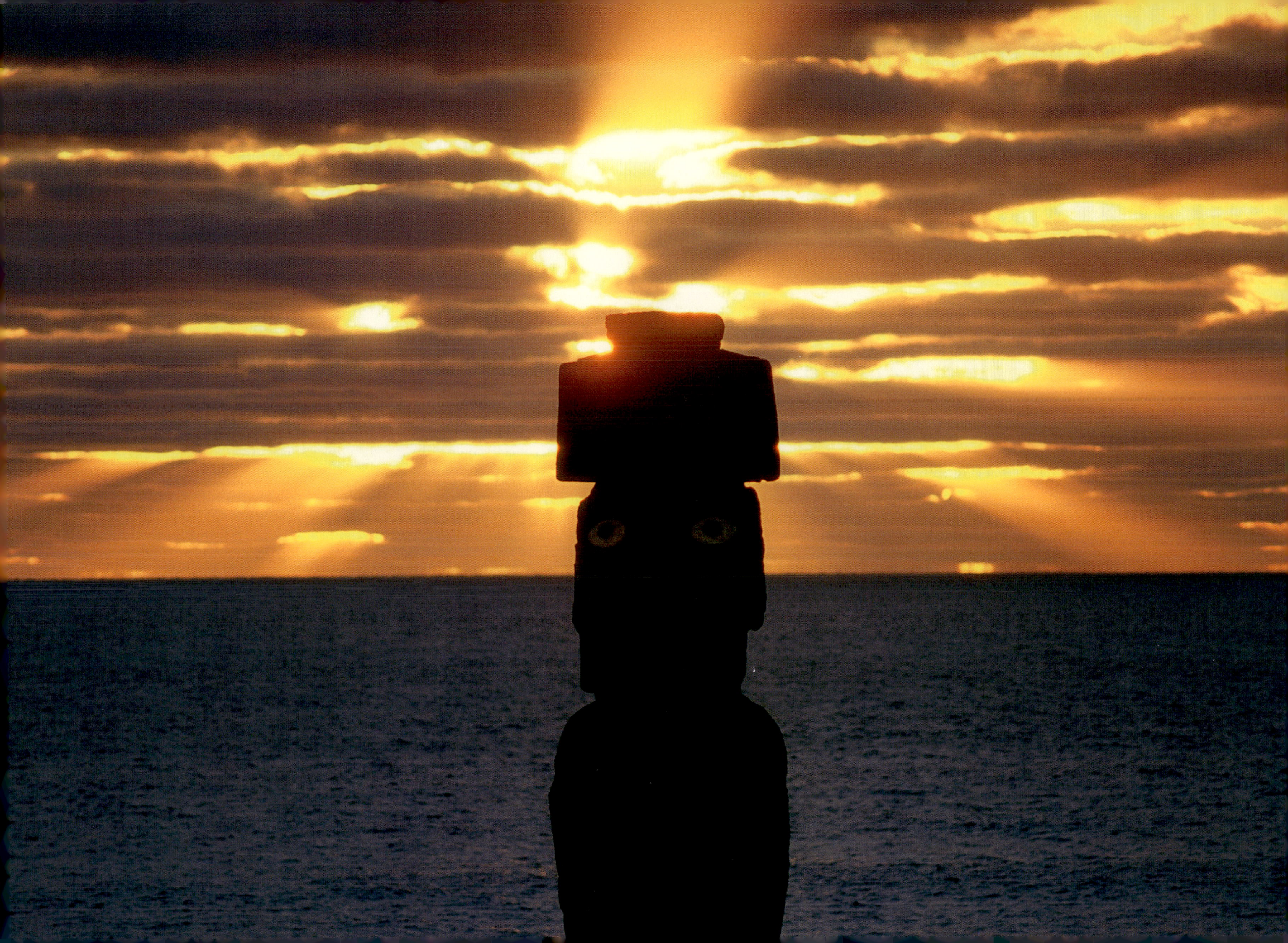

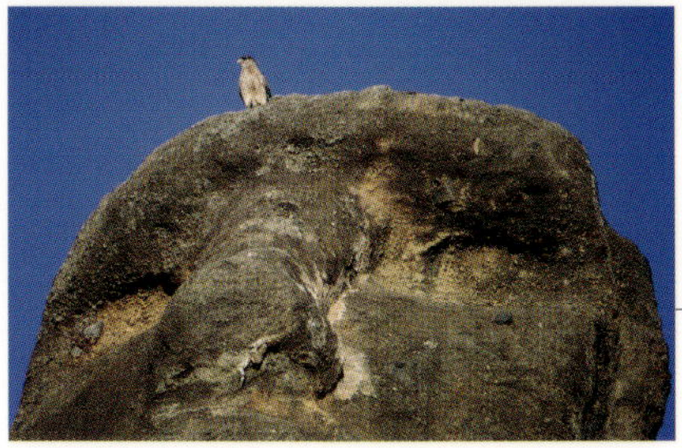

Easter Island

EASTER ISLAND or *Rapa Nui* as it is known by its inhabitants, is a tiny triangular volcanic island of only 166sqkm, lying 3700km from the South American coast and 4000km from Tahiti. The nearest inhabited island is Pitcairn Island 2000km to the southwest. It is the most isolated inhabited island in the world. This isolation contributed to the island's limited variety of plants, animals and also marine life. With no natural harbours and no rivers, the rugged coastline of cliffs is broken only by the beautiful pink coral sand beaches at Anakena and Ovahe, in the north. In this isolation evolved a unique culture expressed in the astronomical and engineering knowledge of the Moai construction. The yet to be deciphered Hieroglyphics script found on the island, is the only form of writing found in the Pacific.

The island was settled by probably two waves of Polynesians from the Marquesas, between 300AD and 700AD. The people brought coconut, bananas, taro, yam, sugar cane and chickens, but no evidence of pigs and dogs. The chicken became widespread as can be seen from the common stone pens constructed for them.

Nearly 1000 Moai which range in height from 2 meters to nearly 21 meters, are spread all over the island, many lying broken, face down. Those that are standing on platforms (Ahu) are orientated according to precise astronomical observations. These statues which were carved between 1000-1680 AD (and probably represent ancestors) are from quarry of Rano Raraku volcano where there are still many Moai at various states of completion.

Although it seems likely that there was contact between South America and Easter Island, all biological, linguistic and archaeological evidence points to a Polynesian homeland, probably the Marquesas via Samoa. Origins of this monumental architecture can be found in the Marquesas, Society, Samoan and Tongan islands dating back thousand of years.

The destruction of the forests by slash-and-burn agriculture, cremation of the dead and maybe transportation of the Moai led to environmental catastrophe. Cut off without timber for ocean-going canoes, warfare and conflict ensued, leading to the toppling of the Moai.

The ceremonial village of Orongo, with its spectacular location on a cliff between the Rano Kau crater and the ocean, was the home of the birdman cult. This cult, which seems to have arisen after the toppling of the Moai, centres on a ritual competition each spring where a representative from each clan tries to be the first to collect migrating seabirds' eggs. This entailed climbing down the Orongo Cliffs and swimming to a small island 1km away, entitling the winner's clan to political leadership for one year.

Contact with Europeans brought disease, slavery and death leading to an almost total collapse of the population to 111 in 1877. Today the population of nearly 3000 (about 2/3 indigenous Polynesians) lives mostly in the town of Hanga Roa.

[**LEFT**] *moai at ahu tahai* [**ABOVE**] *hawk resting on moai*

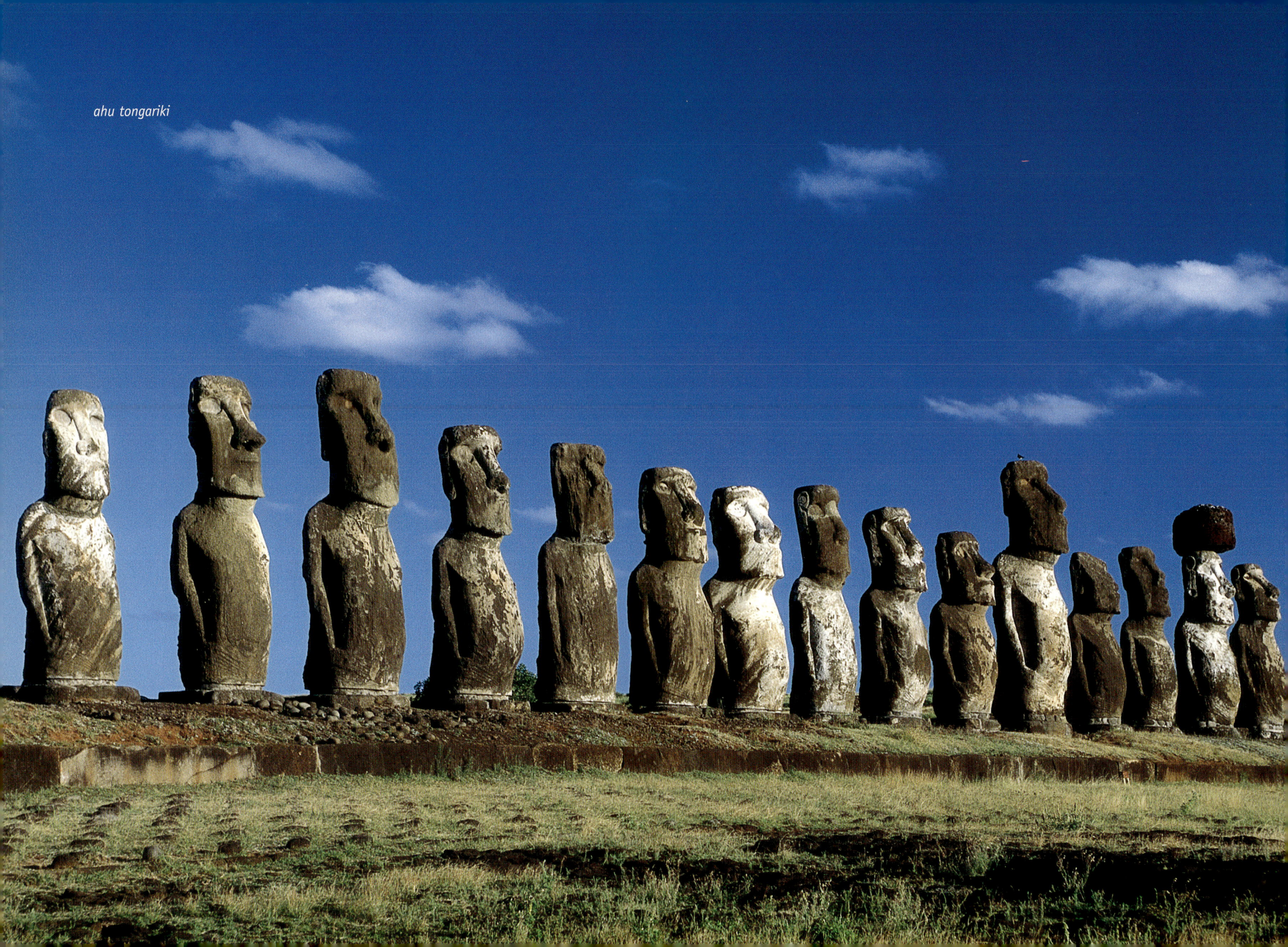

ahu tongariki

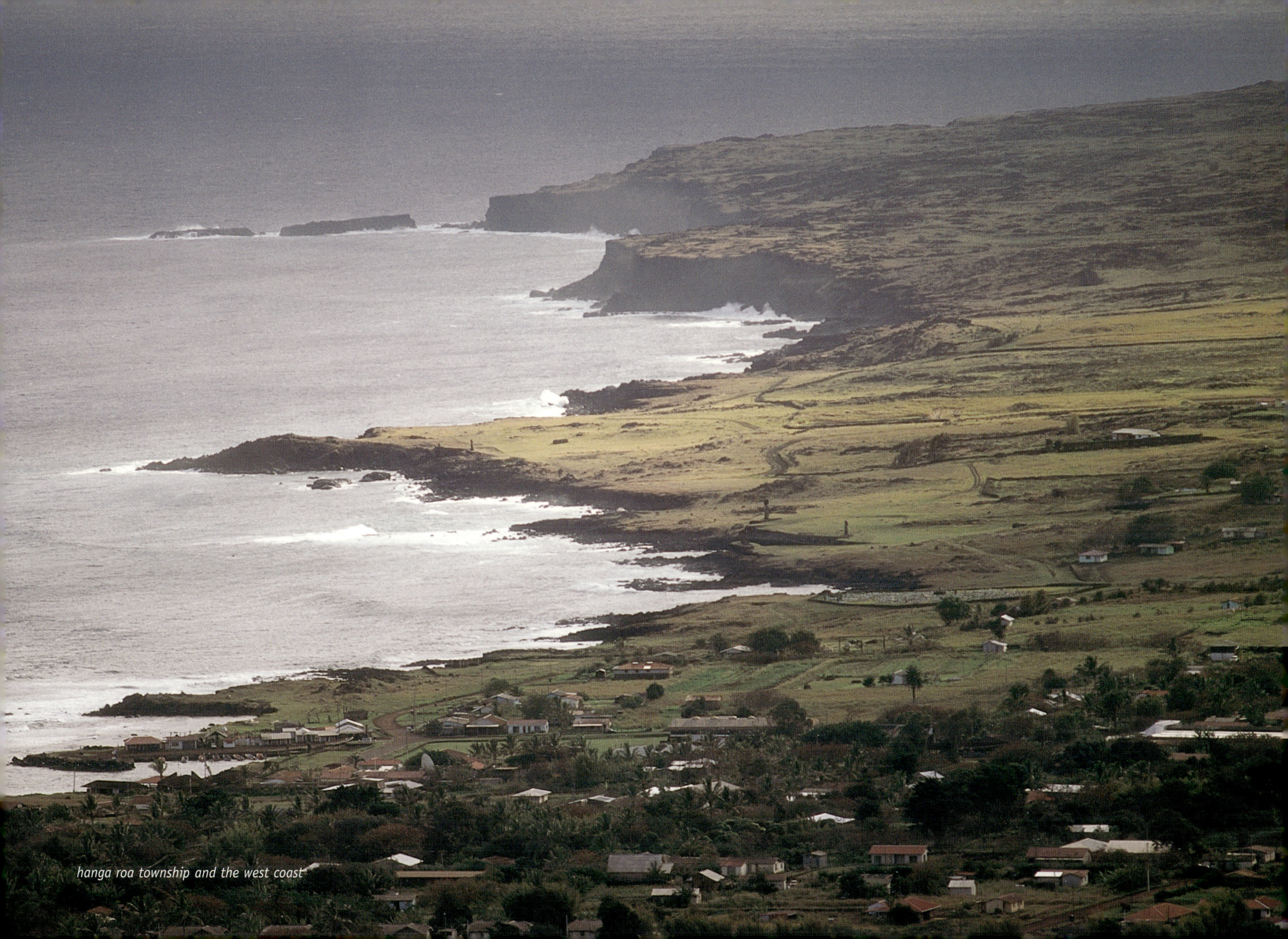

hanga roa township and the west coast

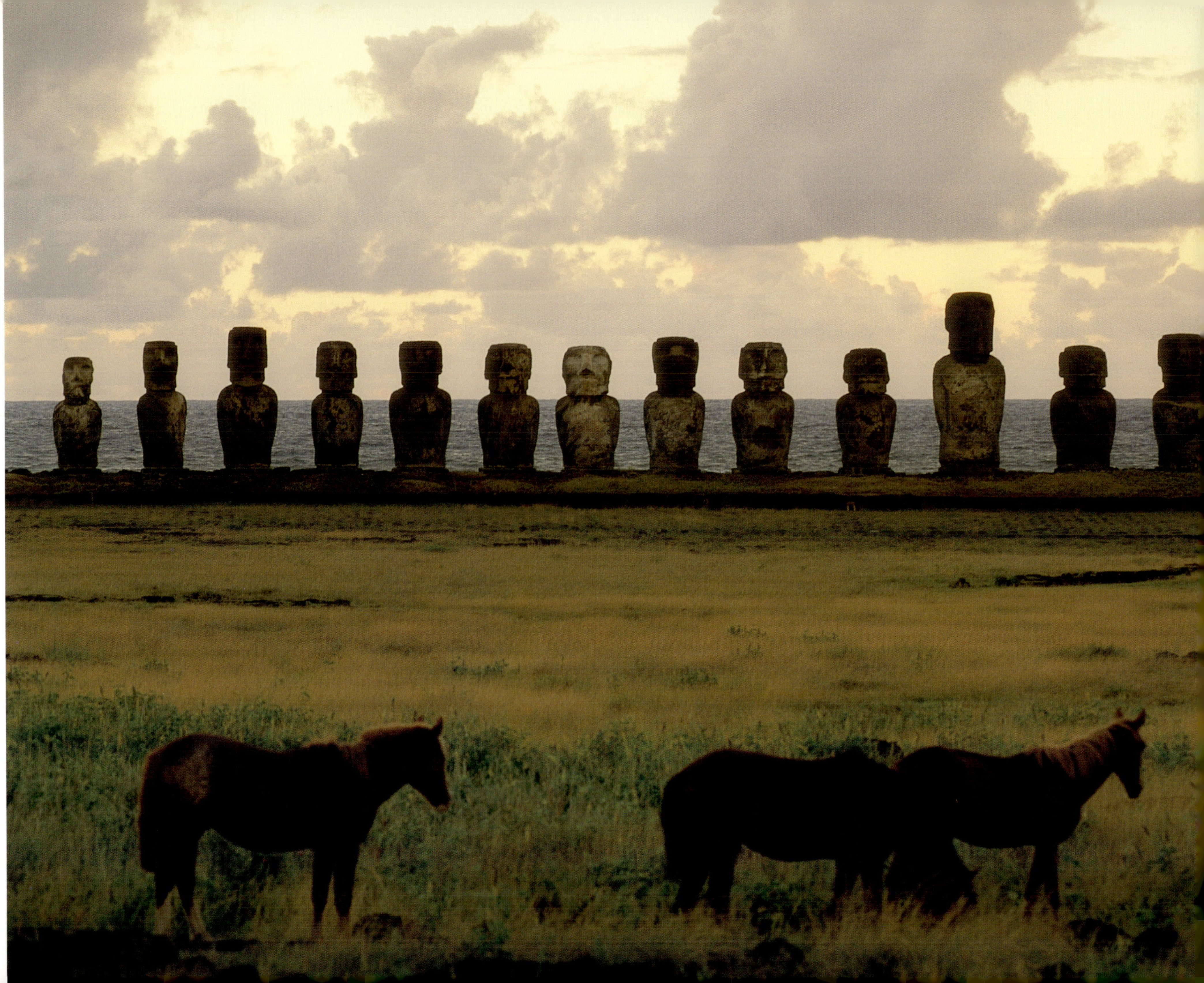

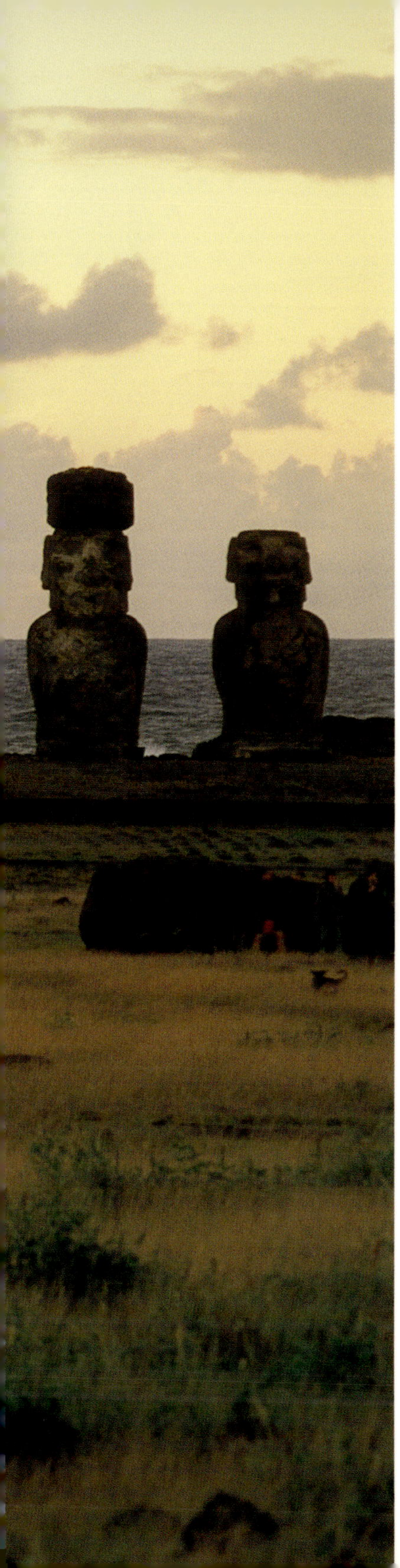

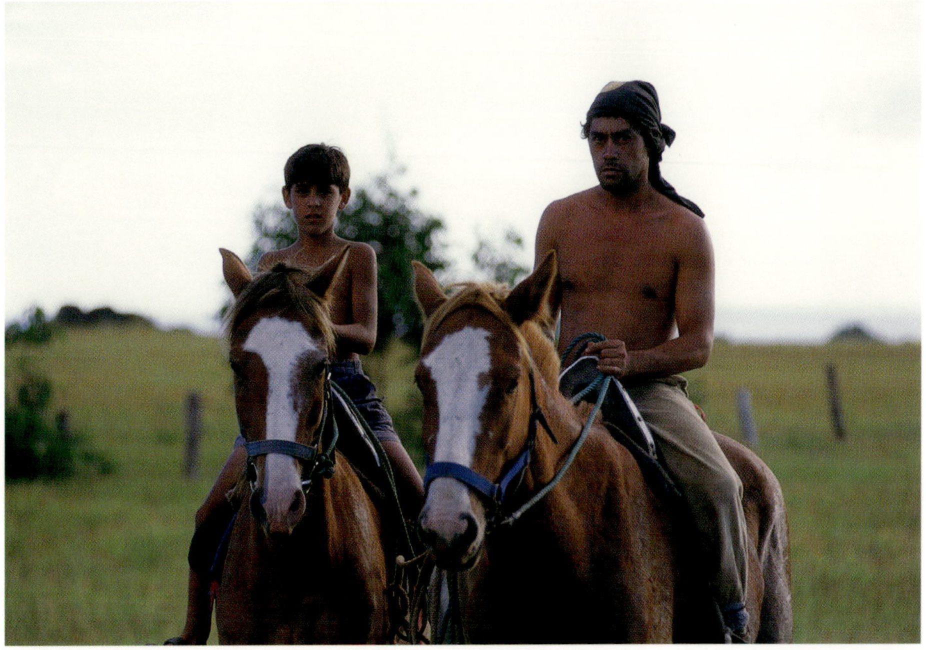

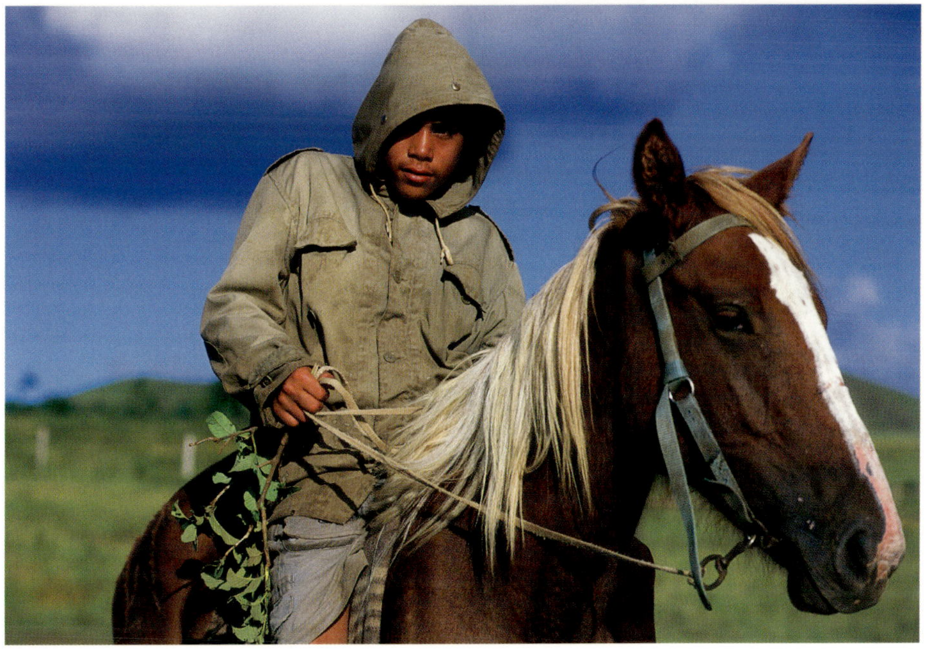

[FAR LEFT] *horses at ahu tongariki* **[ABOVE]** *easter island cowboys*

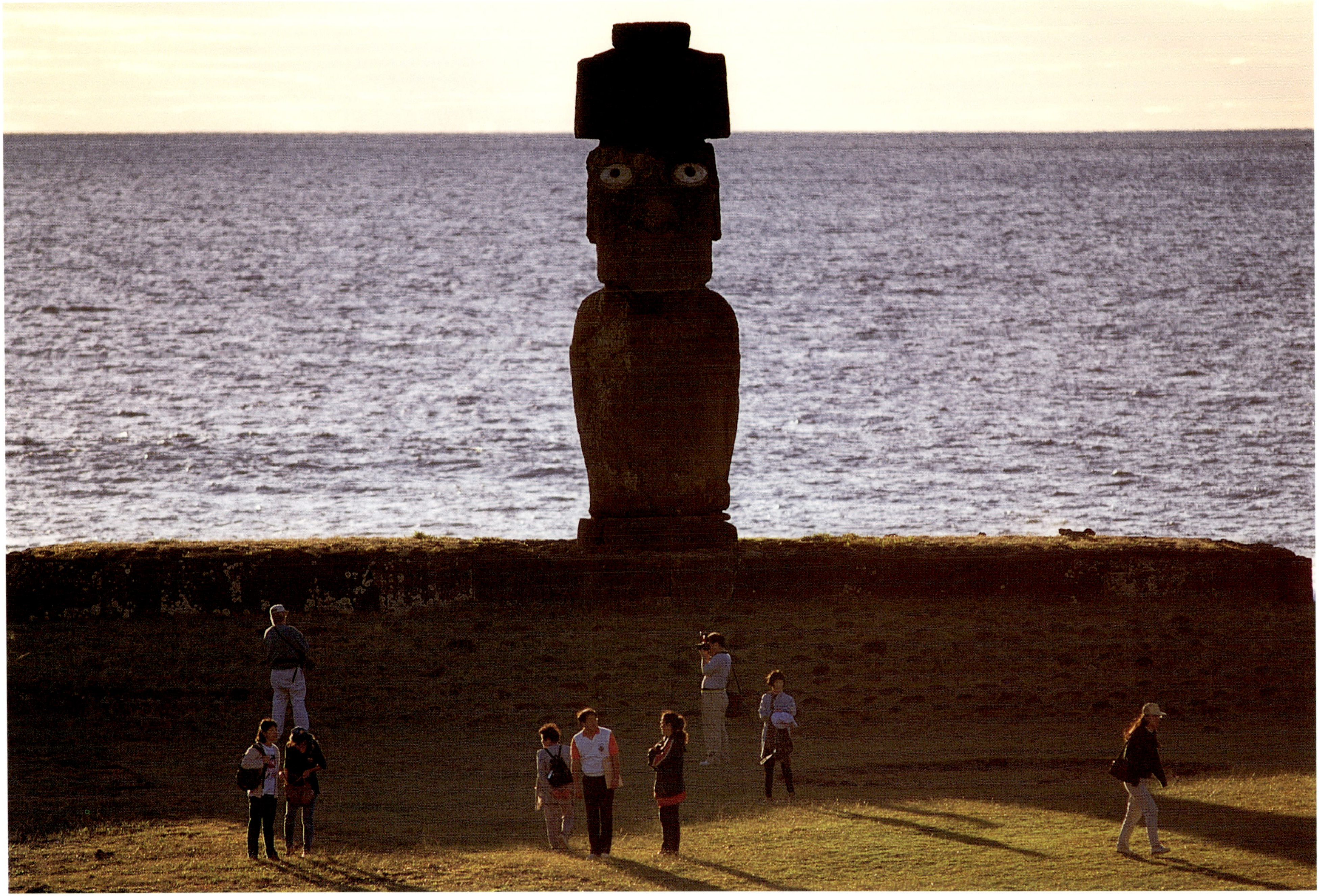

tourists at ahu tahai complex

[RIGHT] *rano kau crater*

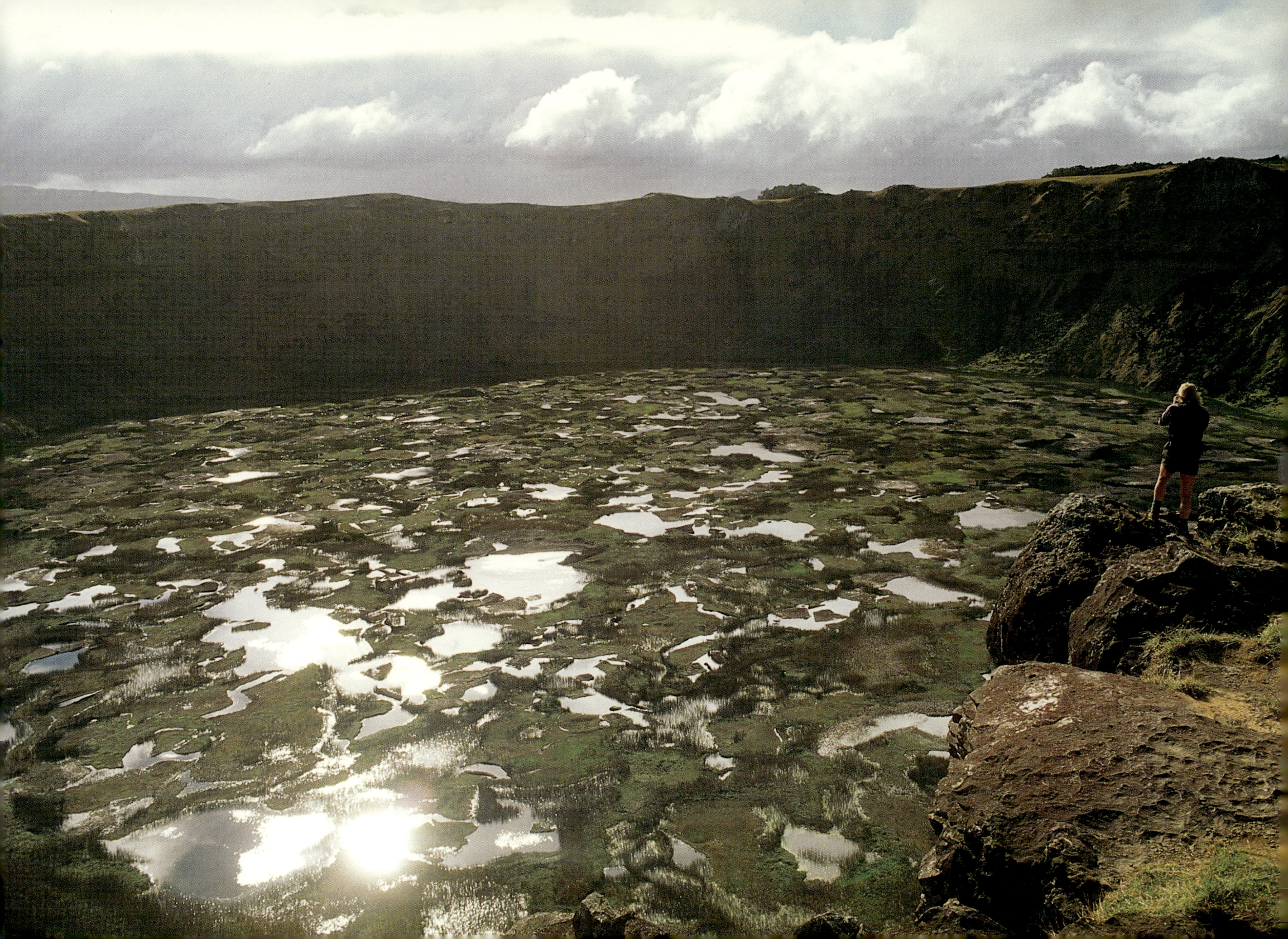

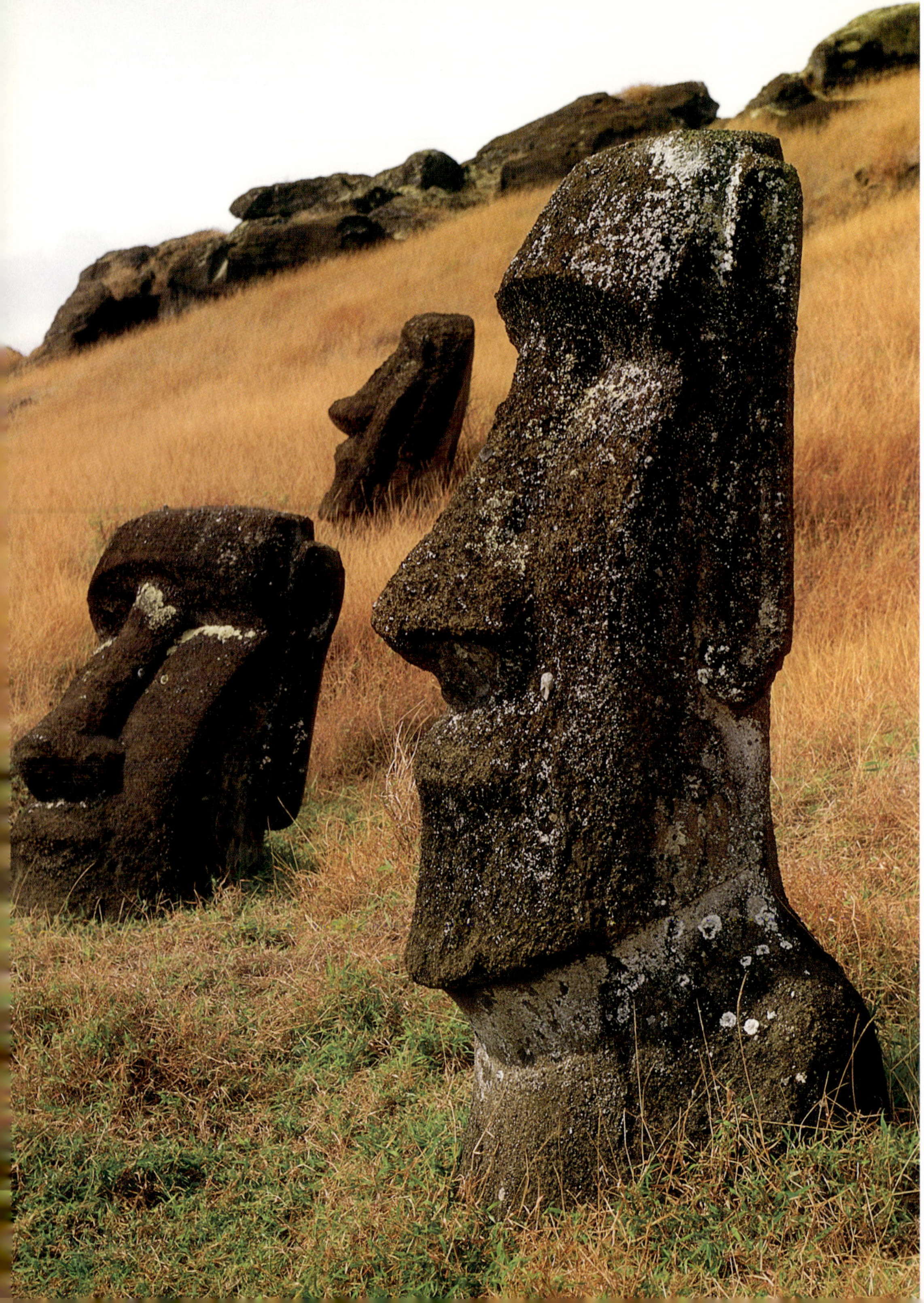

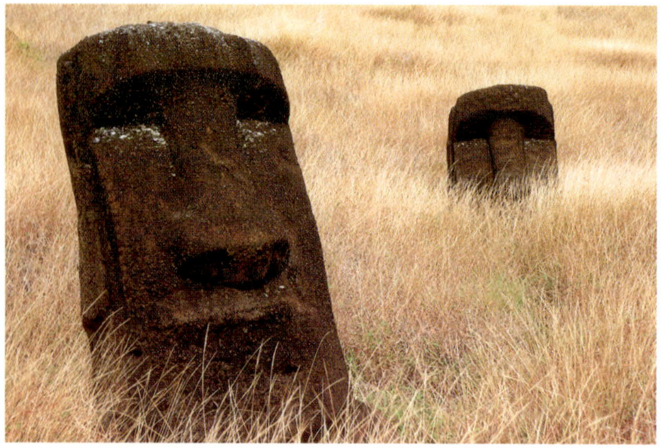

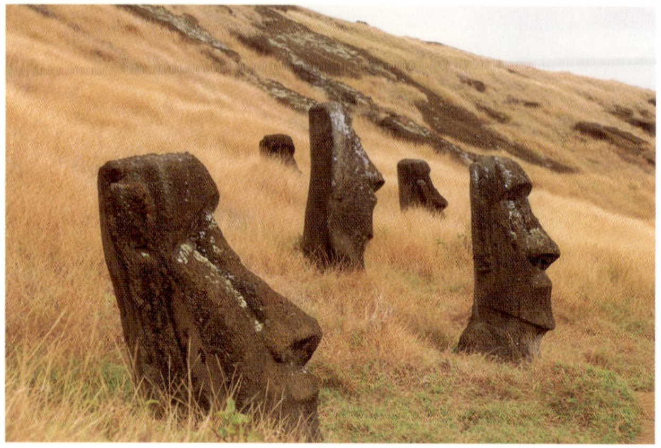

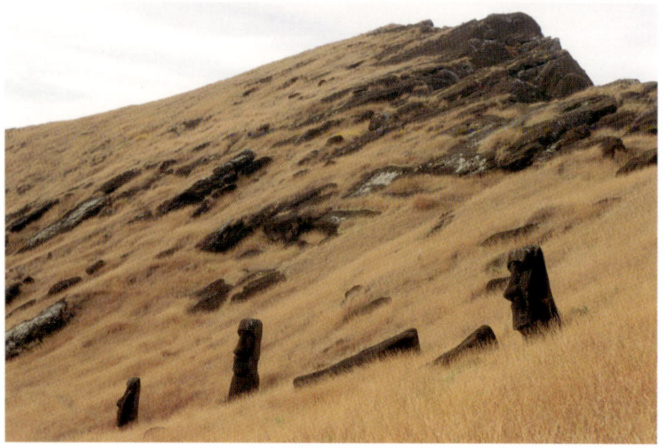

moai at the rano raraku volcano quarry site

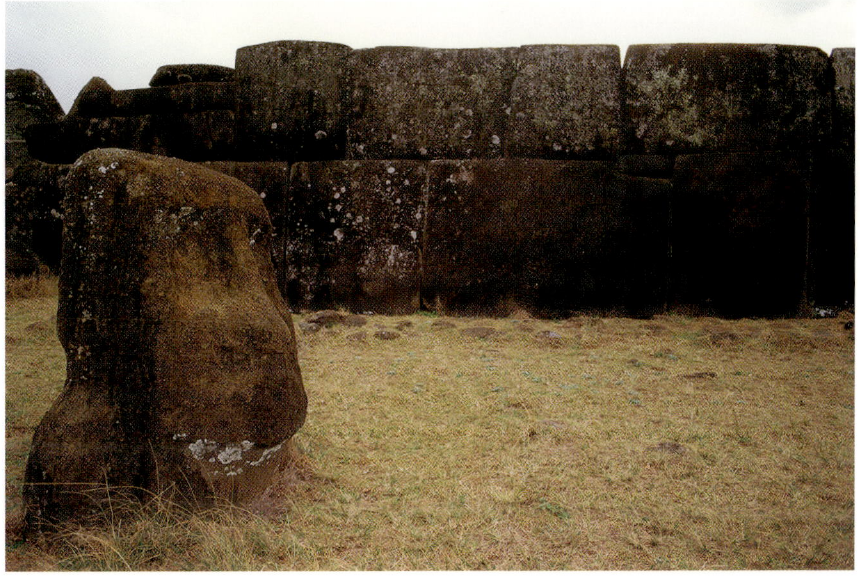

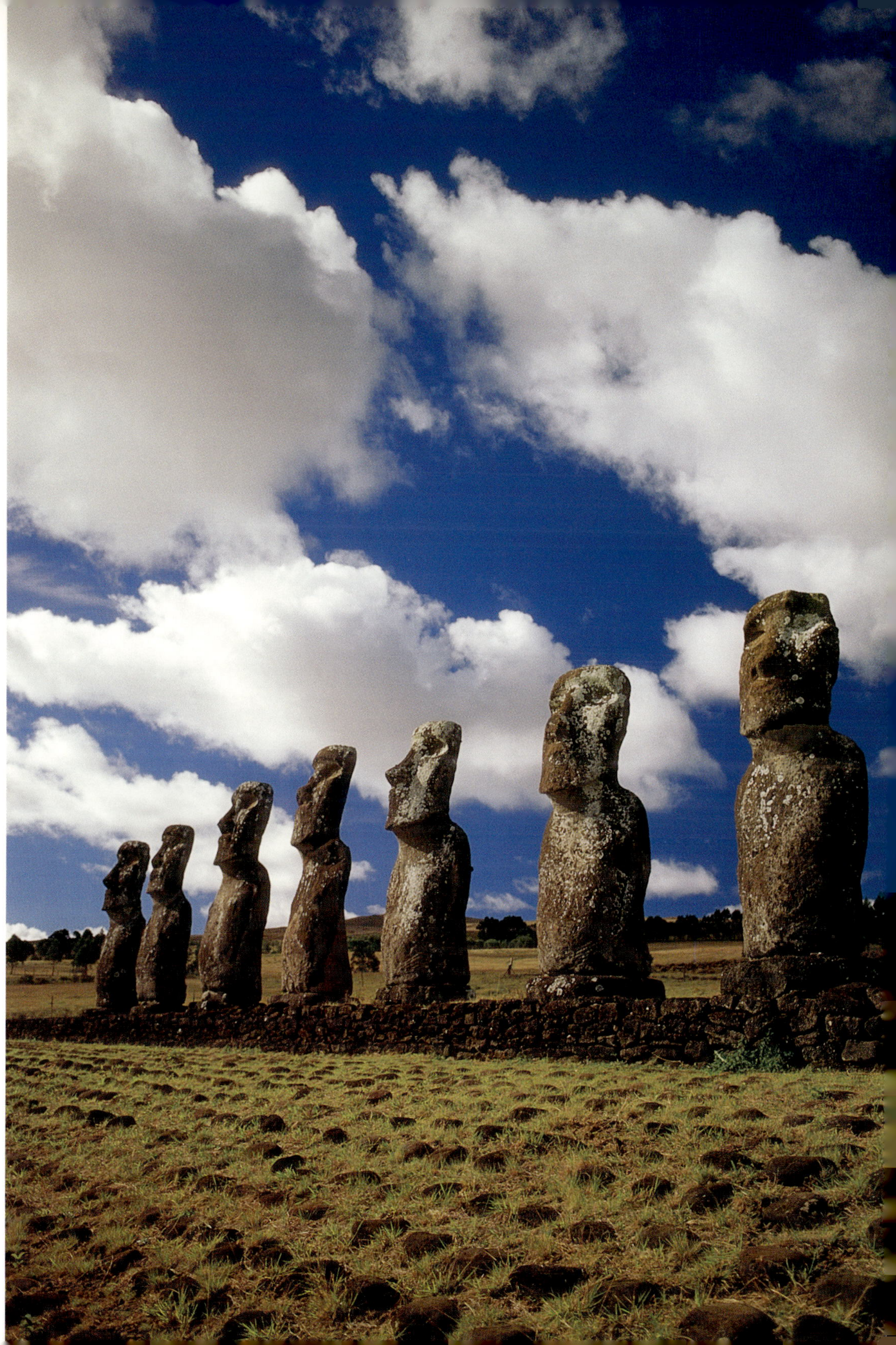

[**ABOVE**] *ahu vinapu* [**RIGHT**] *ahu akivi*

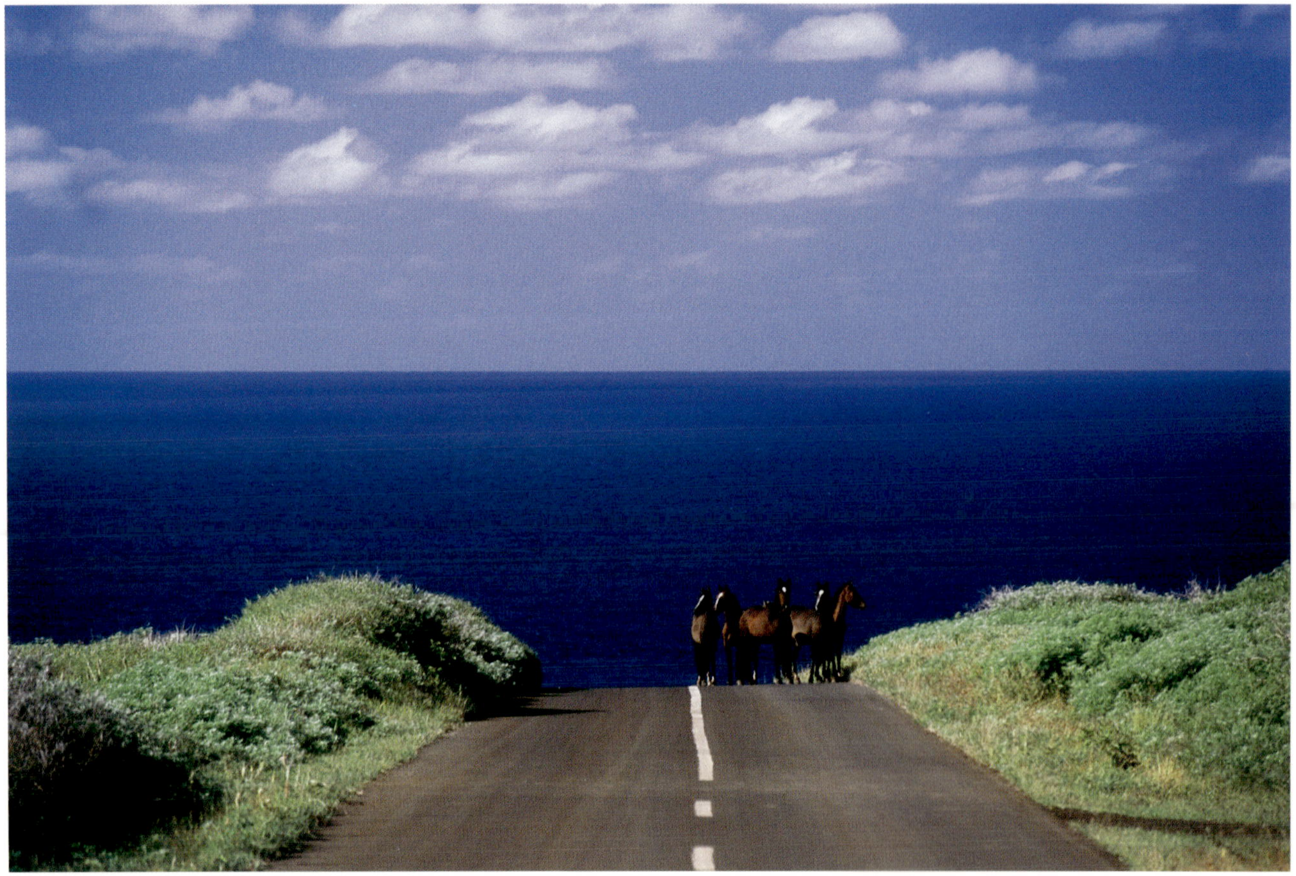

wild horse road block

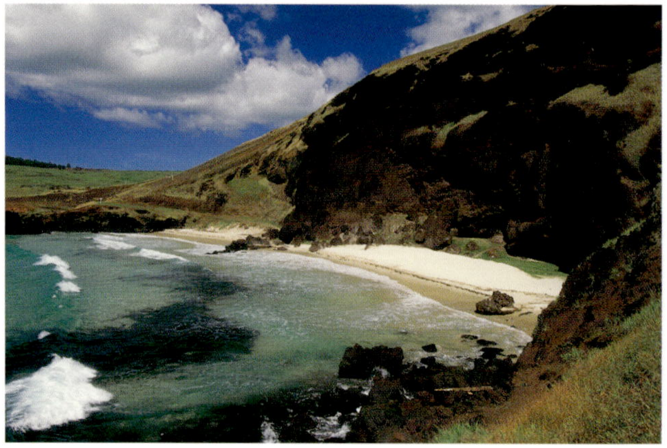

[**RIGHT**] *ovahe beach* [**FAR RIGHT**] *couple on horseback,* anakena beach

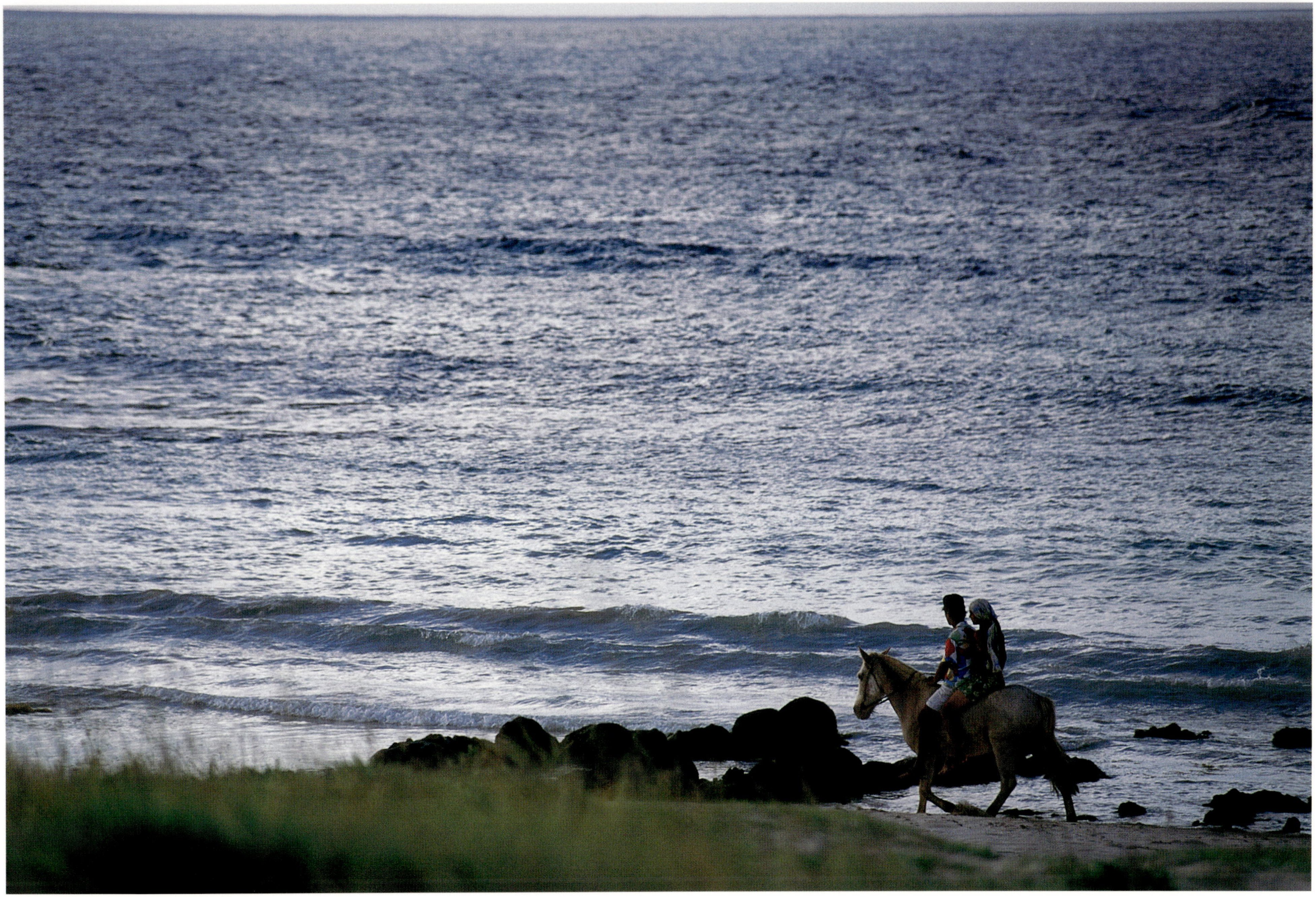

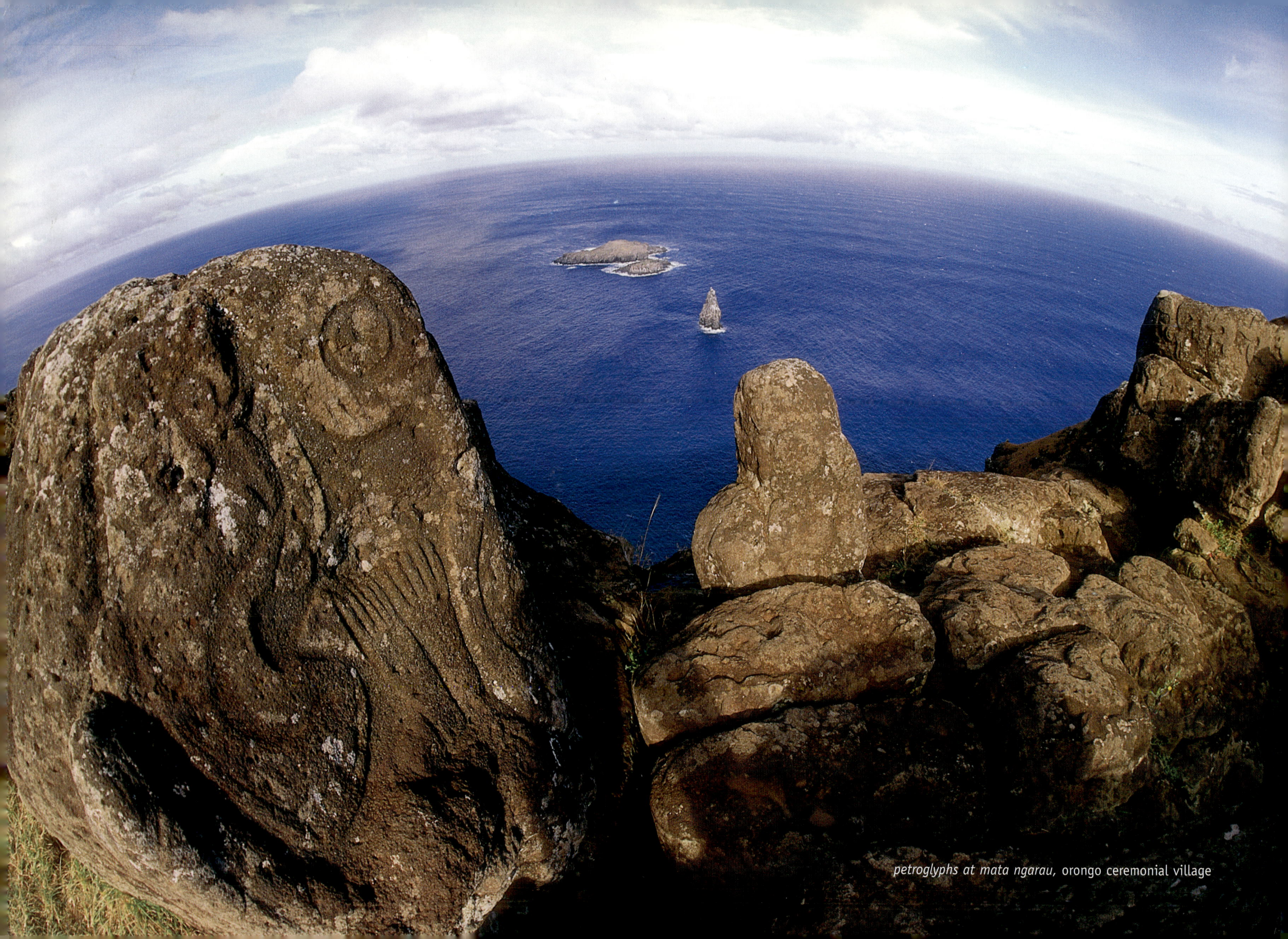

petroglyphs at mata ngarau, orongo ceremonial village

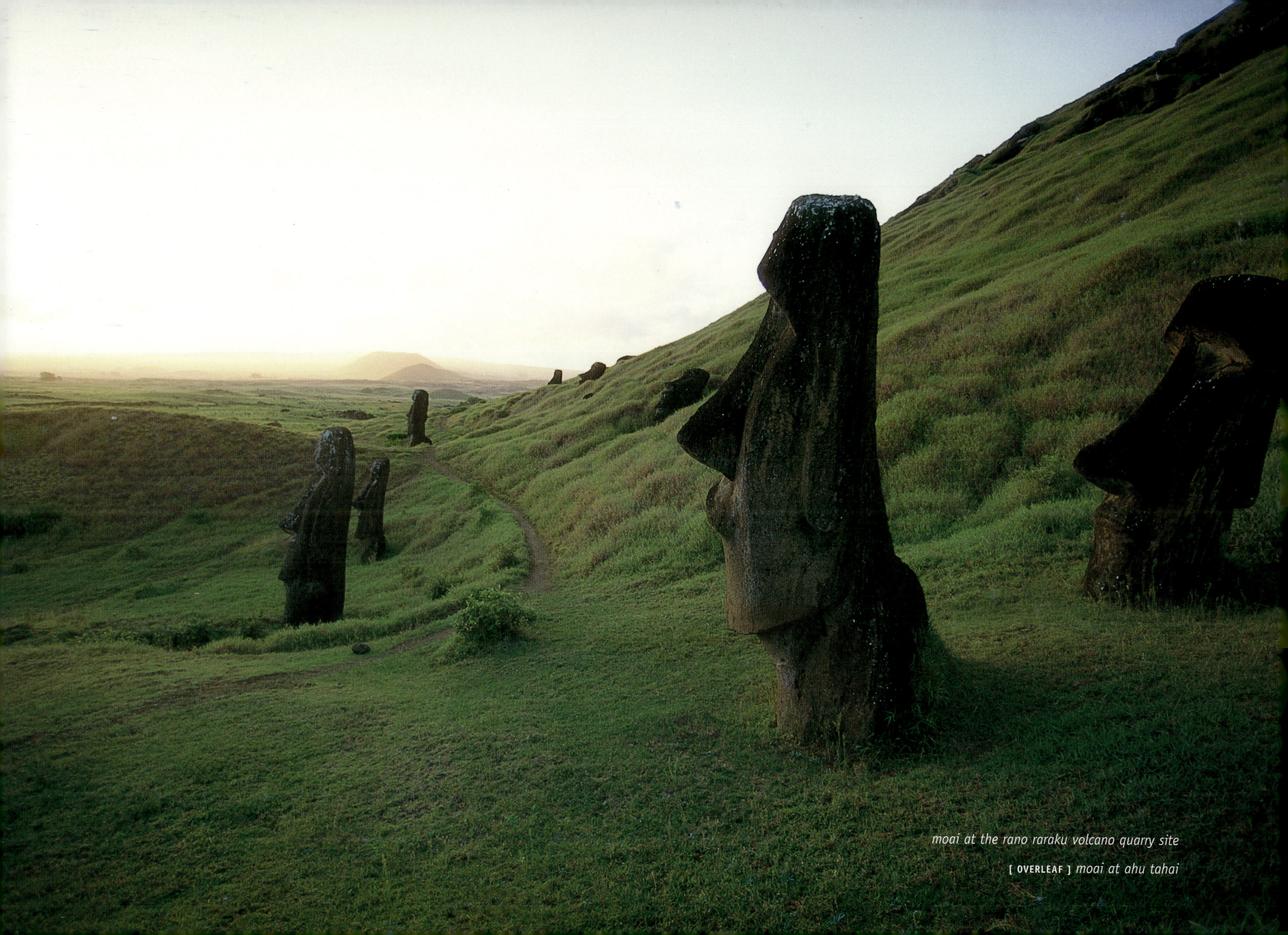

moai at the rano raraku volcano quarry site

[OVERLEAF] *moai at ahu tahai*

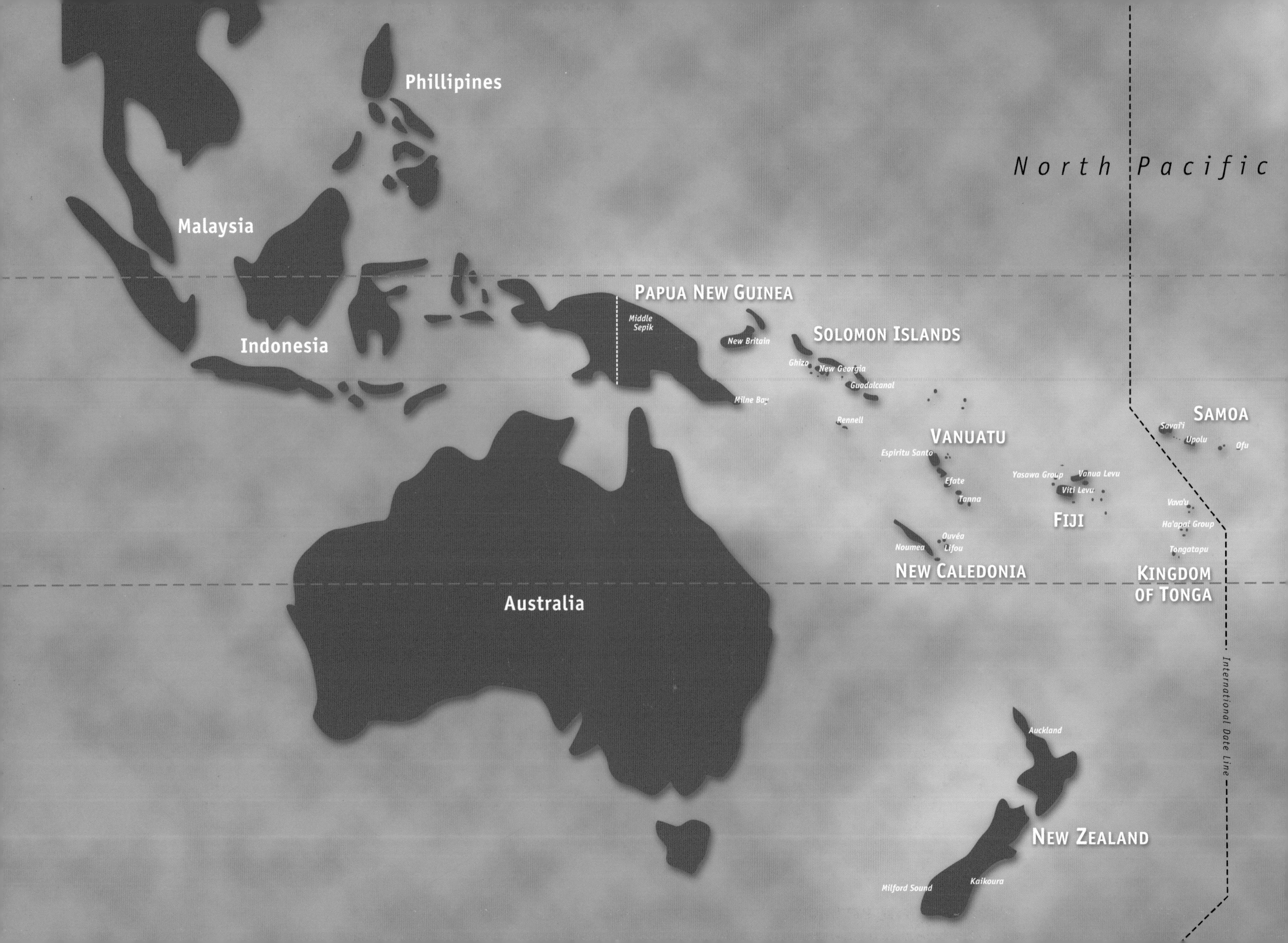
North Pacific
Phillipines
Malaysia
Indonesia
Papua New Guinea
Middle Sepik
New Britain
Milne Bay
Solomon Islands
Ghizo
New Georgia
Guadalcanal
Rennell
Samoa
Savai'i
Upolu
Ofu
Vanuatu
Espiritu Santo
Efate
Tanna
Yasawa Group
Vanua Levu
Viti Levu
Fiji
Vava'u
Ha'apai Group
Tongatapu
Ouvéa
Noumea
Lifou
New Caledonia
Kingdom of Tonga
Australia
International Date Line
Auckland
New Zealand
Milford Sound
Kaikoura

Muhammad صلى الله عليه وسلم Our Way of Life

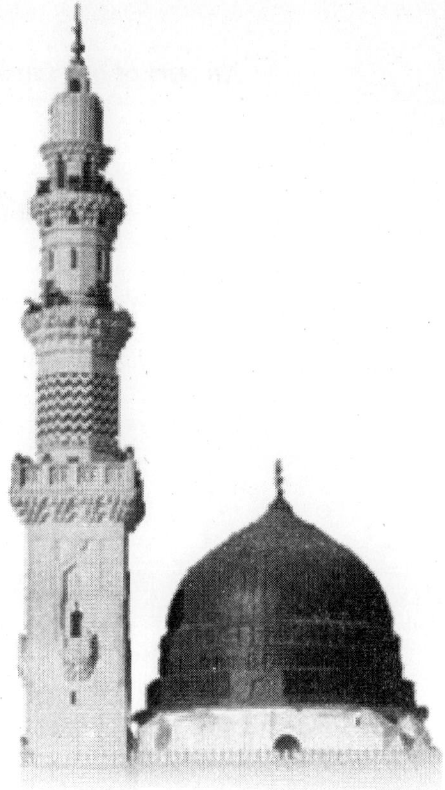

A Coloring Book For Children

Muhammad Ajmal Shamsi

Muhammad ﷺ Our Way of Life (A Coloring Book for Children)

By Muhammad Ajmal Shamsi

ISBN 81-7231-566-X

First Edition : 2004
Reprint : 2014

Published by *Abdus Sami* for :

Islamic Book Service (P) Ltd.
1511-12, Pataudi House, Darya Ganj, **New Delhi**-110 002 **(India)**
Tel.: 011-23244556, 23247899, 23253514, 23269050, 23286551
FAX: 011-23277913 | **e-mail:** info@ibsbookstore.com
Website: www.ibsbookstore.com

Our Associates:

- Azhar Academy Ltd., **London (United Kingdom)**
  Tel. 020-8911-9797
- Lautan Lestari (Lestari Books), **Jakarta (Indonesia)**
  Tel. 0062-21-35-23456
- Husami Book Depot, **Hyderabad (India)**
  Tel. 040-6680-6285

Printed in India